Who Belongs?

D1571133

Who Belongs?

Race, Resources, and Tribal Citizenship in the Native South

MIKAËLA M. ADAMS

OXFORD

UNIVERSITY PRESS

OXFORD
UNIVERSITY PRESS

Oxford University Press is a department of the University of Oxford. It furthers
the University's objective of excellence in research, scholarship, and education
by publishing worldwide. Oxford is a registered trade mark of Oxford University
Press in the UK and certain other countries.

Published in the United States of America by Oxford University Press
198 Madison Avenue, New York, NY 10016, United States of America.

Library of Congress Cataloging-in-Publication Data
Names: Adams, Mikaëla M., author.
Title: Who belongs? : race, resources, and tribal citizenship in the native
South / Mikaëla M. Adams.
Description: New York, N.Y. : Oxford University Press, [2016] |
Includes bibliographical references and index.
Identifiers: LCCN 2016012095 | ISBN 9780190619466 (hardcover ; alk. paper) |
ISBN 9780190055639 (paperback : alk. paper)
Subjects: LCSH: Indians of North America—Tribal citizenship—Southern States. |
Indians of North America—Legal status, laws, etc.—Southern States. |
Indians of North America—Southern States—Politics and government. |
Indians of North America—Southern States—Government relations. |
Indians of North America—Kinship—Southern States. |
Indians of North America—Southern States—Ethnic identity. |
Federally recognized Indian tribes—Southern States.
Classification: LCC E93 .A29 2016 | DDC 975.004/97—dc23
LC record available at http://lccn.loc.gov/2016012095

To my husband, David

CONTENTS

ACKNOWLEDGMENTS

This book would not have been possible without the support, encouragement, and assistance of a number of people. I will be forever grateful to the scholars, teachers, friends, family, and many others who helped me along the way.

I owe an enormous debt of gratitude to my academic advisers, Theda Perdue and Michael D. Green. Theda and Mike were a constant source of support throughout my graduate studies at UNC-Chapel Hill. As advisers, they were my strongest advocates and most honest (and constructive) critics. They showed me how to combine archival materials, ethnographies, and oral histories to reach a fuller picture of the past, and they taught me how to look for and interpret the actions of indigenous peoples in documents where Native voices are absent. Through their instruction and their own excellent example, they showed me how to be an ethnohistorian. Sadly, Mike passed away in 2013. I feel privileged to have known him. I will remember him for his fine scholarship but especially for his generosity, humor, and kindness. Theda continues to be a dedicated mentor and a dear friend. She has read every word I have written and my work is all the better for her insight and advice. Anyone who has worked with Theda and Mike knows just how rare they are as scholars, mentors, and people. I am lucky.

I would like to thank the other members of my dissertation committee at UNC-Chapel Hill for their assistance during the early phase of this project. Daniel M. Cobb's passion for research and teaching inspired my own interest in American Indian history when I first met him as an undergraduate at Miami University. Without him, I might never have pursued a graduate degree in history. Malinda Maynor Lowery has been an amazing mentor and friend. Our discussions over coffee helped me clarify many of the ideas that eventually made their way into the book. Kathleen DuVal is an incredible scholar and teacher. Her meticulous edits proved invaluable as I revised my dissertation into a manuscript. I am grateful for the insights provided by each of these committee members. I would also like to thank Sandra Hoeflich and Danny Bell for their support of my doctoral work at UNC.

A special thanks goes to my editor at Oxford University Press, Susan Ferber. I first met Susan at a conference in 2011. Although I was still a graduate student with only tenuous ideas about how to transform my dissertation into a book, Susan took the time to meet with me and discuss my research. Not only that, but she remembered me—a couple of years later she sent an email to check on my progress. Soon after, I had a book contract. Throughout the revising and editing process, Susan has been an enthusiastic champion of my work. I am grateful for her careful edits and her dedication to making the book the best it can be. I would also like to thank the two anonymous reviewers who provided useful feedback on the first draft of the manuscript. In addition, I am grateful for the hard work of my project manager, Maya Bringe, and my copy editor, Patterson Lamb, during the final stages of the production process.

The archival research that sustains this book would not have been possible without the generous support of the UNC History Department, the UNC Center for the Study of the American South, the UNC Graduate School, the University of Mississippi College of Liberal Arts, and the University of Mississippi Arch Dalrymple III Department of History. Each organization offered me funding that allowed me to travel across the South to conduct my research. I am also grateful to the UNC Graduate School for awarding me the Royster Society of Fellows' Sequoyah Dissertation Fellowship. This non-service fellowship permitted me to devote my last year at UNC to writing. The University of Mississippi Arch Dalrypmple III Department of History generously funded the costs associated with the historical photographs in the book.

A number of archivists and librarians assisted me as I conducted my research. In particular, I would like to thank Brent Burgin at the University of South Carolina, Lancaster, for his generous assistance. Brent introduced me to scholar Thomas Blumer, former chief of the Catawba Indian Nation Donald Rodgers, Catawba elder Fred Sanders, and Catawba enrollment assistant Donna Curtis, each of whom provided me with important information on Catawba tribal citizenship. I would also like to thank Charles Lesser of the South Carolina Department of Archives and History, Maureen Hill and Arlene Royer of the National Archives and Records Administration in Atlanta, Charles B. Greifenstein of the American Philosophical Society, Leanda Gahegan of the National Anthropological Archives, Mary Frances Ronan of the National Archives and Records Administration in Washington, Michael Wright of the National Archives and Records Administration in Fort Worth, and R. Lee Fleming, the former director of the Office of Federal Acknowledgment, for their assistance as I sifted through archival materials and gathered the evidence that allowed me to tell the stories of the six tribes in this study.

I am grateful to the State Archives of Florida, the National Anthropological Archives, the Valentine Richmond History Center, and the American Museum of Natural History for allowing me to reproduce historical photographs from their collections. There is nothing quite as thrilling as seeing a photograph of someone whose story you have read in the archives. I would also like to thank Matthew Lockhart, the editor of the *South Carolina Historical Magazine*, for allowing me to reprint portions of my chapter on the Catawba Indian Nation, which had appeared in the January 2012 issue.

As a graduate student at UNC-Chapel Hill, I was fortunate to become part of a supportive community of American Indian studies scholars. In particular, I would like to thank Julie Reed (now at the University of Tennessee) for her enduring friendship. Her passion for research and her kindness as a person inspire me. I am also grateful to Brooke Bauer, also a good friend, who read and commented on my chapter on the Catawba Indian Nation. In addition, Courtney Lewis and Susannah Walker, of First Nations Graduate Circle, were helpful and encouraging, especially during my final year of writing the dissertation.

Since joining the Arch Dalrymple III Department of History faculty at the University of Mississippi, I have been overwhelmed by the kindness and generosity of my colleagues. Each in their own way has helped shaped me as an academic—from lunchroom chats about teaching to offers of writing advice and editing suggestions. Many have also become close friends. I cannot imagine a better department chair than Joseph P. Ward, who has provided unwavering support throughout my years at the University of Mississippi. I would also like to thank Deirdre Cooper Owens (now at Queens College), Jesse Cromwell, Oliver Dinius, Charles W. Eagles, Chiarella Esposito, Lester L. Field Jr., Joshua First, Shennette Garrett-Scott, Jonathan Gienapp (now at Stanford University), Susan R. Grayzel, Darren E. Grem, April Holm, Joshua H. Howard, Vivian Ibrahim, Zachary Kagan Guthrie, Courtney Kneupper, Marc H. Lerner, Theresa H. Levitt, John R. Neff, John Ondrovcik, Ted M. Ownby, Elizabeth A. Payne, Paul J. Polgar, Jarod Roll, Charles K. Ross, Mohammed Bashir Salau, Sheila Skemp, Antoinette Sutto, Nicolas Trépanier, Annie S. Twitty, Jeffrey R. Watt, Jessica Wilkerson, Charles Wilson, and Noell Howell Wilson. I am also grateful to our department administrative coordinator, Kelly Brown Houston, who has helped me navigate numerous grant applications and travel reimbursement forms as well as many other day-to-day administrative tasks. My colleagues make me look forward to going to the office each day.

In addition to my fellow historians, I would also like to thank the members of the University of Mississippi Native American and Indigenous Studies Working Group. In particular, Heather Allen, Tony Boudreaux, Robbie Ethridge, Maureen Meyers, and Annette Trefzer have been encouraging and supportive of my work. I look forward to building a strong indigenous studies program with them at the University of Mississippi.

I have been fortunate to work with a number of incredible graduate students at the University of Mississippi, many of whom have incorporated indigenous history into their research. In particular, I would like to thank Jillian McClure, Christine Rizzi, Justin Rogers, Gary Rowland, and Jeff Washburn for our many thought-provoking discussions about American Indian studies and for their energy and enthusiasm for historical research and writing. I look forward to seeing them develop as scholars.

I deeply appreciate my network of friends outside of my field, including Özlem Arat, Fernando Chague, Debbie Drysdale, Özgün Erdoğan, Samantha Fairclough, Maria Bailey Gondo, Wafa Hassouneh, Natalia Kolesnikova, Hanna Lee, Maya Mikati, Maria Augusta Mitre, Racha Moussa, Pavan Muttil, Mamta Raveendran, Cinthya Zuniga Reddix, Ken Reddix, Nina Rifkind, Aubrie Langhorst Schroer, Michael Schroer, Guansong Wang, and Lu Wang. They sustained me during graduate school and beyond and have enriched my life in innumerable ways.

My family has been a pillar of support throughout the long process of researching, writing, and revising this book. In particular, I would like to thank my parents, Karen Cummings Adams and David Adams, for their love and encouragement. Somehow they raised six children while traveling around the world and encouraged each of us to follow our passions. From an early age, they fostered my interest in history by taking me and my siblings to museums, historical sites, and ancient ruins. They also taught us to love stories. The many hours we spent in embassies waiting to get visas approved, moreover, helped spark my enduring interest in questions of belonging and citizenship (as well as my hatred for paperwork). I hope I can emulate their example of hard work, love of learning, and social consciousness.

My grandmother, Norma Cummings, or, as I call her, Mormor, has also been incredibly supportive. She accompanied me on trips to the archives, read early drafts of my project, and thoughtfully listened to explanations of my research. I want to grow up to be just like her.

I would also like to thank my multi-talented younger siblings. Knud Adams was my closest confidant and partner-in-crime throughout our itinerant childhood. He, perhaps more than anyone, understands the forces that drive me. Christian Adams used his geographical skills to create the beautiful maps in this book. I am grateful for his patience with my many requests for formatting tweaks and for his overall support of the project. Briagenn Adams never allows me to take myself too seriously—very important for an academic. She reminds me to stay grounded and enjoy life. Tabitha Adams has kept me constantly entertained with her dry wit but also moved by her kind heart. Keir Adams continually inspires me with his strong work ethic and quiet perseverance. I am also grateful to my sister-in-law, Selene Carey, for her friendship and support.

I am deeply thankful for my parents-in-law, Lídia Melo Fragoso and Celso Gonzalez Gonzalez, and my sister-in-law, Lídia Fragoso Gonzalez, who welcomed me into their family with open arms. I finalized much of the conceptual framework for this project during one of our visits to see them in Portugal. I am grateful for their hospitality, love, and care. Despite my poor Portuguese language skills, they never cease to make me feel like I belong (or to feed me the most delicious food and pastries). I am so lucky to have joined their family.

I owe a final and very special thanks to my best friend and husband, David Fragoso Gonzalez. David has watched this project develop from its earliest stages and by now knows the material almost as well as I do. His logical way of thinking helped me clarify many of my own ideas and his thoughtful questions pushed me to sharpen my arguments. He also accompanied me on research trips, listened to me talk about tribal citizenship for hours, and kept me happy and well fed throughout the process. His humor, kindness, and love sustained me throughout. Quite simply, I could not have finished the book without him.

Who Belongs?

Introduction

Citizenship and Sovereignty

In 1994, Sharon Flora wrote to the editor of the *Cherokee One Feather*, the official newspaper of the Eastern Band of Cherokee Indians in North Carolina, "It is unfair that I cannot be recognized as a Cherokee Indian simply because I cannot locate my ancestors' names on the rolls." Referring to the Baker Roll of 1924, which serves as the basis for modern Eastern Band tribal citizenship, Flora expressed her frustration with the tribe's criteria for belonging and asserted that "those of us who cannot enroll . . . feel the same pride in our hearts of being Cherokee that they do, but we are always on the outside looking in."[1] This letter touched on a critical issue in Indian country today: tribal citizenship.[2] Who can lay claim to a legally recognized Indian identity? Who decides whether or not an individual qualifies?

"Indian" is not merely an ethnic or racial identity; rather, it is a political status based on an individual's citizenship in one of several hundred tribal nations that have, or have the potential to have, a legal relationship with the United States.[3] Tribes existed as sovereign political entities on the American continent before Europeans arrived, and they retain important aspects of this pre-contact sovereignty.[4] Over the years, the federal government has acknowledged the unique status of Indian people in treaties, laws, and court cases.[5] In particular, the 1974 Supreme Court case *Morton v. Mancari* recognized Indians not "as a discrete racial group, but, rather as members of quasi-sovereign tribal entities."[6] Although historically the United States often conflated race and nation for Indian tribes, and "Indian" continues to have racial connotations in US law as well as in common parlance, race alone does not identify someone as Indian for most legal purposes.[7] Instead, as legal scholar Matthew L. M. Fletcher has argued, "At the core of modern America Indian law and policy, and at the core of modern American Indian tribal nations, is citizenship."[8]

In modern federal and administrative decisions, the United States has recognized the right of tribal governments to determine their own citizenship criteria. The Supreme Court made this point in its 1978 decision in *Santa Clara Pueblo v. Martinez*.[9] In this case, a Santa Clara Pueblo citizen, Julia Martinez, brought suit against her tribe because its citizenship rules based on patrilineal descent excluded her children. Martinez argued that the pueblo's action violated the 1968 Indian Civil Rights Act.[10] The Supreme Court, however, refused to interfere in the pueblo's authority to regulate its own "internal social relations."[11] Tribes consider the case an important victory for tribal sovereignty. Today, the Bureau of Indian Affairs affirms that "an Indian tribe has the right to determine its own membership for tribal purposes."[12]

Tribal citizenship, however, has a history. Although today the United States recognizes the sovereign right of tribes to define their citizenship, Indian tribes have not always been free to decide who belonged. In the late nineteenth and early twentieth centuries in particular, as the federal government asserted more power over Indian nations and southern states enforced Jim Crow segregation, non-Indian officials frequently claimed this authority for themselves.[13] Working within this colonial framework, tribes fought back by setting their own criteria and by manipulating the language used by white politicians and bureaucrats to serve their own purposes. They developed new tribal citizenship requirements to bolster their political status and protect their economic resources. Modern citizenship criteria are the products of these historic interactions.

This book explores the history of tribal citizenship in six southeastern tribes: the Pamunkey Indian Tribe of Virginia, the Catawba Indian Nation of South Carolina, the Mississippi Band of Choctaw Indians, the Eastern Band of Cherokee Indians of North Carolina, the Seminole Tribe of Florida, and the Miccosukee Tribe of Indians of Florida. It first argues that tribal citizenship is intimately connected to tribal sovereignty. When tribes made decisions about who belonged to their communities and defended those choices against the claims and criticisms of outsiders, they engaged in a political act of self-determination. Examining tribal citizenship underscores the varying ways that tribes have exercised and defended their sovereignty over time and highlights the complicated and often fraught relationship between tribal nations and the settler-colonial government of the United States.[14]

Second, definitions of tribal citizenship underwent a profound change in the late nineteenth and twentieth centuries. Post–Civil War developments in federal Indian policy gave new economic and symbolic value to tribal citizenship, which transformed it into a commodity that tribes vigorously protected. Furthermore, the context of Jim Crow put new pressures on tribes to distinguish themselves racially in order to uphold their political status. Tribes understood that ongoing political acknowledgment of their sovereignty depended on their recognition as "Indian" by white America. As a result, they increasingly adopted racial criteria for tribal citizenship, which reflected views in the Office of Indian Affairs (OIA). The bureaucratization of the OIA in this period led to new federal oversight of tribal affairs and to demands for systemized documentation of tribal citizens. As tribes redefined their relationship with the federal government, their formerly fluid approaches to citizenship became fixed in tribal rolls and constitutions. In many cases, the tribal citizenship criteria developed in the early twentieth century continue to determine who legally qualifies as a tribal citizen today.

Finally, tribes made strategic choices when they decided on their citizenship criteria. Not simply the victims of federal Indian policy or American racial ideologies, Indians actively worked within the constraints they faced to create citizenship criteria that they believed best reflected their community values while protecting their economic resources and political status. Rather than abandon traditional ideas of belonging, tribes searched for ways to make their identity intelligible to white America. Sometimes this entailed making difficult choices that excluded certain people from citizenship, but tribes did what they had to do to survive. Since each tribe's particular circumstances and historical relationship with federal and state governments were unique, the decisions they made varied. The construction of tribal citizenship criteria belies the notion of an essential "Indian" and reveals that citizenship in a tribe is a historically constructed and constantly evolving process. By exploring the stories of six tribes in depth, this book illuminates decision-making processes at a tribal level and lends an ethnohistorical perspective to the study of tribal citizenship.[15]

As legal scholar Kirsty Gover has explained, citizenship rules "constitute the 'self' that is to 'self-govern,' by defining the class of persons entitled to share in tribal resources and participate in tribal politics."[16] By determining their citizenship, tribes create and maintain political boundaries that reinforce their unique legal status in the United States.[17] Citizenship criteria provide tribes with guidelines for deciding who can take advantage of communally owned reservation lands and tribal services, hunting and grazing rights, and tribal per capita payments. In addition, tribal citizenship establishes who can vote in tribal elections as well as who can run for and hold tribal office. Since the 1970s, Congress has increasingly relied on tribal citizenship to determine whether an individual qualifies as an Indian under US law for federal benefits such as health and educational services.[18] Without the right to determine their citizenship, tribes would be powerless to protect their rights and resources from outsiders. To act as nations, tribes must have clear boundaries between citizens and non-citizens.[19]

Tribal sovereignty is a historically contingent, slippery concept.[20] There is nothing inherent about its significance, and as legal scholar Charles

Figure 0.1 Although they experienced similar pressures on their land, resources, and
identity in the biracial world of the Jim Crow South, the Pamunkey Indian Tribe, the
Catawba Indian Nation, the Mississippi Band of Choctaw Indians, the Eastern Band of
Cherokee Indians, the Seminole Tribe of Florida, and the Miccosukee Tribe of Indians
of Florida each developed unique tribal citizenship criteria. Their decisions reflected
their particular histories and legal relationships with federal and state governments.
Map prepared by Christian Adams.

F. Wilkinson has observed, "during the modern era, the existence of tribal
sovereignty, and what it means, has been the subject of heated and extensive
debate."[21] Although tribes exercised sovereignty before the establishment
of the United States, their political power has not existed in a vacuum. As
United States power has waxed, anthropologist Circe Sturm has argued, tribal
sovereignty has relied "less on autonomy and independence than it does on
mutual recognition and interdependence." As a result, tribes have not enjoyed
full authority to define themselves as they see fit. Some tribes never achieved
federal recognition, and thus have had a difficult time exercising any form of
sovereignty. Even those tribes recognized by the federal government "must
manage their public impression and maintain their sense of distinctiveness
or run the risk that their status as sovereign peoples might somehow be challenged."[22] This puts tribes in what anthropologist Jessica Cattelino has called
a "double bind." To be sovereign means a free exercise of power in decision
making, yet tribes find that if they make decisions that do not conform to

American expectations of "Indianness," they risk losing recognition of their sovereignty.[23] The study of tribal citizenship provides insight into the various ways that tribes have employed their political identity as "Indian" to bolster their tribal sovereignty over time.

decisions based on freedom

Originating as a legal concept with the presumed divine powers of monarchs and popes in medieval Europe, "sovereignty" evolved following the eighteenth-century political revolutions in Europe and America as a way to describe the new reciprocal relationship between citizens and the state that replaced the old bonds of personal allegiance of subjects to the king.[24] Despite the term's European origin, Indian tribes exercised sovereign powers at the time of contact between Europe and the Americas.[25] They were politically distinct peoples with defined territorial limits.[26] They governed themselves and delineated who belonged to their communities. This inherent sovereignty of tribal nations predated European arrival and the foundation of the United States.[27]

When Europeans arrived in the Americas, they implicitly recognized the sovereignty of Native nations, but they did not treat Indian tribes on a basis of equality. In their efforts to acquire land and resources and to prevent other European powers from wresting control of the new continents from them, Europeans invented the "Doctrine of Discovery" to assert power over the territories they colonized. This doctrine, as interpreted by Supreme Court Chief Justice John Marshall in 1823, maintained that American Indians were not full sovereigns of the lands they possessed but rather were users of the land. Europeans claimed that the land itself belonged to whichever Christian nation supposedly "discovered" it.[28]

In spite of European assumptions of their superior right to American land, the realities of the colonial world necessitated that they make treaties with Indian nations. As historian Deborah A. Rosen has explained, "limited military capacity in the colonies meant that [Europeans] sometimes had no choice but to acquiesce in the independence of Indian nations."[29] Treaties had emerged as a custom within international law to assert nationhood and recognize national sovereignty, and when European powers made treaties with Indian tribes, they created legally binding compacts that acknowledged the sovereign status of Indian nations.[30]

When the United States declared its independence from Great Britain, the new nation continued to make treaties with Indian tribes. Between 1778 and 1871, the United States ratified 371 treaties with indigenous nations, thereby recognizing their sovereign status.[31] The United States also provided for a relationship between Indian tribes and the federal government in its governing document. The US Constitution expressly stated that only Congress had the power to regulate commerce with Indian tribes.[32] The commerce clause acknowledged that tribal relations with the United States were beyond the purview of individual states and that authority to deal with tribal nations—as sovereign entities—rested solely with the federal government.

Treaties recognized the sovereign status of tribes and established relationships between tribes and the federal government. For a variety of historical reasons, however, not all tribes made treaties with the United States. Some tribes, like the Pamunkeys and Catawbas, made agreements with colonial governments and, after the American Revolution, maintained relations with individual states rather than forming new treaties with the federal government. This situation created problems: although state governments recognized the inherent and retained sovereignty of these tribes, the federal government did not because it had no treaties or government-to-government relationship with them. State-recognized tribes struggled to maintain their national identities without the protections afforded federally recognized tribes. In some cases this worked to their advantage: they were not subject to federal policies that threatened tribal sovereignty. They were more vulnerable, however, to the pressures of land-hungry local whites and the whims of state legislators.

As tribes adapted to the pressures of the new American nation, they began changing their conceptions of belonging. Prior to the nineteenth century, tribal citizenship did not exist apart from kinship. Indians knew who belonged by tracing their familial ties as well as by engaging in shared cultural practices, speaking a common language, residing in the same tribal homeland, and politically affiliating with the tribal body. In the Southeast, these social and political bonds were reinforced by membership in a matrilineal clan. Children belonged to the clan of their mother and owed obligations to their clan relatives that helped bind the community together. Even after southeastern Indians began intermarrying with non-Indians, the importance of kinship continued. As historian Theda Perdue has argued, the children of these unions were readily accepted as long as they had Indian mothers with clan affiliations.[33] Indians also incorporated white and black people into the tribal body through marriage, adoption, or other rituals of kinship. As long as these individuals behaved as relatives and adopted the cultural mores of their Indian families, the tribe did not distinguish between them and other tribal citizens.[34]

Over time, however, Indians confronted new questions of belonging as intermarriage increased, tribal citizens acquired African slaves, and Indians began adopting Euro-American patterns of inheritance. By the late eighteenth and early nineteenth centuries, tribes like the Cherokees found it expedient to move toward a unified tribal identity and centralized system of governance in order to deal more effectively with Americans and to protect their land base.[35] In this process they borrowed Euro-American ideas of citizenship and sovereignty as a way to describe and defend their separate political status. They also adopted Euro-American concepts of race.

  ⊀ Race is not an inherent <u>biological attribute of individuals; it is a social fiction that has to be made and remade.</u>[36] Although Europeans first used "race" as a term in the early sixteenth century, initially it indicated "a category or class of persons or things and carried with it no implication of biological identity."[37] By the eighteenth and early nineteenth centuries, however, Europeans and Euro-Americans began to associate race with biological inheritance as a way to justify their expropriation of indigenous land and African labor. Scientific inquiry during this period, including anthropometric and phrenological measurements, "provided the fodder for an elaboration of the inferiority of others as the final ingredient necessary for rabid, racial, Anglo-Saxonism."[38] Once created, racial categories took on a life of their own. Although ideas of race had no biological basis, they became infused with cultural meanings so that even after the original motivations for constructing racial categories changed, race continued to play a role in structuring the social world.[39] As Circe Sturm has explained, "It is in this context that race is both a falsehood and a fact, being false in its biological, scientific sense and factual in its very real effects on lived experience."[40]

Although the United States made treaties with tribes as sovereign polities, it simultaneously viewed Indians as members of a racial group. The racialization of tribal identity furthered the United States' goal of shrinking tribes and their land base.[41] As Jodi A. Byrd has argued, "Transforming American Indians into a minority within a country of minorities is the fait accompli of the colonial project that disappears sovereignty, land rights, and self-governance as American Indians are finally, if not quite fully, assimilated *into* the United States."[42] The conflation of race and nation also eventually restricted the ability of tribes to incorporate outsiders as full citizens since the United States did not recognize these individuals as "Indian," at least for jurisdictional purposes. Although in colonial times tribes had fully incorporated non-Indians into their societies, the 1846 Supreme Court case, *United States v. Rogers*, held that a white man's race could not be obscured or eliminated based on his acquisition of tribal citizenship.[43] Although tribes continued to include intermarried and adopted non-Indians as tribal citizens until the late nineteenth century, this practice declined.

In addition to denying the tribal citizenship rights of non-Indians, federal officials also began expressing the "biological intermixture between Indians and non-Indians in terms of fractionated blood."[44] When Indians had children with white people, for example, government agents and missionaries assumed that these children, whom they called "mixed bloods" or "half breeds," would take on some of the supposed racial qualities of their non-Indian parent.

"Mixed bloods" were presumed more predisposed to "civilization," and thus less "Indian," which white Americans equated with "savagery." Although early treaty provisions did not distinguish between "mixed bloods" and "full bloods" in terms of eligibility for federal funds or services, "blood" entered the lexicon and contributed to the idea that Indian identity could be diluted and ultimately disappear.[45]

During the late eighteenth and early nineteenth centuries, tribes began internalizing the racial categories of white America, especially when it came to blacks. Having adopted plantation slavery, southern tribes in particular turned to these categories as a way to distinguish themselves from enslaved Africans.[46] They wrote governing documents and passed statutes that specifically restricted marriages between tribal citizens and black people and denied those with African ancestry full tribal citizenship.[47] As the nineteenth century progressed, race became increasingly tied to notions of tribal identity and belonging. Indeed, for some tribes, race became "a cornerstone of the national identity" that tribes used to demand recognition of their separate political status from white America.[48]

While tribes redrew boundaries of belonging in the early nineteenth century, the United States looked for ways to make legal sense of Indian nations. The Supreme Court established the political status of federally recognized Indian tribes when Chief Justice John Marshall characterized tribes as "domestic dependent nations." In three cases, *Johnson v. McIntosh* (1823), *Cherokee Nation v. Georgia* (1831), *and Worcester v. Georgia* (1832), Marshall conceived of a model that called for largely autonomous tribal governments subject to an overriding federal authority, but free of state control.[49] His interpretation maintained that although tribes were under the protection of the "stronger" government of the United States, they had not forsaken their legal claims to self-government and other sovereign rights as a result of that protection. Among these reserved rights was the tribal prerogative to delineate citizenship. The Marshall Trilogy provided the basis for the trust relationship between tribes and the federal government, which bound the United States to protect the political integrity and territorial possessions of tribal nations under its supervision.[50]

Despite the legal relationship that the Supreme Court established between tribes and the United States, land-hungry white Americans were not willing to share the continent with Indian nations, whose citizens they considered racial inferiors. The Andrew Jackson administration pushed through the Indian Removal Act of 1830, which authorized the federal government to make removal treaties with eastern tribes and exchange their land for territory west of the Mississippi.[51] Often conducted fraudulently or signed under duress, these treaties led to the forced removal of thousands of southeastern tribal peoples from the Cherokee, Choctaw, Chickasaw, Creek, and Seminole Nations (commonly referred to as the Five Tribes).[52] When these tribes removed west, they took with them their government-to-government relationship with the United States. The scattered Indians who remained in the South were left without a federal relationship or protection. In the years that followed, remnant tribes like the Mississippi Choctaws, Eastern Band of Cherokees, and the Florida Seminoles, as well as state-recognized tribes like the Catawbas and Pamunkeys, rebuilt their nations and strove to regain external recognition of their tribal sovereignty, including the right to control their citizenship.

Removal shifted notions of tribal belonging by complicating the legal process of distinguishing tribal citizens. Tribal enrollment emerged during these years as a new way of defining "Indianness." Prior to removal, the federal government was interested in population statistics of Indian tribes but less concerned with the question of who belonged to these nations. When the government signed removal treaties, however, officials made promises to tribal citizens. They needed to know who was entitled to land, resources, and funds under the terms of the treaties, and to answer this question, they developed tribal rolls. For the Cherokee Nation, for example, the removal roll determined who was eligible for transportation and subsistence under the Treaty of New Echota. Cherokees left behind in the Southeast relied on a list of people granted reservations in an 1819 treaty to remain legally in their homes. South Carolina promised the Catawbas annual stipends in exchange for land cessions made in the 1840 Treaty of Nation Ford, and state officials compiled a list of tribal citizens eligible for these funds. The increased involvement of federal and state officials in questions of tribal belonging encouraged Indian tribes to reconsider their citizenship criteria. Late nineteenth- and early twentieth-century federal policies and racial legislation made this process more difficult.

Following the Civil War, federal Indian policy underwent a major shift as the United States turned its attention westward and began consolidating its power over the North American continent. The United States had tried to solve its so-called Indian problem by moving tribal nations out of the reach of white society, but this strategy was no longer viable as Americans spread into new territories, built railroads, and staked claims to western lands. With nowhere left to move Indians, the United States began to confine them, first by moving them onto reservations, and then by gradually chipping away at their internal sovereignty through a strategy of weakening tribal governance and subjecting Indian communities to state and federal bureaucracies and legal systems.[53] Tribes that remained in the South already had experienced this erosion of sovereignty following the removal of the Five Tribes to Indian Territory in the 1830s and 1840s. Left on marginal lands with an unclear political status, they were subject to state jurisdiction and unable to exercise full political control over their territory.

In 1871, Congress passed an act announcing that "hereafter no Indian nation or tribe within the territory of the United States shall be acknowledged or recognized as an independent nation, tribe or power with whom the United States may contract by treaty." This act, although it did not abrogate previous treaties and continued to allow Congress to negotiate agreements with tribes, indicated the federal government's intention to freeze Indians in time and deny their ongoing right to separate nationhood.[54] Not long after, Congress passed the Major Crimes Act of 1885, which extended federal criminal jurisdiction over tribal lands.[55] The Supreme Court justified this extension of federal authority with claims of congressional plenary power in the 1886 case *United States v. Kagama*.[56] Congress put its plenary power to use the following year when it passed the General Allotment Act of 1887, which authorized the breakup of tribal land into individually held allotments for tribal citizens and opened up "surplus" land to non-Indian settlement.[57] Policymakers expected allotment to serve as "a mighty pulverizing engine" that would once and for all break up the tribal mass.[58]

The ultimate goal of white reformers in this period was to transform Indians into United States citizens. Concerns over citizenship preoccupied late nineteenth- and early twentieth-century Americans. The emancipation of former slaves and the passage of the Fourteenth Amendment broke down racial barriers to American citizenship. The rise of Jim Crow segregation, meanwhile, created new obstacles to the full political inclusion of minorities.[59] Mass immigration raised issues of naturalization, while restrictive immigration laws, like the Chinese Exclusion Act of 1882, denied the possibility of American citizenship to certain groups.[60] Imperialist expansion in the Caribbean, Pacific, and East Indies created conundrums over how to incorporate the populations of newly acquired territories.[61] American women fought for the franchise and an end to their status as second-class citizens. As new groups vied for inclusion in the American body politic, Americans hotly contested the meaning of citizenship and often turned to concepts of race, gender, class, and nationality to decide whom to include and whom to exclude.[62] In this context of discussion and debate, the United States endeavored to make sense of people who lived within the country's borders but who claimed citizenship in their own tribal nations.

Although the Fourteenth Amendment, ratified in 1868, declared that "All persons born or naturalized in the United States, and subject to the jurisdiction thereof, are citizens of the United States and the State wherein they reside," the citizenship status of Indian people remained unclear in postbellum America. Tribal citizens continued to owe their allegiance to their tribal nations, and since most were "not taxed" or subject to the full jurisdiction of the United States, they did not automatically acquire American citizenship under the Fourteenth Amendment.[63] In 1884, the Supreme Court ruled in *Elk v. Wilkins* that even Indians who left their reservation and joined American society did not gain American citizenship unless they underwent a naturalization process and demonstrated that they were "fi[t] for a civilized life."[64]

At the same time, postbellum federal Indian policy worked to undermine tribal sovereignty and to break up tribal nations with the ultimate goal of assimilating Indians into American society. Reformers argued that Indians could become United States citizens if they abandoned their tribal customs, embraced the American market economy, and cultivated individuality.[65] People like General Richard Henry Pratt, founder of the Carlisle Indian Industrial School in Pennsylvania in 1879, hoped to "kill the Indian and save the man" by destroying tribal cultures and removing Indian children from the supposed negative influences of their kinsmen. At boarding schools, Indian children were prohibited from using their Native languages, practicing their traditional religions, wearing their Native clothes, and using their former names. Through strict discipline and regimented education, reformers hoped to remake Indian children into the image of white citizens, albeit an inferior one.[66] Meanwhile, the General Allotment Act of 1887 established a legal path to United States citizenship for Native people: once they became private property holders and members of American society, their land became taxable and they became US citizens.[67]

Despite efforts to eliminate tribal identities during the allotment era, the political conception of Indian identity never completely went away.[68] Although federal policies undermined the territorial sovereignty of tribal nations, the federal government continued to recognize Indians as citizens of tribes with rights to tribal land and property. When Congress finally passed the Indian Citizenship Act in 1924, which granted United States citizenship to "all non citizen Indians born within the territorial limits of the United States," for example, it stipulated that "the granting of such citizenship shall not in any manner impair or otherwise affect the right of any Indian to tribal or other property."[69] Legal scholar Allison M. Dussias has described the changes to the political status of tribes that took place during these years as a shift from "geographically-based" to "membership-based" tribal sovereignty.[70] Tribal citizens and their property rights—rather than borders drawn on a map—defined the tribal body, its authority, and its reach. Indeed, from an American legal standpoint, tribal citizenship became the very basis of tribal sovereignty.[71] This transition was a dangerous one for tribes. Anthropologist Jean Dennison has pointed out that "rendering American Indians as possessors of particularly marked bodies rather than as citizens in polities controlling a territory" served to further "alienate indigenous populations from their land" and undermine tribal sovereignty.[72] Yet tribes had little choice in the matter. To continue to exist and function as political entities in this new context, tribes had to clearly delineate who belonged.

During the allotment era, tribal citizenship increasingly became connected to individual property rights.[73] Whereas in the past tribes had communally owned vast swaths of territory, by the late nineteenth century the United States had confined tribes to tiny fractions of their former holdings and had promised to divide the remainder among individual Indians. These changes put a new economic premium on tribal citizenship since resources were scarce and only those who belonged to a tribe were entitled to a share. To be a tribal citizen meant having a recognized right to tribal property, which made tribal citizenship itself a form of property.[74] As such, tribes had to defend their citizenship against those who felt little political or cultural allegiance to the tribe but who wished to profit from tribal assets. If a tribe did not defend its citizenship, it stood to lose its property and its political authority. Efforts to clarify and enforce the rights of ownership of allotted tribal lands as well as other tribal resources led to new battles over citizenship. These struggles occurred even within tribes that were never formally allotted since the mere threat of this policy incentivized tribes to consider who belonged as citizens and shareholders of tribal assets.

The rise of Jim Crow segregation during this period further complicated tribal citizenship. Beginning in the 1880s, southern states passed a spate of segregation laws designed to regulate social, economic, and political relationships between whites and non-whites and to prevent interracial contact "from the moment a child was born in a segregated hospital or at home on a segregated city block to the time he or she died and was buried in a 'colored' cemetery."[75] At the core of these segregation laws, which the Supreme Court upheld in the 1896 case *Plessy v. Ferguson,* was an effort to separate people into categories of "white" and "colored" in order to reinforce white supremacy and restore racial boundaries that had collapsed following emancipation.[76] Indians, as a third race, did not fit neatly into either of these categories. Their anomalous status put them in a precarious position. White southerners constantly threatened to ignore their political identity as citizens of tribal nations and instead to lump them together with African Americans in the racial category of "colored."

To add to the problem, turn-of-the-century white Americans widely believed that Indians were a "vanishing race" doomed to extinction. Notions of Indian "blood" and the idea that interracial reproduction was an indicator of assimilation fed the perception that indigenous cultural distinctiveness was in decline and that soon there would be no "real" Indians left.[77] These ideas were magnified in the South since most Americans assumed that all southeastern tribes had migrated west during the removals of the 1830s and 1840s. White southerners suspected that anyone claiming to be "Indian" might actually be black. Indeed, in places like Virginia, white eugenicists actively worked to re-classify Indian populations as "colored" and to deny their political identity.[78] Tribes without federal recognition were particularly vulnerable to these attacks since their political status did not have an official basis in US law. Applying the rules of hypodescent, whites viewed Indians as disappearing whenever they mixed with other populations, especially African Americans.[79] Efforts to "erase" Indians stemmed from racial fears of blacks using "Indianness" as a way station to whiteness, and also from desires to divest tribes of their remain-ing land and resources since the elimination of "Indian" as a political category "would result in more land held as private property by non-Indians."[80]

In the context of Jim Crow America, tribal citizenship took on increased symbolic value. To be recognized as Indian meant escaping classification as "colored" and avoiding some of the harshest manifestations of segregation and racial violence. As historian Katherine Osburn has argued, "Federal Indian policy during the allotment era intersected with the segregated society of the Jim Crow South to create a market for Indian identity."[81] Even beyond the tan-gible land and resources to which tribal citizens were entitled, "Indianness" itself became a form of property that endowed its holders with certain rights and benefits within America's racial hierarchy.[82] This property, however, had value only as long as outsiders recognized its worth. If white Americans per-ceived tribal citizens as illegitimately "Indian" according to the racial ideas of the time, then tribal citizens stood to lose their protections. The symbolic value of "Indianness" created an additional incentive for tribes to police be-longing to ensure that only recognizable "Indians" made it onto the tribal rolls. They knew that each person they included represented the identity of the tribal nation as a whole.

The need to closely monitor the racial identity of tribal citizens became part of what anthropologist Jean Dennison has termed the "logic of recogni-tion." Tribes worried that if they lost their distinct racial and cultural identity through permissive enrollment policies, the American public would no longer see them as "real" Indians.[83] They risked losing their political recognition—whether state or federal—and by extension their tribal sovereignty, land, and resources. As a result of these fears, tribes felt pressured to fit their citizenship criteria within the bounds deemed acceptable by white society. In this context, race became an ever more critical component of Indian identity and tribal citi-zenship, particularly in the South.

The growing economic and symbolic value of tribal citizenship in the late nineteenth and early twentieth centuries inspired thousands of individuals across the South to assert an Indian identity, a development that challenged tribal efforts to police belonging. Many of these people cynically claimed tribal citizenship in order to profit from tribal land and resources.[84] Others genuinely believed family stories of Indian heritage. Some—in particular those who were phenotypically black—used claims of Indian identity to contest the emerging biracial society of the American South. As historian Laura L. Lovett has explained, "For individuals and families classified as 'colored,' appealing to Indian ancestry in family histories or public pageantry used Indianness, as they understood it, to undermine the very definition of the racial category assigned to them by segregation."[85] Claiming Indian identity was a way to escape poverty and discrimination in a society that offered little comfort to its most marginalized citizens.[86]

Whatever their motivations, people who claimed an Indian identity but lacked a tribal connection posed a threat to tribes. By claiming rights to the property of tribal citizenship, they put in jeopardy both tribal resources and political identity.[87] This danger was particularly pronounced for asset-rich tribes because tribal citizenship not only attracted individual claimants but also speculators and lawyers who saw an opportunity to cash in on tribal resources. Traveling across the South, these schemers searched for people with pretentions to Indian ancestry to put on tribal rolls in exchange for a fee and a share of any assets the claimants might receive.[88] To guard against this threat, tribes created new citizenship rules that they hoped would distinguish between legitimate tribal citizens and people who lacked a genuine connection to the tribe.

The link between tribal citizenship and political recognition became more pronounced during the late nineteenth and twentieth centuries as the federal apparatus for managing Indian affairs grew increasingly bureaucratized. During these years, the Office of Indian Affairs underwent a period of professionalization similar to that of other government agencies, businesses, and professions in postbellum America.[89] Previously a relatively weak and ineffective organization, the OIA strengthened institutionally by selecting a professional staff, centralizing reservation control through a systematic inspection system, and delineating clear organizational goals, such as the education and assimilation of tribal citizens.[90] To put their new policies into practice, officials sent agents into tribal communities to monitor and manage tribal affairs.[91] Infused with reformist zeal and progressive ideals, the agents endeavored to account for their charges in a systemized fashion. Their efforts were particularly important for tribes that underwent allotment or other distributions of tribal resources, but they also applied to any tribe that received state or federal services or that sought formal political recognition. Government agents needed to know who was entitled to a share of tribal assets.[92] As a result of these policy shifts, white officials became enmeshed in the inner workings of tribal citizenship. They demanded that tribes clarify, delineate, and document their enrollment criteria and they strove to neatly categorize people into distinct categories of "Indian" and "non-Indian."

As part of their effort to document tribal citizens, officials produced tribal rolls.[93] Created as part of federal census records or to enumerate tribal citizens for the purpose of distributing claims money, allotting land, or extending federal recognition, these rolls endeavored to make Indian people "recordable, predictable, and legible."[94] They included key information about tribal citizens, such as their name, age, address, kinship relationship to other tribal citizens, and degree of Indian blood. Yet although the rolls served similar purposes across tribes, officials applied no uniform standard to their creation. The particular historical context of each tribe shaped how the roll was constructed and who was included or excluded. Depending on the circumstances, reservation agents produced the rolls in consultation with the tribal government, let the tribal body take the lead on citizenship decisions, or took matters into their own hands. More often than not, the creation of tribal rolls entailed a process of mutual accommodation and dialogue in which "Indians partly yielded to and partly gave their own meanings to U.S. law."[95]

Occasionally, the construction of tribal rolls became highly contentious as core members of the tribal community, federal agents, and people who claimed a right to tribal citizenship vied for the power to decide who belonged. These disputes occurred more frequently in resource-rich tribes like the Eastern Band of Cherokee Indians since more people clamored for inclusion on the tribal rolls. Threatened by outsiders who demanded tribal rights and by white officials who presumed to make decisions for them, tribes fervently defended their citizenship. They understood that more was at stake than the simple question of enrollment. Their sovereign authority over tribal citizens, their land and resource base, and their government-to-government relationship with the United States all depended on the determination of their citizenry. Citizenship debates illuminate the inner workings of tribes at crucial moments in their history and reveal the contested nature of United States power.

Ultimately, the tribal rolls created in the late nineteenth and twentieth centuries represented a mere snapshot of the composition of each tribe at a particular historical moment. The products of debates and disputes, these rolls did not necessarily even reflect a true representation of whom Indian people considered tribal citizens at the time.[96] Once finalized, however, the rolls fixed tribal citizenship in place. Indeed, these rolls often became the basis for modern citizenship in the tribe since many tribal constitutions mandated that all future tribal citizens descend from someone on the roll. Today the vast majority of tribes in the United States define descent by reference to a base roll.[97]

The efforts of federal agents to quantify, classify, and enroll Indians were complicated by their own conceptions of race and the messy realities of kinship, identity, and belonging. Indians had intermarried with outsiders since colonial times and some of their descendants had integrated into black and white populations, while others remained closely associated with the tribal body. The United States had no uniform way to decide which of these individuals qualified as tribal citizens. Although the US Constitution used the word "Indian" in two places, it failed to define the term. This left Congress to make its own definitions on an ad hoc basis.[98] To make sense of the complexity, white officials often turned to ideas of race and "blood" to create intelligible categories of people.[99] A person with one Indian parent and one non-Indian parent, for example, had one-half Indian blood. A person with one Indian grandparent and three non-Indian grandparents had one-quarter Indian blood. These calculations were notoriously inaccurate; in the absence of documentary evidence, officials often based blood quantum designations merely on the racial phenotype of the individuals they recorded. By evaluating Indian identity on the basis of "blood," white officials injected a racial component into the political status of "Indian." They also reinforced the idea that a person's identity— both racial and political—could be fractionalized and diluted. Eventually, a number of tribes adopted blood quantum restrictions to tribal citizenship, thereby cementing race into tribal law.[100]

Federal uses of "blood quantum" to define Indian identity became more pronounced under the Indian Reorganization Act (IRA) of 1934. This act, passed under the auspices of Commissioner of Indian Affairs John Collier as part of the Indian New Deal, was intended to undo the destructive policy of allotment and to foster the recreation of cohesive, land-based tribal communities. The act provided funds for the repurchase of tribal lands, extended to Indians the right to form businesses and other organizations, and encouraged tribes to revitalize their self-government by writing tribal constitutions based on a US model.[101] These new constitutions included formal citizenship criteria that codified and fixed tribal enrollment requirements in place. As scholars like Melissa Meyer have pointed out, the IRA "gave long-overdue support to Indian political organizations, but at the expense of indigenous forms and practices."[102]

Although the IRA did not dictate who could qualify for tribal citizenship, it stipulated that the secretary of the interior approve all constitutions organized under its terms. In addition, the act provided a definition of "Indian" for the purpose of determining who could take advantage of the act in the first place. This definition referred to all persons of Indian descent who were citizens of federally recognized tribes, all descendants of tribal citizens residing on a reservation as of June 1, 1934, and any other person "of one-half or more

Indian blood."[103] In this way, tribes seeking formal recognition during these years—like the Mississippi Choctaws—had to abide by federally mandated blood quantum restrictions on their tribal citizenship in order to have their political identity officially acknowledged.[104] But the federal government applied "blood" inconsistently to tribal identity depending on the particular circumstances of different tribes. Although a few previously unacknowledged tribes found their citizenship regimes constrained in this way, overall the constitutions enacted under the terms of the IRA were not heavily reliant on Indian blood quantum. Instead, most tribes that reorganized under the act—like the Catawbas—relied on parental enrollment and residency to make their tribal citizenship decisions.[105]

The IRA formally articulated the conceptual difference between "federally recognized" and "unrecognized" tribes by creating categories of people entitled to a federal relationship. Confusion over what constituted a "tribe," however, persisted, and many tribes—like the Pamunkeys in Virginia—fell through the cracks. For a time, the task of deciding which groups qualified for federal recognition as tribes fell to the secretary of the interior, who relied extensively on the work of Felix S. Cohen, an employee of the Solicitor's Office in the Department of the Interior from 1933 to 1947, who wrote *The Handbook of Federal Indian Law* (1941).[106] Cohen's treatise emphasized the political relationship of tribes to the United States and argued that tribal sovereignty was "perhaps the most basic principle of all Indian law."[107] Cohen also outlined criteria for determining which tribes could be federally recognized. Unlike the IRA, Cohen did not use "blood quantum" as a criterion. Instead, he stressed the de facto treatment of the group as a tribe by the federal government and other tribes and also considered the group's internal political organization.[108]

Despite Cohen's recognition of the political rather than racial character of tribes, tribal sovereignty faced another setback in the 1950s after the federal government implemented its termination policy. In 1953, House Concurrent Resolution 108 recommended the immediate withdrawal of federal aid, services, and protection from federally recognized tribes.[109] Public Law 280, also passed that year, authorized certain state governments to extend their jurisdiction over Indian reservations.[110] Like allotment, termination promised to bring Indians into the mainstream by ending the relationship between tribes and the federal government, and by dividing and distributing commonly held tribal lands and resources.[111] Termination also required the creation of tribal rolls so that tribes could disburse their assets to recognized citizens. This policy prompted tribes like the Catawbas to revise and refine their citizenship criteria.

During these years the federal government also encouraged Indians to relocate from their reservation homes to urban environments that provided them with greater educational and employment opportunities. The relocation program, which officials saw as another way to assimilate Native people into mainstream America, facilitated a dramatic demographic shift in the Indian population. By 1970, around half of the total Indian population in the United States lived in cities. As Kirsty Gover has pointed out, this shift forced tribes to consider new questions about sovereignty and citizenship: "If tribes were no longer geographically discrete, closely inter-related and co-resident, what concept of tribalism could sustain the community?"[112] In response to these demographic changes, tribes like the Mississippi Choctaws and Catawbas removed residency requirements from their citizenship criteria to ensure that the dispersal of tribal citizens did not lead to the demise of the tribe.

Despite the threats of termination and relocation—and perhaps in reaction to these policies—tribal sovereignty reemerged as a valued term within indigenous communities.[113] Throughout the 1960s and 1970s, tribal citizens rallied around the call for self-determination to express their vision of rights for Indian peoples. These efforts culminated in the 1975 Indian Self-Determination and Education Assistance Act, which reversed termination and promised to uphold tribal sovereignty. Despite these gains, however, many tribes continued to rely on the enrollment rules and base rolls established in the early twentieth century.[114] These criteria became a standard by which tribes judged who could legitimately claim a political identity as a tribal citizen. As anthropologist Circe Sturm has pointed out, "the documentary ideal has now become one of the most commonly referenced and consistently applied measures of tribal belonging."[115]

Although tribal citizens sometimes "feel conflicted about tribal regulations and the fact that they privilege written histories over oral histories, they believe the contemporary political moment leaves them with few options."[116] In particular, the foray of certain tribes into the world of high stakes gaming since Congress passed the Indian Gaming Regulatory Act in 1988 has raised the economic stakes of tribal citizenship. To defend their political identity and economic resources from outsiders, tribes need an efficient mechanism to determine who belongs.[117] As was the case in the late nineteenth and early twentieth centuries, "practical administrative considerations—which entail a bureaucratization of indigenous identity—play an important role in shaping the overall discourse and practice" of tribal citizenship today.[118]

The federal government's "logic of recognition" also continues to constrain tribal citizenship decisions. Despite the 1978 Supreme Court ruling in *Santa Clara Pueblo v. Martinez* that affirmed the right of tribes to determine their own citizenship, tribes recognize that their sovereign status and federal-tribal trust relationship are dependent on the "appropriateness" of their enrollment rules. As Kirsty Gover has argued, "Over-inclusive membership rules could legally transform a tribe from a sovereign political entity to a racial association and release the federal government from its trust obligations" if Congress decided that the community was "no longer sufficiently tribe-like to exercise tribal sovereignty."[119]

Tribes seeking federal recognition are particularly vulnerable to government oversight of their citizenship criteria. In 1978, the federal government created the Federal Acknowledgment Process to provide an official administrative review process and mandatory criteria for groups seeking federal recognition.[120] To qualify for recognition, tribes must provide base rolls and citizenship criteria that meet the approval of federal officials.[121] Like Cohen's criteria, the Federal Acknowledgment Process, which still operates today, relies on political continuity and community cohesion rather than race. Nevertheless, racial ideas remain embedded in the process since historically outsiders recognized the separate political status of tribes as "Indian" in part because of the racial identity of their tribal citizens.[122] Race and politics remain inextricably intertwined for Indian identity despite seemingly race-neutral federal policies.[123]

The shifts in federal Indian policy, the racial legislation of Jim Crow, and the bureaucratization of Indian Affairs in the late nineteenth and twentieth centuries all influenced how tribes thought about citizenship. During this period, tribes internalized ideas of Indian blood and to some extent racialized definitions of belonging; however, tribes did not apply these concepts uniformly or universally.[124] The Pamunkeys of Virginia, the Catawbas of South Carolina, the Mississippi Choctaws, the Eastern Band of Cherokees in North Carolina, the Florida Seminoles, and the Miccosukees each developed different requirements for tribal citizenship based on their unique histories and relationships with federal and state officials. Their stories demonstrate that Native peoples do not blindly or universally adopt notions of tribal identity. Instead, using a variety of criteria, such as reservation residency, cultural affiliation, gendered notions of kinship, and racial identity, Indians have created different strategies for delineating who can legitimately claim rights as citizens of their tribes.

When it came to making their citizenship criteria in the late nineteenth and twentieth centuries, tribes were both strategic and resourceful. They chose rules that they felt best reflected their traditional values and ideas of belonging, but they also borrowed from concepts and documentation used by the federal government to make their citizenship criteria intelligible to white America.[125] They looked for ways to protect their land and resources from outsiders and to promote the ongoing recognition of their tribal sovereignty and political status as nations. Ultimately, tribes made decisions on what they believed to be the optimal composition of their communities in ways that they hoped would best promote their ongoing political survival. Sometimes this meant making difficult choices that excluded certain people from tribal citizenship; these were the sacrifices tribes had to make to survive in a hostile environment.

"Policing Belonging, Protecting Identity," the first chapter, examines the Pamunkey Indian Tribe of Virginia. As a state-recognized tribe, the Pamunkeys did not face federal pressure to establish an official citizenship roll until very recently when they sought federal recognition. This did not mean that the tribe was exempt from external influence on its citizenship decisions, but it gave the Pamunkeys flexibility to develop and modify citizenship criteria based on their particular needs at different times. Of primary concern to the Pamunkeys in the late nineteenth and twentieth centuries was the protection of their reservation lands. These 1,200 acres, reserved to them in treaties with the colony of Virginia, represented the heart of the tribe, where core members of the community lived, hunted, fished, farmed, and raised their families. The Pamunkeys' fear of losing control of this land motivated many of their citizenship decisions, particularly after white Virginians equated the Pamunkeys' tribal right to the reservation with their racial identity as "Indian."

To protect their land, the Pamunkeys developed strategies to bolster their Indian identity and increase their visibility in Virginia while simultaneously distancing themselves from African Americans to avoid classification as "colored." They also searched for ways to keep the reservation in the hands of core members of the tribe after some Pamunkeys moved elsewhere and intermarried with whites. The tribe developed unique residency rules, gendered definitions of belonging, and a tiered system of tribal citizenship to meet these challenges, which included prohibiting Pamunkey women who married whites from living on the reservation and denying voting rights to tribal citizens who moved away from the core community. The Pamunkey story reveals one way that a tribe used citizenship criteria to preserve its territorial sovereignty and to bolster its political status.

The second chapter, "From Fluid Lists to Fixed Rolls," explores the experiences of the Catawba Indian Nation of South Carolina. As a state-recognized tribe in the Jim Crow South, the Catawbas faced similar pressures to those experienced by the Pamunkeys. They worried about losing their political status and reservation land if whites failed to acknowledge their Indian identity. The Catawbas had an additional incentive to guard their tribal citizenship from outsiders: each year tribal citizens received per capita payments from the state for lands ceded to South Carolina in 1840. To distribute this money, the tribe had to negotiate their definitions of belonging with state officials who made the payments to ensure that only legitimate community members received a share.

Complicating this process, the tribe underwent several significant social changes in the late nineteenth and early twentieth centuries. After a majority of the tribe converted to Mormonism, a small contingent of Catawbas migrated west with missionaries. Catawbas debated whether these migrants still deserved shares of the tribe's assets. Furthermore, the intermarriage of South Carolina Catawbas with whites raised questions over the status of their children. While confronting these issues, the Catawbas achieved federal recognition, which required the creation of an official tribal roll. The Catawba story demonstrates how one tribe used its citizenship criteria to respond to changing social conditions and traces how the shift from state to federal recognition altered the process of defining citizenship.

The third chapter, "Learning the Language of 'Blood,'" examines the Mississippi Band of Choctaw Indians. Unlike the Pamunkeys and Catawbas, whose tribes remained relatively intact in the post-removal South, the Mississippi Choctaws belonged to a remnant population that stayed behind after the United States forced the Choctaw Nation to relocate to Indian Territory, now Oklahoma. Two provisions of the Choctaw removal treaty shaped their creation of a new polity with a distinct citizenry. The fourteenth article promised allotments of land to Choctaw families that remained in Mississippi and became state citizens, but an unscrupulous federal agent prevented their exercise of this right. As a result, according to the treaty, they continued to be citizens of the Choctaw Nation, in which they no longer lived. At the end of the nineteenth century, Congress created the Dawes Commission to allot the Choctaw Nation's western lands to tribal citizens and to dissolve the tribe, whose residents became citizens of the new state of Oklahoma. The commission assigned allotments to certain Mississippi Choctaws as well and based its enrollment decisions in part on individuals' degree of Indian blood. Those who did not qualify for enrollment, in addition to hundreds more who could not move west because of poverty, lost citizenship rights in the Choctaw Nation.

In the years that followed, the Mississippi Choctaws used what they had learned about federal notions of Indian identity, and particularly ideas of "blood," to recreate a tribal status. In 1918, Congress appropriated funds for their relief and began purchasing land for their use. These federal actions acknowledged the separate status of the Mississippi Choctaws from the Choctaw Nation and began the process by which the tribe decided who legally belonged to it as citizens. The Mississippi Band of Choctaw Indians achieved federal recognition in 1945, at which point the Choctaws developed a tribal constitution that formalized their citizenship criteria. The Mississippi Choctaw story reveals how the remnants of a removed tribe manipulated federal concepts of race and "blood" to create a new tribe, delineate citizenship requirements, and regain tribal resources in the South.

"Contests of Sovereignty," the fourth chapter, focuses on the experiences of the Eastern Band of Cherokee Indians of North Carolina. Like the Mississippi Choctaws, the Eastern Band of Cherokee Indians survived in the South after the forced removal of the Cherokee Nation. Unlike the Mississippi Choctaws, the Eastern Band's political separation from the Cherokee Nation had already commenced prior to the removal era. In treaties made with the federal government in 1817 and 1819, some Cherokees opted to remain on ceded land in North Carolina and become state citizens. Later joined by other Cherokees who escaped removal, these Cherokees formed the core of what became the Eastern Band. Gradually rebuilding a tribal land base in the 1840s and 1850s with the help of a white ally, Eastern Cherokees reasserted a political identity and rebuilt their nation. In 1868 they achieved federal recognition as a separate tribe, and in 1889 they incorporated the tribe under the state laws of North Carolina to affirm their control of tribal resources.

As the Cherokees formalized their legal status, citizenship in the Eastern Band evolved from a clan-based network of kin to a political identity that provided tangible economic and legal rights. Adapting to these new conditions—and helping to create them—the Cherokees aimed to protect their resources from outsiders by limiting access to tribal citizenship. This effort became particularly important after the Band sold valuable tracts of land and tribally owned timber, and distributed the profits to tribal citizens. In addition, the threat of federal allotment of Eastern Band land forced the tribe to consider carefully questions of belonging. During the enrollment process, which culminated with the Baker Roll of 1924, the Eastern Band of Cherokee Indians developed legal citizenship criteria that could stand up to the scrutiny of federal officials while limiting tribal rights to those individuals who belonged to the core Cherokee community centered on the Qualla Boundary. The federal government's involvement in this process and its rejection of criteria established by the Band threatened to destroy the tribe's economic base and its political future. The Eastern Band experience identifies the vital interconnections between the control of tribal citizenship, the protection of tribal resources, and the preservation of tribal sovereignty.

The final chapter, "Nation Building and Self-Determination," explores the story of the Seminole Tribe of Florida and the Miccosukee Tribe of Indians of Florida. Like the Mississippi Choctaws and the Eastern Cherokees, the Seminoles were people left behind in the South following the removal of most tribal citizens to Indian Territory. Linguistically diverse and geographically scattered in late nineteenth-century Florida, the Seminoles were united by their memories of three brutal wars fought against the United States. To preserve their political independence in Florida and to avoid future removal attempts, the Seminoles established rules of conduct and rigorously policed interactions with outsiders.

Increased contact with Americans brought change. Seminoles differed in their responses to missionaries, educators, reservation lands, and economic programs, which opened new divisions that cut deeper than old linguistic and geographical differences. When official political status through federal recognition threatened to lock the tribe into one political identity, tribal citizens responded by breaking into two federally recognized tribes as well as a third group of unorganized Mikasuki-speakers that rejected political affiliation with either tribe. Although they shared a common heritage, Seminole and Miccosukee citizens chose to belong to the tribe that most accurately reflected their worldview. As their divergent histories show, for some tribes, discussions of tribal citizenship not only concerned who belonged but also raised questions about what kind of tribe a person wanted to belong to. The Seminoles and Miccosukees brought ideas of tribal citizenship and tribal sovereignty full circle: they claimed authority over their citizenship decisions, but they also asserted their right to self-determination by joining the tribe that best reflected their values.

Although each chapter examines the particular experiences of one tribal community, taken together they illustrate some of the key issues faced by southern tribes as they made their citizenship decisions in the late nineteenth and twentieth centuries. The Pamunkey story highlights the dangers of the "logic of recognition"—the way that tribes have had to guard their citizenship in order to promote external acknowledgment of their "Indianness." Southern tribes—particularly those without federal recognition—risked reclassification as "colored" if they did not actively distance themselves from black people during the Jim Crow years. The Catawba story showcases the bureaucratization of tribal citizenship and the effects that the transition from state to federal recognition had on tribal citizenship decisions. Federally approved base rolls, as well as legal citizenship criteria set out in tribal constitutions, became the foundation of modern tribal citizenship. The Mississippi Choctaw story illustrates how tribes adopted and adapted federal concepts of "Indianness," and particularly notions of Indian "blood," in order to satisfy external expectations about their identity. By purposefully conflating race and nation, the Mississippi Choctaws were able to transform themselves from a remnant population of a removed tribe into tribal citizens in their own right. The Eastern Cherokee story, however, illustrates that tribes did not adopt federal concepts of "Indianness" blindly. Rather, they engaged in prolonged contests of sovereignty over the meanings of citizenship. Finally, the Florida Seminole and Miccosukee story connects tribal citizenship to self-determination by showing that Indians have not conceived of themselves as simply belonging to a racial group but rather to political entities with distinct goals. By joining the tribe that best reflected their worldview, the Seminoles and Miccosukees

highlighted the national character of Indian tribes and the ongoing commitment of tribal citizens to determining their own futures.

This book does not pass judgment on the citizenship criteria adopted by
any of the tribes under study or attempt to offer solutions to the problems
inherent in modern tribal citizenship debates. These issues are multifaceted,
far-reaching, and different for each tribe. Rather, *Who Belongs?* is intended to
shed light on the complexities of tribal citizenship and explain why some tribes
made the decisions they did about belonging at particular historical moments.
By illuminating the constraints tribes faced, the threats they experienced to
their political sovereignty and economic resources, and the racial context in
which they lived, it demonstrates that tribes' citizenship decisions were neither arbitrary nor malice driven but were difficult choices made under difficult
circumstances. This may be cold comfort to people like Sharon Flora who feel
unfairly excluded from tribal citizenship today, but this book at least begins to
explain those decisions as well as their consequences.

1

Policing Belonging,
Protecting Identity

The Pamunkey Indian Tribe of Virginia

On October 14, 2010, the Pamunkey Indian Tribe of Virginia submitted a petition to the US Department of the Interior for federal recognition as an Indian tribe. After reviewing the application, Director of the Office of Federal Acknowledgment R. Lee Fleming wrote a letter to the tribe's lawyers that described "obvious deficiencies or significant omissions apparent in the documented petition." One problem was that the application lacked specific tribal citizenship requirements, which is a key criterion for federal recognition. Although the Pamunkeys claimed that "all current members descend from 40 direct lineal ancestors," they failed to provide any information other than a statement that "Pamunkey Tribal membership requires sufficient documentation of ancestry back to certain identified Tribe members *and* a social connection to the Tribe and current Tribal members residing on the Pamunkey Indian Reservation." If the Pamunkeys did not fully delineate their citizenship requirements and provide other documentation, Fleming warned, their application faced rejection "because of technical problems."[1]

The failure of the Pamunkeys to spell out their citizenship criteria for the Office of Federal Acknowledgment did not mean that they lacked an understanding of who belonged to their tribe. Indeed, Pamunkey tribal citizenship had a long history fraught with stressful situations and difficult choices. As a small, state-recognized tribe in racially divided Virginia, the Pamunkeys fought bitter battles to preserve their tribal status in the late nineteenth and early twentieth centuries. In this struggle, they marshaled tribal citizenship requirements to bolster their Indian identity and to insist that the Virginia legislature uphold their rights to reservation land. Race became a critical factor to the Pamunkeys as they strove to defend themselves against Jim Crow reclassification as "colored." The tribe also created a tiered system of tribal citizenship based on gender and reservation residency. These distinctions helped ensure that the core Pamunkey community living on the reservation maintained authority over Pamunkey land even as certain community members moved away and married whites. Although their criteria for belonging were not always clear to outsiders, the Pamunkeys had historical reasons for including some and rejecting others from their tribe.

The Pamunkeys inhabited a small tract of land that the colony of Virginia had set aside for them in the seventeenth century. This reservation was part of the larger territory occupied by the Powhatan Confederacy at the time of contact with the English in 1607. White squatters continually made inroads on Pamunkey territory, and a series of cessions reduced the Indians' land base. Following Bacon's Rebellion in 1676, the Indians appealed to the colonial legislature to have their lands officially restored. An order of assembly passed in 1677 confirmed the Pamunkeys' reservation and guaranteed them hunting and fishing rights on Englishmen's unfenced patented lands. Land sales and cessions continued into the eighteenth century, however, as outsiders pressured the Indians. Finally, in 1748, the Virginia Assembly appointed three white trustees to oversee Pamunkey land sales. This began a long process of

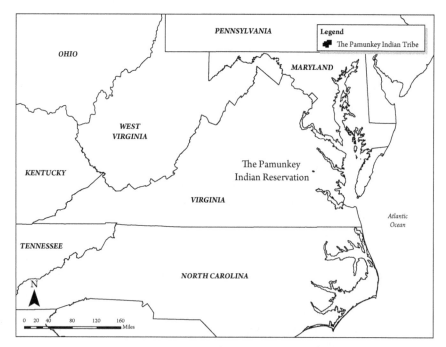

Figure 1.1 Set aside for the tribe by the colony of Virginia in the seventeenth century, the Pamunkey Indian Reservation consists of 1,200 acres located in a bend of the Pamunkey River in King William County. Map prepared by Christian Adams.

white oversight of Pamunkey actions.[2] By the removal era, the Pamunkeys were an often ignored, but legally entrenched part of Virginia.

Unlike many southern tribes, the Pamunkeys never directly faced the threat of westward removal. Small in numbers in the 1830s, the Pamunkeys seemed inconspicuous and innocuous to white observers. Indeed, many Virginians denied the Pamunkeys were Indian at all since they had adopted so much of the surrounding Anglo culture. Instead, they viewed the Pamunkeys as members of the free non-white social strata in Virginia, "persons of color." As such, the Indians were not worth the effort and expense of removal.[3] The Pamunkeys soon found, however, that white attitudes toward their racial identity were just as threatening to their survival in the South as federal removal policy was to other tribes. Pamunkey efforts to defend their Indian identity and to preserve their tribal land base ultimately had profound effects on their definitions of belonging.

Despite the general indifference Virginians displayed toward the Pamunkeys, some whites in the state did seek the dissolution of the Indians' land base during the removal years. In 1836, the Pamunkeys heard a rumor that local whites planned to petition the Virginia General Assembly to sell the reservation on the grounds that non-Pamunkeys, including free blacks, also lived there.[4] In 1842, Thomas W. S. Gregory, a white Virginian, made good on this threat and circulated a petition for the termination of the Pamunkey reservation. Gregory asserted that "the claims of the Indian no longer exist—his blood has so largely mingled with the negro race as to have obliterated all striking features of Indian extraction." He argued that the presence of a legally constituted free non-white community put white Virginians in danger and described the reservation as "the haunts of vice, where the worthless and abandoned whiteman may resort and find everything to gratify his depraved appetite; where spirituous liquors are retailed without license; the ready asylum of runaway slaves, and a secure harbor for everyone who wished concealment."[5] He called for the Indians' immediate expulsion from the state.

The Pamunkeys responded to Gregory's actions with two counter petitions to the General Assembly. In particular, they refuted the accusation that they had married with free blacks "until their Indian character has vanished."[6] They asserted that they were hardworking and honest people who lived together like a large extended family and took care of each other. Moreover, they insisted, many people on the reservation were fully Indian and others were more than half Indian in ancestry.[7] The tribe's white trustees supported their claims, and the General Assembly rejected Gregory's petition. The Pamunkey reservation was safe. The experience, however, taught the Pamunkeys that in the future they would have to be careful about their associations with outsiders in order to protect their Indian identity and, by extension, their land rights in Virginia.

Although the 1843 petition failed to drive the Pamunkeys from their homes, Virginia whites continued to question their racial identity. After John Brown's unsuccessful raid at Harpers Ferry in 1859, the state temporarily disarmed the Pamunkeys.[8] This move not only hurt Pamunkey hunters economically but also threatened their Indian identity by conflating them with free blacks. When the Pamunkeys protested, the governor of Virginia suggested that officials take an annual census to determine who was entitled to treatment as a "tributary Indian." The governor added that "if any become one fourth mixed with the Negro race then they may be treated as free negroes or mulattoes."[9] The state never compiled the promised censuses. Like the 1843 petition, however, the governor's remarks warned the Pamunkeys about the consequences of association with African Americans.

Officially, Virginia recognized the Pamunkeys as an Indian tribe based on colonial-era treaties with them, yet the state's treatment of them did not foster good feelings. When Virginia seceded from the Union in 1861, a number of Pamunkeys fled to Canada to avoid conscription in the Confederate service. Some reasoned that as long as Virginia declined to treat them as equal citizens, they had no obligation to fight for the state. As Frank Sweat testified to the Southern Claims Commission after the war, "I have some Indian blood in my veins and was not permitted to vote or sit in the jury box. I was but one step from a slave."[10] Other Pamunkeys went further and joined Union forces, serving as soldiers, guides, and seamen.[11] They may have thought that a Union victory would bring recognition of their rights in Virginia. Contrary to their expectations, however, the Confederate defeat did not alter the racial attitudes of white Virginians. Instead, the Pamunkeys found themselves subject to even stricter social and racial codes.[12]

After the Civil War, the Indians' fears of identity loss grew more pronounced. White Virginians increasingly divided the state's population into two categories: "white" and "colored." This system of social and legal classification left little room for Virginia Indians. Uninformed reporters asserted that "their aboriginal blood is so mingled with the imported African that their identity as Indians is almost lost and merged in the negro or mulatto."[13] Such claims disturbed Pamunkeys who feared a repeat of earlier efforts to break up their reservation. Determined to avoid racial as well as tribal extinction in the eyes of whites, the Pamunkeys fought back by refusing the label of "colored," developing their own ideas about race, and building segregated institutions. These efforts, born out of a desperate need to defend their Indian identity, had a lasting legacy on the way the tribe defined belonging.

Segregation hit Virginia even before the official end of Reconstruction. Churches that had once welcomed parishioners of any color barred blacks and Indians as soon as the Civil War ended. Pamunkeys, most of whom had belonged to the Colosse Baptist Church in King William County, found themselves without a religious home.[14] Refusing to attend black churches, in 1865 they established a separate place of worship on the reservation "under the trees during the summer, and in the members' homes in winter."[15] The next year they constructed the Pamunkey Indian Baptist Church.[16] The dedication of the first Indian church in Virginia reportedly "was a joyous one for that group of earnest Christian Indians," one that represented a triumph over the limitations of biracial segregation in the South.[17]

The tribe permitted only Indian or white ministers to preach at the new church.[18] They designed this rule to emphasize that the church was "Indian," not "colored." The Pamunkeys also fostered relationships with white Baptists by joining the Dover Baptist Association in Virginia, which was willing to accept them as a separate congregation. The tribe sent delegates to annual meetings of this organization. White members marveled at the "curious looking men" with "real copper" complexions and "long, black and straight" hair who attended the meetings, but did not turn them away.[19] At various points, the association even appointed white ministers to serve the tribe.[20] By taking an active role in the Dover Baptist Association, the Pamunkeys highlighted their ongoing dedication to their faith and their religious, if not political, equality to whites.

On the reservation, the Pamunkey Indian Baptist Church became a center for community gathering and received "the hearty support of the whole tribe."[21] The church held services every Sunday, which nearly all the Pamunkeys on the reservation attended.[22] One Pamunkey woman recalled, "What I remember about church on the reservation is that you didn't think about whether or not you were going to go. You went to church on Sunday morning because it was something you did with the whole family." Church attendance was "something that the entire community did together" and "most of the activities in the community were centered on the church." Children attended Sunday school and adults joined together in singing, preaching, and prayer. The church helped emphasize community belonging and also the specific roles of tribal citizens. For example, Pamunkey men and women sat on different sides of the church aisle, a division that reflected their different responsibilities and gender roles.[23] Church membership also reinforced tribal identity by including community members but excluding those whom the Pamunkeys considered racial inferiors. Indeed, observers noted that "the membership of the church and that of the whole tribe [were] almost coextensive."[24] Born out of Virginia's efforts to segregate "white" from "colored," the Pamunkey Indian Baptist Church became a strong marker of Pamunkey identity.

Segregated schools had a similar effect. The Pamunkeys refused to send their children to "colored" schools and petitioned the governor of Virginia to

establish a free, Indian school on their reservation.[25] Virginia finally heeded
this plea in 1877. The governor stipulated, however, that the Pamunkeys pay
school taxes to help support the institution. He also insisted that public support of the reservation school did not entitle the Indians to any other political rights in Virginia. According to white Virginians, the Pamunkeys were not
entitled to full state citizenship because of their status as "tributary Indians."
Their land was exempt from taxation, and as they were not subject to the bur-
dens of citizenship, neither did they deserve the privileges.[26] The Pamunkeys
accepted these terms in order to send their children to school.

Finding a teacher for the reservation school, however, proved problem-
atic. When the state appointed a black teacher to educate Pamunkey children, the Indians sent her back to Richmond.[27] They did, however, accept
white teachers. In later years, Pamunkey youths also attended Bacone High
School in Oklahoma and the Cherokee Boarding School in North Carolina,
both designed to serve Indian students.[28] Some of these students left the reservation permanently, but others returned to teach Pamunkey children.[29]
The Pamunkeys provided their own teachers to ensure that there was no
question about the status of their school as an "Indian" rather than "colored"
institution.[30]

Over time, the reservation school, like the Pamunkey Indian Baptist
Church, became a community focal point and a symbol of Pamunkey identity. Pamunkey children felt welcome there, even when surrounding whites
rejected them on account of race. Tribal citizen Louis Steward, who was born
in 1916, recalled that he and his siblings had tried to attend a white school in
Richmond while their parents worked in the city, but school officials kicked
them out on the grounds that they "had too much black blood." Instead of enrolling in a "colored" school, the children returned to the reservation and attended school there.[31] Tribal citizens shared common memories of the small
schoolhouse that contributed to their sense of separation from local black and
white populations. Proud of their separate education system, Pamunkey parents were distressed when Virginia integrated schools in the 1960s.[32] While
it lasted, the school provided the Pamunkeys with an institutional marker of
their distinct ethnic identity.[33]

In addition to establishing their own segregated institutions, the Pamunkeys
defended themselves against outside assumptions about their racial identity.
When a white neighbor taunted a Pamunkey man about being a "mulatto" in
1889, for example, the Indian took the matter to court and proved "that he had
no negro blood in his veins."[34] In a similar case in 1904, the Pamunkey chief
traveled to Richmond to consult a lawyer to seek "damages against a white
man of wealth . . . who is alleged to have said on a train that the tribe was com-
posed of 'half-niggers.' "[35] In addition to suing people who labeled them black,

Pamunkeys who visited Virginia cities refused to use services designated as "colored." In West Point, for example, Pamunkeys annoyed local whites by insisting on patronizing white barbershops.[36] Pamunkeys refused to accept the racial categorization to which whites assigned them. Instead they continually challenged Virginia color codes to preserve their Indian identity.

The Pamunkeys fought one of their most successful battles against Jim Crow over railroad coaches. In 1855, the Richmond and York River Railroad had run a track through part of the reservation. The Pamunkeys resented this action because the company failed to compensate them for the land.[37] Nevertheless, the Indians became frequent railroad customers, taking the train into the state capital to work and to purchase supplies. In July 1900, however, railroad companies began complying with a new Virginia law that demanded the segregation of railroad coaches by race.[38] The Pamunkeys decried the interpretation of the law, which compelled them to ride in Jim Crow coaches.[39] According to a journalist, the "order of the company requiring the red men to go into coaches provided for colored people has made them howling mad."[40] Their anger only increased after train conductors physically ejected Pamunkey travelers from white coaches.[41] The Indians refused to accept the law and planned ways to combat it.

The first effort of the Pamunkeys to defeat the new law took place in the King William County court. Initially, the court ruled against their suit and insisted they belonged in the "colored" coaches.[42] Not easily dissuaded, the Pamunkeys held a tribal meeting a few days later and appointed a committee to appeal directly to the Southern Railroad Company. They told company officials that they had been "treated with indignity," and they protested that "some of the most aristocratic families" in Virginia claimed descent from Pocahontas and other historic Natives, while maintaining a white racial identity.[43] They argued that if these whites traveled in white coaches, Pamunkeys should, too. Their persistent assertion of their rights finally captured the attention of the superintendent of the Richmond Division of the Southern Railroad.[44] In late August, he forwarded a telegram to the Pamunkey chief: "Please notify Chief Dennis, of the Pamunkey Indian tribe, that the matter is all right now in regard to riding in cars with the whites."[45] A small concession on the part of the railroad company, this decision represented a major victory for the Pamunkeys. Through their refusal to accept classification as "colored," the Indians overcame Virginia's Jim Crow conveyance codes and forced whites to recognize their Indian identity.

Following their fight to ride in white coaches, the tribe began issuing official certificates of tribal citizenship. These passports clearly identified the Pamunkeys as Indian, "to prevent annoyance when traveling."[46] If train conductors questioned their right to board white coaches, the Pamunkeys

simply pulled out their certificates. The Pamunkeys hoped that official documents would cement their identity as Indian in the eyes of white Virginians.
Nevertheless, they knew that the battle against racial reclassification was far
from over. Whites recognized their rights as Indians only so long as they maintained distance from blacks.

Although the Pamunkeys conceded that whites were their equals—and
hoped that whites recognized them as such as well—they considered "blacks
far beneath their social level."[47] Visitors to the reservation often commented on
the Pamunkeys' "race pride."[48] To showcase the perceived differences in their
positions, Pamunkeys hired local African Americans to work as farm laborers on the reservation.[49] These men and women farmed Pamunkey land, but
they did not socialize with their employers. By overseeing black laborers, the
Pamunkeys established not only that they were above such menial work but
also that they belonged to a different class of people than African Americans.

Above all, Pamunkeys decried intermarriage between tribal citizens and
African Americans. James Mooney, an ethnographer who visited the tribe in
the late nineteenth century, explained that their "one great dread is that their
wasted numbers may lose their identity by absorption in the black race."[50] To
prevent the ethnic extinction predicted for them by many Virginia whites, the
Pamunkeys developed strict codes to limit relationships between tribal citizens and black people. They prohibited social contact with African Americans
and refused "to allow marriages or even visiting between the young people."[51]
The tribal council formalized this position in its 1886 reservation laws. The
very first resolution stated that "No member of the Pamunkey Indian Tribe
shall intermarry with anny [sic] Nation except White or Indian under penalty
of forfeiting their rights in Town."[52]

For Pamunkeys who dared marry African Americans, the tribe's reaction
was draconian. Family members turned their backs on kin because of race.
In the 1970s, anthropologist Helen C. Rountree met a phenotypically black
man who claimed Pamunkey ancestry. Jesse L. S. Pendleton explained that his
Pamunkey grandmother, Roxanna Miles, had married a black boat captain.
Shunned by the Indian community, the couple moved to Newport News and
raised a family. As a child, Pendleton visited the reservation a few times with
his grandmother, but he developed the impression that tribal citizens were
"clannish and hostile to outsiders." Although Miles tried to maintain contact
with her Pamunkey relatives, the tribe rejected her children and grandchildren
on account of their race. This rebuff led to bitter feelings. Pendleton claimed
that "There wasn't much of anybody [his grandmother] didn't hate." Indeed,
Miles may have suffered self-hatred as well. Pendleton—who was raised primarily by his grandmother—grew up ashamed of "being colored," an attitude
he may have acquired from Miles.[53]

According to some reports, the Pamunkeys took their efforts to exclude blacks from tribal citizenship even further. A journalist asserted in 1902 that the Pamunkeys had "excluded from membership in their tribe a large number of those who showed plainly the marks of negro ancestry."[54] Another reporter described a tribal committee set up in the late 1880s "to exclude from their reservation certain black sheep who have crept into their fold." Stipulating that tribal citizens prove at least one-fourth Indian ancestry, this committee denied tribal rights to those who could not.[55] The question of black ancestry in the tribe became a deeply sensitive issue for the Pamunkeys. They refused to talk about the subject with outsiders, and they even avoided the topic among themselves.[56] As late as the 1970s, the Pamunkeys insisted that researchers recognize their prolonged efforts "to maintain their blood lines."[57]

Pamunkeys not only rejected relationships with African Americans, but they also tried to bolster their Indian identity through intermarriage with people from other Native communities. By the late nineteenth century, most members of the small tribe were closely related to every other person on the reservation.[58] This tight network of kin made finding suitable marriage partners within the tribe difficult.[59] Tribal citizens understood the dangers of incest, but they preferred Indian spouses to white or black partners. They hoped that marriage with Indians from other tribes would "restore the blood of their tribe and save themselves from extinction."[60] Such marriages also promised to highlight their Indian identity to Virginia whites.

Historically, Pamunkeys occasionally engaged in relationships with Indians outside of Virginia. In the mid-nineteenth century, for example, a Pamunkey man named John Mush (or Marsh) married a Catawba woman and went to live with his wife's tribe in South Carolina. The couple's children also married Catawbas.[61] Members of this family visited their Pamunkey relatives on several occasions. In the late 1880s, the Catawba family of Ep Harris, Margaret Harris, and their daughter, Maggie, journeyed to Virginia and lived among the Pamunkeys for two years.[62] Tuscarora Indians from North Carolina, like Peter Cussic, also made homes among the Pamunkeys.[63] The Pamunkeys were glad to have such individuals live with them because they provided the community with potential spouses.[64] Indeed, some Pamunkey men urged visiting Indian women to marry them. A journalist reported in 1900 that the reservation's schoolteacher, a woman who claimed to have Indian ancestry, finally resigned after she grew tired of the persistent efforts of Pamunkey men, including the chief, to court her.[65]

To increase the number of unions with citizens of other tribes in the late nineteenth century, Pamunkey leaders devised plans to attract non-Virginia Indians to the state. The tribal council entered into negotiations with the Eastern Band of Cherokee Indians in North Carolina, for example, "to procure brides for their unmarried sons and husbands for their unmarried daughters." Southern newspapers romanticized these efforts, claiming that "The male Pamunkeys understand the eastern Cherokee women to be exceptionally pretty, modest and sensible, and the female Pamunkeys regard the eastern Cherokee braves as handsome, loyal and industrious, calculated to make model husbands." Whether or not this was the case, the Pamunkeys certainly preferred Cherokees to local non-Indians as partners. The tribal council even sent Pamunkey emissaries to North Carolina to visit Cherokee Chief Nimrod J. Smith. They hoped that a personal appeal might "bring the negotiations to a favorable conclusion."[66]

In addition to courting the Cherokees, the Pamunkey tribal council sent a representative to the 1893 World's Columbian Exposition in Chicago. William Terrill Bradby traveled to Richmond before his trip to obtain from the governor a certificate that attested to the tribe's ownership of reservation land. Bradby hoped that the promise of land would lure western Indians to Virginia as marriage partners for Pamunkeys.[67] Once in Chicago, Bradby introduced himself to the head of the ethnological department of the World's Fair and became an honorary assistant in the department.[68] He met Indians from western tribes at the exposition and tried to convince them "to join the Pamunkeys in an effort to keep the blood lines purely aboriginal."[69]

Pamunkey efforts to draw Cherokees and western Indians to Virginia ultimately failed, but their hard work was not wasted. Although they did not bring home spouses, their search for Native husbands and wives attracted attention from white reporters and lawmakers. Indeed, the Pamunkeys made sure this was the case. Prior to their visits to North Carolina and Chicago, they sent emissaries to the state governor in Richmond, purportedly to receive "valuable suggestions from him as to the best manner" of securing "the contemplated alliance[s]." The governor may not have known how to help them find partners, but the delegations left a strong impression that the Indians were doing everything in their power to restore "the good Pamunkey breed again." White reporters from the *Atlanta Constitution* and the *Washington Post* relished the story, comparing the Pamunkey case to "that of the primitive Romans and the Sabines" and rooting for the Indians to find spouses.[70] This publicity drew attention to the Pamunkeys' assertion of Indian identity. Thus, even without non-Virginia Indian spouses, the Pamunkeys reinforced white perceptions of their status as Indian.

The Pamunkeys were more successful at arranging marriages with Indians from other Virginia tribes. The Pamunkeys had a long history of interaction with the Mattaponis and Chickahominies in particular, and the tribe raised no objection to tribal citizens marrying within these groups.[71] At the turn of the century, several Pamunkeys resided among the Chickahominies in Charles

Figure 1.2 William Terrill Bradby (pictured) traveled to the 1893 World's Columbian Exposition in Chicago to seek western Indian spouses for the Pamunkeys. Although his overtures failed, he helped draw media attention to the Pamunkeys' efforts to maintain a racially "Indian" identity in Jim Crow Virginia. Photographer: De Lancey W. Gill. Date: 1899. Courtesy of the National Anthropological Archives, Smithsonian Institution (BAE GN 00893 06197600).

City and New Kent Counties and "both bands are much intermarried."[72] The bonds of kinship were so firm between the Pamunkeys and the Mattaponis— who lived on a reservation a mere ten miles from the Pamunkeys—that for many years the two groups acted politically as one tribe. Over time, however, differences between the tribes separated them into distinct entities.

The Mattaponis lived on a seventy-acre reservation along the Mattaponi River.[73] Like the Pamunkeys, they had established early treaty relationships with the colony of Virginia that acknowledged their presence and affirmed their rights to their reservation land. At one point their reservation was connected to the Pamunkey reservation by a small strip of land; however, oral tradition suggests that whites tricked the Indians into selling this tract for a barrel of rum sometime before the nineteenth century.[74] By the late nineteenth century, the forty or so Mattaponis who resided on the reservation lived "principally from lumbering and farming." Unlike the Pamunkeys, they had "no chief or council." Instead they combined their political affairs with those of the Pamunkeys.[75] Anthropologists who visited the two tribes in the early twentieth century observed "no differences in community life" between them and noted that extensive intermarriages had "completely merged [the Pamunkeys and Mattaponis] in blood."[76]

Despite external similarities, Pamunkeys and Mattaponis made internal distinctions between their citizens. Although formally the tribes shared a single political organization, in practice the Mattaponis recognized their own headmen. The ten miles between the tribes created different community needs and goals, which grew more pronounced after the first ethnographers visited the tribes in the late nineteenth century. Rountree has suggested that Mattaponis may not have agreed with some of the activism that researchers inspired among the Pamunkeys.[77] They may have distanced themselves from Pamunkey cultural revitalization projects and the tribe's efforts to project a "pure" Indian identity to outsiders.

Another possibility is that racial tensions led to a split in the political organization of the tribes. Ethnographer James Mooney reported that Mattaponis had "more negro than Indian blood in them," but declared that Pamunkeys were "tolerably pure from mixture with other colors."[78] If he made similar observations to the Indians, the Pamunkeys may have felt it expedient to separate themselves politically from individuals with perceived black ancestry. Whatever the cause, the Mattaponi and Pamunkey tribes officially split in 1894. That year, the Virginia General Assembly appointed white trustees for the Mattaponis and the tribe wrote its own reservation laws.[79] From that point on, the Indians made distinctions between Mattaponi and Pamunkey tribal citizens.

Despite perceived racial differences between the tribes, the Mattaponis established taboos against intermarriage between Indians and blacks that were just as strict as those of their Pamunkey neighbors. Rountree reported in the 1970s that "No mixed couple would be allowed to live on the reservation; the tribe would disown them."[80] In recognition of Mattaponi efforts to maintain racial distance from blacks, Pamunkeys continued to marry Mattaponis despite the political separation of the tribes. Social and cultural ties between the tribes continued even after they legally divided their political citizenship.

The Pamunkeys remained a particularly vibrant Indian community in late nineteenth- and early twentieth-century Virginia, a fact that impressed researchers. When Mooney visited them in the 1890s, he discovered that they "have maintained their organization as a tribe under colonial and state government, and have kept up more of the Indian form and tradition than any of the [other Virginia tribes]."[81] The Pamunkeys were proud of their relationship with the state, and the tribal council kept copies of their treaties with Virginia, which the councilmen showed to reservation visitors.[82] The state held their reservation land "in trust for their benefit" and also promised tribal citizens rights to hunting, fishing, and gathering on surrounding public lands.[83] Although Virginia did not pay the tribe annuities, it exempted tribal citizens from state taxes.[84] The governor appointed white trustees to manage external tribal affairs, and every four years the Indians elected a chief and headmen to deal with internal issues.[85] To vote, eligible male citizens over eighteen years old deposited either a grain of corn or a bean, each representing one of two candidates, in a ballot box, and the man with the most votes won.[86] In later years, the Pamunkey tribal council also chose the tribe's white trustees. Annual picnics bought men of the tribe and the white trustees together, where they renewed their alliance.[87]

Pamunkey land consisted of a 1,200-acre reservation located in a bend of the Pamunkey River in King William County. Much of this territory was boggy swampland and underbrush, but in the northern area the Indians held around 300 acres suitable for homes and gardens. By the 1890s, the arable land was reportedly "in a good state of cultivation."[88] The Indians lived in weatherboarded, frame homes with two to four rooms.[89] They grew corn, potatoes, and had a few fruit trees.[90] Their preferred modes of subsistence, however, were hunting and fishing. Deer and wild turkey abounded on the reservation, and Pamunkey fishermen also took "large quantities of herring and shad by seine, according to the season, with ducks, reedbirds, and an occasional sturgeon."[91] Indeed, the Pamunkeys valued hunting and fishing so much that they refused "to vote upon selling or burning the woods on their reservation because this would destroy the game."[92] Both activities were communal endeavors. All able-bodied men joined in the annual tribute drive, which provided game to the Virginia governor in lieu of state taxes.[93] Fishermen also worked together, spending an average of four hours a day in their boats from early spring to fall.[94] To supplement their incomes, the Indians sold their fish, game, furs, and surplus farm products in Richmond and Baltimore.[95] By the late nineteenth century, the reservation had both a post office and a railroad station, which helped Pamunkey hunters and fishermen bring their products to market.[96] The reservation provided the Indians with their livelihoods, and reservation life contributed to the Pamunkeys' sense of tribal identity.

The Pamunkeys developed a unique system of land use that incorporated notions of communal ownership and private tenure. As a whole, the reservation belonged to the tribe, not to individual tribal citizens. This communal ownership was reinforced by state law: the tribe could not legally alienate or divide the land unless the Virginia legislature approved.[97] Pamunkey families claimed parcels of land, however, where they built homes and planted gardens.[98] Although tribal citizens bought and sold houses among themselves, land was not heritable: each new generation had to present a land request to the tribal council and have its choice accepted.[99] In addition to the home plots, the tribe divided marshland into six hunting territories bid on annually by individual tribal citizens.[100] The highest bidder rented the land for the duration of the year, and no other tribal citizen had the right to hunt on the plot without permission. In later years, some Pamunkeys sublet their plots to white sportsmen from Richmond, especially if they were too old to hunt themselves.[101] Tribal citizens continued to hunt on these sublet lands, however, while the lessees were away.[102] Rental fees paid by tribal citizens went to the tribal treasury and were used to maintain the reservation roads and provide other tribal services. Access to tribal lands was a privilege of tribal citizenship.

The Pamunkeys had lost their native language by the mid-nineteenth century, yet they were "by no means culturally barren."[103] Mooney reported that middle-aged citizens of the tribe remembered their parents having conversational knowledge of the old language half a century before, and Pamunkeys continued to pass down "elements of folk-belief, medicine lore, local legend and social practices" even after use of the Pamunkey language faded.[104] Pamunkey parents taught their children about the glory days of the Powhatan Confederacy: Opechancanough, the militant brother of Powhatan, was their hero.[105] They boasted that they were the descendants of Powhatan's warriors and they loved "to tell how bravely and stubbornly their forefathers resisted the encroachments of the whites."[106] They also told more recent tales of resistance. A favorite story was that of William Terrill Bradby's escape from Confederate soldiers during the Civil War. According to the tale, the soldiers rounded up Pamunkey men who refused to fight and marched them to Richmond for execution. Along the way, Bradby outmaneuvered his captors by pretending he had lost a boot. As the Confederates looked for the shoe, Bradby ran into the woods. Although the soldiers fired at him, he evaded capture by using his superior knowledge of the landscape. After swimming across a creek, Bradby hid in a railroad culvert until he heard that the governor had pardoned the Pamunkey men. The Pamunkeys proudly named his hiding place "Terrill's Culvert."[107] Such stories reminded the Pamunkeys of their persistent struggle for survival and fostered a sense of community pride in their shared history.

Pamunkey children grew up with an intimate knowledge of tribal land. From an early age, they learned to distinguish such things as different types of mud beds in the marshlands along the river. Fishermen made reference to "woods mud," "marsh mud," "floaty-bed mud," and "river mud," and boys acquired "expertness in traversing these dangerous endroits ... as soon as they learned to walk." The Indians also took note of natural signals like the hoots of the barred owl, which called out the tides to remind the fishermen to tend to their nets. Pamunkeys believed that blooming field pansies announced the run of shad in late March. For this reason, they called these pansies "shad flowers." Although they were Baptists, they revered the Pamunkey River as "old man river" and "folk-lore pil[ed] up around the seeking of fish."[108] Pamunkeys also retained healing knowledge that linked them to their land. Although they sent for white doctors if medical cases grew serious, they treated minor illnesses with teas made from local roots and herbs.[109]

Although for the most part, Pamunkeys dressed like local whites, the Indians used some distinctive elements of clothing.[110] John Garland Pollard, who visited the tribe as part of a Bureau of American Ethnology investigation in the early 1890s, reported that the Pamunkeys had "an inclination to the excessive use of gaudy colors in their attire."[111] Ethnographers were even more intrigued by the Pamunkey tradition of weaving turkey feathers to create elaborate mantles. Mattaponi and Pamunkey informants told researchers about earlier times when women made "capes so covered with turkey-feathers as to be warm and durable as well as beautiful." Mothers passed down this cultural knowledge to their daughters. By the 1920s, anthropologist Frank G. Speck described Margaret Adams, "the oldest woman at Pamunkey town," as the tribe's finest weaver of turkey feather garments.[112] Men and women also made jewelry to adorn their outfits. Pamunkey women did beadwork, which was time-consuming but provided them with distinctive decorations both to wear and to sell.[113] Chief Paul Miles collected animal bones and combined them with baked clay beads to create "a pretty bauble to add to his Indian costume, perhaps to sell to some visitor as a souvenir."[114] Unique ornaments and clothing helped to mark the Pamunkeys' Indian identity and to separate them from outsiders.

The Pamunkeys were also skilled pottery-makers. In oral interviews, Pamunkeys recalled that they had made pottery on the reservation "ever since we can remember." Primarily a female pursuit, women taught their daughters how to collect and mold clay.[115] They used white clay found about six feet beneath the surface of the soil in certain areas of the reservation and passed down knowledge of the location of clay mines from one generation to the next. In the 1940s, an elderly Pamunkey woman asserted that her grandmother, born around 1796, collected clay from the same mine she used.

Figure 1.3 Although for the most part Pamunkeys dressed like their white neighbors, they used some distinctive decorative pieces. In this photograph, Theodora Octavia Dennis Cook donned a turkey-feather mantle made by Margaret Adams, whom anthropologist Frank G. Speck described as the tribe's finest weaver of turkey-feather garments. Photographer: Frank G. Speck. Date: 1919. Courtesy of the National Anthropological Archives, Smithsonian Institution (SPC Se Powhatan Confederacy Pamunkey BAE 1-8 01793000).

Any tribal citizen could "use the clay from private property without (being guilty of) trespassing," and no one owned the land of the reservation's main clay mine.[116] To emphasize the common ownership of the tribe's natural resources, the opening of a clay mine was a community affair: "the whole tribe, men, women, and children, were present, and each family took home a share of the clay."[117]

Once they collected the clay, Pamunkey women dried it, beat it, passed it through a sieve, and pounded it in a mortar. They added burned freshwater mussels, "flesh as well as shells," to the prepared clay to serve as temper, and then saturated the mixture with water. Once kneaded, the "substance is then shaped with a mussel shell to the shape of the article desired and placed in the sun to dry." Potters rubbed dried pieces with a stone to produce a gloss, heated them with a slow fire, and finally burned them in a kiln.[118] Although Pamunkey artists may have drawn on the techniques of visiting Catawba potters and borrowed some European pottery forms, the articles they produced were "tempered and shaped by native methods."[119] In particular, their use of mussels connected the pottery to the Pamunkeys' livelihood as fishermen, just as the clay connected them to the land.

The Pamunkeys made pottery for their own use and to sell to white neighbors, but by the end of the nineteenth century, the rise of cheap, manufactured earthenware began undercutting this craft and only a few elderly Pamunkeys continued to build pots.[120] Scholarly interest in Pamunkey pottery, however, helped revive the tradition.[121] In the early twentieth century, potters began collecting shells along the river to make fresh designs on their wares. Pocahontas Cook, for example, decorated her jars by imprinting "the contour of such mollusks upon the surface in serial order." Other Indians used fossilized shark teeth to create comb-like indentations on clay pipe stems. Drawing inspiration from the river that sustained them, Pamunkey potters cut "criss-cross marks upon the wooden paddle used to ornament the surface of the pot," which reflected the cross-hatched patterns of shad nets.[122] Like their distinctive jewelry and turkey-feather clothing, Pamunkey pottery became a cultural symbol that the Indians used to showcase their identity to outsiders.

Ethnographic interest in Pamunkey crafts inspired Virginia state legislators to take notice of tribal art as well. In 1932, the state began an educational program to revive and commercialize native arts and crafts.[123] Legislators hoped the program would relieve some of the poverty on the reservation caused by the Great Depression. When members of the State Board of Education asked the Pamunkeys what sort of program they thought would be most useful, tribal councilmen suggested a pottery school.[124] The Pamunkeys eagerly participated in the program and welcomed a pottery instructor who arrived on the reservation to teach the Indians new techniques. The methods differed from traditional practices and included the use of commercial glazes and a modern kiln. The changes, however, allowed Pamunkey potters to experiment with styles and to produce a greater supply of pieces to sell to tourists.[125] The pottery school also provided a social environment for Pamunkey women. Anthropologist Theodore Stern reported that "At the school, they relax at their work and talk: for rarely does an operation require such concentration that the potter cannot converse at the same time."[126] In this way, the pottery school helped strengthen community bonds in much the same way that clay mine openings had brought Pamunkey people together. Pottery, like distinctive dress, helped Pamunkeys delineate who was part of their community.

In the late nineteenth and early twentieth centuries, Pamunkeys exploited a growing public interest in the past by embracing the story of Pocahontas and John Smith. White Virginians were proud of this account because it rivaled the one of the Pilgrims at Plymouth and gave the South a place in white America's founding. Many white Virginians claimed descent from Pocahontas, which gave them prestige as members of one of the first families of Virginia. The Pamunkeys created their own dramatic reenactment of the tale, and several prominent tribal councilmen starred in the production.[127] They published fliers in 1898 that announced their performance of a "Green Corn Dance, Pamunkey Indian Marriage, Snake Dance by Deerfoot, War Dance, [and] Capture of Capt. John Smith and the saving of his life by Pocahontas."[128] In 1899, the Pamunkeys sent a delegation to Richmond to ask the governor to fund their production company on a trip to the Paris Exposition, where they hoped to perform for an international audience.[129] Although they never made it to Paris, the Pamunkeys continued to display their history for local white spectators. In 1935, the State Board of Education helped sponsor a pageant that included twenty-five Pamunkey actors from the reservation. The play reenacted "the meeting of their tribesmen with the men of Capt. John Smith and subsequent events in the relationships between whites and Indians."[130] Pamunkeys saw plays and pageants as a way to make their Indian identity and long history in Virginia visible to white audiences.

The Pamunkeys also increased their political visibility during these years by making elaborate productions out of their annual visits to the state governor in Richmond. The tribe had paid symbolic annual tribute to the governor since the seventeenth century, but in the late nineteenth and early twentieth centuries they made this gesture more public and drew the attention of reporters.[131] In 1907, for example, tribal leaders carried into the city a freshly killed deer "swung on a sapling cut on the reservation." Chief G. M. Cook used the spectacle as an opportunity to make a public speech in which he proclaimed that "the Virginia Governor had always been considerate of his people and that the red men desired to express their good will in the only way open to them."[132] With these words, Cook not only affirmed the state's relationship with the tribe but also showcased the Pamunkeys' cultural persistence as hunters. The following year, the Pamunkeys' visit coincided with Thanksgiving, and a delegation carried to Richmond "half a dozen wild turkeys and a saddle of venison."[133] By providing the governor with his Thanksgiving dinner, the Pamunkeys drew on depictions of the Pilgrims and the first Thanksgiving to express both their Indian identity and their long-lasting friendship with white Americans.

Pamunkey visibility drew further attention from researchers, but with mixed results. James Mooney demonstrated that the Pamunkeys were not on the verge of extinction by publishing a list of thirty-nine Pamunkey heads of households that he compiled in 1901. This census included Pamunkeys on the reservation as well as a few who had migrated elsewhere, indicated their marriage partners and the number of children in their families, and noted which Pamunkeys had married Mattaponi, other Indian, or white spouses. Most tribal citizens, Mooney showed, married other Pamunkeys. He recorded just three white wives, one Mattaponi wife, and one "alien" husband. Although he did not name married women or minors, he enumerated them, bringing the Pamunkey population up to 146 individuals.[134] According to Mooney, he compiled the census "from information furnished in conference by the principal men of each band, and [the census] may therefore be considered as an official

Figure 1.4 Since the seventeenth century, the Pamunkeys had paid symbolic annual tribute of game to the governor of Virginia in lieu of state taxes. These visits became elaborate productions in the late nineteenth and early twentieth centuries as the Pamunkeys strove to demonstrate their Indian identity for white audiences. Date: c. 1926–1930. Courtesy of the Cook Collection, Valentine Richmond History Center (image no. 1377).

statement of their membership as recognized by themselves."[135] Beginning in the early twentieth century, the Pamunkey tribal council also began creating "voter lists" of male tribal citizens with voting privileges on the reservation. Like Mooney's census, these lists did not name Pamunkey women and minor children, but they provided further evidence of the political existence of the tribe.[136]

Anthropologist Frank G. Speck, who visited the tribe in the 1920s, addressed the issue of Pamunkey intermarriage. Combating local stereotypes about the Pamunkeys' supposed loss of Indian identity, he asserted that elimination of the tribe on the ground of "there being no longer pure-blood Indians among them . . . would involve a maze of controversy, for it would mean that many existing Indians groups all over North, Central, and South America, maintaining active tribal tradition, even government, would be consigned to the anomaly of classification as 'whites' or 'colored people.' "[137] In the view of researchers like Mooney and Speck, the Pamunkeys were just as "Indian" as any other tribe.

Unfortunately for Virginia Indians, the work of ethnographers and anthropologists as well as the cultural revitalization efforts of tribes like the Pamunkeys brought unwelcome attention. White Virginians uncomfortable with the idea of an anomalous "third race" in the state lashed out at the claims of researchers. Anthropological work on Virginia tribes particularly riled the head of Virginia's Bureau of Vital Statistics, Walter Ashby Plecker.[138] Plecker staunchly believed that only two races existed in Virginia: "white" and "colored." As a eugenicist, he held that "The worst forms of undesirables born amongst us are those when parents are of different races" and he argued that "the intermarriage of the white race with mixed stock must be made impossible."[139] Plecker assumed that anyone asserting Indian identity was in fact attempting to "pass" as white in order to intermarry with whites, and thus saw Indianness as a dangerous way station between blackness and whiteness.[140] Plecker made it his mission to prove all people in Virginia who claimed to be Indians were actually the descendants of African Americans.[141] He banned Frank G. Speck's 1928 *Chapters on the Ethnology of the Powhatan Tribes of Virginia* and looked for ways to legally destroy the Indian identity of Virginia Natives.[142]

Plecker bolstered his efforts with state laws. On March 8, 1924, the Virginia legislature passed the Act to Preserve Racial Integrity, which aimed to identify so-called "near white" people who had taken advantage of segregated white services despite distant black ancestry. White Virginians worried that these individuals contaminated the supposedly pure racial stock of whites in the state through their proximity in schools and other public institutions, as well as through instances of intermarriage. Although many of the people targeted

Figure 1.5 Due to anti-miscegenation laws that restricted marriages with whites and fears of racial reclassification that discouraged them from marrying blacks, most Pamunkeys married other Pamunkeys. In this photograph, Pamunkey Chief George Major Cook posed with his Pamunkey wife, Theodora Octavia Dennis Cook, and their children. Photographer: De Lancey W. Gill. Date: 1899. Courtesy of the National Anthropological Archives, Smithsonian Institution (BAE GN 00880 06196100).

were "scarcely distinguishable as colored," the new law decreed that even one drop of African "blood" made them black. The law defined white people as those "with no trace of the blood of another race, except that a person with one-sixteenth of the American Indian, if there is no other race mixture, may be classed as white," an exception that accommodated prominent white Virginians who claimed descent from Pocahontas. The act instructed clerks of court to investigate the racial claims of those requesting marriage licenses and made it a felony "for any person willfully or knowingly to make a registration certificate false as to color or race." Violators of the law faced a year in prison.[143] Plecker believed that the Virginia Racial Integrity Act "definitely places upon the Bureau of Vital Statistics the responsibility of correctly classifying racially the population of the State in vital statistics records."[144]

An act unanimously passed by the Virginia Legislature in 1930 refined the Racial Integrity Act. Designed to protect unsuspecting "pure" white children from contact with "white children of mixed blood" in schools, it classed "anyone with any ascertainable degree of negro blood . . . as a colored person."[145] The act made an exception, however, for citizens of the Pamunkey and Mattaponi tribes. Individuals "with one-fourth or more Indian blood and less than one-sixteenth negro blood" could be classed as Indian rather than as "colored" as long as they lived on their reservations.[146] The act also insisted that Indians promise "to marry only with others of the same racial and tribal classification."[147] These exceptions placated tribal citizens, who had declared that they would rather "be banished to the wilds of Siberia" than to "submit to a loathsome, humiliating Negroid classification."[148] The act placed new legal strictures on notions of tribal belonging, however, by limiting the amount of both black and white ancestry tribal citizens could possess in order to have rights as Indians on the reservations. It also set a geographical boundary to recognized Pamunkey and Mattaponi identity. Outsiders' racial definitions of Indian identity increasingly affected how reservation Virginia Indians thought about tribal citizenship.

The new state law did not exempt Pamunkeys and Mattaponis from Plecker's attacks. He maintained that these groups had always been classified as "free negroes" in historical records, and he described the amendment to the act that recognized the Indian identity of the Pamunkeys and Mattaponis as "jocular." Although forced to comply with the law, Plecker declared that "When they leave the reservation, they take their proper classification as colored."[149] He made sure that Indians could not attend white schools and he warned white hospitals not to treat Indian patients. He even provided hospital staff "with lists of names including all native Indians" so they would know whom to turn away.[150] In a 1924 health bulletin, Plecker insisted that "the term 'Indian' will no longer be accepted" on birth certificates, except for those of "known pure Indian blood, or those mixed with white."[151] He did not believe any such people lived in the state. If midwives challenged him, he responded with threats. In a letter to midwife Mary F. Adkins in 1942, for example, Plecker warned that if she failed "to make out a correct certificate, giving the race of both parents as colored," "it may become necessary to revoke your permit and advertise you to the midwives, local registrars, and others . . . as being no longer permitted to practice midwifery."[152] Plecker informed another midwife, Martha V. Wood, that "giving the wrong color in registering a birth certificate is a penitentiary offense."[153] Plecker even went so far as to post notices on the backs of previously issued "Indian" birth certificates that insisted that the bearer was actually black.[154] In Plecker's view, there were "no descendants of Virginia Indians claiming or reported to be Indians who are unmixed with negro blood."[155]

To legitimize his work of racial reclassification, Plecker employed a genealogist to trace "practically all of the families of our so-called 'Indian' groups back to the 1830 U.S. Census." This census had listed "free negroes" and

Plecker assumed that all of these individuals were black. He did not take into account that nineteenth-century census takers often listed Indians in this category as well. Plecker was proud of the Bureau's efforts to rat out supposed pseudo-Indians through genealogy. He bragged in a 1943 letter that "Hitler's genealogical study of the Jews is not more complete."[156] This statement was particularly shocking considering the recent entry of the United States into the Second World War.

Virginia Indians ran into new racial classification issues when America went to war in late 1941. The military segregated servicemen into "white" and "colored" units, and the State Headquarters for Selective Service in Richmond directed local boards to delay registering Indians until they could make "the proper determination of classification." Although Indians supposedly received classification as white, any rumor of black ancestry was enough to record them as "colored." The boards individually reviewed the cases of more than 170 individuals.[157] Plecker weighed in on the issue and insisted that Virginia classify as "negro" all Indians entering military services in the state.[158]

Although they wanted to fight for the United States, Indian servicemen protested attempts to reclassify them. In July 1942, the Pamunkeys sent a petition to the state governor expressing their distress. They declared that their "whole pride of living is in our Tribe, and its recognition by our great Commonwealth," and asked the governor, "is our pride and happiness to be made a casualty of this war?"[159] When the state failed to protect their Indian status in the armed forces, some Indians preferred prison to enrollment as "colored." In 1943, a Virginia judge sentenced two Indian men to two years in jail after they refused to enroll with the draft board other than as Indian.[160] Advocates for Virginia Indians wrote to the commissioner of Indian affairs and complained that Plecker's efforts were "a real injustice to many Indians who have worked and sacrificed over many years to maintain their recognition of status."[161] Pamunkeys and other Virginia Indians beseeched the Office of Indian Affairs to help them in their battle against reclassification.

As a state-recognized tribe, the Pamunkeys had never established a treaty relationship with the federal government. This meant that, although they maintained a political tradition and held reservation lands, the federal government did not officially recognize their tribal status. Allies of the Pamunkeys thought that if the tribe secured federal recognition, they would be better equipped to defend themselves against Plecker's attacks and to protect their resources. When Commissioner of Indian Affairs John Collier implemented the Indian Reorganization Act (IRA) in 1934, for example, white allies of the tribe wrote to the Indian Office to ask whether the federal government could help the Pamunkeys buy more land.[162] Assistant Commissioner of Indian Affairs William Zimmerman was not encouraging. He did not think it fair "to divert any funds which could be used for the benefit of Indians who are now and who have been for generations wards of the Federal Government" to aid state tribes like the Pamunkeys.[163] Although under the terms of the act citizens of unrecognized tribes could receive federal benefits if they proved that they were "one-half or more Indian blood," Zimmerman wrote that "even if it should be determined that these Indians are eligible, in accordance with this provision, I seriously question the advisability of Federal intervention in the affairs of this group."[164] The Pamunkeys remained unrecognized.

Nonetheless, John Collier made personal efforts to help the tribe. After receiving a number of appeals from Virginia Indians, the commissioner confronted Plecker directly. In a series of letters, Collier questioned the validity of the Bureau of Vital Statistics' use of genealogical records and census listings to determine the racial identities of Native Virginians. Collier pointed out that these methods were "known to be susceptible to a high degree of error" and argued that "Ethnological students of Virginia Indians are generally of the opinion that the physical features of these groups incline more to the Indian than to the negro or white." The commissioner asserted that it seemed "grossly unfair to classify as negroes persons who are obviously more Indian than anything else even if there are negroid characteristics present." He asked Plecker to develop "a more realistic definition of an Indian" that did not simply presume "colored" identity based on rumored black ancestry.[165]

In response to Collier's letters, Plecker vilified the state's Indian population and condemned the efforts of anthropologists to assist tribal revitalization projects.[166] Despite Plecker's antagonism, such scholars continued to work with Indians in the state to prove their ethnic identity. One man in particular, James Coates, made it his mission to combat the Virginia Bureau of Vital Statistics. After Plecker sent out a circular in 1943 to local registrars, doctors, nurses, clerks of court, school superintendents, and public health workers that allegedly exposed certain individuals as black, Coates did his own research into the complicated genealogies of Virginia Indians.[167] He collected testimony from white Virginians who confirmed that the Pamunkeys were "good hard working people and have tried to uphold their race and traditions."[168] In another petition, white citizens in King William and New Kent Counties called on the State of Virginia to recognize the Indian identity of the Pamunkeys and objected to the claims of "certain prejudiced individuals" that the Pamunkeys had black ancestry.[169] Such support from undeniably white Virginians bolstered the Pamunkeys' claims and helped combat Plecker's assertions.

Coates knew that official tribal documentation of citizens would help Virginia tribes prove their Indian identity by making the line between tribal citizens and non-tribal "colored" people less ambiguous. Consequently, he sent letters to the chiefs of Virginia tribes asking them each to produce a list of tribal citizens in good standing. Coates expected these lists to serve as formal rolls that legally defined tribal citizenship to show "exactly who we are fighting for in our effort to obtain official recognition and proper classification as native Virginia Indians." He strategically recommended to the chiefs that no one "be permitted to appear on the list whose good standing and blood relation is other than pure Indian or Indian and white." This suggestion had the effect of encouraging tribes once again to purge from citizenship individuals with rumored black ancestry. The Chickahominies and other non-reservation communities quickly responded to Coates with citizenship lists.[170] The Pamunkey chief wrote to Coates, telling him "that his council had finally decided to compile the census [he] requested some months ago"; however, no roll was forthcoming for several years.[171]

Finally, in 1954, the tribe prepared a governing document that provided the Pamunkeys with written laws and ordinances.[172] They may have done so in response to an amendment passed by the Virginia General Assembly that confirmed state-recognized Indian identity for "members of Indian tribes existing in this Commonwealth having one-fourth or more of Indian blood and less than one-sixteenth of Negro blood."[173] The "Laws of the Pamunkey Indians" did not include specific criteria for tribal citizenship, other than to note that qualifying Pamunkey men over age eighteen were entitled to "a voice and vote in the affairs of the tribe."[174] Tribal ordinances specified, however, that "No member of the Pamunkey Indian Tribe shall intermarry with any person except those of white or Indian blood" or risk losing their citizenship. This stipulation complied with both Coates's recommendation that the tribe preserve racial purity and the state's warning that only individuals with less than one-sixteenth African American "blood" qualified as Indian. The Pamunkeys appended a list of "all male citizens residing on the reservation as of July 1, 1954," as well as "a list of all male citizens living off the reservation as of that date" to the document.[175] This roll, however, was neither officially approved by the state nor recognized by the federal government. Instead, it remained a flexible list subject to change at the tribe's discretion.

Anthropologists like Speck and Coates encouraged Virginia Indians to develop strategies to distinguish tribal citizens officially from outsiders. Speck made another suggestion, however, that the Pamunkeys declined to accept. Beginning in the 1920s, Speck encouraged the descendants of all the Powhatan groups in Virginia to organize into corporate associations and consolidate their forces. Speck believed the Indians had power in numbers and that by working together, they could "avert obliteration of their names and racial tradition."[176] Tribes without reservation land, like the Chickahominies, welcomed this opportunity. The Pamunkeys saw the situation differently. In their view, association with other Virginia tribes weakened rather than strengthened their identity claims. Tecumseh Deerfoot Cook explained the tribe's concerns to Coates in 1944: "Some of these people whom Dr. Speck wants us to unite with are not even recognized as Indians by the State of Virginia. . . . [W]e feel that it is best to fight for Pamunkey Tribe exclusively and let the other tribes fight for themselves."[177] Although Pamunkeys certainly took interest in the fate of other Virginia tribes, with whom they intermarried, their primary concern was to preserve their particular tribal identity. In this way, Pamunkeys distinguished their citizenship not only from non-Indian outsiders but also from other Virginia tribes.

Walter Ashby Plecker finally retired from the Virginia Bureau of Vital Statistics in 1946 and died shortly thereafter. The next registrar continued a weaker version of Plecker's policies; in 1959, however, a new registrar abandoned these practices altogether and destroyed Plecker's Racial Integrity File.[178] Conditions improved for Virginia Indians after Plecker departed, but his actions left a lasting legacy for the Pamunkeys. They had defended their Indian identity against the claims of outsiders since the early nineteenth century, and Plecker's work showed them how quickly they could lose ground if they did not vigilantly police the racial identities of their tribal citizens. Years after Plecker's death, the Indians "still hate[d] his memory." Moreover, they continued to agonize over questions of race. After conducting fieldwork with the tribe in the early 1970s, Rountree explained that to the Pamunkeys the color bar was "literally everything."[179] The tribal citizenship criteria created by the Pamunkeys during and shortly after Plecker's term as head of the Bureau of Vital Statistics reflected their racial reclassification fears.

Although white Virginians like Plecker fought to prevent marriages between Indians and whites in the late nineteenth and early twentieth centuries, such unions occurred. The Pamunkeys had a long history of intermarriage with whites. William Terrill Bradby informed Mooney, for example, that "the numerous Bradbys of the Pamunkey and Chickahominy tribes all have descent from a white man, his great-grandfather." Such relationships continued into the twentieth century, whether or not the state legally recognized them.[180] When they could not find marriage partners within their own community or among the citizens of other Virginia tribes, the only option acceptable to the Pamunkeys was marriage with whites.[181] Unlike black intermarriage, white intermarriage did not threaten the Pamunkeys' Indian identity. White Virginians generally perceived the children of these unions as Indian, not white. White intermarriage, however, raised new concerns for the tribe, especially in regard to protecting tribal resources. Pamunkeys also worried about the influence white spouses might exert over tribal affairs. They developed tribal rules to address these concerns.

In the colonial era, Pamunkeys traced descent through the female line.[182] Chiefs, known as "weroances," acquired their positions by matrilineal inheritance: a ruling position passed from a female ancestor to her sons, then daughters, then the sons and daughters of her oldest daughter. Pamunkeys also historically recognized female rulers. The weroansqua Cockacoeske, for example, led the tribe in the mid-seventeenth century.[183] Between 1664 and 1723, at least six Pamunkey women served in prominent leadership positions.[184] Matrilineal inheritance meant that Pamunkey identity rested on the identity of an individual's mother. Pamunkey women bore and raised Pamunkey children, no matter the racial identity of the fathers. Over the years, however, contact with patriarchal Euro-Americans shifted Pamunkey constructions of gender. As the Indians became more male-focused and Pamunkey women lost some of their economic power, the tribe began modeling its notions of descent and female citizenship rights on those of the surrounding Anglo-Virginian society. This set off a process by which Pamunkeys created a tiered system of citizenship that denied certain tribal citizens full political rights on the reservation.

By the late nineteenth century, the Pamunkeys had abandoned ideas of matrilineal descent in favor of bilateral inheritance. The children of both Indian fathers and Indian mothers had rights as tribal citizens, so long as they could prove their lineage and other Pamunkeys recognized their tribal connection.[185] In a nod to Virginia's racial statutes that defined as Indian those who lived on state reservations "with one-fourth or more Indian blood and less than one-sixteenth negro blood," however, the tribe adopted blood quantum restrictions for reservation residency.[186] To live on the reservation, Pamunkeys had to be at least a "quarter blood" Indian.[187] Tribal citizens still considered individuals without the necessary ancestry to be kin, but these people did not enjoy all the privileges of tribal citizenship, such as access to reservation lands or voting rights in tribal elections. Even more controversial were the differences in citizenship rights the tribe granted male and female Pamunkeys.[188]

Pamunkey voting practices reflected gender imbalances on the reservation. The tribe's political tradition was a point of pride for the Indians: it represented an unbroken continuation of their tribal sovereignty across years of hardship. They limited political rights in the tribe, however, to Pamunkey men. A young man became an eligible voter when he turned eighteen and paid a voter registration fee of $1. He could vote in every election thereafter, so long as he paid the tribe $6 a year in taxes and maintained residency on the reservation. In earlier times, the tribe had imposed an upper age limit of sixty-five years on voter participation, but by the mid-twentieth century this stipulation had disappeared as the reservation population aged.[189] Men over sixty did not have to attend tribal meetings, but they still voted. The tribe imposed a $1 fine on younger men who missed meetings without an excuse. The Pamunkeys codified these rules in their 1954 governing document.[190] Pamunkey women, on the other hand, did not have voting rights, no matter their age or resident status, a franchise initially modeled on that of the state of Virginia.[191] Even after women gained voting rights in the United States, however, the tribe continued to deny Pamunkey women the vote.[192]

Although they may have influenced the voting habits of their husbands and sons, Pamunkey women resented their lack of direct political power.[193] In 1939, the state supervisor of Trade and Industrial Education reported that there were "considerable controversies between the men-folk and the women-folk" on the reservation.[194] Dissatisfaction apparently grew. By the 1970s, Rountree noted that certain Pamunkey women were "not entirely happy" with the voting situation, "for they feel that women have as much sense as men."[195] Some Pamunkey men sympathized with their mothers, sisters, and wives and tried to effect change in the tribe's voting policy. In the 1970s, for example, Edward Bradby advocated female suffrage until the tribe stripped him of his own voting rights due to his failure to meet the tribe's residency requirement.[196] In his opinion, reservation women were "harder workers than the men and they should have the right."[197] The chief at the time, Tecumseh Deerfoot Cook, also recognized "that some women want the vote, and the law may have to be changed in the future."[198] Ultimately, however, Pamunkey women could not muster enough male support to turn their desire into reality.[199] Many men on the reservation were "reactionary on that subject" and blocked efforts to promote female suffrage.[200] They believed that there was not "much to interest women in politics, and they have so much to do at home."[201] Although the Pamunkey chief and tribal council considered the issue of women's voting rights in 1969 and 1976, they took no action to change tribal law.[202]

An issue that rankled Pamunkey women even more than voting rights was that of reservation residency. Pamunkey tradition allowed "a man of the tribe to bring his alien wife to the reservation, but a girl who marries an outsider has to depart and reside off the reservation."[203] This rule had deep origins and was related to Pamunkey fears of being reclassified as "colored." In 1818, the *Virginia Herald* reported that two black men had married Pamunkey women and moved to the reservation. In response, the Pamunkeys called a meeting with their trustees and insisted that "their law orders that no individual who is not a descendant of a Pamunkey Indian shall settle among them."[204] By the twentieth century, the tribe also barred white men with Pamunkey wives from living on the reservation.[205]

Pamunkey men reasoned that intermarried white men had no place on the reservation because they lacked political rights in the tribe. If they lived there, they would take up "land that could otherwise be allotted to men who could be active in reservation affairs."[206] Only Indian men could vote and it was impossible for a white man to become a naturalized citizen in the tribe since the state of Virginia only recognized as "Indian" those with a quarter or more Indian "blood." Therefore, Pamunkey men asserted, "if he were in his right mind [a white man] would not want to live there, anyway."[207] Pamunkey women wondered if another motivation was at play. One woman speculated that "the more whites who come onto the reservation to live, the less the Indians will be in control."[208] Tribal elders, she claimed, feared that "the white men will take over."[209] White women, like Pamunkey women, had no political voice in the tribe, so white wives did not threaten Pamunkey authority over the reservation.[210] Tribal leaders worried, however, that white husbands would not take disfranchisement lightly.

The tribal policy against the residency of white husbands and their Pamunkey wives preserved Pamunkey control over tribal land, but it affected the reservation population. Once they married whites, Pamunkey women had to move away and raise their children elsewhere. Without enough young families to take the place of their elders, the reservation population aged. By the 1980s, only sixty Indians remained on the reservation, most of them elderly.[211] In contrast, the Mattaponis had a similar rule about intermarriage and residency, but it was not strictly enforced.[212] Leniency regarding the residency of women with white husbands attracted more young people to the Mattaponi reservation and encouraged them to stay.

The controversy over white husbands and Pamunkey reservation residency continued into the late twentieth century. In 1989, the media picked up the story when the twin granddaughters of former chief Tecumseh Deerfoot Cook married white men and challenged the tribe's policy. Kim Cook Taylor and Cam Cook Porter wanted permission to live on the reservation with their husbands. As Porter put it, "My roots are here and there are advantages to living here. I want to live here." Sick of male-dominated Pamunkey politics, the sisters declared "This is the 1980's and this is America, not the 1600's and Jamestown." [213] They circulated a petition on the reservation and sought signatures from Pamunkeys who lived off the reservation in places like New Jersey and Tennessee. They predicted that "as many as 20 Indian women who married whites would return to the reservation if the laws are changed and the racial barrier is broken."[214] The sisters collected over two dozen signatures, and the tribal council agreed to meet with them once they completed the petition drive.[215] Although the Pamunkey chief agreed that eventually the tribe would have to change its policy or risk "totally disappear[ing]," the issue remained unresolved.[216]

Pamunkey women also continued to fight for political inclusion. In 1988, nine female tribal members formed the Committee of Pamunkey Indian Women's Rights Issues and petitioned the tribal council for an explicit statement regarding "the rights and privileges of the Indian women." The tribal council deliberated the issue, but in 1990 denied a motion to enfranchise Pamunkey women and to allow them to reside on the reservation with non-Indian husbands. Women continued to exert pressure on tribal leaders, however, and by 1998 the views of the tribal government on residency rights began to change. That year, eligible Pamunkey voters agreed to allow a Pamunkey woman and her white husband to build a home on tribal land.[217] This ruling ended the gendered division of reservation residency rights.

Over the next decade, the tribe further deliberated female voting. The work of anthropologist John H. Moore in 2006, in particular, revealed the deep dissatisfaction of Pamunkey women with the tribal government. As one woman complained, the tribe should "at least give the women a voice and listen to the women."[218] Pamunkey women sent letters and petitions to the tribal government and also spoke to reporters about the injustice of their situation. The latter action incurred the wrath of certain members of the tribal council, who insisted that the women should work within the tribal government structure rather than airing the tribe's dirty laundry in public.[219] Yet the women were not deterred. Indeed, they linked their fight for a voice and a vote in the tribe to the Pamunkeys' bid for federal recognition. In 2011, for example, Mildred "Gentle Rain" Moore complained to reporters that "a woman [Cockacoeske] saved this tribe, yet our women cannot serve as council members or even vote. If we attend tribal councils, we must remain silent. What will they do about women's rights if they ever get federal recognition?"[220]

Ultimately, the women's activism paid off. At a special tribal meeting held on July 12, 2012, Pamunkey men voted to extend the franchise to female tribal citizens and to afford them the same political rights as men. A victory for Pamunkey women, this decision was also a strategic move on the part of the tribe in its fight for federal recognition. In their revised petition for acknowledgment, the Pamunkeys pointed to the new law as "clear evidence of the Tribe's self-determination and self-governance" as well as "the flexibility of the tribal government as it codifies and amends rules." These actions, the tribe argued, fulfilled the federal government's requirement that tribes seeking recognition demonstrate historical and ongoing political influence over their citizens.[221]

Just as women belonged to the tribe but lacked full citizenship rights until recently, men who migrated away from the reservation continued to be Pamunkeys but did not have all the privileges that came with reservation residency. Pamunkeys had long been a mobile people. Although strongly connected to the reservation by kinship and historical ties, individual Indians could not always make a living for their families if they stayed there.[222] State laws during the Jim Crow years made finding gainful employment difficult.

Lured by the promise of better jobs and less discrimination, many Pamunkeys migrated to cities where their race was not known or to northern states.[223] In 1901, for example, Mooney recorded that Pamunkeys lived in Philadelphia, Richmond, Petersburg, Newport News, and New York.[224] In the 1920s, Speck noted that the Pamunkeys on the reservation numbered about 150 people, but had they "been able to keep together without the young men having to emigrate to the cities to find employment, the number would now be much larger."[225] Jim Crow legislation affected Pamunkey migration patterns in other ways as well. Some Indians chose to move away in order to "pass" as white. Louis Stewart, for example, recalled that his paternal uncle, George Stewart, married a white woman and never returned to the reservation because "he didn't want trouble" for his daughters, who worked outside of Richmond at the Phillip Morris factory, which only hired whites.[226]

Upon leaving the reservation, some Pamunkeys found jobs in maritime and fishing industries that utilized their intimate knowledge of the Pamunkey River.[227] Other Indians trained as mechanics and plumbers. Some became day laborers in Richmond and Baltimore. The Depression years saw the return to the reservation of a number of Indians who could no longer find work in the cities. These migrants, however, soon discovered "that if times are bad in the cities, neither are they flourishing on the reservation, the ancient pursuits of agriculture and trapping having declined in profit."[228] Lack of opportunity at home forced them to move away again.

The involvement of the United States in the First and Second World Wars also encouraged Pamunkeys to leave the reservation. Numerous Pamunkey men signed up to fight for the United States, and some even gave their lives. In 1918, for example, twenty-four-year-old Private Joseph I. Miles died in France from wounds he received in action.[229] Fourteen tribal citizens served in the Second World War. Pamunkeys who enlisted in the military necessarily left the reservation during their time in training camps and in combat overseas. When they returned to the United States, some men chose to pursue careers in the armed forces and moved permanently away from the reservation.[230]

Pamunkey migrations accelerated after the Second World War. Young people, in particular, "[broke] the bonds of the reservation—choosing to work and marry and live beyond its confines."[231] These young people may not have wanted to leave, but economic necessity forced them to find jobs away from home. Some attended college and found employment as accountants, executives, and occupational therapists in cities.[232] Others made conscious decisions to relocate because they objected to reservation politics and tribal rules. Edna Bradby Allmond, a Chickahominy, and her Mattaponi-Pamunkey husband, for example, lived just off of the reservation because they disliked "how houses on [the] reservation can only be sold to other Indians."[233] Although they retained their connection to the tribal community, by the 1950s at least nineteen Pamunkeys lived elsewhere in the state and forty-five resided outside Virginia.[234] In 1965, only twenty-nine individuals lived permanently on the reservation. Many of these were older Pamunkeys who came back in their re-tirement "to farm and fish for shad."[235] Whether they migrated out of necessity or by choice, their decisions came with costs.

While they lived away from the reservation, Pamunkeys forfeited their po-litical rights as tribal citizens. Men who were absent from the reservation for more than six months lost their right to vote in tribal elections.[236] This rule ap-plied whether the men lived one mile or hundreds of miles away. If they stayed away for more than two years, they also lost their land: their plot reverted to the tribe and became available to someone else.[237] The tribe reasoned that these individuals were "more orientated toward the outside world" and there-fore did not deserve political and land rights during their absence.[238] Indeed, in the late nineteenth century, ethnographer Albert Samuel Gatschet insisted that the tribe no longer recognized as full Pamunkeys "those Indz who live outside the settlement."[239] These individuals did not lose their tribal connec-tion, however, as long as they chose to maintain it. Every August, the tribe held a "well-attended homecoming, with Indians who live away from the reserva-tion coming home for an afternoon service which forms the beginning of a week-long revival." Young Pamunkeys also returned to the reservation at other times to visit older relatives. Many migrants came back permanently once they retired.[240] These individuals remained Pamunkeys while they were away; they simply did not have all the rights of tribal citizens.

The Pamunkeys denied citizenship rights to off-reservation Indians, but they fully reincorporated returning migrants. Pamunkey men regained the right to vote and hold political office if they returned to the reservation and spent at least half the year with the tribe. Chief Paul Miles, for example, spent seven years as a linesman on river steamers before returning to the reservation and taking on a leadership role in the 1920s and 1930s.[241] Similarly, Tecumseh Deerfoot Cook worked at the Campbell Soup Company in Philadelphia for two decades before returning to Virginia. He became chief in 1942 and served in that capacity for the next forty years.[242] If migrants returned and spent at least sixty days a year on the reservation, they also kept their home plots.[243] Pamunkey men always had the potential for full citizenship rights. These rights simply depended on reservation residency.

The tiered system of citizenship created by the tribe allowed for fluidity in Pamunkey notions of belonging. The number of people in residence on tribal land was "only a fraction of the people genealogically entitled to live on the reservation."[244] In 1964, a reporter noted that "Though the resident members number less than 100, both the Pamunkeys and the Mattaponis claim as many as 400 tribesmen each."[245] From an outsider's perspective this ambiguous mix of "core," "fringe," and "genealogically eligible" people made Pamunkey tribal citizenship confusing and imprecise.[246] For the Pamunkeys, it was simply a matter of knowing their relatives. Only those on the reservation, however, had full tribal rights. In this way, Pamunkeys married whites and migrated freely without losing their identity, but the tribe protected its land base from outside interests by limiting the legal rights of non-residents.

Over the years, Pamunkeys established citizenship criteria and categories that reflected their need to protect their Indian identity and tribal land from outsiders. They created racial barriers to citizenship to protect against "colored" reclassification, and they created a tiered system of citizenship to ensure that Pamunkeys always controlled the reservation. Despite establishing these standards, the Pamunkeys did not create a formal citizenship roll. James Mooney's 1901 census, published in 1907, provided an unofficial count of the tribal population, as did tribal lists of eligible voters and federal censuses. The 1954 roll supplied another list of tribal citizens. These lists, however, lacked official standing and neither the state nor the federal government called on the Pamunkeys to create a formal roll. The non-binding format of these lists reflected Pamunkey desires to monitor tribal citizenship closely. Formal criteria may have permitted certain people to claim technical citizenship, but fluid definitions based on historical and ongoing needs allowed the tribe to maintain strict control over who belonged.

Without federally approved tribal citizenship criteria and an official tribal roll, the Pamunkeys defined tribal belonging on their own terms in the late twentieth and early twenty-first centuries. In general, proof of belonging rested on the memories of recognized tribal citizens.[247] If tribal citizens recalled the genealogies of applicants for citizenship, they included those individuals as Pamunkeys. If not, they denied them the right to live on the reservation. In their 2010 petition for federal recognition, the Pamunkeys claimed that citizenship depended on direct lineal descent from forty ancestors as well as "in-person interviews" of applicants. The Pamunkeys also mentioned the 1954 list, although they did not provide a copy of this roll to the Office of Federal Acknowledgment. The roll they provided the Office included 182 recognized tribal citizens, all descended from the original forty.[248]

After R. Lee Fleming wrote to the tribe and warned them about the deficiencies in their recognition petition, the Pamunkeys further clarified their citizenship criteria in a revision filed on July 11, 2012.[249] To qualify for citizenship today, individuals must prove that they are a *"direct lineal descendent"* of a Pamunkey Indian listed on one or more census records, including the Pamunkey Indian Reservation Census of 1908, rolls of Pamunkey voters taken in the first decade of the twentieth century, and the 1900 and 1910 US

Censuses of the Pamunkey Indian Reservation.[250] These requirements restrict citizenship to individuals with a genealogical connection to Pamunkeys who lived on the reservation in the early twentieth century. In addition, applicants for citizenship "must prove *social connection* to the Tribe and current Tribal members residing on the Reservation and the Tribe in general." The chief and tribal council determine social connection by evaluating applicants' written or oral statements about "all known and remembered contact they have had throughout their lifetime with those Tribal members residing on the Reservation." Applicants must also provide three "resident Tribal members as references who will attest that the applicant has been in social contact." Parents who wish to enroll their children also must provide this evidence since "Membership of the parent will not automatically grant membership to a minor," especially if the parent "has lost social contact."[251]

The Pamunkeys also reaffirmed the laws and ordinances passed by the tribe in 1954.[252] These rules include restrictions on voting for non-resident tribal citizens and those who fail to pay the tribal resident tax, which the tribe raised from $6 to $25 a year in 2003.[253] If Pamunkeys return to the reservation for a six-month period and pay the tax, they are "restored to voice and vote."[254] Thus, although Pamunkey women now have the same voting rights as Pamunkey men, the tribe maintains a tiered system of citizenship based on reservation residency.

The revised petition did not provide documentation that the Pamunkeys had amended the tribal ordinance against black intermarriage.[255] In September 2014, members of the Congressional Black Caucus urged the Justice Department to investigate discrimination within the tribe before the Bureau of Indian Affairs rendered a final decision on Pamunkey recognition. In response, Pamunkey Chief Kevin Brown pointed out that the institutionalized racism of the state of Virginia had prompted the tribe to include racist policies in the past to protect the Indian identity of its citizens, but he maintained that these policies were "never an attack on, or reflective of, ill-will toward African-Americans." Brown insisted that the intermarriage ban was "antiquated and now repealed."[256] The tribe's new citizenship roll, dated October 18, 2012, includes 203 individuals, around forty of whom live on the Pamunkey reservation.[257]

Many of the historical struggles the Pamunkeys faced in their effort to preserve their reservation and Indian identity came as a result of their status as a state tribe. Without federal recognition, the Pamunkeys lacked assurances that whites would acknowledge them as Indians, especially during the Jim Crow years. To avoid extinction through legislation or amalgamation, real or imagined, the Pamunkeys had to make hard decisions about belonging. In particular, they used social distance from African Americans to prove that they deserved separate categorization. Virginia's biracial codes threatened Pamunkey identity, but also, more tangibly, reclassification as "colored" threatened Pamunkey land. If whites did not believe that they were Indian, they feared, Virginia might not uphold its treaty obligations to the tribe, including common ownership of their reservation. Distinguishing Pamunkey tribal citizens from black people was thus a matter of both political and economic survival. The tribe's decision to create a tiered system of citizenship also reflected its goal of preserving the tribal land base. Until recently, the tribe denied full rights to Pamunkey women—especially those who married whites—and off-reservation Pamunkeys because Pamunkey men on the reservation feared losing control of the land. Historical factors, experiences, and fears influenced how the Pamunkeys decided who belonged.

Concerns about land rights and legal status explain the recent efforts of the Pamunkey Indian Tribe to obtain federal recognition. In early 2014, Assistant Secretary for Indian Affairs Kevin K. Washburn issued a proposed finding on the Pamunkey recognition petition in which he declared that the tribe met all seven mandatory criteria for acknowledgment.[258] Following this finding, Pamunkey recognition went into a probationary period in which third parties could comment on the merits or flaws of the petition. During these months, a number of political enemies of the tribe endeavored to block Pamunkey recognition for economic reasons. The casino giant MGM, for example, was building a $1.2 billion gambling complex in Maryland, just across the Potomac from Virginia, and feared competition from the Pamunkeys. The anti-casino group Stand Up for California worried that Pamunkey recognition would open the door for small tribes in California to also gain acknowledgment and open casinos. Local Virginia businesses, meanwhile, feared that federal status would permit the tribe to sell gasoline, alcohol, and cigarettes more cheaply than non-Indians.[259] To forestall Pamunkey recognition, these organizations cynically repeated many of Plecker's early twentieth-century arguments. Stand Up for California, for example, insisted that several tribal citizens were in fact descendants of pre–Civil War free blacks, not Indians, and that the list that the tribe provided as proof of tribal citizenship was therefore unreliable.[260] Tribal enemies also persuaded the Congressional Black Caucus and a group of Democratic congresswomen to question the tribe's legitimacy based on their "long and clear practice of discriminating against women, African Americans and other non-Pamunkey tribal members."[261] The efforts of these groups to discredit the tribe delayed Pamunkey recognition and revealed the ways that outside perceptions of tribal citizenship continue to influence official acknowledgment of tribal sovereignty.

Despite the lobbying efforts of tribal enemies, on July 2, 2015, the Bureau of Indian Affairs rendered a favorable decision on Pamunkey recognition.[262] On the day before the ruling went into effect, however, Stand Up for California filed another request for reconsideration, which put a further hold on the tribe's status. Once again, the organization cast aspersions on the Pamunkeys' Indian identity by asserting that tribal citizens have black ancestry.[263] The Interior Department's Board of Indian Appeals reviewed the case and ultimately rejected Stand Up for California's request. On January 28, 2016, the Pamunkey Indian Tribe became the 567th federally recognized tribe. Legal recognition of their status as "Indian" brings to an end the Pamunkeys' long struggle to preserve their ethnic identity and reservation land.[264]

As the Pamunkeys have discovered, the path to federal recognition brings with it its own challenges since federal oversight means that internal tribal decisions about belonging are increasingly subject to outside scrutiny. The "logic of recognition," which shaped tribal decisions on belonging in the late nineteenth and twentieth centuries, continues to influence how tribes define their citizenship today.

From Fluid Lists to Fixed Rolls

The Catawba Indian Nation of South Carolina

In January 2000, Cynthia Ann Walsh wrote a heated email to the editors of the *Rock Hill Herald*. The descendant of Catawba Indians who migrated west in the last decades of the nineteenth century, Walsh could not understand why her family had been excluded from the citizenship rolls of the Catawba Indian Nation in South Carolina. "The Bureau [of Indian Affairs] simply is unable or unwilling to make up their minds what the criteria [for citizenship] ought to be," she charged. "I find it an outrage that a federal agency has acted with such willful contempt for the clear language of federal laws entrusted to it to apply and enforce."[1] Walsh and her family blamed their exclusion from the tribe on the mishandling of Catawba citizenship rolls by federal officials and the Catawba Indian Nation. They demanded clear qualifications for citizenship so they could make their case for inclusion in the tribe.

Despite Walsh's allegations of modern mystifying of Catawba enrollment criteria, defining Catawba tribal citizenship had never been simple. Before 1943 it was a fluid process that involved ongoing negotiations between Catawbas and South Carolina agents over per capita state appropriations payments made to tribal citizens. Social changes such as the arrival of Mormon missionaries on the reservation, the departure of some Catawbas for the West, and increasing intermarriage between Catawbas and outsiders led to decades of discussions, debates, and decisions on the meaning of belonging. The tribe, through the state, granted some Catawbas access to state appropriations, but denied the rights of others whom they did not consider tribal citizens. State appropriations lists reflected their changing ideas. The citizenship roll of 1943, which Interior Department officials compiled after the tribe gained federal recognition, was only a snapshot of this complex process, but it legally fixed Catawba tribal citizenship. For those left off, the roll seemed arbitrary and imposed by outsiders. Yet the tribe had been actively involved in creating its citizenship criteria all along, even if the Catawbas had not always uniformly agreed with

[handwritten marginalia: sense of belonging redefined]

enrollment decisions. The 1943 roll ended the flexibility of Catawba tribal belonging, but it provided the Indians with an important legal tool to define concretely their political identity and to draw up official boundaries of citizenship.

The Catawbas, like the Pamunkeys, belonged to a state-recognized tribe that remained in the South following removal. Although the Catawbas had sustained a friendly alliance with the state of South Carolina for decades, white settlers enviously eyed the Indians' extensive landholdings. Reduced in numbers by warfare and disease, the Catawbas could not farm all of their land, so they supplemented their incomes by renting much of their territory to white leaseholders beginning in the late eighteenth century. Initially this arrangement worked well, and Catawba community ties strengthened through leasing tribal land. By the 1830s, however, white lessees began to resent this situation. Year after year, these tenants sent petitions to the state legislature to demand that the Indians give up their reservation and transfer title of the

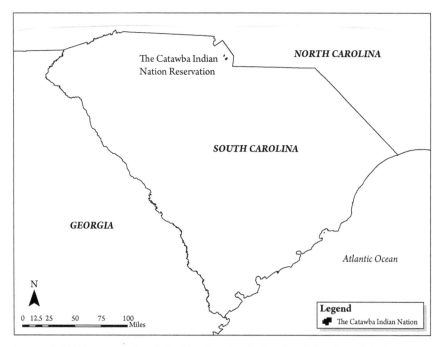

Figure 2.1 When Catawbas drifted back to South Carolina following a failed removal attempt in the 1840s, their state-appointed financial agent secured for them a small tract of land on the Catawba River. Although this 630-acre plot was meager compensation for the 144,000 acres of farmland the Catawbas had ceded to South Carolina, the "Old Reservation" provided the Indians with a place to regroup and rebuild as a nation. A land claims settlement with South Carolina and the federal government in 1993 provided the Catawba Indian Nation with funds to purchase additional land. Map prepared by Christian Adams.

lands to whites. In 1832, the state appointed commissioners to negotiate with the Catawbas for the sale of their land.[2]

Under pressure from the state, white tenants, and other non-Indian tres- *agreement*
passers, the Catawbas finally signed the Treaty of Nation Ford in 1840. They *for*
agreed to give up their land in exchange for $5,000 that the state promised *removal*
to use to purchase a new reservation in North Carolina. South Carolina
also agreed to pay the Indians $2,500 when they left their current homes
and $1,500 a year for nine years.[3] This was meager compensation for the
144,000 acres of rich farmland ceded by the Indians, but the Catawbas had
little choice but to sign. The treaty left the Catawbas without a place in South
Carolina. Divided over where to go, some Catawbas drifted westward and
joined the Eastern Cherokees in the mountains of North Carolina. Others
considered moving across the Mississippi River and settling among the
Choctaws and Chickasaws in Indian Territory. Still others preferred to stay
where they were. For a time, at least, the Catawbas seemed disjointed and
dissolved as a people.

South Carolina eventually abandoned its efforts to remove the Catawbas.
State officials failed to purchase a suitable replacement for the lands the
Catawbas ceded in 1840 or to appropriate the entirety of the promised treaty
money. Instead of acquiring a new reservation for them in North Carolina, in
1842 their financial agent secured for the Catawbas a small tract of land on
the Catawba River. The soil was poor, the terrain was hilly, and the land was
covered in forest. Nevertheless, this tract, known as the "Old Reservation,"
became home for the Indians who returned to South Carolina in the mid-
nineteenth century. The tribe gradually regrouped and reorganized a political
system on and around this land.[4]

Instead of the funds provided by the treaty, in 1849 the South Carolina
governor promised to pay the Catawbas a 6 percent annual interest on their
withheld funds. The state made these small annual payments to the tribe until
the 1940s, except during the Civil War.[5] From 1840 to 1910, state appropriations totaled about $86,900. From the 1910s through the 1930s, the state paid
the tribe about $9,500 annually. Some of the money funded a small school for
Catawba children on the reservation in South Carolina.[6] The financial agent
paid the reservation's teacher, physician, and others who provided services to
the tribe.[7] The remaining funds were "doled out in small per capita payments,"
ranging from $20 to $40 for each tribal citizen. The Catawbas survived on this
money, combined with what they could produce in their small gardens and
cornfields, by hunting and fishing, or through selling their pottery.[8] State officials believed that these payments sufficiently compensated the Catawbas for
the land they lost in the 1840 treaty.[9] The Catawbas maintained that the state
owed them a just settlement for the thousands of acres ceded at Nation Ford,

but they took the state payments as temporary compensation for their considerable loss.[10]

To determine which Catawbas were eligible for state payments, the tribe's financial agent kept annually updated lists of tribal citizens. These lists included the names of individual Indians ordered in family groups and noted whether each person was married or single. The lists recognized both male and female household heads and indicated how much state money each individual received.[11] Until 1883, the agent published the lists each year in the state's reports and resolutions file. After that date, they were no longer published, although agents continued to compile lists in order to distribute payments.[12] Each year the Catawbas provided their agent with the names of people they believed the state should include.[13] State payments created an incentive for Catawbas to consider formally what it meant to belong to the tribe, a process that profound social changes made more difficult.

Like the Pamunkeys, the Catawbas began distancing themselves from African Americans early in the nineteenth century after witnessing whites' racial attitudes to blacks and observing—and participating in—slave systems.[14] This process began early in Catawba history as the Indians forged military and trade alliances with white Americans, but it took on new urgency in the late nineteenth and early twentieth centuries with the rise of Jim Crow segregation. As Indians, the Catawbas suffered racial prejudice at the hands of their white neighbors that only heightened following Reconstruction and the establishment of strict racial codes in the South. Aware of whites' even greater antipathy toward African Americans, the Catawbas, according to anthropologist Frank G. Speck, lived "in obsessed fear of being regarded as 'colored' and classified with negroes."[15] The Catawbas discovered that harboring racial prejudice against black people helped distinguish them from African Americans in the eyes of whites.[16] By setting up strict racial boundaries, the Catawbas attempted to preserve their separate Indian identity at a time when whites threatened to lump them into the category of "colored." These ideas, in turn, limited whom Catawbas viewed as potential marriage partners and helped create racial boundaries to Catawba citizenship.

Even though the Indians lived in a region with a large African American population, they made every effort to avoid contact with blacks, a fact that astonished Special Indian Agent Charles L. Davis in 1911. Davis observed no friction between the Catawbas and their black neighbors, but he reported that "It seems to be simply the resolution of the little band to keep clear of the colored population for their own wellbeing."[17] The Catawbas refused to marry African Americans or even to engage in illicit sexual relationships with black neighbors. If any such unions existed, they remained hidden and unacknowledged. Most white observers agreed with the Catawbas' assertion that "there is not a drop of negro blood in their veins."[18] Even those skeptical of the Indians' claims to racial purity, "judging merely from the complexion of one or two families," had to acknowledge that "if there is colored blood it dates many years back, and is quite limited in scope."[19] For the Catawbas, as for the Pamunkeys, racial labeling as "colored" threatened the tribe's survival as well as the legal rights and social privileges of tribal citizens.

Mormon missionaries arrived in the context of this move toward hardening racial ideas and contributed to the trend. Hoping to convert the region's white population in the early 1880s, missionaries redirected their attention after a chance encounter with Catawbas at Rock Hill. They integrated themselves into Catawba community life, built a church, and set about educating Catawba children. Although local whites resisted their efforts—one Mormon elder was whipped by a mob while another received a flesh wound to the chin after local whites fired on him—the Indians protected the missionaries and welcomed them into their homes.[20] The first Catawbas to convert to the new faith were Robert Harris, Pinkney Head, John Saunders, and Jim Harris. These influential men soon induced other tribal citizens to follow their example. By 1934, 95 percent of the Catawbas participated in Mormon meetings.[21]

The Mormon message appealed to the Catawbas because it provided a counter-narrative to the racial prejudice of white South Carolinians against Indians. Although the Mormons, like other whites at the time, believed in the superiority of the white race, they also believed in the mutability of racial lines, at least when it came to Indians. They taught the Catawbas that they were members of a lost tribe of Israel, the Lamanites, who had been punished by God but who were still capable of salvation. Missionaries promised the Indians that sincere repentance, faithfulness to the gospel, and purity of life would "surely obtain for you forgiveness from God and . . . restore you to his favor."[22] They guaranteed the Catawbas not only spiritual transformation but also physical transfiguration. The descendants of the converted would eventually become white as a sign of God's forgiveness.[23] As Catawba leader Sam Blue explained, the Mormons "brought a book [that was the] direct history of our fore father[s], which we had no other history before this book came along."[24] According to historian Douglas Summers Brown, the Mormon message "gave them a place—and a respectable place—among the peoples of the world."[25]

Although the Mormon message infused the Catawbas with renewed pride that counteracted the racial discrimination they faced at the hands of other whites, the Mormons were less charitable toward African Americans. Whereas the Book of Mormon promised Indians that if they converted, their descendants would eventually gain the privilege of whiteness, no such redemption was offered blacks.[26] Mormon missionaries among the Catawbas taught that in ancient times God and the devil fought an epic battle. One-third of the world's spirits fought for God and became Mormons. Another third fought with the devil and became those who reject Mormonism. The final third "remained neutral, and constitute the Negro race," marked as disgraced by their color.[27] Mormon missionaries directed their Catawba converts to have nothing to do with the members of this so-called degraded race. At a conference held on the Catawba reservation in 1908, the presiding Mormon official told the Indians of the "glorious promises that God had made to the house of Israel, and reminded his hearers of their ancestry." He went on to instruct them to be "industrious, sober, honest, law-abiding and not to contaminate themselves and their posterity by intermarrying with the negro race."[28] The Catawbas readily complied with this final command.

The combination of Catawba fears of being reclassified as "colored" and the direct exhortations of Mormon missionaries to avoid intermarriage with blacks led to the deepening of negative Catawba attitudes toward African Americans. By the 1930s, one government official proclaimed that these Indians did "not mix with negroes, nor interbreed with them," and that "negroes have a wholesome fear of the Indians and do not come upon the reservation."[29] For the Indians, non-interaction with blacks was a point of pride and also a way of appealing to the sympathy of their white neighbors. Appeals to whites by demonstrating common racial thought partially paid off. Special Agent Davis insisted that "This one thing has done much to retain the respect and sympathy of the white population of the vicinity."[30] In terms of tribal citizenship, Catawba attitudes toward blacks meant that although the tribe, unlike the Pamunkeys, did not officially bar citizenship to those who married blacks, such a decree was unnecessary. Intermarriage with African Americans was unthinkable and black-Catawbas did not exist in the eyes of the tribe.

In addition to influencing Catawba racial thought, Mormon missionaries also encouraged some Catawba converts to move west. This effort ultimately had profound ramifications for the tribal citizenship rolls. Beginning in the late nineteenth century, missionaries sent tribal citizens to Salt Lake City and elsewhere in the West where they received further instruction and helped build the Mormon community.[31] In 1887, for example, five Catawba families— headed by James Patterson, John Alonzo Canty, Alexander Timms, Hillary Harris, and Pinkney Head—departed with the Latter-Day Saints for southern Colorado.[32] Sometimes Catawbas returned to South Carolina, but often they did not. Those Catawbas who stayed in the West built new lives for themselves, intermarried with whites and Latinos, and spread out to new homes in Utah, Colorado, New Mexico, and other western states. Although these Catawbas retained a sense of their Indian heritage and of their kin ties to the people they left behind, their geographical distance from the core Catawba community in South Carolina eventually called into question their rights as tribal citizens.

When Catawbas moved out of state, South Carolina faced a dilemma. Should state appropriation payments owed the tribe be paid to non-residents? At first, state agents continued disbursing payments to Catawbas who migrated. In 1887, the attorney general of South Carolina advised that Catawbas were "entitled to their pro rata share of such fund . . . so long as they belong to the tribe, and not upon their residence in this state."[33] Pinkney Head and his family drew their appropriations for two years after leaving South Carolina.[34] Then the payments stopped. Under pressure from officials who had received complaints from South Carolina Catawbas about dwindling per capita payments, the agents refused to pay any more money to Catawbas outside of the state.[35] In 1892, this stance was formalized when the state legislature passed a resolution prohibiting payment to those Indians who left South Carolina.[36] From then on, the financial agent excluded western Catawbas from the appropriations lists.

Despite numerous appeals by Catawbas in the West and elsewhere, in 1905 South Carolina reaffirmed the ruling against paying Catawbas out of state. According to the new state attorney general, only those Indians on the reservation could get a share of the tribe's assets.[37] In 1909, the assistant attorney general interpreted the law to mean "permanent residence in the State" and denied appropriations even to those Catawbas who returned to South Carolina after time away.[38] Although not every agent enforced the rule with such rigor, by the early twentieth century, South Carolina officials reserved payments for South Carolina residents only. Special Agent Davis explained in 1911 that "the State naturally objects to distributing what it terms gratuities to residents of other states."[39] This position infuriated western Catawbas who believed the state was cheating them out of their heritage and inheritance. In 1892, for example, Nancy Harris from Gainesville, Texas, complained to the South Carolina governor that she and her children had been cut out of their "just Rites." Invoking the Catawbas' long history of friendship with the United States, she demanded that the governor imagine himself in her situation: "if you was to move over in Georgia or north C would the members of the legetlater [*sic*] have a rite to take your home from you?"[40]

Some western Catawbas made direct appeals to the federal government for recognition of their rights as tribal citizens. In 1895, a group calling themselves "the Catawba Indian Association" in Fort Smith, Arkansas, held a convention and sent a petition to Washington, DC, asking for land allotments.[41] This association represented 257 Catawbas and their descendants from Indian Territory, Oklahoma Territory, Arkansas, and Texas who had migrated west during the mid-nineteenth-century removal attempts of the tribe.[42] They beseeched the federal government to investigate their situation and "to secure the Catawba Indians equal rights to share in the Public Domain the same as other Indians."[43] They wanted to know if, as non-reservation Indians, they had rights to land or property in South Carolina, and also whether they could benefit from homesteading laws in their states and territories of residence.[44] The commissioner of Indian affairs replied that he saw no reason why these Indians should not "take up lands in severalty" in the West, but he remained silent on their right to South Carolina Catawba assets.[45]

In lieu of asking for rights as South Carolina Catawbas, some individuals who migrated west asked the government to grant them citizenship in western tribes. In 1896, the commissioner of Indian affairs received a petition from Pinkney Head and seventy-five other Catawbas in Sanford, Colorado, "who claim to have once resided in South Carolina but are no longer 'recognized' by said State." The petitioners asked to become citizens of the Ute Indian tribe on the Uintah Reservation, "receiving and enjoying in common with them all rights and privileges and the protection of the government." This petition did not reflect a relinquishment of Catawba identity on the part of Pinkney Head and his relatives but simply showed that these Catawbas were looking for alternative ways to receive benefits in their new western homes. With South Carolina's refusal to grant them shares of the state's appropriation payments, union with the Utes seemed a viable alternative. Although Pinkey Head and his relatives may have hoped for allotments as Utes under the terms of the General Allotment Act of 1887, the federal government had no intention of adding to the rolls of western tribes.[46] The unintended consequence of this petition was to make both state officials and South Carolina Catawbas believe that Pinkney Head's group had given up their rights in the Catawba Indian Nation.

South Carolina officials did not want to pay appropriations to Indians outside of the state, and South Carolina Catawbas supported this decision. In part, their motivations were financial. Desperately poor with few opportunities for employment, late nineteenth- and early twentieth-century Catawbas often depended on state money for survival. As one agent explained to the governor of South Carolina, the Catawbas frequently bought goods on credit with the promise that they would pay back storekeepers once their appropriations came in. In this way, they were advanced both money and supplies that were critical for their daily needs even when they could not find jobs.[47] Catawbas took pride in maintaining "their good name in matter of credit," yet the small amount of money they received barely covered living expenses.[48] A white woman married to a Catawba man recalled that the meager appropriations were "usually spent three or four times over before the year rolled around."[49] The Catawbas realized that if appropriations money went out of state, they would be left with even less credit and fewer means of feeding their families. For this reason, according to the agent, "The Indians have made a rule that if one of their number does not live on the reservation or in the State six months before they are paid off they will not be entitled to a share."[50] The decision to restrict the rights of western Catawbas was not simply imposed by the state but was something that South Carolina Catawbas also approved and promoted.

Catawba desires to restrict payments to tribal citizens in the state reflected their financial needs but also showcased their cultural ideas about belonging. To be a Catawba, an individual had to be part of the Indian community. The core of that community was centered on and around the reservation lands in South Carolina, and for the Catawbas, physical presence on that land correlated with community belonging. As one Catawba man described it, "Reservation life when I grew up was a caring, sharing extended family."[51] Catawbas who moved away from South Carolina were not able to participate in the events and traditions that defined Catawba identity. They might maintain kin ties to the core Catawba community and they might eventually return and reintegrate into community life, but as long as they lived apart from the Catawbas in South Carolina, they held a different status in the eyes of those Indians who remained in the state. In particular, western Catawbas who had migrated away generations before seemed undeserving of an equal share of the tribe's assets. As Chief James Harris explained to reporters in 1907, he had no problem with sharing payments with tribal citizens who returned to South Carolina and resumed their tribal connection, but he objected to Catawbas coming back for money and departing again as soon "as they are paid off."[52]

Life on and near the reservation provided the Indians with knowledge of how to be Catawba that people raised elsewhere did not acquire. Although outside observers frequently assumed that Catawba culture was fading, community members continued to pass on unique life ways to their children as well as to adapt and develop new cultural practices to maintain ethnic boundaries.[53] The Catawba language mostly disappeared in the early twentieth century (the last speaker died in 1959), but Catawba worldviews persisted. Stories were a particularly important form of Catawba identity expression. In the 1930s, Catawba elder Bob Harris explained "that story-telling was intended to develop the mind, to make children think, to teach them about the ways of life."[54] Among the old people who lived on the reservation "were always many tellers of tales who educated and frightened and amused the children, and entertained the adults."[55] South Carolina Catawbas grew up hearing stories that projected a specific worldview and ethos. Those who lived away from South Carolina did not share this experience.

From their elders, Catawbas learned about "wild Indians," who were mischievous creatures with a proclivity for distressing small children. In an oral interview, Nola Campbell recalled that the older Catawbas warned her not to go out and play at night lest the wild Indians get her.[56] Mrs. Roy Brown similarly recalled that the wild Indians, who were "little people, like little elves," lay in wait beneath floorboards. If children sat on a crack, the wild Indians pulled their feet through.[57] According to Catawba tradition, these little people lived in the old Catawba cemetery and elsewhere along the Catawba River, so only South Carolina Catawbas had to worry about them.[58] They ate acorns, tree roots, fungi, turtles, and tadpoles.[59] If they captured children, they took them away and tied their hair in tree branches.[60] One woman remembered that the wild Indians stole her younger brother. When the family found him, he was shivering and alone on a tree stump in the middle of a pond. The wild Indians had sucked all the blood out of one of his arms, but in return the little people had given him healing knowledge.[61] Stories of wild Indians terrified Catawba children, but they also provided common childhood memories that tied Catawbas to their landscape and taught children important lessons— especially about obeying their parents at bedtime.

Catawbas told many stories specific to the terrain of their homeland. Community members knew, for example, that "the baldness which character- izes the Roan Mountain" arose from three ancient battles the Catawbas fought against enemy tribes. After the Catawbas carried the day, "the Great Spirit caused the forests to wither from the three peaks of the Roan Mountain where the battles were fought." In their place grew crimson flowers, "nourished by the blood of the slain."[62] South Carolina Catawbas also knew about a place in the Catawba River where noises heard among the rocks were "said to be caused by old Indians crossing there." At another point near the reservation, tribal citizens sometimes heard ghostly Catawbas dancing and singing. One man even claimed he "once saw a woman dressed in the ancient manner with bow and arrows and a bundle on her back" down by the river. She vanished from view as quickly as she appeared.[63] Nola Campbell remembered a story about a mysterious white horse that "walked up and down that road past where Georgia and Douglas Harris lived."[64] Although she never saw the horse herself, the story was ingrained in her memory in part because of the familiar geo- graphical space that it evoked. Non-resident Catawbas could not have shared the knowledge relayed by such stories because they did not have the same fa- miliarity with the landscape of South Carolina.

In the 1930s, anthropologist Frank G. Speck worried that younger members of the tribe were beginning to forget the stories of their ancestors as a result of their instruction at Euro-American schools. He argued that the Catawba chil- dren he encountered possessed "practically no knowledge of the native tales and traditions which made animal life and nature in general so mysterious to their ancestors."[65] It may have been true that knowledge systems were chang- ing on the reservation; however, this did not mean the end of storytelling tra- ditions. Catawbas often adapted Euro-American tales to make them fit within the world the Indians knew. For example, Speck recorded a Catawba story reminiscent of the Judeo-Christian account of Noah's Ark. In the Catawba version, "it rained so much that the river rose," an idea that would have been familiar to people who lived along the Catawba River and occasionally dealt with severe floods, such as the Great Flood of 1916. Instead of escaping on an ark, the Catawbas in the story climbed up trees on an island and remained there for a long time. Finally, like Noah, they sent a dove to discover if the land had dried. The dove returned, but instead of an olive leaf, "it brought back corn in its mouth."[66] For the Catawbas, the introduction of this new story, adapted into a Catawba framework, did not mean a loss of tradition. It simply signaled the evolving nature of their culture and the addition of new tales to their repertoire of stories.

In addition to providing an environment for shared storytelling, residence on or near the reservation also provided Catawbas with the opportunity for participation in community activities such as dancing. Like stories, dancing evolved as a Catawba tradition. Older Indians recalled earlier times when their people "made a fire outside and danced around it." Traditional dances were led by old men and continued long into the night.[67] These physical expressions of identity were reserved strictly for community members. According to Margaret Brown, who spoke with Speck in the 1920s, years earlier a black man who worked on the reservation had attempted to join in the festivities. Up until that point the young man had been treated with "considerable freedom" on the reservation, but when he tried to join the Catawba dancers, his employers turned on him. The black man "fled through the woods, the horde behind him. . . . It is said they might have killed him had they caught him then."[68] This event reflected the Catawbas' hardening ideas of race. It also revealed their sense that dancing was a critical marker of Catawba identity reserved only for members of the community.

Traditional dances began to fade by the late nineteenth century, in part due to the influence of Mormon missionaries.[69] Dancing, however, did not end on the reservation. Certain tribal citizens like Sam Blue made it their mission to preserve knowledge of traditional Catawba practices like dancing, and they passed this information on to their children and grandchildren.[70] In addition, as with stories, the Catawbas adapted Euro-American dances to serve as new forms of Catawba identity expression. Nola Campbell remembered that every Saturday night Catawbas gathered at a different tribal citizen's house and held square dances. Even though the homes were small, they would simply "tear the beds down and throw them in the back room and just dance up a breeze in their living room." Such dances were not as exclusive as the traditional Catawba dances. Campbell recalled that her relatives sometimes hired "a colored man by the name of Charlie Crawford to pick a guitar" while an intermarried Cherokee named Major Beck played the fiddle.[71] Nevertheless, they served as important gatherings where friends and relatives met, laughed, and shared a good time. Western Catawbas missed out on this opportunity.

A particularly critical marker of Catawba identity on the reservation that withstood the test of time was pottery building.[72] Mothers taught their daughters how to dig, wash, and knead clay and the best ways to build pots. Arzada Sanders recalled that she learned to make "the old timey pottery" such as "big bowls for holding flowers" and big pots decorated with "heads and three legs" by watching her mother and grandmother.[73] Similarly, Isabel George remembered how her mother made her beat clay as a child. After she prepared her mother's clay, she got a small piece of clay and practiced building her own pots. Even when at play, George recalled, she dug out "old red, stiff mud" to practice shaping pots like her mother.[74] By the time a young Catawba woman married, she was "normally able to continue the tradition as a master potter in her own household."[75]

Pottery building was a family affair. Women were in charge, but their husbands and children helped them by digging clay and scraping and polishing pots.[76] The rubbing rocks used to smooth finished pieces became family heirlooms passed through generations. Mrs. Roy Brown noted that one had belonged to her great aunt and must have been at least a century old.[77] Catawba potters crafted "fantastic designs" on many of their wares, including representations of "squirrels, turtles, birds, pots, shoes, and other familiar objects." Not only did potters showcase their artistic talents, but their creations also provided valuable income for their families. As Frances Wade recalled, "My mother could make pottery. That's the way we got our clothes when we went to school."[78] In the 1890s, Catawba women carried "their wares to Rock Hill, where they [would] barter them for old clothes or anything that [was] offered for them."[79] In later years they sold pots at Winthrop College and to tourists and collectors who visited the reservation.[80]

Catawba pottery, like stories, was a product of a particular landscape. Potters knew the locations of the best clay holes and they were careful to keep these places in good order. One potter recalled that clay was dug so often from a particular place that "now the hole is big." Catawbas kept the clay fresh by filling the hole with dirt between visits.[81] They used two different types of clay, "a fine-grained stiff variety called 'pipe clay'" and "a course, lighter, crumbly kind known as 'pan clay.'" In 1908, the Catawbas mined three sites in South Carolina for pan clay and five for pipe clay. They would work each clay hole until "it becomes troublesome to keep free of water, then abandon it and begin another one near by."[82] Knowledge of clay holes and pottery building was intimately tied to the natural landscape and cultural environment of South Carolina.

Figure 2.2 Catawba women made distinctive pottery that they sold to local whites, tourists, and collectors to supplement their family incomes. In this photograph, Sarah Harris, the mother of Chief David Adam Harris, and a young Catawba girl posed with some of Harris's larger pieces. Date: 1908. Courtesy of the National Anthropological Archives, Smithsonian Institution (SPC Se Catawba NM 48736 01757300).

In addition to providing raw materials for manufactured goods, the land around the reservation contained plants and animals critical for Catawba healing practices. Many reservation Indians believed that evil spirits or ghosts caused sickness. Fortunately, Catawbas knew how to prepare medicine for recovery.[83] The bark of slippery elm, for example, treated consumption and "the chills might be cured by rolling up a granddaddy-long-legs in a dough and swallowing it." Parents gave babies tea made out of powdered turtle hearts to ensure long life.[84] When they had headaches, Catawbas wrapped their heads with snakeskin.[85] According to Gilbert Blue, who became chief of the tribe in the 1970s, a local herb called fireweed had power as "a potence builder in males." He said that his grandfather, Sam Blue, used to swear by fireweed, "and he himself had twenty-three children."[86] Some natural remedies were exported by migrating Catawbas. For example, Susannah Harris married a Cherokee named Samson Owl and moved to North Carolina, but she recalled that a rabbit's foot could be used as a love charm and that sassafras wood should not be burned in the summer or the burner would tell lies.[87] Thomas Morrison, who

moved to Arkansas as a child and later returned to South Carolina, also retained a wealth of Catawba healing knowledge.[88] For the most part, however,
medicinal knowledge, like stories, dances, and pottery, remained community-
specific information related to life on the reservation in South Carolina.

Reservation life was important to Catawba identity, but barriers between
South Carolina and western Catawbas were not impermeable. If individuals
rejoined the community in South Carolina, the core Catawbas on the reservation welcomed them and granted them equal rights to tribal assets. An example of this flexibility was the case of Thomas Morrison. When he was a child,
Morrison and his parents fled an 1853 smallpox outbreak in South Carolina
and settled in Arkansas.[89] In the 1880s, he returned to South Carolina as a
grown man. According to Speck, Morrison was well known to the Indians as
a "medicine doctor." The Catawbas respected his knowledge of the traditional
Catawba art of curing and welcomed his reintegration into community life.
Morrison ingratiated himself by refusing to charge Indians for his services,
although he collected payments from local whites whom he treated. He taught
Catawba leader Sam Blue much of his knowledge, especially "herbs and nature
potencies" for healing. Morrison even served as an interim chief of the tribe
in 1886. He stayed in South Carolina for several years, and during this time
he drew a share of the tribal funds from the state. Eventually he returned to
Arkansas, but while he lived in South Carolina he was a full and active community member.[90] Morrison's story illustrates that South Carolina Catawbas
did not deny the Catawba identities of those who moved west or reject the possibility of their rejoining the tribe; they simply believed that these individuals should return to the community before they received payments as tribal
citizens.

Although South Carolina Catawbas may have agreed with the state's restrictions on paying appropriations to western Catawbas, they were less pleased
when South Carolina denied funds to Catawba children who attended out-of-
state boarding schools. Beginning in the 1890s, a steady stream of Catawba
youth left home to study at the Cherokee Boarding School in North Carolina
and at the Carlisle Indian Industrial School in Pennsylvania. Catawbas had
mixed feelings about the boarding schools. Although parents wanted their
children to have new opportunities, they worried about their well-being, especially when students like Rosa Harris returned from Carlisle in poor health.[91]
The death of Wade Ayers at Carlisle in 1903 following a smallpox vaccination
was a severe blow to the tribal community.[92] Parents wondered if it were worth
sending their children away. They also worried about how children's absence
from South Carolina would affect family finances.

When Catawba children left South Carolina to attend boarding school, the
state cut off their annual appropriations payments. This situation put Catawba

parents in a bind. Although they saw graduates of Carlisle return "to their people masters of a trade, industrious and thrifty," they worried about how the family would manage in the meantime. As a result, many parents "were more than ready to keep their children home and thereby deprive them of the benefits which they might have received at Carlisle." Advocates for Indian education tried to address this problem. Mrs. R. E. Dunlap, a teacher at the Catawba Indian School on the reservation, wrote to the governor of South Carolina and pleaded the children's case.[93] Through her efforts, the issue reached the level of a scandal, and for a time, Catawba students received their state pensions. Gradually, however, the disbursing agents for the state began denying pupils their payments once again.[94] Despite the appeals of federal agents to the commissioner of Indian affairs on the matter, the Catawbas, as a state-recognized tribe, had to deal with state officials rather than with the federal government. The issue of state appropriations and boarding school students continued to fester without clear resolution.

State residency played into evolving Catawba notions of belonging, but so too did shifting ideas of kinship. Kinship traditionally had defined Catawba tribal belonging, and as a matrilineal society the Catawbas customarily traced kin exclusively through the mother's line. Over time, however, the Catawbas began to rethink their views on kin. Repeatedly decimated by disease over the course of the nineteenth century, the tribe's population had dwindled to around 100 by 1900. With only a few Catawba spouses to choose from, tribal citizens began looking elsewhere for marriage partners. Exogamous marriages, however, had consequences for Catawba ideas of tribal citizenship. If only one parent was Catawba, did a child really belong to the tribe? Did inheritance patterns apply equally to the children of male and female Catawbas? What status would non-Catawba spouses hold in the tribe? The resolution of these questions had important implications for the tribe.

As time passed, it grew more difficult for the Indians to find non-related partners within their tight-knit community.[95] Southern Indians had long-standing taboos against incest, particularly between members of the same clan, and these concerns were heightened by personal experiences with the results of such unions. Frank G. Speck's Catawba informants told him in the 1930s that if close relatives married, "something might happen to produce spoiled (defective) children. . . . Their minds might not be good."[96] Similarly, tribal citizen Howard George's grandfather warned him that "some of his people married like that into people and said then their children were born blind."[97] Like the Pamunkeys, Catawbas worried about the effects that years of endogamy might have on the vitality of future generations. Rather than engage in relationships with close kin, Catawbas sought spouses outside the tribe.

Intermarriage with other Indians was one option the Catawbas pursued to remedy the problem of marriage within a small, closely related community. In the early nineteenth century, for example, a Catawba woman married a Pamunkey man named John Mush (or Marsh). This Pamunkey left his relatives in Virginia and moved onto Catawba land. He and his wife had several children, and he eventually died among her people around 1860. According to ethnographer James Mooney, who visited the tribe in the late nineteenth century, the Mush children all married Catawbas. By the 1880s, there were at least twelve members of this family out of a reservation population of barely 100. Although Mooney suggested that some of the other Catawbas disliked the Mush family on account of their "sullen disposition," they nonetheless considered the family Catawba.[98] After all, the Mush children descended from a Catawba mother.

Although they had been traditional enemies, Catawbas also began marrying Cherokees in the mid-nineteenth century after some of the tribe moved to North Carolina following the Treaty of Nation Ford. Most Catawbas eventually returned to South Carolina after "latent tribal jealousies broke out," but a few remained—mostly intermarried women. Contact between the two tribes continued and Catawbas and Cherokees occasionally married each other. Mooney reported that in 1898 two Catawba women, Nettie Harris Owl and Susannah Harris Owl, lived among the Eastern Band, both married to Cherokee men. These women were expert potters and shared their methods with their husbands' tribe.[99] Susannah later became a key Catawba informant for Speck in the early twentieth century.[100] She had begun her married life among her own people, but then moved to her husband's reservation so that their children could attend the Cherokee school.[101]

Over the years, a few Cherokees also moved to the Catawba reservation, usually accompanying Catawba spouses. In some cases, intermarriages between the two tribes spanned generations and included multiple family ties. Joseph Sanders, a Catawba man, met Lily Beck, a Cherokee woman, in the first decade of the twentieth century while he was visiting friends in North Carolina. The pair soon moved back to the Catawba reservation and married.[102] Not long after, Beck's grown son from a previous relationship, Fletcher Beck, went to South Carolina to visit his mother. The young man found a Catawba partner as well and married in 1914.[103] Lily Beck's brother, Major Beck, also visited the Catawbas. His Catawba wife later recalled "He never did go back. I guess the young girls would not let him go back."[104] When he moved to the Catawba reservation and married Lula Beck, Major Beck gave up his claims to Cherokee tribal citizenship. The couple's children appeared on the Catawba appropriations list; other cousins who lived in North Carolina enrolled as Cherokees.[105]

Catawbas who married Cherokees had to make choices about the legal identity of their children. Some, hoping to benefit from Eastern Band timber money and claims settlements, enrolled their children in that tribe. When they did this, however, their children forfeited their rights as Catawbas because neither the federal government nor South Carolina tolerated dual tribal citizenship. Commenting on one such case in 1909, the assistant attorney general for South Carolina insisted that if "the father is Cherokee" and if the family's two children were "enrolled for participation in the settlement with the eastern Cherokees," then these children were "certainly not entitled to the provision made by the State of South Carolina for the Catawba." In his view, this held true even though the children's mother was Catawba and the family had moved back to South Carolina.[106] Other families welcomed the opportunity to list their children as Catawbas from the start. This was especially true for certain members of the Beck family whose rights as Cherokees were questioned because the family had lived apart from the Eastern Band for many years in Georgia.[107] Unable to enroll as Cherokees, the Becks who married Catawbas moved to South Carolina and registered their children with the Indian agent there.

Non-Catawba Indian spouses provided one solution for the problem of Catawbas marrying close kin, but this was not practical for everyone on the reservation. Catawbas had much more contact with non-Indians in the surrounding counties of South Carolina than they did with Indians from other states. Although they refused to marry African Americans, Catawbas were open to relationships with whites. Catawba women had begun marrying white traders in the eighteenth century, a practice revived in the nineteenth. Whether due to the uneven effects of disease, alcohol, and stress or to random chance in a small population, Catawba women outnumbered men in the late nineteenth century. This meant that Catawba men usually could find Catawba wives, but eligible bachelors were not as available to Catawba women. Genealogist Ian Watson has proposed that this gender imbalance encouraged Catawba women to seek relationships with whites.[108] Whether the unions were brief or permanent, Catawbas considered children resulting from these relationships fully Catawba. They inherited their right to a place on the tribe's appropriations list through their mother's line.

Catawba women led the way in interracial relationships, but Catawba men also began marrying white spouses.[109] Job opportunities on nearby farms or in town exposed these men to whites and budding friendships with white men led to interactions with their white sisters and cousins. Evelyn MacAbee George, a white woman, recalled that her cousin encouraged her romance with a Catawba youth. The daughter of an overseer, she met her future husband when he came to work at the farm. Her cousin became friends with the young

Catawba man and began telling Evelyn "things that Mac said and telling Mac things that [she] said that [they] did not say." He eventually arranged a date for the pair.[110] Although some white families objected to these matches, others, like the MacAbees, accepted their Catawba sons-in-law.[111]

The anti-miscegenation laws of South Carolina complicated interracial relationships. Although Radical Republicans had repealed such laws after the Civil War, state legislators enacted new sanctions in 1879.[112] Not only did the new law bar marriages between blacks and whites, but it also prohibited intermarriage between whites and Indians. State legislators reinforced this ruling in subsequent legal codes. In 1918, a Catawba man named Ben P. Harris wrote to the attorney general of the state to inquire about "intermarriage of races." The attorney general replied by quoting Section 385 of South Carolina's Code of Laws of 1912: "It shall be unlawful for any white man to intermarry with any women of either the Indian or negro races, or any mulatto, mestizo, of half-breed, or for any white woman to intermarry with any person other than a white man." The law declared that marriages in violation of this rule would be "utterly null and void and of non effect." Moreover, people engaging in such unions were guilty of a misdemeanor and could be fined $500 and imprisoned for a year.[113] Despite legal barriers, however, Catawba men and women continued to marry whites. They simply went to a preacher without registering the marriage in court or lied about their racial identity when they applied for a marriage license.[114] Even if South Carolina did not legally sanction these unions, interracial partners lived together as husband and wife and white families and tribal citizens recognized them as spouses.

Although Catawbas accepted interracial couples, it took time for white spouses to become integrated into Catawba community life. Catawbas interacted with whites on a regular basis, but "because of the treatment that they received at their hands," some Indians felt bitter toward and suspicious of whites who joined the reservation community. One white woman who married a Catawba remembered that she "did everything to make friends with them," including freely dividing produce from her garden with her neighbors, yet she "felt like they resented [her]." Only after years of patience did she finally feel that they "accepted [her] as one of them." Once fully incorporated into community life, however, the woman explained that the Catawbas were "just as close to me as my own kin."[115] Through bonds of kinship and friendship, intermarried whites eventually became part of the reservation community.

Some intermarried white women integrated so fully into the Catawba community that they took up Catawba traditions such as pottery building. Mae Bodiford Blue, who married a son of Chief Sam Blue, recalled that when her husband lost his job, her father-in-law encouraged her to make pots. Mae took his advice and soon fashioned sculptures of ducks, turtles, and canoes as well

Figure 2.3 In 1918, Ben P. Harris (pictured) wrote to the attorney general of South Carolina to inquire about the "intermarriage of races" and the legal rights of his children by a white woman. He was disappointed to learn that such marriages were null and void in the eyes of the state. Despite legal barriers, however, Catawba men and women continued to marry whites, even if their unions were not legally sanctioned. Photographer: De Lancey W. Gill. Date: 1899. Courtesy of the National Anthropological Archives, Smithsonian Institution (AE GN 03814B/Broken Negative File 06679700).

as ashtrays and other pieces to sell. She found out that she "had a knack for doing this" and subsequently contributed to her family's income through pottery sales.[116] Nola Campbell recalled that her white mother, Maggie Price Harris, also built pottery.[117]

For a time, Catawba women did not mind that their white sisters- and daughters-in-law built pots. When the Indians went to sell their wares at

Winthrop College and elsewhere, they emphasized the Catawba-origin of the pots no matter the identity of the individual artist. Pottery was typically fashioned in a communal setting with extended families sharing in the process and in the production of the final pieces. As long as white women contributed to Catawba family economies, Catawbas welcomed their efforts.[118] Over time, however, some Catawba women worried about how the presence of white potters might affect outside perceptions of this Catawba tradition. When pottery building was no longer essential for family incomes, a few Catawba women began to object to white women representing the community with their pieces. In an oral interview conducted in 1977, Frances Wade recounted how one Catawba woman, Doris Blue, demanded that Mae Bodiford Blue end her practice of building pots. She did so after a buyer specifically visited Mae to buy Catawba pottery.[119] This shifting attitude suggests that as the importance of Catawba pottery as an economic practice waned, its importance as a cultural—and racial—marker grew.

Non-Catawba spouses held an ambiguous position on the reservation. At times they seemed like fully included members of the community, yet they lacked the rights of tribal citizens. Non-Indian spouses were not permitted to attend tribal meetings, for example, and if widowed, they had to leave the reservation. The Catawbas designed these rules to protect the community. Although outsiders could become kin, the Catawbas held them at arm's length legally to ensure that Catawba rights and resources remained reserved for tribal citizens alone. These rulings extended to the payment of state appropriations. Intermarried whites lived in the Catawba community, had Catawba children, and even appeared on reservation censuses, but they never drew payments from the state. The names on the appropriations lists exclusively belonged to individuals who claimed Catawba "blood."

Leola Watts's experiences illustrate the rigidity of the rule against white people drawing a stipend. Watts was born in the late nineteenth century, the daughter of a white woman. At the time of her conception, Watts's mother lived with a black man. Suspecting his partner of infidelity, the man swore he would kill her if the baby were not born black. According to oral tradition, Watts's mother knew the baby would be white, so she hid her labor and gave birth in a nearby barn. She then took the infant to her Catawba neighbors, James and Mary Jane Watts, and begged them to raise her.[120] The Watts took in the child and brought her up within the Catawba community. Leola Watts learned the traditions of her adopted parents. She wore her hair long, built pottery, and even learned to speak a few Catawba phrases. She married a prominent member of the tribe, Nelson Blue, who was the son of Chief Sam Blue, and bore several children.[121] Despite Watts's full integration into the Catawba community, however, her racial identity precluded her from inclusion on the South Carolina appropriations lists.

In addition to denying citizenship to intermarried and adopted whites, Catawbas also initially excluded the children of non-Catawba mothers. As a matrilineal people, Catawbas considered only the children of Catawba women to be Catawba. When Catawba women began intermarrying other Indians and whites, these relationships posed no problems since their children enjoyed all the privileges of tribal citizenship. The intermarriage of Catawba men and outsiders, however, was a different story. Special Agent Charles L. Davis reported in 1911 that "with the Catawbas of South Carolina, children of white mothers are wholly excluded."[122] He noted that the reservation included ninety-seven people descending from Catawba mothers and thirteen people descending from white mothers; yet the state, adopting the tribe's rule, only allocated money to those with Catawba mothers. In his estimation, this restriction protected "the enrollment from having illegitimate whites charged to it," a problem that Davis had seen happen among the Eastern Band of Cherokee Indians.[123] For the Catawba fathers of half-white children, however, this rule seemed to place an undue burden on their families.

The first Catawba father to demand recognition of his half-white children was Jefferson Davis Ayers in 1894. That year, he applied for appropriations money from the financial agent for his children. When the agent denied his request, Ayers hired a lawyer. Other tribal citizens considered Ayers's demands outrageous. They threatened to hold the agent responsible for the money if he acquiesced to Ayers, and when Ayers confronted them in the streets of Rock Hill, "they denounced him for delaying the payment of the money." One Catawba man, John Brown, was so incensed that he physically attacked Ayers. Only the intervention of nearby Catawba women prevented the breakout of a serious fight.[124] The financial agent submitted the case to the state attorney general for resolution. In his reply, the attorney general proclaimed, "It must be taken for granted that the Legislature intended the distribution to be made to the Catawba Indians as heretofore. I would most certainly follow their *law* on the subject and not our *law*."[125] The Ayers children lost their payments and the Catawba tribe maintained its right to rule on matters of belonging.

After the Ayers incident, the issue of appropriations for the children of non-Catawba mothers diminished for a time, although it never disappeared. In 1904, a newspaper article referred to the "strange condition" among the Catawbas: "The children, if born of white mothers even in wedlock, are deprived of the pension share, while a child of an Indian mother with a white father may realize the benefits whether the parents are married or not."[126] Catawba notions of tribal belonging conflicted with Euro-American concepts of legitimacy, making the Indians' position difficult for outsiders to

Figure 2.4 As a matrilineal people, Catawbas initially considered only the children of Catawba women to be Catawba. After Catawba men who married white women protested this situation and the state attorney general supported them, the tribe changed its ruling in 1917. In this photograph, Catawba women and their children posed on the Catawba reservation in South Carolina. Date: 1908. Courtesy of the National Anthropological Archives, Smithsonian Institution (SPC Se Catawba NM 48736 01757000).

understand. As more Catawba men married white women in the early twentieth century, they, too, questioned the tribe's position and once again began clamoring for their children's rights.

In 1915, a Catawba man, like Ayers before him, approached the financial agent and inquired about the rights of his children. The wife of this unnamed man was "half white and half Indian," but because her mother was white, both she and her children were left off the appropriations list. The financial agent appealed to the state attorney general for advice. Unlike his predecessor, this official ruled against the tribe. He argued that there was no distinction between the mixed-ancestry children of Catawba mothers and Catawba fathers and that both should get equal shares of the tribe's resources. The tribe immediately protested the decision and hired lawyers to file an injunction. Catawba fathers on the other side of the dispute hired their own attorneys and geared up for battle. The judge in the case dismissed the Catawba's appeal for an injunction on the attorney general's ruling, but the case lingered in the courts.[127] A month later, there was still no clear resolution.[128]

Outsiders believed the children of Catawba fathers and white mothers deserved rights, but the tribe took longer to come around to this point of view. Finally, in 1917, Chief David Adam "Toad" Harris took it upon himself to change the tribal law. According to oral tradition, Harris did this as much for personal as for political reasons.[129] Although previously married to a Catawba, the chief began a relationship with a white woman named Dorothy Price. Rumors circulated that Harris murdered his Catawba wife, Della George, so that he could marry Price. Having been tried and acquitted for the crime, Harris turned his attention to the Catawba inheritance law. To ensure the inclusion of his children by Price, he convinced the tribe to place the children of white women on the appropriations lists.[130] Harris apparently paid politically for the scandal. He was kicked out of the Mormon Church on the reservation and lost the next tribal election. Sam Blue replaced him as chief in 1918.[131]

In 1921, the South Carolina attorney general confirmed the tribe's new position on intermarriage. When tribal citizen Ben P. Harris wrote to verify the eligibility of his children for payments, the attorney general responded that although such children were illegitimate due to the state's anti-miscegenation laws, they "certainly could not be classed as white persons or citizens of the State" if their father were Indian, so they must be Catawbas. The attorney general also issued a warning to those Catawbas who might complain about the decision, which revealed his stance on miscegenation: "If counting these children as Catawba Indians reduces the pro rata of the appropriation made by the General Assembly from year to year for the support of this tribe, the Catawba Indians have no one to blame for the condition but themselves. They certainly cannot consistently oppose having these children participate in the appropriation and at the same time continue to practice these illegitimate relationships."[132] For white South Carolinians, Indian "blood" made these children Catawba regardless of the identity of their mother. Although not all Catawbas agreed, the tribe grudgingly accepted the children of white mothers onto the appropriations lists.

The inclusion of the children of white mothers on tribal rolls was a welcome relief to Catawba fathers who married outside the tribe. The end of matrilineal inheritance, however, brought a new dilemma: illegitimacy. Whereas there was never a question about the identity of children of Catawba mothers, children who claimed Catawba fathers had few ways to unequivocally prove their ancestry in an era before DNA testing. Agents complained that some unscrupulous whites contracted marriages with the Catawbas "for the express purpose of an outside white trying to share in that last farthing which is left to these people."[133] They worried about white children illegitimately finding their

Figure 2.5 According to oral tradition, Chief David Adam "Toad" Harris (pictured) changed the tribal law that excluded from citizenship the children of non-Catawba women. He did so after he married a white woman so that their children would appear on the state appropriations lists. Photographer: De Lancey W. Gill. Date: 1905. Courtesy of the National Anthropological Archives, Smithsonian Institution (negative 3812 B).

way on to the appropriations lists and they closely policed the racial identities of the individuals claiming payments. Agents demanded "to have some proof showing that these applicants have Indian blood in their veins, since their mother is a white woman" and required sworn affidavits attesting to parentage.[134] Whereas the Catawbas, with Mormon support, erected a barrier between blacks and Indians, state officials tried to ensure that there was also a boundary between whites and Catawbas. State money went only to Catawbas by blood, forcing the Indians to delineate and codify kinship and belonging.

The rights of individuals to appear on South Carolina's appropriations lists for the Catawbas evolved over the course of the late nineteenth and early twentieth centuries as tribal citizens and state officials negotiated the terms of inclusion. These lists determined which Indians were entitled to a share of the tribe's assets and the presence of individuals on these lists became an important marker of community belonging. Race, residency, and inheritance rules all played a role in making these determinations. The flexibility of the appropriations lists left room for the tribe to explore their evolving ideas about Catawba identity. This fluidity, however, was not to last. The state could no longer ignore the Indians' poverty in the 1930s, and when the tribe sought the resolution of ongoing land claims in South Carolina, the federal government got involved. Ultimately, the Interior Department replaced state appropriations lists with an official roll that fixed Catawba tribal citizenship. Once in place, this roll became the basis for all future Catawba citizenship decisions.

Since the Treaty of Nation Ford in 1840, Catawbas had steadfastly maintained that the state had given them a raw deal. The treaty had promised a new reservation in North Carolina where the Indians could make a new life, but this land never materialized. Instead, South Carolina reserved for them a tiny and barren fraction of the thousands of acres they had ceded. Convinced that the state had violated their rights, the Indians held that South Carolina needed to make up for its false promises. In particular, they cast their eyes on tracts of land that they had leased to white settlers before the 1840 treaty. Although supposedly South Carolina took over these leases under the terms of the treaty, the state had not properly compensated the tribe for the loss. When the leases began expiring in the early twentieth century, Catawbas hired lawyers to look into their claims.

White people living on the land began worrying that the Catawbas had a legitimate case. Newspapers stories announced, "The Catawba Indians May Recover Land," and warned that the Indians "have a good claim." Even if the tribe was unsuccessful in its bid, the Catawbas' assertions put "a cloud on the title to over 9,000 acres of land" held by white South Carolinians.[135] South Carolina took the matter seriously enough that the issue even went before the state legislature to determine whether officials could arrange a compromise.[136] State officials dreaded the matter going to court "as the Indians' lands are now worth many thousands of dollars."[137]

The extreme poverty of Catawbas on the reservation also attracted the attention of state officials. Since the Treaty of Nation Ford, the Catawbas had suffered economically on their reduced lands. In 1894, one journalist described their condition as "wretched indeed."[138] Yet, worse was still to come. The Great Depression of the 1930s hit the rural Catawbas hard and deprived them of most opportunities they had for work outside the reservation.[139] Chief Sam Blue despaired that his people were in a "starving condition" because their land was "so poor and rough" they could not earn a living on it. Only seven members of the tribe had full-time jobs in 1934, and despite their yearly appropriations payments, the Indians could not pay their bills.[140] Year after year, individual Catawbas racked up debt as they struggled to make ends meet. In 1936, the State Auditing Department reported that the tribe owed more than $9,200 to its creditors.[141] By that time, the Catawbas had defaulted on so many bills that their agent reported the impending loss of medical care. He explained that "The local doctors are reluctant, in fact most of them are declining to render medical aid on account of the non-payment of the accumulated bills."[142] President Franklin D. Roosevelt's plans to combat the Depression and the appointment of a new commissioner of Indian affairs, John Collier, who was sympathetic to the plight of the country's Natives, prompted the chief to beg Washington for relief.[143]

After receiving numerous pleas from state officials and the Catawbas to address their impoverished condition, the Indian Office finally sent an agent to South Carolina to investigate the situation. D'Arcy McNickle, an enrolled Salish Kootenai and a longtime Indian activist, visited the reservation and advised the commissioner of Indian affairs to enter into negotiations with the State Budget Commission to learn whether a cooperative arrangement could be worked out between state and federal officials for the care of the tribe. He reported that the state was prepared to spend $100,000 to purchase new lands for the Catawbas and to rehabilitate the tribe. The state expected this money to serve as a settlement with the Catawbas for unfulfilled treaty obligations and to release South Carolina from future responsibilities to the tribe. The Catawbas, McNickle said, were in favor of this idea, so long as they could keep their old reservation which housed "the burying place of their people for many generations now."[144] All that was left was for the federal government to support the plan.

In response to McNickle's letter, in 1937 legislators in Congress presented a bill for the relief of the Catawba Indians. This bill authorized the secretary of the interior to enter into a contract with the state of South Carolina "for the agricultural assistance, industrial advancement, and social welfare, including relief, of the Catawba Indians."[145] Although initially opposed by Assistant Secretary of the Interior Ebert K. Burlew, who challenged the Catawbas' Indian identity and right to federal services, in 1941 Congress finally authorized a small appropriation of $7,500 to enable the Office of Indian Affairs to begin working out a plan with South Carolina.[146] The entry of the United States into the Second World War delayed these efforts, but in 1943, the Interior Department, the state of South Carolina, and the Catawba tribe finally reached an agreement.

The memorandum of understanding that resulted from these negotiations was divided into three parts. First, the state of South Carolina promised to contribute $75,000 to purchase federal trust lands for the Catawbas and to pay $9,500 annually for two years to aid in "rehabilitating" the tribe. In addition, the state agreed to protect the rights of Catawbas as citizens of South Carolina "without discrimination," including their right to attend white public schools and state institutions of higher learning. Second, the Catawba tribe agreed "to organize on the basis of recommendations of the Office of Indian Affairs for the effective transaction of community business" and "to carry on the program of rehabilitation" as prescribed by federal and state officials. Finally, the Office of Indian Affairs promised to contribute annually to the welfare of the Catawbas, to aid in the development of arts and crafts programs on the reservation, to create educational programs for the Catawbas, to provide medical services to the Indians, and to offer Catawbas loans and grants for economic development.[147] In effect, this act granted federal acknowledgment to the Catawbas, shifting their status from a state-recognized to a federally recognized tribe.

As part of the memorandum of understanding, the federal government required the compilation of an official tribal citizenship roll. D'Arcy McNickle encouraged this action even before officials finalized the memorandum. In 1940, he predicted that once the federal government started providing services to the Catawbas, "individuals will begin drifting in from North Carolina and elsewhere" to demand rights.[148] A roll promised to provide a concrete basis for tribal citizenship and to ensure that federal resources went to the right people. To expedite the process, federal agents turned to the appropriations lists held by the tribe's financial agent.[149] These lists had long identified Catawbas for the distribution of state annuities and it seemed natural that they would serve a similar purpose for the federal government. Federal agents did not consult the Catawba chief, councilmen, or tribal elders on the question of citizenship, but instead relied exclusively on state records to make the 1943 roll.[150] For the most part, South Carolina Catawbas did not seem troubled by this. When they noticed the following year that officials had omitted a few of their number, they simply sent a letter to their new federal agent and requested "that their names be added to the Catawba Tribal Roll and the per-capita payment of $18 be made to each of them."[151] The government complied with this request.

The final roll included 306 names, almost none of which belonged to Catawbas who had migrated to the West.[152] The exclusion of Catawbas outside of South Carolina perhaps occurred simply as a matter of course as agents transferred names from the state list to the federal roll, but it also may have been an intentional decision made by South Carolina legislators who objected to using the funds they had promised for people living outside of the state. South Carolina Catawbas did not protest this decision.

Although the Roll of 1943 excluded western Catawbas from tribal citizenship, there were a couple of exceptions. Two brothers, Ben E. Rich Garcia and Edward Guy Garcia, had returned to the reservation in South Carolina in the late 1930s and married Catawba women. The Garcia brothers descended from western Catawba grandparents who left South Carolina with Mormon missionaries in the 1880s.[153] Despite the family's long absence from the core

Catawba community, the tribe welcomed the brothers back into the fold and allowed them to live on the reservation.[154] Although these men initially did not appear on the financial agent's appropriations list, the tribal council voted to include them.[155] This decision was reminiscent of earlier moments in Catawba history when returning Indians like Thomas Morrison reintegrated into the tribe even after long absences. As long as such individuals proved that they were willing to rejoin the community and act as kin, the South Carolina Catawbas had no objection to their full inclusion.

Perhaps the Garcia brothers acted strategically in their decision to return to South Carolina at that particular moment. For years, western Catawbas had monitored the situation in South Carolina, periodically inquiring about their rights as Indians and asserting their Catawba identity. In 1921, for example, Wilford M. Canty in Sanford, Colorado, wrote the Office of Indian Affairs, "I would like to know if I can get my share of Indian land here in Colorado. I belong to the Catawba Tribe."[156] The Indian Office continually denied such requests, yet western Catawbas remained vigilant of opportunities. As rumors spread about a possible agreement among the state, the federal government, and the Catawba tribe in South Carolina, western Catawba letters flowed into Washington.[157] Garcia family members asked their state senator in Colorado to write a letter on their behalf. Senator Edwin C. Johnson told the Indian Office that this family was "interested in securing their share in the deal and are anxious to learn whether it will be necessary for them to return to South Carolina in order to claim their portion."[158]

When the commissioner of Indian affairs informed western Catawbas that the plan for the tribe included the purchase of new lands in South Carolina and that "the members of the Catawba Tribe residing elsewhere could only share in the benefits by returning to South Carolina," members of the Garcia family confronted a difficult choice.[159] Family members recalled that they had left South Carolina to begin with because "the land that was given us or left to us was land that is no good." They worried about returning to a place where people had to build "pots to sell that they may have enough to keep themselves alive."[160] Yet, certain family members decided to try their luck in South Carolina. When Ben E. Rich Garcia and Edward Guy Garcia met and married Irene Minerva Beck and Juanita Betty Blue on the Catawba reservation, they decided to stay. This decision guaranteed their place on the 1943 roll.

Although the Garcia brothers made it onto the Catawba tribal roll, their siblings in the West did not.[161] Their sister, Viola Elizabeth Garcia Schneider, remained in Colorado, and she did not appear on the South Carolina appropriations list. Such an omission created an unusual circumstance whereby full siblings held different political statuses, based exclusively on their geographical location. Western Catawbas felt frustrated by their exclusion. Viola's daughter,

Cynthia Ann Walsh, later explained on her family's citizenship petition in the 1990s that both her mother and her aunt had attended the Haskell Institute in Kansas and graduated as Catawba Indians. She insisted that the tribe and their agent even had granted her mother an official "Certificate Degree of Indian Blood" in 1937.[162] Despite this recognition of the family's ethnic and racial identity as Catawba, the 1943 roll omitted these individuals, thereby denying them citizenship in the tribe.

Despite the problems associated with the 1943 roll, the Catawbas accepted it and made it the basis of citizenship in their new constitution, which they created as part of the memorandum of understanding. The second article of the constitution defined citizenship as "All persons of Indian blood whose names appear on the tribal roll of July, 1, 1943, as recognized by the State of South Carolina" and "All children born to any member of the Catawba Tribe, who is a resident of the State of South Carolina at the time of the birth of said children."[163] With this document, the tribe emphasized Catawba ancestry by "blood"—highlighting the ongoing importance of both kinship and race— and South Carolina residency as key markers of belonging. They also codified the 1943 roll as the basis for citizenship in the tribe. On May 20, 1944, the Catawbas held an election to ratify this constitution. Only 30 percent of the tribe voted, but all the votes favored the proposed constitution.[164]

Voting citizens of the tribe approved the new constitution's exclusion of western Catawbas, but in the years after they finalized the roll, problems arose. Just as the state appropriations lists had once excluded Catawba children attending out-of-state boarding schools, the new roll failed to include South Carolina Catawbas serving in the armed forces and stationed elsewhere at the time of its completion. This was a blow to the tribe because "just about every man of the tribe of fighting age" had enlisted to serve in the Second World War.[165] Away in Europe or on training bases scattered across the United States, the appropriations lists excluded these Catawba men during their absence from South Carolina. This exclusion carried over onto the 1943 roll. At first tribal citizens did not notice the mistake. Only when the threat of the government's termination policy promised to divide the tribe's federal land and resources did servicemen and veterans realize their omission.

Beginning in the 1950s, the United States promoted a new policy in its dealings with Indian tribes. Known as "termination," this policy sought to end the federal relationship with tribal nations and transition Indian people into ordinary American citizens. Similar to the nineteenth-century allotment policy, termination called for the detribalization of reservation land and the division of tribal assets among citizens. Ultimately the government hoped to end all treaty obligations including services to tribes. This policy intended to "modernize" American Indians and bring them into mainstream American life. The Catawbas looked like perfect candidates for termination. In 1959, the Committee on Interior and Insular Affairs in the House of Representatives recommended the ratification of a bill—H.R. 6128—that provided for "the division of the tribal assets of the Catawba Indian Tribe of South Carolina."[166]

Some Catawbas supported the idea of termination. The memorandum of understanding had promised much but had failed to deliver. In 1956, Chief Sam Blue complained that "We Catawba Indians are dissatisfied with the way we are treated by the Government Agent and his employees when the State of S.C. turned us over to the Federal Government." Although the agreement had called for an economic rehabilitation program for the Indians, Catawbas insisted that "nothing has been done about it so far to help the Catawbas."[167] Impoverished despite federal promises, many Catawbas believed they would be better off with fee simple title to their land. The termination act promised approximately $1,500 to each Catawba family out of the tribes' assets, which consisted primarily of land valued at approximately $254,000.[168]

Federal officials and South Carolina congressmen encouraged those Catawbas in favor of termination. Representative Robert Hemphill visited the tribe and persuaded many that "the memorandum of understanding has been of no advantage to the Tribe." When tribal citizens worried about how tribal assets would be divided under the provisions of the act, Hemphill read them the citizenship clause of the 1944 constitution and promised that the tribe could also vote to include servicemen outside of South Carolina.[169] Taking his advice, the tribal council passed a resolution on May 21, 1960, to amend the citizenship provision of the tribal constitution. Directing their comments to the secretary of the interior, they declared that recognized tribal citizens desired that the roll include servicemen and their children born outside of South Carolina.[170] With this resolution, the Catawbas asserted their sovereign right to define tribal citizenship. They did not pass a similar resolution to include western Catawbas. South Carolina Catawbas believed that members of the core community deserved rights—whether home or away—but they did not extend the same privileges to Catawbas who had left the reservation permanently years before.

Satisfied that the core community would receive shares of tribal land and resources under the termination act, the tribe finally agreed to accept H.R. 6128, although only a small portion of the tribe voted on the issue. As part of the termination act, the federal government required a new roll for the Catawbas to record each Indian born on or before July 2, 1960.[171] Each citizen whose name appeared on this final roll was "entitled to receive an approximately equal share of the Tribe's assets that are held in trust by the United States."[172] Government officials compiled the new roll based on the 1943 roll and on the tribe's insistence on the inclusion of servicemen, veterans, and their children. Finalized in early 1961, the new roll named 631 individuals as tribal citizens.[173] Most of these Catawbas resided in South Carolina, but a few had moved to other states sometime during the two decades that followed the memorandum of understanding.[174] Although they lived out of state, they belonged to the tribe because their names appeared on the 1943 roll.

The Catawba termination act undid the memorandum of understanding and ended the tribe's federal relationship, but it did not affect the status of Catawbas in South Carolina as state Indians. The tribe retained its state reservation, but officials divided or sold all of the federal lands. This action reduced land held in common by the Catawbas from 4,018 to 630 acres.[175] Gradually, even the land held onto by Catawba families was alienated. Chief Gilbert Blue recalled that many Catawbas ended up losing their land "for the sake of money in the hand."[176] Although a temporary solution for immediate poverty, once this money was gone, the Catawbas were left with nothing but the 630-acre state reservation. South Carolina's timely legalization of marriages between whites and Catawbas gave intermarried whites legal rights to the Catawbas' now detribalized federal lands and accelerated the process of dispossession.[177]

Termination left the Catawbas "a loose knit people" without a federal relationship or an official tribal government. The Indians, however, did not abandon their tribal identity or the value they placed on their state reservation as a marker of that identity. With most of their federal lands gone, Catawbas rallied around the state reservation, and when local whites began moving "dangerously close to the reservation line" and illegally cutting Catawba timber, tribal citizens began to reorganize politically.[178] In 1973, the tribe reestablished tribal and executive councils.[179] Two years later, the tribe incorporated under the laws of South Carolina as a non-profit. This move—similar to a strategy employed by the Eastern Band of Cherokee Indians nearly a century before— gave the Catawbas a legal existence despite their lack of federal recognition. It also allowed the Catawbas to take advantage of some federal assistance programs designed for Indian tribes.[180]

As part of the Catawbas' efforts to reorganize themselves in the years after termination, tribal citizens drew up a new constitution. The 1975 constitution built on the 1944 constitution but made a few changes in the wording of its citizenship clause.[181] It required that citizens descend from those who appeared on the 1943 and 1961 rolls and be of Indian blood, but, unlike the 1944 constitution, it made no mention of the provision that future enrollees be born in South Carolina. By this time, a number of enrolled citizens had moved away from the state to earn livings elsewhere. With the 1943 and 1961 rolls as a barrier separating these people from descendants of the western Catawbas who left the state in the nineteenth century, geographical boundaries to citizenship no longer seemed essential. Enrolled citizens were now free to move out of state and still retain their political rights in the tribe.

The new tribal constitution also aimed to protect Catawbas from opportunistic whites. Now that marriage between whites and Indians was legal, white spouses could potentially claim rights to tribal assets through their Catawba husbands and wives. To ensure that this did not happen, the tribal council resolved that "non-Indian spouses of deceased or divorced Catawbas who do not have children may not reside on the reservation longer than six months."[182] This resolution recognized the reality of increasing intermarriage but protected the remaining tribal lands from alienation. The Catawba Indian Nation continues to operate under the 1975 constitution today. In July 2015, the tribe made a bid to institute a revised and updated constitution that would "improve the nation's ability to work with federal agencies and other groups on issues affecting the tribe." The initiative failed, however, after not enough tribal citizens voted to approve it.[183]

With the 1975 constitution in hand, tribal leaders turned their attention to the Catawbas' long-standing land claims. Despite the 1943 agreement, the Catawbas believed that both the state and federal government had yet to make amends for the Treaty of Nation Ford. The Catawba claim rested on two central issues. First, tribal citizens insisted that the state had failed to carry out the terms of the Treaty of Nation Ford.[184] The second point the tribe made was that the treaty itself was illegal. According to the Trade and Intercourse Act of 1790, all treaties with Indian nations had to be conducted under congressional authorization and ratified by the Senate. South Carolina negotiated the 1840 treaty without congressional approval or federal oversight. According to federal law, the Indians insisted, the Treaty of Nation Ford was null and void.[185] The Native American Rights Fund helped the Catawbas bring their case before state and federal officials, and after nearly two decades of legal wrangling, the parties finally reached an agreement.[186] In October 1993, President Bill Clinton signed the Catawba Indian Tribe of South Carolina Land Claims Settlement Act into law.[187]

The Settlement Act promised the Catawbas $50 million over five years from federal, state, and local governments, and from title insurance companies. The tribe placed these payments in five trust funds for the purpose of land acquisition, economic development, education, elderly assistance, and per capita payments to tribal citizens. The act also authorized the tribe to buy 3,000 acres of tax-exempt land to expand its reservation and restored tribal powers of self-government as well as the tribe's relationship with the United States. Once again, the Catawbas were a federally recognized tribe. In terms of the per capita payments, the act stipulated that 15 percent of the settlement funds be divided among enrolled tribal citizens.[188] This stipulation revived the question of who was entitled to a share of Catawba resources.

As legislators drew up the Settlement Act of 1993, several South Carolina officials suggested that the tribe include a blood quantum requirement for citizenship.[189] The attorney general of South Carolina wanted this restriction because "of the minute portion of Catawba blood which will undoubtedly be possessed by future generations." As tribal citizens intermarried with non-Indians and Catawba blood diluted, such a provision "would place the Catawbas eventually in precisely the same circumstances as any other American citizens," and the state would no longer be responsible for the Catawbas because they would no longer qualify as Indian.[190] In 1993, state legislators proposed a one-eighth blood quantum requirement for state services.[191] Tribal citizens, however, decided that blood quantum would be difficult if not impossible to determine with any accuracy, and they used their sovereign authority to reject any such citizenship requirement. Instead, the tribe settled on lineal descent from the rolls of 1943 and 1961 as the primary criterion for tribal inclusion. Although the state did not get its way about blood quantum, it managed to include a caveat in the settlement that revoked all state services to the tribe after ninety-nine years from the date of the act. This rule does not affect the Catawba Indian Nation's federal status or federal services, but many tribal citizens feel frustrated by South Carolina's persistent efforts to renege on its responsibilities for the tribe.[192] In effect, the outcome may be the same as the proposed blood quantum requirement and may eventually end state services and tax exemptions for Catawba Indians.

The Settlement Act of 1993 called for the creation of a new tribal roll in order to determine which Indians were entitled to benefit from the act's provisions, including per capita shares from a fund of $7.5 million.[193] To ensure that no one was left off the new roll, the federal government mandated that the Catawba Indian Nation publish the roll several times in local newspapers and allow for appeals.[194] The Catawbas complied with this ruling and the federal government also published the roll in the federal register in November 1994. After three years of appeals, the federal government added 113 additional names to the roll. Most of these belonged to infants born to enrolled tribal citizens; none belonged to western Catawbas.[195]

Western Catawbas continued to appeal their exclusion from the tribal rolls into the 1990s. For these individuals, tribal citizenship was not just about the money they might receive but about recognition of their Catawba heritage and family histories. One western Catawba even offered "to sign away all claims to a share of $50 million in settlement money if the tribe in South Carolina will add his and his family's name to its membership roll." In a statement to the *Rock Hill Herald*, Wayne Head insisted that he was not interested in money.

His family "just want[ed] the right to be on the roll and reestablish our ties with our heritage."[196]

South Carolina Catawbas had mixed feelings about granting citizenship to western Catawbas. Some, like Chief Gilbert Blue, suggested that the western Catawbas wait until after the 1993 settlement's cash payments were distributed to renew their appeal. At that point, Blue suggested, there would be no objection to the western Catawba's inclusion, as long as they could prove their claims.[197] In 2011, tribal elder Fred Sanders called their exclusion "an injustice." He maintained that although they are not enrolled, these individuals are still Catawba.[198] Other tribal citizens, however, were less certain about the rights of western Catawbas. As an article in the Catawba Indian Nation's official newspaper pointed out, "while the effect of Catawba culture may be boundless, there are limits to the legal recognition of membership in the Catawba tribe."[199] Many tribal citizens objected to the inclusion of individuals who rarely visited South Carolina and who retained no political connection to the tribe. By 2000, even Chief Gilbert Blue had changed his position on the western Catawbas. Stating that tribal citizenship rested on both heritage and social connection to the tribe, he insisted that "even though someone might be of Catawba blood, if they weren't on an earlier roll, they can't be included."[200] The western Catawbas made another appeal for inclusion to the Bureau of Indian Affairs in 2000, but officials denied their request because they could not prove direct lineal descent from people on the 1943 and 1961 rolls.[201]

The new roll was finally published in 2000 and served as a basis for the per capita distributions made to tribal citizens. Each Catawba born before the date of the Settlement Act—October 27, 1993—was entitled to a share. Today the tribe relies on lineal descent from the 1943, 1961, and 2000 rolls to define belonging, but the Catawba tribal council also holds a working roll for citizens which includes South Carolina Catawbas mistakenly left off the 2000 per capita roll.[202] To resolve the problem of illegitimacy, the tribe currently requires DNA testing for the children of Catawba men and non-Indian women if the couple is unmarried.[203] The rolls provide a basis for determining which Catawbas are entitled to tribal services and federal benefits. Today there are more than 2,800 enrolled tribal citizens, a little over half of whom live away from the reservation in South Carolina.[204]

Tribal citizenship in the Catawba Indian Nation of South Carolina has a complicated history based on the tribe's relationships with both state and federal officials. Appropriations lists that followed the Treaty of Nation Ford forced state agents and Catawbas to develop criteria for tribal citizenship. These early lists evolved based on the changing needs of the tribe. As the Catawbas interacted with outsiders in South Carolina and converted to Mormonism, their society underwent several transformations that affected the way the Indians thought about belonging. The racial climate of South Carolina and the views of Mormon missionaries encouraged the Catawbas to distance themselves from African Americans, which created an unofficial racial barrier to inclusion. When some Catawbas moved west, the tribe decided to withhold state payments from these individuals. Finally, as tribal citizens increasingly married whites, the Catawbas at first excluded the children of intermarried white women, but then decided to accept all mixed-ancestry children. State officials weighed in on these decisions and occasionally developed rules that the tribe opposed, such as the decision to deny appropriations to Catawba children away at boarding school. Overall, however, the creation of the appropriations lists was a negotiated process that reflected Catawba ideas about belonging rather than simply the imposition of citizenship criteria by outsiders.

The involvement of federal officials in Catawba affairs in the 1940s changed the meaning of Catawba tribal citizenship. Instead of allowing for a flexible list that the Indians could alter from year to year, federal officials demanded an official and permanent roll. The appropriations lists served as a basis for the roll of 1943 and in this way reflected the tribe's vision at that particular historical moment. The roll also created a new legal and political status for tribal citizens. Officially, the Catawbas still had the power to make changes to the roll as an inherent right of tribal sovereignty. They did so when they updated the roll in 1961 and 2000. Yet, both officials and enrolled tribal citizens came to see an individual's presence on these rolls as the standard for belonging to the Catawba Indian Nation. Indeed, the rolls served as a legal tool that the tribe used to refuse citizenship to those it deemed ineligible. The Catawbas of South Carolina had long denied rights to western Catawbas who departed the reservation in the late nineteenth century; the citizenship rolls gave this denial an official legal basis.

Formalizing the Catawba tribal roll came with costs and benefits. The rolls put an end to the organic nature of earlier Catawba citizenship. No longer a negotiated process, citizenship became fixed. This shift hurt those who continue to feel a strong attachment to Catawba cultural and ethnic identity but whose names do not appear on the official rolls. The citizenship rolls, however, also provided the tribe with a means to protect itself. Distinctions between citizens and non-citizens are a necessary defense for any sovereign entity, particularly one with limited land and resources. By setting legal boundaries to tribal citizenship, the rolls protect the Catawba Indian Nation from the claims of individuals who no longer retain close connections to the core Catawba community.

3

Learning the Language of "Blood"

The Mississippi Band of Choctaw Indians

In 1913, the Choctaw Nation in Oklahoma sent a memorial to Congress to implore legislators not to reopen its citizenship rolls to include Mississippi Choctaw claimants. The federal government had closed these rolls in 1907 as part of its allotment program in Indian Territory, but Mississippi Representative Pat Harrison charged that the rolls had unfairly excluded Choctaws who remained in his state. Fearing that Harrison's bill to reopen the rolls would cause undue delays in the distribution of its tribal property and diminish the value of per capita shares, the Choctaw Nation protested that the Mississippi Choctaws had enjoyed ample opportunities to move west and enroll in the Choctaw Nation; that some had failed to do so was not its fault. "The Mississippi Choctaw Indian," the memorial asserted, "by reason of long separation from the Indians of the West, has come to be a class by himself." No longer entitled to citizenship in the Choctaw Nation, "these Indians present as distinct characteristics and difference from the Choctaw Indians in Oklahoma as though they were members of an entirely different tribe."[1]

The memorial of the Choctaw Nation came at the end of a decades-long struggle to define the citizenship rights of Mississippi Choctaws. Under the fourteenth article of the Choctaw removal treaty in 1830, the federal government had permitted some Choctaws to remain in Mississippi, take land allotments, and become state citizens. The article had specified, however, that Choctaws who made this choice would not lose their citizenship in the Choctaw Nation. Years passed and a series of small-scale removals sent many Mississippi Choctaws to Indian Territory, where they acquired full rights in the Choctaw Nation. A core group in Mississippi, however, refused to leave. In the late nineteenth century, the citizenship status of this remnant population came to a head when the federal government began allotting tribal lands in Indian Territory to tribal citizens. Did Mississippi Choctaws who remained in the South have any right to Choctaw Nation lands in the West?

If so, how could the Choctaw Nation and federal officials identify these claimants?

Ultimately, the rights of Mississippi Choctaws to Choctaw Nation citizenship rested on three factors: treaty rights, Choctaw "blood," and residency in Indian Territory. Not all Mississippi Choctaws met these requirements, however, and when the rolls closed in 1907 more than 1,000 Mississippi Choctaws were left without an official tribal identity. In the years that followed, these Indians regrouped, attracted federal attention, and finally secured a political status distinct from that of the Choctaw Nation. In the process, they created their own citizenship criteria, which drew on their experiences fighting for rights in the Choctaw Nation and the realities of living in the Jim Crow South. The story of the Mississippi Band of Choctaw Indians reveals how the members of a remnant Native population lost citizenship in one Indian nation, but then used the lessons they learned about federal perceptions of Indianness, and particularly ideas about Indian "blood," to rebuild a legal tribal identity.

[margin note: defining rights & identity]

The Choctaw Nation was the first of the large southeastern tribes to sign a removal treaty with the United States following the passage of the Indian Removal Act on May 28, 1830. Four months after President Andrew Jackson signed the act into law, federal officials pressured Choctaw leaders into ceding their rich lower Mississippi valley farmlands in the Treaty of Dancing Rabbit Creek. The Choctaws were deeply divided about removal, however, and to persuade them to sign the treaty, the United States had to make concessions.[2] Although most of the tribe promised to relocate to western lands they had acquired in an earlier treaty, the federal government allowed some Choctaws to remain in the South.[3] Article 14 promised that those Indians who wanted to stay could apply for 640-acre land allotments in Mississippi and become citizens of the state. The article specified, however, that Choctaws who made this decision "shall not lose the privilege of a Choctaw citizen."[4]

United States officials imagined that only acculturated Choctaws would take advantage of Article 14. They had underestimated Choctaw attachment to their homeland, however, and more than 5,000 culturally conservative Choctaws refused to leave. According to the terms of the treaty, those who stayed had six months to register with Agent William Ward for an allotment. As it turned out, Ward was an incompetent alcoholic who had little regard for Indian treaty rights. Instead of upholding the promises of Article 14, Ward refused most Choctaws an allotment in Mississippi.[5] In the end, only 143 Choctaws received land patents; the rest became squatters.[6]

Forced onto marginal lands and denied the privileges of state citizenship, the Mississippi Choctaws faced bleak prospects by the mid-nineteenth century, but they survived. Although they lost a formal political body with the westward departure of the Choctaw Nation, they preserved a distinct cultural

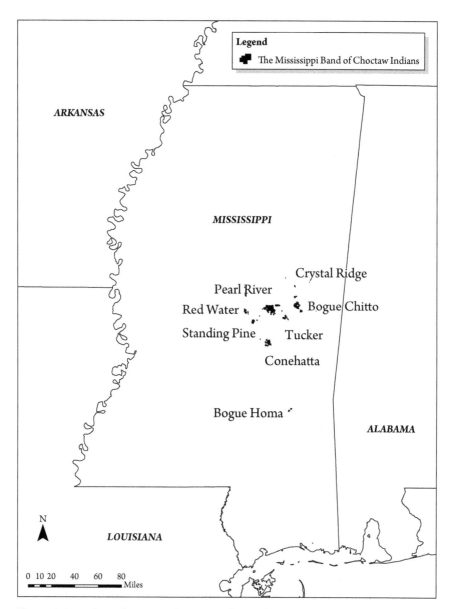

Legend

■ The Mississippi Band of Choctaw Indians

ARKANSAS

MISSISSIPPI

Crystal Ridge

Pearl River

Red Water   Bogue Chitto

Standing Pine   Tucker

Conehatta

Bogue Homa

ALABAMA

N

LOUISIANA

0 10 20   40   60   80
Miles

Figure 3.1 By the early twentieth century, those Choctaws who remained in Mississippi had coalesced into seven main settlements: Bogue Chitto, Bogue Homa, Conehatta, Pearl River, Red Water, Standing Pine, and Tucker. In 1918, the federal government began purchasing land for the use of the Choctaws in and around these communities. This land was put in trust with the federal government in 1939. In the late twentieth century, the Mississippi Band of Choctaw Indians added an eighth settlement at Crystal Ridge. Today the Choctaw Indian Reservation contains more than 35,000 acres of land. Map prepared by Christian Adams.

identity. Gradually, these Choctaws converged into a number of small settlements in east-central Mississippi: Bogue Chitto, Bogue Homa, Conehatta,
Pearl River, Red Water, Standing Pine, and Tucker.[7] After the Civil War, two
small groups of Choctaws also moved to Louisiana.[8] Within these communities, language, attachment to the land, cultural practices, kinship, and social
interactions helped determine who belonged. These markers of identity defined individuals as Choctaw, even though they could not exercise their rights
as Choctaw Nation citizens due to their distance from Indian Territory.

An ongoing marker of Choctaw identity in Mississippi was the use of the
Choctaw language. For those Choctaws who remained in the South, this
knowledge was nearly universal. Some Choctaw parents even made use of the
written language developed by missionaries in the early nineteenth century
and taught their children to read and write in Choctaw.[9] Isolated from outsiders, the Choctaws knew "so little of English that only the males are able to use it
as a medium of conversation."[10] A few of these men could speak English "pretty
well and give you pretty good satisfaction, but as a rule they do not speak
English well."[11] Fluency in Choctaw and difficulty speaking English marked
individuals as Choctaw because this indicated that they had grown up in one
of the Choctaw communities. Indeed, Choctaws could even tell to which of
the communities an individual belonged: each settlement had a slightly different dialect.[12]

The Choctaws who remained in the South also shared a strong connection
to their homeland that was spiritual as well as physical. The Choctaws believed that their people had emerged from Nanih Waiya, a mound in Winston
County, Mississippi. According to one version of their creation story, "ages ago
their ancestors were created in this mound and thence issued forth into the
light of day."[13] After they surfaced from the mound, the Great Spirit gave them
their tribal laws and charged them "to watch all the natural things that the
Creator's got here."[14] Staying in the South and caring for the land thus became
a sacred duty. Both the mound and the tale it evoked reinforced the sense that
Choctaws were a distinct people with unique ties to Mississippi.

Choctaw gender roles reflected their connection to the land. Choctaw
men provided for their families by hunting and fishing. Observers noted that
they were "remarkable marksmen" who still used bows and arrows in the late
nineteenth century to take down game "between fifty and sixty yards" away.[15]
By watching their elders and stalking their prey, Choctaw boys learned the
habits of their quarry and discovered the best places to make a kill. Simpson
Tubby, who was born in 1867, recalled that from an early age he "knew where
the beaver, the otter and the raccoon had their homes."[16] Another Choctaw
man remembered shooting crayfish and birds when he "wasn't old enough to
go hunting with the older men."[17] Boys also used "rabbit sticks" carved from

hickory wood and blowguns made of swamp cane to kill smaller game.[18] In fulfilling their roles as hunters, they became familiar with the local landscape and developed confidence as young Choctaw men.

Choctaw women also contributed to family economies by cultivating small plots of land.[19] Their principal crop was corn, but women also grew beans, peas, and potatoes. In addition to cultivating crops, Choctaw women gathered wild tubers, nuts, and acorns. They picked sassafras leaves and crushed them into a powder that thickened soup.[20] Women also prepared a number of unique dishes by pounding, boiling, and baking corn.[21] Like boys who watched their fathers and uncles to learn how to hunt, Choctaw girls learned farming, gathering, and cooking techniques from their mothers and aunts. Just as hunting made Choctaw men familiar with the local landscape, farming and gathering provided Choctaw women with intimate knowledge of their surroundings in Mississippi. These complementary and gendered economic pursuits provided Choctaw men and women with clear community roles that contributed to their sense of place and belonging.

After the Civil War, many Mississippi Choctaws turned to sharecropping to make a living. With this shift in economic production, the responsibility for farm work became centered on men rather than women because they made the contractual arrangements with landowners. Nevertheless, Choctaw men continued to hunt and fish and women "never ceased working in the fields."[22] In the early twentieth century, Simpson Tubby described fishing as "all the pleasure the Indian [man] has."[23] Women, meanwhile, cultivated household gardens in addition to picking cotton alongside their husbands. Mary Lou Farmer, who was born in 1917, recalled how she and her sisters plowed fields, picked cotton, harvested corn, peas, and peanuts, stripped cane, and made syrup.[24] Cooking also persisted as a female responsibility, and women added new foods to their culinary repertoire as landowners supplied Choctaw tenants with flour, rice, salt, coffee, and syrup in addition to the traditional cornmeal, beans, and peas.[25] The gendered nature of farm work changed by the 1870s and 1880s, but Choctaw men retained their identity as hunters while Choctaw women remained closely associated with the production of crops that fed Choctaw families.

Choctaws in Mississippi had a distinct material culture. They made a variety of items that they used in their daily lives and sometimes sold to outsiders to provide their families with additional income. Employing local raw materials, Choctaw women produced household goods like soap, pots, and baskets, whereas Choctaw men made hunting tools and other objects associated with men's work. Choctaws fabricated wooden mortars for pounding corn from "the trunk of a Postoak or black gum" tree by plastering the sides with wet clay and shaping the interior with fire.[26] Choctaw women fashioned intricate baskets from strips of swamp cane, while men used this local material to make blowguns.[27] The materials and techniques used by the Choctaws connected them to both the land and the people who had gone before them and distinguished them from other Mississippians.[28]

The Choctaws' most important sense of shared identity came from frequent visits and community gatherings where they renewed bonds of kinship

Figure 3.2 Choctaw women fashioned intricate baskets from local materials like swamp cane, palmetto stems, white oak, and honeysuckle vines. They used these baskets to store and carry food, sift corn, and pick cotton. Women also sold their wares to outsiders to supplement their family incomes. In this photograph, a Choctaw woman named Haylaema posed with a large "kishi" basket, which she strapped to her back with a leather loop. Date: 1909. Courtesy of the National Anthropological Archives, Smithsonian Institution (BAE GN 01102B22 06227100).

and friendship. Relatives and neighbors regularly visited each other's homes, where they received warm welcome and shared food.[29] Observers noted that the Choctaws "love to see one another and spend much of their spare time just sitting out on the front porch or in the front yard visiting."[30] The Indians also gathered to mark special rites of passage, such as marriages and funerals. Unique nuptial customs that involved symbolic gift exchanges between in-laws established and reinforced kinship obligations between various Choctaw families.[31] Families also supported each other during times of grief. Choctaw funerary services included an elaborate "pole-planting" ceremony that marked the gravesite with decorated poles, followed by a "Big Cry" of ritualized weeping and feasting.[32] These gatherings bound Choctaws together in joy and sorrow and strengthened their sense of community.

In addition to informal gatherings and rites of passage, Choctaws met several times a year to hold feasts, dances, and ballgames. In particular, the traditional sport of stickball drew great crowds.[33] A rough sport that involved two teams whose players vied for points by tossing a ball at opposing goal posts using "a pair of tongs with cups at the end," stickball allowed the various Choctaw settlements to meet and engage in friendly competition.[34] By playing these games in front of white spectators, the Choctaws also projected their separate identity in Mississippi at a time when their anomalous presence in the state threatened their status as Indian. Although Choctaw men wore clothing similar to that of non-Indians in their regular life, on game days they "donned the primitive Indian dress, each player being as nearly nude as decency would allow." They streaked their faces with red, yellow, and black paint and sounded out "war whoops" as challenges to members of the opposing team.[35] These performances demonstrated that they were different from other "free people of color" and thus warranted special consideration from local whites.

The establishment of churches and schools in Choctaw communities in the late nineteenth century challenged some traditional customs.[36] Although a few Choctaws continued to perform their distinctive marriage ceremonies even after Catholic, Baptist, and Methodist missionaries began proselytizing in the 1880s, many switched to marrying "after the style of white people."[37] Similarly, funeral customs changed with the introduction of Christian mortuary rituals. Although ritual wailing continued, Henry S. Halbert, a white man who had extensive contact with the Mississippi Choctaws, reported that the last pole-pulling ceremony took place in February 1885.[38] Some Christian Choctaws began eschewing stickball games because they disapproved of the gambling and drinking that took place during the matches. Occasionally these sentiments led to conflicts between converted and unconverted Indians.[39] Many elderly Choctaws, in particular, believed "in the old way of worshipping" and resented the admonishments of other Choctaws to change their behavior.[40] Charlie Denson, a Choctaw man born in 1923, for example, recalled that his grandfather "didn't believe in no Christian people" and refused to join a church.[41]

Although not everyone embraced Christianity, the churches and schools offered new places for Choctaws to be "Choctaw." Church services, including the singing, were conducted in the Choctaw language.[42] Choctaws attended these services accompanied by their families and friends. Churches and schools also provided Choctaws with the opportunity to take on leadership roles and to create new social organizations centered on these institutions.[43] The purchase of land for the Indians by the Catholic Church at the Holy Rosary Mission in the Tucker community, moreover, provided the Choctaws a permanent space to live and farm that they had not enjoyed since they lost their fourteenth article allotments.[44] Although white people oversaw and managed the Indian churches and schools, these segregated institutions helped bring structure to Choctaw community life and reinforced their sense of ethnic identity.

The Choctaws bolstered their distinctive identity through endogamous marriage practices. For the most part, Choctaws only wed other Choctaws, which led outsiders to regard their communities as maintaining "an unusual degree of racial purity."[45] They avoided forming connections with white people in part as a result of their distrust of white settlers who had deprived them of their land, but also because they understood that they faced punishment if they crossed the strict color line in Mississippi.[46] They also avoided unions with black people. Like the Pamunkeys and Catawbas, Choctaws worried that association with African Americans would jeopardize their status in the South, and, before the Civil War, even tempt local whites to enslave them. For this reason, any black person "under the restrictions of slavery, never was a visitor to the Choctaw's cabin."[47] Without the protection of recognized reservation lands after the war, racial reclassification posed a threat to Choctaw squatters and sharecroppers. Halbert observed that by the early twentieth century, there were "comparatively very few [Choctaws] who have white blood. Of negro admixture, there is practically none."[48]

Although the majority of Choctaws wed within their communities, there were a few exceptions. Prior to removal, white traders had married Choctaw women, which gave them access to extensive kinship networks. The mixed-ancestry children born of these unions used their mother's clan status and their father's language and business skills to rise to important positions in the tribe as interpreters, intermediaries, and entrepreneurs. By the time of the removal treaty, about 20 percent of the tribe were "mixed blood."[49] Most of these families moved west; however, a few groups of mixed-ancestry Choctaws remained in Mississippi. Greenwood Leflore, the former chief of the Western District of the Choctaw Nation, for example, stayed on a 1,000-acre allotment. Living as a southern planter and slaveholder, Leflore enjoyed a place of prominence in Mississippi society. He even served twice in the state house of representatives and once in the state senate.[50]

Most of the mixed-ancestry families that remained in Mississippi eventually merged into the larger white population. Leflore, for example, married a white spouse, as did his children and grandchildren.[51] As the generations passed, these individuals lost touch with the core Choctaw communities. Although they recounted their Choctaw heritage in family stories, they socialized exclusively with whites and no longer identified racially as Indian. Choctaws living in the core communities in Mississippi knew of these people, but they no longer recognized them as Choctaw.

Not all Choctaws who married white people, however, lost their tribal connection. Brothers Tom and Simpson Tubby, for example, both married white women and fathered children in the late nineteenth century, but they continued to speak the Choctaw language and to maintain social ties to other tribal citizens.[52] Simpson Tubby, a Methodist preacher, taught at the Tubby Rock Indian School for Mississippi Choctaws in Neshoba County in the early years of the twentieth century.[53] In the 1930s, he became a principal informant on Choctaw culture for the anthropologist John R. Swanton.[54]

The children of Choctaw mothers and white fathers usually identified as Choctaw because they grew up surrounded by their maternal relatives. Wash Bell, for example, was the son of a "full-blood" Choctaw woman and a half-white father. He married a "full-blood" Choctaw named Winnie and fathered at least six children. His brother, Harges Bell, also married a Choctaw woman.[55] These "mixed bloods" may have identified as Choctaw in part because of their kin connections to other Choctaws but also because of white racial prejudice, especially after the passage of Jim Crow laws in the years following Reconstruction. Denied the privileges of whiteness because of their phenotypically Indian appearance, they turned to their Choctaw relatives for social support. The "full-blood" Choctaws accepted them based on their kin ties and their familiarity with the Choctaw language and culture. Indeed, as far as other Choctaws were concerned, their degree of "blood" had very little to do with their identity as Choctaw.

Occasionally, Mississippi Choctaws formed unions with African Americans. After the Civil War, slavery no longer served as a boundary between blacks and Indians. Picking cotton as sharecroppers, "side by side with blacks," provided an opportunity for socializing, which occasionally led to intermarriage.[56] For example, Bill Martin, a "full-blood" Choctaw, married Rhody, who was "part Choctaw and part Negro," sometime in the late nineteenth century. The couple had eight children, at least one of whom also married a black spouse.[57] Jim Jack Johnson, also a "full-blood" Choctaw, married a black woman name Dehlia. The couple had seven children.[58] Three of the children of Billie Willis, another "full-blood" Choctaw, and his wife, Lou, who was "half white and half Choctaw," also married black people. The couple fully acknowledged their African American in-laws as well as their black-Choctaw grandchildren.[59]

Although close Choctaw relatives recognized them as kin, the children of Choctaws and black people tended to marry African Americans rather than Choctaws and they gradually formed communities separate from those of the "full-blood" Indians. Racial prejudice on the part of the Choctaws as well as the desire of interracial couples to send their children to English-speaking "colored" schools encouraged this divide. In 1899, according to a Choctaw man named Willie Philip, nearly every resident of a distinct community in Kemper County, Mississippi, was "mixed with the colored people, having inter-married with them ever since the war."[60] Although Choctaws recognized their shared heritage with the "Sukanatches," as they called these people, they questioned their Choctaw identity. As Philip pointed out, "they are all like colored folks, and don't speak Indian like we do."[61] For the Mississippi Choctaws, loss of the Choctaw language in particular suggested that the Sukanatches were no longer really Choctaw. As Halbert reported in 1911, "All negroes that have a trace of Choctaw blood are classed as and associate with negroes. They speak the English language alone."[62] Distanced from their Choctaw relatives by linguistic differences and racial prejudice, black-Choctaws simply became black in the eyes of both white officials and "full-blood" Choctaws.

Language, culture, kinship, and isolation helped the Mississippi Choctaws define who belonged to their communities in the late nineteenth century. During these years, the Mississippi Choctaws always knew that in addition to belonging to local communities, they were also Choctaw Nation citizens. After the Civil War, numerous small parties of Choctaws migrated west to take advantage of their citizenship rights.[63] When they arrived in Indian Territory, the Choctaw Nation welcomed them with acts that specifically recognized these "late arrivals."[64] Despite this incentive to move, many Choctaws opted to stay in their homelands. Although technically entitled to Choctaw Nation citizenship, those who remained in Mississippi could not exercise their rights unless they moved to Indian Territory.

The issue of who qualified as a Choctaw Nation citizen came to a head after Congress passed the General Allotment Act in 1887. United States legislators hoped that this act, which called for the division of tribal lands into allotments for tribal citizens, would encourage Indians to adopt "the habits of civilized life" and eventually exchange their tribal identity for United States citizenship.[65] Ironically, to begin this process of assimilation, the federal government first had to identify who qualified as a *tribal* citizen. The government thus got

into the business of determining Indian identity so as to divide tribal land
and resources. In the process, federal officials injected their own ideas about
race and "blood" into definitions of tribal citizenship. These actions had far-
reaching consequences for the citizenship rights of the Mississippi Choctaws.

After the federal government extended its allotment policy to the Choctaw
Nation in the Curtis Act of 1898, it sent a Dawes Commission official named
Archibald S. McKennon to Mississippi to identify Choctaws based on their
fourteenth article claims. When McKennon arrived in Mississippi in early
1899, however, he quickly discovered that the government's charge was easier
issued than fulfilled. Most of the Indians he interviewed had no way to trace
their ancestors back to fourteenth article claimants.[66] In the nearly seventy
years that had passed since the treaty signing, names had changed and most
Choctaws had not kept genealogical records.[67] McKennon complained in his
final report that "the commission finds it impossible to trace descendants now
bearing English names to ancestors bearing Indian names."[68]

Despite his failure to collect genealogical proof that Choctaws in Mississippi
were the heirs of fourteenth article claimants, McKennon was convinced
that the Indians he met ought to be recognized as Choctaw. For McKennon,
their phenotype alone presented clear evidence that they were entitled to
recognition.[69] Rather than abandon his task, McKennon decided that those
who showed a "predominance of Choctaw blood and characteristics" should
be identified without proof. Those who looked "half [Choctaw] or anything
less," however, still had to provide genealogical evidence to get on the roll.[70]
To determine who qualified under this so-called "full-blood rule of evidence,"
McKennon made notes about the appearance of the individuals he questioned.[71] He used these phenotypical judgments to decide whether applicants
were entitled to enrollment as "full blood," or if they were "half blood," "apparently white," or "black." In addition to racial markers, McKennon also used
cultural clues to help him decide on the identity of an applicant. In the case
of Meely Sam, a seventy-year-old Choctaw woman, for example, McKennon
noted that she was "Full blood. Don't speak English." Looking like an Indian
and speaking Choctaw assured Sam a place on the roll.[72]

Sometimes McKennon was so convinced that an applicant looked "full
blood," that he enrolled him as such contrary to his own testimony. John
Frenchman, for example, admitted that he was "half Choctaw and half French,"
but McKennon enrolled him as "full blood."[73] Similarly, Tom Tubby, who had
a Choctaw father, noted that his mother was half white and half Cherokee.
McKennon nevertheless wrote "Tom Tubby apparently full blood" and included him on the roll.[74] In contrast to these verdicts, McKennon decided that
other applicants were not Choctaw because their ancestors had intermarried
with whites or blacks. He reserved his harshest judgments for black-Choctaw

applicants like Mary Campbell, whom he told, "you may have Indian blood, but that would not entitle you to register here."[75] McKennon also refused to enroll children who had black mothers, even if he recognized their fathers as "full blood."[76] Although these children had just as much Choctaw ancestry as white-Choctaws whom McKennon did enroll, the commissioner concluded that their black parentage negated their Choctaw identity.[77] McKennon privileged his own racial judgments over the self-identification of the applicants he interviewed.

To complicate matters further, attorneys and speculators interfered with McKennon's work, a theme that continued throughout the Choctaw enrollment process, as well as that of many other tribes. Hoping to make easy money, these individuals cajoled the Indians into signing contracts with them by promising aid with enrollment in exchange for half of the Choctaws' land allotments in Indian Territory. Speculators bolstered their efforts by falsely identifying themselves with the government commission. As Mississippi Choctaw Scott Bell testified, a contractor associated with the attorney Charles F. Winton "said they were working for the Commission, and I thought it was true. . . . I thought I had to do that to get what was coming to me."[78]

Some Mississippi Choctaws made deals only to discover later that they had been duped. Others, after meeting with the speculators and providing them with the names of their family members, thought there was no need to appear before McKennon. As Riley Willis explained, "we came here, and as soon as we got here we saw Winton, and he took all our names. Don't know that there was anything else."[79] When McKennon learned of these actions, he summoned Winton before him and accused the attorney of "greatly confusing these Indians, and troubling them." By the time McKennon made his discovery, however, the damage was already done. Many Choctaws were "shy of coming in" as a result of the contracts and never appeared before the commission. Winton protested that these Indians would not have come anyway because they distrusted the government's removal plan.[80] Either way, hundreds of Choctaws failed to make it on the roll.

In the end, McKennon's roll was far from complete. Around 150 Choctaws from the culturally conservative Bogue Chitto community in Neshoba County, for example, refused to appear before the commission. Other Indians from Jones and Smith Counties also failed to meet the commission, some because of distance, others due to mistrust of federal intentions. The black-Choctaw Sukanatches in Kemper County similarly never appeared before McKennon, although their racial phenotype makes it doubtful that the commissioner would have registered them even if they had come.[81] Despite these omissions, McKennon sent his roll to Congress for approval on March 10, 1899. The list included 1,923 names. Of this number, McKennon reported, "there are two families, and probably a few other persons, who are mixed bloods, while all the others are full-blood Choctaw Indians."[82]

Not long after McKennon submitted his roll, Congress passed an act on May 31, 1900, that promised Mississippi Choctaws rights in Indian Territory if they removed. A major purpose of the act was to repair some of the damage done by attorneys and speculators. It voided all contracts made with the Mississippi Choctaws that created "any lien on their lands."[83] The act also specified that if any Mississippi Choctaw identified by the Dawes Commission went to Indian Territory prior to the approval of the final citizenship rolls, he or she could enroll and receive an allotment.[84] In the months that followed, thousands of claimants—whether identified by McKennon or not—poured into Indian Territory, set up residence, and claimed Mississippi Choctaw identity.[85] In an ironic twist, however, the "full-blood" Choctaws identified by McKennon were among those least likely to move because they were too poor. Voiding their contracts with speculators while requiring them to settle in Indian Territory to gain citizenship rights put Mississippi Choctaws in a bind. As lawyers for the "full bloods" pointed out, "the result was that the only chance that the Indians had for removal by private means was taken away."[86]

"Full-blood" Choctaws may have found it difficult to remove, but other claimants did not. As the Mississippi Choctaws complained to the US Senate in 1902, "many thousand persons have set up claims pretending they were Mississippi Choctaws."[87] Most of these people had no Choctaw ancestry at all—they simply hoped to gain a share of Choctaw Nation resources. These false claimants brought with them fraudulent testimony and forged documents to "prove" their right to Choctaw Nation citizenship.[88] By the end of the enrollment process in 1907, at least 24,634 individuals had made official applications for citizenship before the Dawes Commission.[89] The unscrupulous claims of this "horde of adventurers," the Mississippi Choctaws complained, "put in jeopardy the rights of the real Mississippi Choctaws by virtue of manifest frauds perpetuated in the name of the Mississippi Choctaws by said pretenders."[90]

Inundated by a "tidal wave of fraud, perjury and graft," the Choctaw Nation in Indian Territory began adopting a hardline attitude toward Mississippi Choctaw claimants.[91] Whereas in the past the Choctaw Nation had embraced "late arrivals" from Mississippi, western Choctaws now looked on new migrants with suspicion and animosity. Fearing that these claimants would cut into the wealth of its citizens, the Choctaw Nation put pressure on the Dawes Commission to overturn the McKennon Roll and to start new enrollment hearings.[92] Ultimately, the secretary of the interior refused to approve the McKennon Roll on the grounds that it was inaccurate, although he did not formally disapprove it either. Left in limbo, the McKennon Roll identified

Mississippi Choctaws but did not grant them Choctaw Nation citizenship. In the meantime, the Dawes Commission began new enrollment hearings "to attempt a more complete and accurate roll."[93]

When the Dawes Commission began new enrollment hearings in 1900, the Choctaw Nation took an active role in examining the applicants. Hiring the legal firm of Mansfield, McMurray, and Cornish to defend its resources from false claimants, the Choctaw Nation deployed these attorneys to cross-examine the applicants and challenge their legitimacy.[94] The Choctaw Nation also questioned the "full-blood rule of evidence." From its perspective, this rule violated Choctaw Nation sovereignty because it granted rights to people who had not legally established their treaty claims. Following these complaints, the Dawes Commission reversed its stance on full-blood Mississippi Choctaws and insisted that they prove their descent from fourteenth article claimants and not merely appear "Indian." Lawyers for the "full bloods" protested the change, and in 1901 the US attorney general wrote an opinion that since the government had recognized the full-blood rule, rights had been established under it. The secretary of the interior refused to act, however, and the issue remained unresolved.[95] The question of who had rights as a Choctaw Nation citizen persisted.

Although the federal government had no clear criteria to identify those Mississippi Choctaws who were entitled to citizenship, the Dawes Commission continued to interview applicants for enrollment in the early years of the twentieth century. Like McKennon, the commissioners found this task troublesome. Although thousands of people clamored for rights as Mississippi Choctaws, the Indians McKennon had identified as "full blood" were among the hardest for the commission to locate. Living in isolated settlements, these Choctaws did not always see the advertisements posted about the Dawes Commission's work. Even when they heard about the commission, some Choctaws reasoned that since they had registered with McKennon, they had no need to enroll a second time.[96] Simpson Tubby, for example, was fishing on the Pearl River on the day that a representative of the commission came looking for him. Since he assumed that his interview with McKennon three years earlier was sufficient, he made no effort to track down the representative and reenroll.[97] Choctaw parents sometimes brought their young children before the commissioners for enrollment, but refused "to present old cases" for themselves.[98] Other Choctaws tried to talk to the commissioners but found their efforts thwarted when the commission initially failed to provide an adequate interpreter who could translate Choctaw words into English.[99]

In addition to encountering logistical obstacles, some Choctaws viewed the Dawes Commission warily. Reportedly, they "got it out amongst themselves that it was some white man's trick; that maybe they were going to be hurt—in some way hauled up to Washington, or something else—and a great many of them did not go."[100] Attorneys and speculators encouraged these feelings by pressuring the Indians to sign new contracts with them before they met the commissioners. Attorneys Charles F. Winton and Robert L. Owen, for example, began making fresh contracts with the Mississippi Choctaws and advised their clients "not to appear again before the Commission" if they had already enrolled with McKennon.[101] Eventually, the Dawes Commission sent Special Agent Charles H. Sawyer to Mississippi to locate these "delinquent Choctaws."[102] Although Sawyer found many of the Indians, hundreds enrolled by McKennon never came before the commissioners and thus did not appear on the new roll.

When they found Choctaws to interview, the Dawes Commission used a series of questions to determine the identity of these individuals. In particular, the commissioners tried to establish the applicants' connection to fourteenth article claimants by demanding genealogical evidence of descent. Like McKennon, however, the members of the commission were often frustrated by applicants' limited knowledge of their family history. Lucy Jim, for example, spoke the Choctaw language fluently and had "every appearance of being a full blood Choctaw Indian," yet she did "not know the names of her ancestors farther back than her mother and father" and knew nothing about whether her relatives had "ever received any land in the State of Mississippi as beneficiaries under the provisions of the fourteenth article of the treaty of Dancing Rabbit Creek."[103] When applicants were unable to provide genealogical information, the commissioners turned to racial evaluations to determine their degree of Indian blood.

The commissioners used three main techniques to determine the "blood quantum" of the applicants they interviewed. First, they grilled them on their ancestry. Were they full blood? Were their parents both full blood? Even if an applicant answered in the affirmative, the commissioners sometimes repeated the questions several times. Andy Folsom testified that he descended from two full-blood parents, for example, but the commissioners demanded, "You are sure that both of your parents, Martin Folsom and Mary West, were full bloods?" Not satisfied with his answer, they made him swear an affidavit attesting to his mother's blood degree.[104]

Second, the commissioners recorded whether an applicant spoke the Choctaw language. In particular, they took note if an applicant had answered questions "through a sworn interpreter of the Choctaw language." Lack of English language skills seemed a good indicator that someone was a full-blood Choctaw, especially if the person in question also looked phenotypically Indian. Conversely, the commissioners suspected the claims of individuals who did "not speak or understand the Choctaw language."[105] Andy Folsom's lack of fluency in Choctaw was one reason the commissioners doubted his parents were full-blood Choctaws.[106]

Finally, the commissioners insisted that all applicants "personally appear" before them so that they could make "a notation . . . as to his or her personal appearance and characteristics."[107] Like McKennon, the commissioners made racial judgments about each claimant's phenotype. In notes typed at the end of the interviews, they declared that certain applicants had "every appearance and characteristic of a full blood," while the look of others "would not indicate that [they were] possessed of that much Indian blood."[108] In the case of Cornelia Tubby, the commissioners noted that she was "lighter complected," although she "has the face and characteristics of a Choctaw." Her brother, Jeff, on the other hand "would easily pass for a full-blood."[109]

Still other applicants, according to the commissioners, looked "white" or "negro." In these cases, the commissioners wrote that the applicants showed "no indication whatever of being possessed of Choctaw Indian blood." The commissioners had especially little tolerance for phenotypically black applicants. Susie Cambric, for example, claimed to be one-quarter Choctaw and three-quarters black. When she told the commissioners that her father was half Choctaw, they challenged her by demanding, "You think everyone who has any Choctaw blood has the right to come here and make application?"[110] At the time she made her application in April 1901, there was still no clear definition of who qualified as a Mississippi Choctaw. Nevertheless, the question directed toward Cambric implied that the commissioners had already made up their mind about certain applicants.

To evaluate the blood quantum of the people they interviewed, the commissioners had to balance out the testimony, language skills, and physical appearance of the applicants.[111] From their perspective, any hint of non-Indian ancestry disqualified a person from full-blood status. The interview exchanges, however, suggest that Choctaws did not always agree with the commissioners' interpretations. In many cases, when initially asked if they were full blood, Choctaw applicants insisted that they were. Only after digging into the family's history did the Dawes Commission reveal non-Indian ancestry. Sampson Tubbee, for example, claimed that he, his wife, Caroline, and his minor grandchild, Eben, were all full bloods. Tubbee spoke little English and answered his questions through a Choctaw interpreter; presumably his wife was also fluent in Choctaw. The couple lived among Choctaws and had married according to Choctaw custom.[112] Witnesses for the couple testified that they "look[ed] like" full bloods and that the Choctaw community recognized them as such.[113] From Tubbee's perspective, there was no question of their status as "full-blood" Choctaws—linguistic, cultural, and phenotypical markers established their identity. Nevertheless, under questioning, Tubbee admitted that his wife's father was in fact not full blood, but "about half." After revealing this fact, the commissioners stated, "Your wife, then, is a three quarter blood Choctaw, instead of a full blood Indian." Confused by this distinction, which did not match the reality of the couple's life together or their self-perception as Choctaw, Tubbee replied, "Yes, I think so." He went on to insist, however, that his grandson was full blood. Yet, by the commissioners' logic, Eben could not have been full blood because he descended from Caroline, whom they now considered "three quarter blood." Even if all of the child's other relatives were full-blood Choctaw, the highest blood quantum the boy could claim was fifteen-sixteenths.[114]

Similar examples of the education of Choctaw applicants on the meaning of "blood" appear throughout the enrollment records. Tom Stephen, like Sampson Tubbee, insisted that both he and his wife were full blood, but then he let slip that his wife's father was "half blood."[115] Identified full-blood Victoria Lafontain asserted her husband was Mississippi Choctaw, although his father was French.[116] John Farve insisted that he was full blood, but his brother testified that their father was a "one-half or three-quarter blood Choctaw Indian."[117] In all of these cases, the Dawes Commission reevaluated the applicants' status with little regard to how the Choctaws themselves constructed their identity. These decisions had serious implications once the federal government and the Choctaw Nation finally agreed on criteria for identifying the Mississippi Choctaws.

As the Dawes Commission pressed on with its interviews, the Choctaw Nation, the Chickasaw Nation (which had joint property interests in Indian Territory with the Choctaw Nation), and the US Congress worked on drafting an agreement that would once and for all delineate who was entitled to identification as Mississippi Choctaw. On March 24, 1902, the Choctaw and Chickasaw Nations sent a proposal to Congress stating that only those Mississippi Choctaws "duly identified" by the Dawes Commission would have rights. The Choctaw Nation narrowly interpreted these words to embrace only individuals with genealogical proof of descent from a fourteenth article claimant, which did not include claims based solely on the "full-blood rule of evidence."[118] By this time, Choctaws in Indian Territory were well aware that "the enrollment of anyone as a citizen of the Choctaw Nation would diminish the interest of the individual members" when the federal government divided their land.[119] Choctaw Nation officials found it prudent, therefore, to protect national assets through a strict interpretation of Choctaw citizenship criteria.

Distraught that the proposal of the Choctaw and Chickasaw Nations excluded them from citizenship, the Mississippi Choctaws, with the help of their lawyers, petitioned Congress for consideration of the full-blood rule.[120] In this memorial, the Indians emphasized that they were "full-blood Mississippi

Choctaws, speaking the Choctaw language," and implored that any proposal for Choctaw Nation citizenship include those who had appeared on the McKennon Roll as well as "such full-blooded Mississippi Choctaw Indians as may be identified by said Commission." The memorial also called for the identification of "the wives, children, and grandchildren of all such full-blood Choctaws," regardless of the blood quantum of these relatives. This provision challenged the Dawes Commission's emphasis on blood degree over kin connections. Appealing to their treaty rights, the Mississippi Choctaws asked for "Simple justice."[121]

Congressmen sympathized with the full-blood Mississippi Choctaws and the Senate even took up an amendment "embodying these suggestions."[122] The Choctaw and Chickasaw Nations in Indian Territory, however, objected. After a heated debate, the Senate Committee on Indian Affairs instructed the Choctaw Nation "to take care of these full bloods."[123] Eventually the two sides hammered out a compromise that only "full-blood Mississippi Choctaw Indians and the descendants of any Mississippi Choctaw Indians whether of full or mixed blood who received a patent to land under the said fourteenth article" would be identified as Mississippi Choctaw. The agreement, which Congress ratified on July 1, 1902, also specified that claimants make applications for themselves in person, which allowed government officials to continue to scrutinize their racial appearance.[124] With these provisions in place, the federal government fixed proof of treaty rights and Choctaw "blood" as two critical markers of Mississippi Choctaw citizenship.

The Dawes Commission immediately began reviewing the testimony it had compiled in the preceding years to rule on the status of the claimants.[125] It was in this process that the weight of the words spoken by applicants during their interviews became apparent. The commission rejected hundreds of "mixed-blood" applicants because they failed to provide sufficient proof of their descent from beneficiaries of the fourteenth article of the Treaty of Dancing Rabbit Creek. The commission excluded Colonel L. Young, Cornelius Young, and their minor children, for example, because although the men knew the names of their alleged progenitors, there was "nothing in the testimony submitted by the applicants herein which would tend to show that the persons through whom they claim, are identical with those mentioned in the records."[126] In a similar case, Jim Pittman, an alleged "one quarter or one third Choctaw Indian," claimed descent from his maternal great-grandmother, Susanna Graham, who took advantage of the fourteenth article. Pittman's "line of descent," however, was "very imperfectly traced by him personally," and the commissioners denied his application.[127]

Phenotypically black applicants had a particularly difficult time convincing the commissioners of their descent from Choctaw ancestors. A significant number of these applicants appeared before the Dawes Commission at Meridian, Mississippi.[128] Although some may have been pretenders who hoped to escape the strictures of Jim Crow Mississippi by taking on a more profitable ethnic identity, others undoubtedly had Choctaw heritage. Without proof of lineal descent from fourteenth article claimants, however, they had no chance of enrollment. In particular, if these applicants descended from a slave woman or had ever been slaves themselves, the commissioners considered their claims invalid. Although the Dawes Commission kept a separate enrollment list for Choctaw Nation freedmen in Indian Territory, they determined that "no freedman is entitled to identification as a Mississippi Choctaw."[129] Even if the applicants descended from a free black woman, the commissioners opined that such a woman "could not convey any Choctaw rights upon her child unless she was legally married to a Choctaw Indian."[130] Without proof of marriage, the commissioners denied them enrollment regardless of whether their alleged father descended from a fourteenth article claimant. The commissioners denied enrollment to both phenotypically white and phenotypically black applicants who failed to prove descent from fourteenth article claimants. The fact that they focused on the condition of servitude and illegitimacy of black applicants, however, suggests that racial ideas and the inheritance rights of slaves factored heavily into their personal thoughts on the rights of black-Choctaw claimants.

The Dawes Commission made strict decisions when it came to the enrollment rights of "mixed-blood" Choctaws who appeared phenotypically white or black. They were equally firm, however, when it came to phenotypically Indian "mixed bloods" who could not prove their ancestry. Individuals who lived in core Choctaw communities, who spoke the Choctaw language, and who married other Choctaws found themselves excluded from the rolls because during their interview they had admitted distant non-Indian ancestry. David Farve, for example, had ruined the chances of enrollment for both himself and his brother, John Farve, when he disclosed that their father had been "one-half or three-quarter blood." Although the brothers had married full-blood women and their mother was full blood, the Dawes Commission rejected their application.[131] Similarly, Tom Clemmons, who was married to a full-blood woman and who spoke and understood the Choctaw language, failed to gain recognition because his father was a white man.[132] In a particularly revealing case, the commission rejected the application of Dennis Frenchman "because he stated in his application that *he thought* he was part white." In fact, his father had testified that he was full blood, and a number of "other old Indians who knew his ancestors also testified that he was a full blood." Nevertheless, the words Frenchman spoke before the commission were enough to condemn him to a status of "mixed blood" and make both him and his children ineligible for Choctaw Nation citizenship.[133]

Even those Mississippi Choctaws whom the Dawes Commission identified as full blood did not automatically receive citizenship in the Choctaw Nation. Under the terms of the government's compromise with the Choctaw and Chickasaw Nations, applicants had six months to move to Indian Territory, where they had to live continuously for a year before they could enroll and receive an allotment as a Choctaw Nation citizen. If an applicant failed to prove continuous residence within four years of arrival, the government would consider his land abandoned, his citizenship terminated, and his allotment salable "at public auction for cash."[134] Establishing and maintaining long-term residency in Indian Territory thus became the third critical marker of Mississippi Choctaw citizenship.

In February, the federal government approved the names of 2,534 identified Mississippi Choctaws and a month later Congress appropriated $20,000 to notify and remove them to Indian Territory before the six-month deadline expired in August 1903.[135] The secretary of the interior did not order the Dawes Commission to appoint a special agent to remove the Choctaws until early July. The commission failed to respond until the end of the month, however, since its members were on vacation.[136] Little more than two weeks before the deadline, Special Agent H. Van V. Smith finally arrived in Mississippi to prepare the Choctaws for removal.[137]

Smith immediately began sending notices to Mississippi Choctaws informing them of this opportunity to move to Indian Territory at government expense.[138] He warned them that if they did not go west, their rights would expire.[139] Some Choctaws responded, and over the next two weeks a few hundred Indians gathered in Meridian, Mississippi with "their baggage and household effects."[140] Yet Smith did not reach all of the Choctaws. Despite his efforts to encourage the Choctaws to catch the train bound for Indian Territory, hundreds failed to comply with the removal provision. By remaining in Mississippi, these Choctaws forfeited their right to Choctaw Nation citizenship and land in Indian Territory.

Identified full-blood Choctaws in Mississippi failed to remove for a variety of reasons. Some simply never received notice of the removal deadline. Many of these Indians lived in rural areas, miles from a post office, and did not see the notice in time to comply with Smith's directives.[141] Other Choctaws lacked funds to hire wagons to take their families to the train depot. Smith reported to the Dawes Commission that "at least 99 percent of these Indians have not a dollar in the world."[142] Illness prevented others from removing. George Thomas, for example, explained that "on account of the condition of [his] wife's health she will not be able to make the journey" and asked the agent if the couple could get their land "without removing to and making settlement in the Choctaw-Chickasaw country." Smith replied that they could not.[143]

Similarly, Emma Pis-ah-ton-tamah from Bayou Lacomb, Louisiana, pleaded that she was "in very bad health and hardly able to stand the move to the Indian Territory." Nevertheless, by law she had to remove before the deadline or forfeit her rights.[144]

The deadline for removal fell in mid-August. Many Indians wrote to Smith and explained that although they wished to remove, they were "undecided on account of the condition of [their] crops."[145] Impoverished Choctaw farmers often were indebted to white landowners. John Williams, for example, owed "about one hundred dollars." Although he wanted his allotment in Indian Territory, he sought to sell his claim to pay his debts, a course of action for which there was no provision.[146] Jim Wallace, another full-blood Choctaw, found himself in a similar bind. Although he owed just "five dollars for rations" to a white man, his creditor refused to let him leave Mississippi until he paid up. Wallace informed Smith of his dilemma, but Smith could do nothing to help him under the terms of the law.[147]

White landowners impeded Mississippi Choctaw removal efforts in other ways as well. Smith learned from "very reliable parties" that local whites had "done all in their power to keep the Indians from moving."[148] Unwilling to give up a cheap source of labor, they threatened Choctaw sharecroppers with arrest if they abandoned their farm-labor contracts without permission.[149] In some cases, landowners outright lied to the Choctaws by telling them that Smith "had no authority from the Government to remove them" and that the special agent's efforts were simply a ploy "to entice them to Meridian and have them sign contracts for the sale of their prospective allotments in the Indian Territory."[150]

Speculators similarly persuaded Indians not to go to Meridian because they hoped that the Choctaws would make contracts with them instead. Representing American ranchers in the West, these speculators wanted to exchange removal aid for leases on grazing lands in Indian Territory.[151] Smith complained to the Dawes Commission that the speculators "made all sorts of misrepresentations as to the real purpose of the government in offering to aid indigent and identified full-bloods to remove."[152] Although Smith tried to inform the Choctaws that "these and similar reports were absolutely false and circulated only for the purpose of misleading and confusing the Indian," he found it impossible to reach all of the Indians before their removal deadline expired, the "time being so short and the means of communication so uncertain."[153] As a result, many Choctaws missed their chance to remove to Indian Territory.

In the end, Smith oversaw the removal of just 259 full-blood Choctaws from Meridian. A few months later, the federal government removed an additional twenty-six Indians whom the Dawes Commission had identified at a later date. Other Mississippi Choctaws either paid their own way or got help from their lawyers.[154] Attorney Charles F. Winton, for example, moved around 200 Choctaws at his own expense.[155] Several hundred more went west with speculators who aided them in exchange for leases on their allotments in Indian Territory.[156] Over 1,000 full-blood Mississippi Choctaws, however, never made the journey.[157]

Even those Choctaws who managed to remove did not always establish the permanent residency in Indian Territory necessary to guarantee them Choctaw Nation citizenship. Life in Indian Territory was harsh, and many migrants longed to return to their homelands.[158] Callie Dixon, for example, recalled that when she, her husband, and her four children arrived in Indian Territory, they "lived in a house that had holes which were stopped up with mud." The family stayed there for several months before determining that "the whites tricked us into coming over here."[159] Other Choctaws agreed with this assessment. After going to Indian Territory and looking over the land for themselves, they decided that the "climate didn't suit us."[160] Comby Wallace, for example, returned to Mississippi after just one year out west.[161]

When Mississippi Choctaws left Indian Territory, which became the state of Oklahoma in 1907, within four years of their arrival, they forfeited their citizenship in the Choctaw Nation. Throughout the late 1910s and 1920s, the federal government made annuity rolls of Choctaw Nation citizens who were entitled to per capita payments that resulted from the sale of tribal property. Each person listed on these rolls was "entitled to share in the lands and moneys of said tribe, except as noted thereon." The people "noted thereon" included Mississippi Choctaws who failed to prove long-term residency in Oklahoma. Although their names appeared on the rolls and some of them even received their allotments, their entries included a note stating, "citizenship cancelled."[162]

While people officially identified as Mississippi Choctaws grappled with the decision of whether to remove to Indian Territory, the Dawes Commission endeavored to wrap up the Choctaw Nation enrollment process. In preparation for closing the final roll, the secretary of the interior finally laid to rest the claims of applicants who had appeared on the McKennon Roll. After reviewing the list, the secretary concluded on March 1, 1907, that it should be disapproved "for the purpose of disposing of these cases, so that no further trouble might arise regarding them." As a result, 539 Choctaws who had failed to resubmit their cases to the Dawes Commission lost rights in the Choctaw Nation.[163] Three days later, the Choctaw Nation citizenship rolls closed altogether. Less than half of the 1,923 people identified by McKennon appeared on this final roll, either because they had not resubmitted applications or because they did not move to Indian Territory. Of the 2,534 applicants approved by the Dawes Commission in 1903, only 1,578 made it on the roll as citizens of the

Choctaw Nation. In addition to those who had removed following identification by the Dawes Commission, 181 Mississippi Choctaws migrants who had
arrived in Indian Territory in the late 1880s and 1890s also made it onto the
roll. These names brought the final enrollment for Mississippi Choctaws up to
1,759.[164] Over 1,000 "full-blood" Choctaws, however, remained in Mississippi.
Stripped of their rights as Choctaw Nation citizens, they were left without a
nation.[165]

Although the Choctaw Nation rolls had closed, the efforts of Mississippi
Choctaw claimants to gain a share of Choctaw Nation property did not end.
Thousands of acres of farmland remained unallotted after enrolled Choctaw
Nation citizens received their 320-acre shares, and there remained "undis-
tributed coal and asphalt lands" worth millions of dollars.[166] These resources
presented "a tantalizing object," and lawyers for the full-blood Choctaws as
well as for thousands of more dubious claimants filed appeals with the federal
government, insisting that the Dawes Commission had unfairly excluded their
clients.[167]

Some of these efforts were quickly revealed as frauds. In 1910, for example, the *Atlanta Constitution* exposed an attorney who purportedly "had
been making an effort to have about 10,000 negroes enrolled, which, he said,
would net the promoter $25,000,000 or $30,000,000 if permitted to be per-
fected."[168] Other schemes, however, were more difficult to dismiss. A lawyer
and self-proclaimed Choctaw named Alexander P. Powell from the legal firm
of Crews & Cantwell spent months traveling around Mississippi, Alabama,
Louisiana, and Texas collecting signatures from supposed Choctaw descendants. Charging his clients a contingency fee and, if the firm won their case,
30 percent of the proceeds, Powell did his best to uncover as many "Choctaws"
as possible. Indians popped up "from behind every bush and stump." Powell
quickly collected 2,000 signatures.[169]

Although some of the individuals represented by Crews & Cantwell undoubtedly knew their claims were false, others sincerely believed they had
rights as Choctaws. Family tradition convinced them of their distant Indian
ancestry, even though most had no modern association with the Choctaw
communities in Mississippi.[170] Several hundred of these claimants eventually formed an organization called "The Society of Mississippi Choctaws."
Members of this society lived all the way from Bayou La Batre, Alabama,
to Mesa City, Arizona.[171] None spoke the Choctaw language or lived in a
Choctaw community, yet they claimed they had "Indian blood" and that this
alone entitled them to rights.[172] Although eager to claim a Choctaw identity
in order to benefit from Choctaw Nation resources, members of this society
carefully guarded their status as phenotypically white people in the Jim Crow
South: they refused membership to anyone suspected of African ancestry, and

they walked a fine line between claiming Indian heritage and preserving the privileges of their white racial identity.

The efforts of Powell and the lobbying of Crews & Cantwell eventually attracted the attention of Mississippi Representative Bryon Patton (Pat) Harrison, who had been elected to Congress in 1911 by Mississippi's sixth district. Just after he took his seat, attorney Harry J. Cantwell visited Harrison in Washington, DC, and in February 1912, Harrison introduced a bill to reopen the Choctaw Nation rolls. Harrison argued that not all qualified fourteenth article claimants had received allotments in Oklahoma and that those excluded when the rolls closed in 1907 should have a chance to resubmit their cases before the secretary of the interior. The bill also allowed claimants to be represented by the counsel of their choice and upheld existing legal contracts between lawyers and their clients.[173]

While the bill was pending and attorneys like Powell scoured the countryside for anyone with a hint of Choctaw ancestry, other lawyers focused their efforts on the identified full-blood Choctaws who had failed to remove west. Choctaws living within the core communities in Mississippi had watched with dismay as the federal government closed the rolls and deprived them of their citizenship in the Choctaw Nation. Indeed, in the month before the closing date, lawyers had submitted to Congress petitions signed by full-blood Choctaws in Mississippi, asking that the rolls not be closed. Choctaw leaders like Simpson Tubby, who as a Methodist minister was one of the few Indians literate in English in Mississippi, wrote letters to the president, the secretary of the interior, and Congress to request an extension of the deadline.[174] These Choctaws continued to insist on their rights into the next decade. Encouraged by attorneys, they organized meetings in county courthouses across Mississippi and discussed how best to pursue their claims against the federal government.[175]

In 1913, the "full-blood" Mississippi Choctaws established a general council to push for federal recognition of their rights. Each of the Choctaw communities sent delegates to Meridian on May 10. At first the delegates had difficulty locating a meeting place since most of the hotels in town refused to accommodate Indians. Finally, under pressure from attorney James E. Arnold, the owner of the Great Southern Hotel agreed to open a dining room and parlor to the Choctaws.[176] Once settled into the hotel, Acting Chairman Simpson Tubby called the delegates to order and officially organized the Mississippi, Alabama, and Louisiana Choctaw Council. The delegates then unanimously elected Wesley Johnson, a Choctaw man from Leake County, as "permanent chief."[177] Although they violated a state law that prohibited the Indians from organizing a tribal government, for the first time in more than eighty years the Mississippi Choctaws had a unified political structure.

At the meeting, the Choctaws appointed Arnold as their "representative in Washington" and hired another attorney, William E. Richardson, "to render whatever legal services were necessary in the prosecution of their rights."[178] These lawyers helped the Indians draft a memorial to Congress to call attention to the plight of the "real" Choctaws left behind in the South. To distinguish themselves from the claimants represented by Crews & Cantwell, the Choctaws employed the language of blood. They insisted that they were "full-blood Choctaws" and that they also were "for the most part speaking only the Choctaw language, living in their own communities in the State of Mississippi, and following the habits and customs of Indian life." Despite the promises made in the Treaty of Dancing Rabbit Creek, these Choctaws had "never received the supervisory control and guardianship of the Federal Government." Federal officials had "left [them] to care for themselves as best they could."[179] With these words, the Choctaws connected their high blood degree to linguistic and cultural markers of their Choctaw identity, and tied both to their treaty rights in Mississippi. They insisted that the United States recognize them as Indians and uphold its treaty obligations.

With the Choctaw memorial in hand, Arnold and Richardson traveled to Washington, DC, to present the case to Congress. They sent copies to the president, to the secretary of the interior, and to the chairmen of both the Senate and the House Committees on Indian Affairs.[180] They also testified on behalf of the full-blood Choctaws before the House Committee on Indian Affairs and presented letters from local whites that testified to the dreadful conditions faced by the Indians in Mississippi. Officials from Newton County, Mississippi, for example, wrote that the Choctaws were "almost in destitute circumstances." Boll weevils had infested their cotton plants, and local farmers provided almost no employment for them.[181] They needed help.[182] If their claim to treaty rights proved unconvincing, the lawyers hoped that at least sympathy might move Congress to act charitably.

Wesley Johnson, Culbertson Davis, and Emil John offered further evidence of the Choctaw situation. These Choctaw men—two from Mississippi and one from Louisiana—traveled to the capital in January 1914 to make their claims in person, despite their own poverty and the difficulty of traveling through the Jim Crow South. As Arnold complained to Congress, the brakeman on the train that carried the Choctaws to Washington initially refused to board the delegates unless they traveled in "the coach with the colored people." After their lawyer protested, the conductor finally permitted them to ride in the smoker coach for white men. Arnold also related how Johnson owned only cotton pants and had neither coat nor socks. He had suffered terribly from the cold until his attorneys prevailed on him to accept a gift of heavier garments.[183] By telling Congress about the indignities and poverty faced by the delegates,

Arnold once again appealed to federal sympathies as a strategy to get aid for his Choctaw clients.

Over the course of the next month, the three Choctaw delegates met with many members of Congress as well as with Commissioner of Indian Affairs Cato Sells, Secretary of the Interior Franklin K. Lane, and even President Woodrow Wilson.[184] During these meetings, the delegates once again laid out the claims of the full-blood Choctaws. They insisted that half of the people identified as Mississippi Choctaws had been denied their rights. The Mississippi Choctaws who removed in 1903 had received land and education for their children in Oklahoma, but the "Choctaws in Mississippi are growing up under the old conditions, their children uneducated, and their condition generally is deplorable."[185]

The Choctaw delegates and their attorneys made sure to emphasize the high blood degree of the Indians they represented. Frustrated that so many people across the South claimed to be Choctaw and fearful that these claimants might derail their own efforts, the Mississippi Choctaws used blood as a boundary to distinguish legitimate Choctaws from false claimants.[186] Although the delegates knew that some of the people they represented had non-Indian ancestry despite living in Choctaw communities and speaking the language, they recognized that their best hope of gaining federal attention lay in using the racial terminology employed by federal officials. They used "full blood" as an index to make their Indianness intelligible to the federal government.

Although most members of Congress were impressed by Johnson, Davis, and John, the Choctaw delegates and their attorneys were not the only people making claims in Washington.[187] When the Harrison bill came up for discussion, lawyers for supposed "mixed-blood" claimants also appeared before the House Committee on Indian Affairs to demand justice for their clients. Their testimony revealed the contested nature of Choctaw identity and the varying ways that "blood" could be employed strategically to assert tribal rights. Harry J. Cantwell, for example, protested the full-blood rule as a benchmark for Mississippi Choctaw enrollment since, he insisted, "a full-blood Choctaw means nothing more than a full-blood American."[188] Luke Conerly, who represented the Society of Mississippi Choctaws, directly challenged the Dawes Commission's methods of assessing which Indians qualified as full blood. He protested, "I hold that there is no rule by which you can determine a full-blooded Choctaw." According to Conerly, no "ethnological study" was sufficient to make such a determination, especially considering the many historical instances of intermarriage between whites and Indians.[189] Cantwell and Conerly made fair points as they challenged the legitimacy of "blood" as a marker of Choctaw identity. Both endeavored to separate the political identity of Choctaw claimants based on their alleged

Figure 3.3 Ahojeobe, or Emil John (pictured), was one of three Choctaw delegates who traveled to Washington, DC, in January 1914 to demand federal attention for those Choctaws left behind in the South. Ahojeobe belonged to a Choctaw community in Louisiana. When the Mississippi Band of Choctaw Indians gained federal recognition in 1945, the tribe's new constitution imposed geographic boundaries to tribal citizenship that inadvertently excluded Choctaws in Louisiana. Some Louisiana Choctaws eventually gained separate federal recognition as the Jena Bank of Choctaw Indians in 1995. Date: 1909. Courtesy of the National Anthropological Archives, Smithsonian Institution (BAE GN 01102B13 06226200).

descent from fourteenth article beneficiaries from their racial identity as defined by degree of Indian "blood." Considering that they represented clients with distant and often spurious claims to Choctaw ancestry who had no current connection to a tribal community, however, their efforts to discredit the full-blood rule also revealed the danger the Choctaw Nation faced if citizenship rolls were thrown open with no boundaries to separate legitimate from false claimants.

Lawyers for the Choctaw Nation also actively engaged in these hearings. Unlike the attorneys for the Mississippi claimants, these lawyers were less interested in questions of blood and more interested in treaty rights and the sovereign power of the Choctaw Nation to decide who belonged as citizens. P. J. Hurley, the principal attorney for the Choctaw Nation, energetically defended the Choctaw Nation's right to reject the citizenship claims of Mississippi Choctaws whether or not they were "full bloods." In a forty-four-page memorial he prepared to educate federal officials on the matter, Hurley pointed out that the Choctaws who removed under the Treaty of Dancing Rabbit Creek had suffered terribly on the Trail of Tears and in the years that followed. Mississippi Choctaws, who had not taken part in these struggles or in the efforts to rebuild the Choctaw Nation in the West, should not now claim an equal share in that improved tribal property in Oklahoma. He insisted that the Choctaw Nation had "always been ready to deal with great liberality toward their absentee brothers," but that at no point did they consider any Mississippi Choctaw "entitled to citizenship or to any of the benefits arising therefrom without taking up his residence in the Choctaw-Chickasaw country and showing his desire to affiliate with them."[190] Moreover, the efforts of lawyers to reopen the rolls had delayed the distribution of funds belonging to the Choctaw Nation.[191] Not only were Mississippi Choctaws demanding land and resources that did not belong to them, but the claimants were also preventing the rightful owners from benefiting from the sale of Choctaw Nation property.

Eager to make sense of the competing arguments of the full-blood Choctaws, the Choctaw claimants, and the Choctaw Nation, Congress sent Inspector James McLaughlin to investigate the various contracts formed between lawyers and Mississippi Choctaw claimants. McLaughlin uncovered quite a scheme. He learned that speculators like Powell had contracted with hundreds of applicants in order to profit from fees of up to a third of any money gained from the Harrison bill.[192] Moreover, the firm of Crews & Cantwell had financed its search for Choctaw descendants with the help of a Texan banker named S. L. Huribut.[193] To make their effort worthwhile, Huribut and the lawyers had chartered the Texas-Oklahoma Investment Company under the laws of the Territory of Arizona and sold stock to American citizens in the company whose only asset was the promise of Choctaw Nation land and money.[194] The company's articles of incorporation provided for a capital stock of $100,000, or 1,000 shares at $100 each.[195] The lawyers used the money from these sales for their expenses and to lobby the federal government to reopen the tribal rolls. For Crews & Cantwell, reopening the rolls was not about getting justice for their clients—whether or not they were really Choctaw—but instead about enriching both themselves and their white investors who looked forward to profiting from unallotted Choctaw Nation lands.[196] With nearly 10,000 alleged Choctaw clients, the lawyers expected the return on this investment to run into the millions of dollars.[197]

The discovery of the activities of the Texas-Oklahoma Investment Company was the final straw for many members of Congress. Although some were sympathetic to the cause of the full-blood Mississippi Choctaws, the widespread fraud that surrounded efforts to reopen the Choctaw Nation rolls was overwhelming. Representatives from Oklahoma, in particular, complained about the exorbitant fees that attorneys hoped to earn "by drumming up claimants in Mississippi."[198] They recognized that any money taken from the Choctaw-Chickasaw funds to pay claimants in Mississippi was money taken out of their state. Other congressmen feared that the federal government would be held liable if Congress reopened the rolls and admitted false claimants. Representative Harrison tried to address some of these concerns by amending his bill so that it specifically targeted identified full-blood Mississippi Choctaws.[199] Despite this effort to distinguish legitimate Choctaws from false claimants, the House Committee on Indian Affairs reported to Congress that the passage of the Harrison bill "would completely upset and undo 11 years of careful, painstaking work of the Interior Department in settling the affairs of the Five Civilized Tribes" and "open up a Pandora's box of troubles." Congress rejected the Harrison bill and the 1907 Choctaw Nation rolls remained final.[200]

Although members of Congress declined to reopen the Choctaw Nation rolls, the activities of the lawyers for the full-blood Choctaws and other claimants in the first two decades of the twentieth century served to keep the Mississippi Choctaws—particularly the "full bloods"—on the federal radar. Some congressmen wondered if these Indians deserved federal attention, despite not having rights as Choctaw Nation citizens. Indeed, the Choctaw Nation suggested as much itself: P. J. Hurley argued that that the Choctaw Nation did not object to the United States offering relief for the Mississippi Choctaws, as long as it paid the cost.[201] After the Harrison bill failed, Congress appropriated $1,000 in May 1916 to send an Office of Indian Affairs employee, John Reeves, to Mississippi to survey these Indians and investigate their condition.[202] The following year, Congress sent another committee to Mississippi to interview the Indians who remained in the state.[203] Mississippi Choctaws regarded these interviews as an opportunity to appeal once again to the federal government for recognition of their treaty rights. Well aware of what they had lost when the Choctaw Nation rolls closed, they applied what they had learned about "blood," treaty rights, and residency during the enrollment process to make a case for their tribal legitimacy.

Like the Mississippi Choctaw delegates in Washington three years before, the Indians interviewed by the 1917 committee distinguished themselves from false claimants by emphasizing their high blood degree. Culbertson Davis, who had traveled to the capital in 1914, for example, told the federal investigators that he did not know of any mixed bloods in Mississippi. He insisted, "All of them have gone to Oklahoma." Similarly, Phillip Dixon conceded that some mixed-blood Indians might live in Mississippi but that he knew nothing about them. Simpson Tubby denied that Choctaws intermarried with whites, although Tubby's own mother had been half-white and he himself had married a white woman.[204] As historian Katherine Osburn has pointed out, the Mississippi Choctaws used claims of "unadulterated" ancestry and the language of "blood" to bolster their Indian identity in the eyes of white officials.[205] Although they perhaps knew that their definition of who qualified as a "full blood" differed from that of the committee members, they used this language to compel whites to recognize their legitimacy as Indians.

In addition to emphasizing their racial identity, the Choctaws who testified before the committee also pointed to their treaty rights and their political status as citizens of a tribal nation. Explicitly making this connection, Simpson Tubby told the committee, "I have been trying to study a little about the different nations and the welfare of the different nations I see that the Mississippi Indians have been treated worse than any nation I know, neglected longer than any nation." Focusing on Choctaw treaty rights, Tubby continued, "we see what the Government has done for all the tribes, the different tribes of Indians, but the Mississippi Choctaw has not had anything at all, as I notice, since the fourteenth article of the Dancing Rabbit treaty."[206] Tubby insisted that the federal government recognize the Mississippi Choctaws as belonging to a tribal nation with rights guaranteed by treaty.

To remedy the effects of federal neglect, Mississippi Choctaws asked that the government set aside money for them from the more than $5 million that it had received from the sale of unallotted lands in the Choctaw Nation. They pointed out that Mississippi Choctaws would have been entitled to that land had the federal government removed them as the law intended.[207] The Choctaws, however, no longer wanted to go west and insisted that the government help them where they were. When a committee member asked W. A. Morris if he "wouldn't want to go anywhere else," he replied, "No, sir: this is my native home."[208] In making these appeals, the Choctaws challenged the residency requirement for Choctaw Nation citizenship and demanded tribal rights even if they remained in their Mississippi homelands.

Members of the investigating committee, however, were more interested in the poverty of the Indians who remained in the state than they were in treaty rights. Many early twentieth-century Choctaws worked for white farmers on

shares. Dependent on their landlords for food and supplies, Choctaw sharecroppers fell deeper and deeper into debt. Other Choctaws were day laborers who primarily picked cotton or cut cordwood. They competed for these
jobs with African Americans, however, and often found themselves without
employment.[209] Poverty meant that few Choctaws could afford medical attention. They had "just a few little churches and a few little schools, very weak."
Choctaw children were so poorly clad that some could not attend school since
they "didn't have clothing suitable to keep them warm." Most Choctaws lived
in dilapidated wood cabins with dirt floors and no windows. When asked by
the committee why so few Choctaws owned their own homes, Simpson Tubby
explained simply that they had no land.[210]

   With no land, no money, and few prospects for improvement through education in Mississippi, the Choctaws' future seemed bleak indeed. Sympathetic
to their plight, members of the Senate Committee on Indian Affairs proposed
setting aside money for them in the 1917 Indian appropriations bill. Senator
John Sharp Williams of Mississippi emphasized the high blood degree of the
Mississippi Choctaws, asserting that "the men I really want to take care of

Figure 3.4 When the Choctaw Nation roll closed in 1907, more than 1,000 "full-
blood" Choctaws remained in Mississippi. Deprived of their tribal citizenship and
their share of Choctaw assets, the Choctaws in Mississippi lived in impoverished
conditions. Nevertheless, the Choctaws held firmly to their indigenous identity and
continued to demand their tribal rights. In this photograph, Louisa and Will Jim posed
on the front porch of their wooden clapboard home near Philadelphia, Mississippi.
Photographer: Henry Bascom Collins. Date: 1925. Courtesy of the National
Anthropological Archives, Smithsonian Institution (SPC Se Choctaw NAA 4974
01773200).

are the Choctaws who are of full blood." Buying into the idea that high blood quantum equated to tribal legitimacy, he proposed that the government make provision for those Choctaws who were "either full or half bloods or maybe some quarter bloods." Oklahoma Senator Robert L. Owen, who had represented many Mississippi Choctaws during their enrollment struggle, recognized their attachment to Mississippi and argued for a federal school for them. Despite the efforts of these senators to secure funding for the Mississippi Choctaws, others in Congress were not convinced that these Indians warranted federal attention. Senator Asle Gronna of North Dakota, for example, protested that because the Mississippi Choctaws lacked a federal relationship, the federal government owed them nothing. He argued that funds should first go to recognized tribes, like the Sioux, who also needed schools and services.[211] With these protests in mind, the committee tabled the issue for another year.

Finally, in early 1918, Commissioner of Indian Affairs Cato Sells took a tour of the South to discover how the government might help "certain over-looked and neglected tribes and remnants of tribes of Indians."[212] After seeing for himself the poor conditions faced by the Choctaws, Sells encouraged Congress to appropriate funds to open an agency for the "full-blood" Indians left in Mississippi. At its next meeting, the House Committee on Appropriations set aside $75,000 for land, housing, economic development, and education, as well as for an agency staff composed of an agent, physician, farmer, and matron.[213] By establishing the Choctaw Agency in Mississippi, the federal government granted de facto recognition to the tribal status of the Indians remaining in the state. Although the Mississippi Choctaws had lost citizenship in the Choctaw Nation, the federal government acknowledged them as an Indian tribe entitled to a federal relationship.

A few years later, in 1926, the agency superintendents began compiling an annual census of the Indians they served in Mississippi. The first two censuses did not record the blood quantum of the Choctaws, but this changed in 1928 when Superintendent R. J. Enochs specifically wrote in a "degree of blood" column. On that census, Enochs documented every single Choctaw as "full blood," regardless of whether the Dawes Commission previously had identified that person as possessing non-Indian ancestry. Simpson Tubby and his son Edgar, for example, both appeared as "full blood" on the census, despite the fact that the Dawes Commission had rejected them as "mixed blood."[214] This reclassification of "mixed bloods" suggests that Enochs—and the superintendents who followed him—at least partially deferred to Choctaw notions of belonging. In contrast to the Dawes commissioners who had rejected claimants with any hint of white or black ancestry, the superintendents worked in close association with the Indians and, as a result, Choctaws managed to change the meaning of "blood" to fit their own notions of belonging.

Although agency superintendents accepted as "full blood" Choctaws who had distant non-Indian ancestry, they were less forgiving about individuals who had more recently intermarried. Jim Crow Mississippi outlawed marriage between blacks and whites, and superintendents praised the Indians for the distance they maintained from other racial groups. Enochs particularly discouraged "intermingling" with African Americans and wrote in his 1927 annual report that "the Choctaw is a very different individual from the negro and the mixing of the two would certainly produce an inferior being to the full-blood Choctaw."[215] Enochs's efforts paid off. In 1929, he bragged that the Choctaws were "becoming prouder and prouder of their virtue and of their racial purity, and that they are, therefore, becoming more and more virtuous every year."[216]

In the rare cases where Choctaws did cross the color line, the agency superintendents responded by excluding their children from the tribal census. In particular, they discounted individuals with black ancestry, who disappeared from agency records. Daisy Miller, a woman whom John Reeves had identified as a "half-blood Choctaw" in his 1916 report, as well as her children by a black

Figure 3.5 In 1918, Congress appropriated funds to open an agency for those Choctaws left in Mississippi. Agency officials, who were often drawn from the local white population, encouraged Choctaws to maintain their "racial purity" by rejecting intermarriage with other populations, in particular African Americans. In this photograph, a group of fifteen Choctaws posed with their agency farmer, T. J. Scott. Although Scott was a devoted ally of the Choctaws, he was also a member of the Ku Klux Klan. Photographer: Henry Bascom Collins. Date: 1925. Courtesy of the National Anthropological Archives, Smithsonian Institution (SPC Se Choctaw NM No # Collins 01778500).

man, did not appear on the census at all. This was also the case for Mag Gracie, a "one-half negro and one-half Choctaw," and her four children, "two of whom are one-fourth Indian and three-fourths negro; the other two being one-fourth Indian, one-fourth negro, and one-half white."[217] Like black-Choctaw families in the past, they merged with the surrounding African American population, spoke English, and no longer socialized with other Choctaw families. Sociologist John Holbrook Peterson reported that when the Choctaw Agency compiled a list of Indian households in 1968, "the existence of these families was mentioned, but no one seriously considered placing them on the list." For this reason, "the claim that all Choctaws are legally full blood continue[d] to be largely correct," although, as anthropologist Pamela Coe ironically noted, "much of the Negro population is part Indian."[218]

Left off the censuses, phenotypically black and white people with Choctaw ancestry did not pursue claims against the Choctaw Agency because, quite simply, there was little incentive to do so. The segregated agency schools were no better equipped than the local "white" and "colored" institutions and language barriers for the culturally Choctaw children meant that lessons proceeded slowly. Although the agency purchased land for the Indians' use in Mississippi, this acreage was not given to the Choctaws as allotments or even as a reservation until it was finally put in trust with the federal government in 1939. Instead, the Indians were supposed to pay back the worth of the property to the government through their farm labor.[219] In addition, unlike many other tribes, the Mississippi Choctaws received no federal annuities in the form of per capita payments. Those who wished to assert a Choctaw identity solely for financial reasons found little to gain by making demands of the Choctaw Agency in Mississippi. For this reason, the superintendents did not have to be as scrupulous as the Dawes Commission when it came to tracing people's family histories and policing blood quantums. Instead, they relied more on Choctaws' self-identification as "full blood," as long as the Indians did not blatantly confuse the color line through intermarriage.

Mississippi Choctaws may have conceived of "blood" in different ways than federal officials, but the idea of blood and the perception that "full bloods" had a more legitimate claim to Indian identity rubbed off. After the passage of the Indian Reorganization Act (IRA) in 1934, for example, the Mississippi Choctaws used their status as "full bloods" to bolster their efforts to reorganize a tribal government. Despite setting up an agency for the Mississippi Choctaws in 1918, the federal government questioned whether these Indians belonged to a recognized tribe entitled to reorganize under the provisions of the IRA since they had lost citizenship in the Choctaw Nation in 1907.[220] Section 19 of the IRA, however, permitted individuals who were one-half or more Indian blood to participate in the legislation even if they lacked political

recognition.[221] Fortunately for the Choctaws, they were already all too familiar with the federal government's language of blood. After years of promoting
themselves as "full blood" to agency officials based on their kinship affiliations, cultural practices, and general refusal to marry outsiders, nearly every
single Choctaw appeared on the agency census as "full blood." Out of a population of 1,908 Choctaws in 1937, only five individuals did not make the cut.[222]
Based on blood, then, the Mississippi Choctaws could reorganize.

When the tribe adopted a constitution in 1945, the Choctaws codified what
they had learned about "blood." They used the 1940 Choctaw Agency census
as a base roll and stipulated that only Choctaws of "one-half (1/2) or more
Indian blood, resident in Mississippi" qualified as citizens.[223] These criteria
conformed to the IRA's requirement that unrecognized Indians have one-
half or more Indian "blood" to reorganize, which in turn reflected the federal
obsession with "blood" that had first solidified during the allotment era. The
residency requirement served to distinguish Choctaws in Mississippi from
those who had won citizenship in the Choctaw Nation West, but it also inadvertently excluded a few Choctaw families who lived in Louisiana. Some
Louisiana Choctaws eventually reorganized as the Jena Bank of Choctaw
Indians in 1974 and won separate recognition from the federal government
in 1995.[224] Although the Mississippi Band of Choctaw Indians modified its
governing document in 1969 and 1975 and got rid of its residency requirement
in order to accommodate tribal citizens who had relocated to out-of-state cities
and to farms in Tennessee in the 1950s and 1960s, the Band upheld its one-half
Choctaw blood quantum requirement, which remains a primary criterion for
citizenship.[225]

Today the Band, which includes more than 10,500 members, continues to
abide by the requirements set out in its revised constitution of 1975.[226] Tribal
citizens must descend from Mississippi Choctaws listed on the 1940 tribal
census and be at least one-half Choctaw by blood. The citizenship article as-
serts that the tribal council has "the power to pass ordinances, subject to the
approval of the Secretary of the Interior, governing future membership," but
insists that "no person of less than one-half degree of Choctaw blood shall be
admitted to membership" in the Band.[227] The Band also requires that all applicants for tribal citizenship include ancestry charts, long-form birth certificates, and paternity affidavits and DNA tests (if needed) to prove their descent
from Choctaws listed on the 1940 roll.[228] These stipulations are reminiscent
of the "genealogical proof of descent" that McKennon and the Dawes commissioners so eagerly sought from Mississippi Choctaw claimants more than
a century earlier.

The persistence of the blood quantum requirement and its strict implementation reveals the deep legacy of federal Indian policy in Mississippi. It also

reflects the ongoing tendency of Mississippi Choctaws to marry within their communities. Finally, the Mississippi Choctaws' growing economic success perhaps reinforces their commitment to a blood quantum requirement. Since constructing an eighty-acre industrial park on reservation lands in 1979 and attracting businesses and building casinos, the once-impoverished Mississippi Band of Choctaw Indians has become one of the largest private employers in the state of Mississippi.[229] With more resources to defend, tribal citizens may find it in their best interest to uphold blood quantum restrictions to ward off pretenders who for generations have tried to claim rights and property based on their assertions of distant Choctaw ancestry.

The Choctaws who remained in Mississippi after the second removal learned all too well what it took to qualify as "Indian" in the eyes of the federal government. Only "full bloods" made it onto the Dawes Commission rolls and had their tribal citizenship recognized by the United States. A "full-blood" status also helped the Choctaws regain a federal agency in Mississippi in 1918. As they dealt with agency officials, the Choctaws learned to manipulate the meanings of "blood" in order to include friends and relatives with distant non-Indian ancestry. They discovered that to preserve their status as "full-blood" Indians, however, they had to eschew further intermarriage. The efforts of the Mississippi Choctaws to project a "full-blood" identity paid off. The tribe re-organized under the terms of the IRA and in 1945 created its own constitution and political status as the Mississippi Band of Choctaw Indians. The tribe's citizenship criteria, however, continue to reflect the federal government's long-term obsession with Indian blood.

The story of the Mississippi Band of Choctaw Indians illustrates the ways that federal policy, access to tribal resources, racial ideologies, and struggles to preserve tribal sovereignty intersect to produce markers of Indian identity. Federal allotment policy caused the Mississippi Choctaws to lose their political status when Choctaw Nation lands were divided and distributed to recognized tribal citizens. The racial ideologies of early twentieth-century government officials, however, provided these disenrolled Choctaws with the opportunity to reclaim an Indian identity. Mississippi Choctaws used and manipulated the language of blood to reassert their tribal sovereignty in their southeastern homelands. By learning about and adapting to federal expectations of what it meant to be "Indian," the Mississippi Choctaws survived and created "an entirely different tribe."[230]

4

Contests of Sovereignty

The Eastern Band of Cherokee Indians of North Carolina

On June 4, 1924, Congress passed an act calling for the final disposition of the land, money, and property of the Eastern Band of Cherokee Indians. The climax of years of legal battles concerning the distribution of tribal resources, this act promised to settle once and for all the question of Eastern Band tribal citizenship and lay to rest the turmoil over who was entitled to a share of Cherokee assets. Following the instructions of the Interior Department, federal agent Fred A. Baker set out to western North Carolina to compile an official list of tribal citizens. What he found was a tribal council he described as "reasonable and honorable" but nonetheless determined "to limit the membership in the Band to as low a number as possible." As Baker explained in his report to the Department, the desire of council was "natural under the circumstances, as it is clear that the greater the number enrolled the less value the share of each member will be."[1]

Over the course of the late nineteenth and twentieth centuries, citizenship in the Eastern Band of Cherokee Indians evolved from clan-based kin to a political identity that provided tangible economic and legal rights. Three interrelated factors—the acquisition of tribal land, the movement of "white Indians" onto Cherokee territory, and the increase in federal oversight of Eastern Band affairs—prompted the tribal council to consider belonging in new ways. Tribal resources and tribal citizenship became inextricably intertwined as the Cherokees rebuilt a homeland and decided who had the right to share in their common property. When the tribal council began making per capita distributions of tribal funds generated through timber and land sales to tribal citizens, "white Indians" with spurious claims to Cherokee ancestry asserted that they too belonged to the tribe, a notion that the core Cherokee community rejected. Federal officials weighed in on these debates and required the tribal council to develop legal definitions of tribal citizenship that could withstand the scrutiny of lawyers and bureaucrats. The federal government refused to trust the council's subjective, though informed, assessments of belonging; the Cherokees had to justify each decision about who belonged. In an effort to protect their economic resources and political rights, the core Cherokee community developed criteria that they expected government officials to uphold. When they did not, the Cherokees fought back. The roll of the Eastern Band of Cherokee Indians, created in the 1920s, was the product of decades of struggle.

The Cherokees, like other southeastern tribes, faced tremendous challenges in the century after removal to survive in a world that denied the continued existence of southern Indians. Like the Mississippi Choctaws who remained in the South following the removal of the Choctaw Nation to Indian Territory, the Eastern Cherokees were a remnant population that broke away from the larger political body of the Cherokee Nation. The forced expulsion of the Cherokee Nation in the late 1830s displaced more than 13,000 people.[2] Not all Cherokees, however, left their southeastern homelands. In Georgia, twenty-two elite, plantation- and slave-owning Cherokee families won the right to remain when the state legislature passed the Cherokee Indian

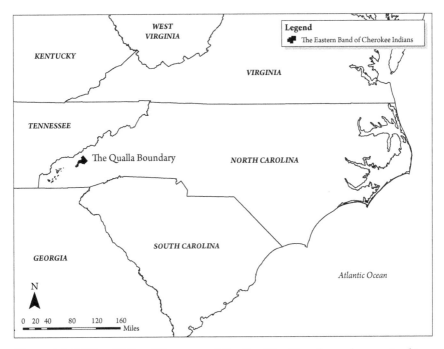

Figure 4.1 William Holland Thomas, a white ally of the Cherokees who remained in North Carolina following removal, helped the tribe rebuild a land base in the 1840s and 1850s. In 1874, the Eastern Band of Cherokee Indians won legal title to this land, which they called the Qualla Boundary. The tribe put this land in trust with the federal government in 1919. Today the Eastern Band of Cherokee Indian lands consist of nearly 65,000 acres. Map prepared by Christian Adams.

Citizenship Act in 1838. These families repurchased their confiscated property from the state and pledged to live as Georgia citizens.[3] In Tennessee,
a less prosperous and more culturally conservative contingent of Cherokees
also escaped removal. Fleeing to the Ducktown Basin, located in the southeastern corner of Polk County, they survived by farming and trading in the
mountains. Eventually racial tensions with their non-Indian neighbors forced
these Indians to find homes elsewhere, either in the removed Cherokee Nation
or among other Cherokee people who stayed in North Carolina.[4] People of
Cherokee descent also continued to live elsewhere in Georgia, Tennessee,
and Alabama.[5]

By far the largest and most clearly defined group of Cherokees that remained
in the South lived in North Carolina. Unlike the Georgia and Tennessee
Cherokees who largely assimilated or moved, North Carolina Cherokees took
advantage of their numerically significant population and their legal relationship with the state to rebuild a tribal identity. They based their rights on land
cession treaties made in 1817 and 1819. A clause in the 1819 treaty permitted
each Cherokee head of family to remain in western North Carolina, apply for
a 640-acre reservation within the ceded territory, and become a state citizen.[6]
Unlike the Treaty of Dancing Rabbit Creek, which had permitted Choctaws
who remained in Mississippi to retain citizenship rights in the Choctaw
Nation, no such stipulation promised these Cherokees ongoing rights in the
Cherokee Nation.[7] Following removal, the Cherokees who remained in North
Carolina severed their political connection to the Cherokee Nation West, although a few eastern Cherokees migrated to Indian Territory and rejoined
the Cherokee Nation in the late nineteenth century. A Supreme Court case in
1885 affirmed this political separation.[8]

Just as the state of Mississippi denied Choctaws their promised allotments,
North Carolina erroneously deprived the Cherokee reservees of their land
by offering it for sale to white settlers. The state compensated them for this
loss, however, by paying for the land and permitting the Cherokees to settle
elsewhere in the region.[9] Gradually, Cherokees in North Carolina purchased
a new tribal land base. With a homeland to defend, as well as an ongoing sense
of political and cultural distinctiveness as Cherokee, they consolidated and
emerged as a new political entity: the Eastern Band of Cherokee Indians.

In the years that followed removal, the Cherokees turned to a local white
businessman and political ally, William Holland Thomas, to help them rebuild
a tribal land base. Familiar with the tribe since childhood, Thomas became the
Band's legal counsel and confidant by 1831. He served as their representative
in Washington, DC, during the removal crisis and in the subsequent years,
Thomas helped those Indians who remained in North Carolina to consolidate their lands and rebuild their lives. Through the 1840s and 1850s, Thomas

acquired new lands for the Eastern Band to reestablish a Cherokee tribal territory in the South.[10] These lands became the social center and economic base that the Cherokees fought to defend by limiting tribal citizenship.

Thomas's aid served the Cherokees well in the years before the Civil War, but after the war their ally's health failed, leaving his financial relationship with the Cherokees in a muddle. Although the tribe's political status seemed more assured during these years—in 1868 the federal government recognized the Eastern Band of Cherokee Indians as a separate tribe—their economic situation grew precarious. Thomas had purchased Cherokee land under his own name using Cherokee funds; when his creditors came knocking, they collected title to lands for which the Cherokees had partially paid. In 1874 the Cherokees took their case to court. After a thorough investigation, the US Circuit Court for the Western District of North Carolina ruled in their favor. The Cherokees paid Thomas's creditors $7,000, which they still owed for the land, and received legal title to the tract, which they called the Qualla Boundary. The 1874 court decision placed a new geographical restriction on tribal citizenship: ownership of the common territory was limited to "the Eastern Band of Cherokee Indians living in the State of North Carolina, as a tribe or community, and whether living at this time at Qualla or elsewhere in the State."[11] In the following decades, the Eastern Band used the language of the 1874 court decision to deny tribal citizenship to individuals of Cherokee ancestry who lived outside North Carolina.

Despite gaining clear title to their landholdings, the Cherokees faced ongoing threats to their resources. A continual problem was trespassing. Even after the 1874 court decision, non-Indian trespassers regularly made inroads on the Qualla Boundary and on other Cherokee lands, pushing Indians out. Whites intimidated Cherokees and drove them from their homes, their agent asserted, "by threats and violence." Regarding "the Indian as his lawful prey," white North Carolinians "forcibly [took] personal property" and "rented land and refused to pay the rent."[12] The fact that the Cherokees held their land in common but lacked any corporate legal standing in state and federal courts further complicated the issue: "Trespassers thus enter their lands and unceremoniously squat upon them, and when the Indian goes into court, it is assumed that being an Indian he has no right to be heard there."[13]

Control over tribal land and the creation of legal political boundaries were especially important to late nineteenth-century Cherokees as outsiders began clamoring for tribal rights.[14] Government policies such as the General Allotment Act of 1887, which promised to break up tribal land bases and distribute tracts to individual tribal citizens, encouraged intruders who hoped to gain access to Cherokee lands by squatting on them and asserting Cherokee ancestry. Core community members dubbed these intruders "white Indians" and complained that they wanted tribal citizenship only to secure economic benefits.[15]

A census compiled by Joseph G. Hester in 1884 reflected growing concerns over the influence of "white Indians." A pending suit by the Eastern Band against the Cherokee Nation for a proportionate share of the proceeds from past land sales and claims prompted this enumeration, and Hester, a government official unaffiliated with either tribe, encouraged the Eastern Cherokees to inflate the roll: "The more Indians you have East of the Mississippi River, the more money you will get for your part, your share will be larger of these funds you are to secure." The tribal councilmen were not convinced and during a "pretty stormy session," they objected to the inclusion of "white Indian" families.[16] Hester ignored their protests. His roll included 2,956 names, which was more than a 50 percent increase in Eastern Band citizenship over what officials had reported on the federal census of 1880.[17] Members of the core Cherokee community desperately searched for ways to reverse this trend toward inflating their numbers.

By 1889, the Cherokees had had enough. Determined to defend Cherokee territory against intruders and to control access to tribal resources, the tribal council headed by Nimrod J. Smith developed an innovative solution: incorporation under the state laws of North Carolina. Incorporation helped protect the Band against trespassers by validating the Eastern Cherokees' tribal organization and communal ownership of tribal lands. Indeed, the sixth section of the Band's articles of incorporation specified that "it shall be unlawful for any person or persons to cut, fell, or destroy any timber trees or wood or to range any stock horses or cattle or make any entries or surveys or in any manner to trespass on any of the land held in common by the said Indians in any of the said counties and all such persons so offending shall be guilty of a misdemeanor and punishable by fine or imprisonment at the discretion of the Court."[18] As a state corporation, the tribe gained standing in court to pursue violations. Incorporation also gave the tribe greater power to sell timber and land without federal interference. It provided the Cherokees with a concrete political identity that served as a means to distinguish tribal citizenship claims based on Cherokee heritage from actual political affiliation with the Eastern Band.

Acting as a corporate board, the tribal council codified its position against "white Indian" intruders by revising the Band's corporate charter in 1895 to provide that "no person shall be entitled to the enjoyment of any lands belonging to the Eastern Band of Cherokee Indians as a corporation or as a tribe, or any profits accruing therefrom, or any monies which may belong to said Band as a corporation or as a tribe, unless such person be of at least one-sixteenth (1/16) of Eastern Cherokee blood."[19] Ratified by the state of North Carolina on March 8, 1897, this act enabled the Band to limit its citizenship to those it

Figure 4.2 To defend Cherokee lands in North Carolina from trespassers and "white Indian" claimants, Principal Chief Nimrod Jarrett Smith (pictured) incorporated the Eastern Band under the state laws of North Carolina in 1889. Incorporation helped validate the Cherokees' tribal organization and communal ownership of the Qualla Boundary. Photographer: Thomas Donaldson. Date: c. 1891. Courtesy of the National Anthropological Archives, Smithsonian Institution (SPC Se Cherokee BAE 1-19 01759200).

deemed real Cherokees. The tribal councilmen hoped that by taking this legal step, they could enforce citizenship criteria that the state and federal governments would recognize and uphold. Like the Mississippi Choctaws, they used the language of blood to make their Indianness intelligible to United States officials and to create boundaries between legitimate tribal citizens and false claimants.

The Eastern Band's need to codify citizenship criteria for the benefit of white officials reflected a growing federal presence on the Qualla Boundary. When the federal government recognized the Eastern Band of Cherokee Indians as a distinct tribe in 1868, it promised to provide the Eastern Cherokees with the same services as other tribes. Federal recognition proved both a blessing and a curse. The Cherokees felt relatively secure in their position as "Indian" compared to other southeastern tribes like the Pamunkeys and the Catawbas, which at the time had only state recognition of their tribal status. Cherokee identity had an official basis in US law. Recognition granted the Interior Department supervision over Cherokee affairs, however, which meant that the tribe had to seek federal approval for many of its decisions.[20]

A significant manifestation of the federal government's presence on the Qualla Boundary was the reservation school system. In 1875, the Indian Office appointed a Baptist minister as special agent to the Cherokees, and he began establishing schools among the Indians. This early effort ended in failure by 1879, the victim of tribal factionalism and bureaucratic mismanagement.[21] Despite the setback, government interest in educating the Eastern Cherokees continued. In May 1881, the Quakers contracted with the United States to provide schools, which included four day schools for children in outlying districts and a boarding school at Cherokee for "the large boys and girls" as well as those who lived more than a mile and a half from the other schools.[22] In 1892, the federal government took over the Quaker schools after an Indian appropriations act authorized the Cherokee Boarding School superintendent in North Carolina to act as agent for the Eastern Band.[23] In the view of the Indian Office, the primary responsibility of government officials on reservations was educational.

Although the Indian Office claimed to serve its tribal clients through education, non-Indian outsiders managed and controlled the schools, leaving the Cherokees with little say over who could or could not attend. School officials frequently accepted the children of non-citizens of the Band, as long as they physically appeared to have some Indian ancestry. As one superintendent explained, Cherokee schools were "under the direction of the Government, wholly" and "membership in the Band [was] not considered" when admitting children to these institutions. School officials used only one criterion to permit children to attend—"whether they have Indian blood." Although officials insisted that "their admission [was] solely for educational purposes and not to determine their property rights" in the Band, by admitting non-citizens to programs designed for the Eastern Band, the government opened a door for outsiders to lay claim to other Cherokee resources as well.[24] These schools, along with the influx of near-white settlers who hoped to claim a share of allotted Cherokee land, served as a double threat to Cherokee culture, social life, economic resources, and tribal sovereignty.[25]

Fears of white Indian infiltration and federal interference pushed Cherokees to develop new citizenship criteria in the late nineteenth and early twentieth centuries. Ongoing concerns over tribal resources served as the final catalyst for these efforts. Incorporation provided the Eastern Band with freedom to use their lands as they saw fit, and soon the tribal council made deals with lumber companies to turn their forested territory, which was largely uninhabited, into tangible profits. They sold timber rights on the Cathcart Tract for $15,000 in the 1890s, which provided employment for Cherokees in logging and milling operations as well as funds to pay back taxes.[26] The council distributed funds from other timber sales to tribal citizens as per capita payments. In 1900, for example, each tribal citizen received $4 from the "Timber Fund."[27] The 1906 sale of the Love Tract for $245,000 promised tribal citizens large payouts over several years.[28]

Despite the per capita payments, not all tribal citizens agreed with the timber and land contracts signed by the tribal council. Dissension stemmed from concern over the tribal land sales and awareness of the federal policy of allotment. Dissatisfaction with the per capita payments as well as pro-allotment rhetoric led some Indians to think that they would make more money if they managed their lands individually through allotment.[29] All Cherokees, however, worried about who was entitled to a share of Eastern Band property and funds. Who was entitled to money from land sales and timber contracts? If federal officials allotted the Qualla Boundary, who would get a share? The Eastern Band needed an official roll.

The first effort to make an official list of tribal citizens came shortly after the finalization of the Love Tract sale. The tribal council, well aware that most of its constituency wished "to get as much of this money as they can get as soon as possible," set about compiling a new Eastern Band roll in 1907 that they could use to distribute funds from the Love Tract sale.[30] This "Council Roll," as they called it, was a preemptive measure on the part of the councilmen since they knew that the federal government intended to draw up its own list of eligible tribal citizens. Cherokees hoped that by presenting federal agents with a tribal roll as a fait accompli, they could avoid any enrollment controversies by clearly delineating the individuals they considered citizens of the Eastern Band.

Basing their list on the 1884 Hester census, which the federal government had commissioned to distribute claim payments, as well as on the Eastern Band corporation's one-sixteenth blood quantum requirement, the council compiled a roll of 1,528 names.[31] The roll included substantial documentation, including the Hester Roll number, Indian name, English name, degree of Indian blood, the roll numbers of parents for those born after 1884, and

Figure 4.3 Eastern Band of Cherokee councilmen, like those pictured, vigorously defended Cherokee land, resources, and identity during the tribal citizenship debates of the late nineteenth and early twentieth centuries. Fears of "white Indian" infiltration and federal interference in Cherokee affairs pushed the tribal council to develop new citizenship criteria that reflected older Cherokee values but adhered to the standards and expectations of white officials. This was no easy task. Photographer: Thomas Donaldson. Date: 1891. From Thomas Donaldson, *Extra Census Bulletin, Indians: Eastern Band of Cherokees of North Carolina* (Washington, DC: United States Census Printing Office, 1892), 20.

the residence of enrollees. The council noted whether citizens had married outside the tribe and the racial identity of their spouses. They approved individuals of one-sixteenth or more blood quantum, but rejected their children, if less than one-sixteenth Cherokee blood. The tribal council recognized other individuals as being of Cherokee blood, but nonetheless denied them rights in the Band. Mark Wolfe and Mary Emmerline, for example, had both married Crow Indians and subsequently moved to the Crow Agency in Montana. According to the tribal council, these siblings were "not eligible here."[32] The Council Roll revealed that the tribal council considered blood quantum and residency as two of the most important markers of belonging. Both of these criteria harkened back to the legally defined political identity of Eastern Band citizens that had begun with the 1874 land case and the 1889 incorporation of the tribe. Approved by thirteen council members and ratified on November 30, 1907, the Council Roll reflected the tribal council's intent to define the Eastern Band's citizenry narrowly.

The year after the tribe compiled the Council Roll, the federal government sent its own official, Frank C. Churchill, to make a list of Eastern Band citizens. This effort came at the request of the federal agent stationed at Qualla who believed the tribe had unfairly excluded many individuals deserving of citizenship rights.[33] Over a period of more than six months, Churchill visited the counties of Swain, Jackson, Graham, and Cherokee and took testimony from numerous applicants to determine their eligibility for enrollment. Upon completing his task, he addressed the tribal council and asked that they assemble the people in order to hear the roll called. At the subsequent meeting, Churchill listed 2,277 names.[34]

The tribal council, although respectful of Churchill's work, was dissatisfied with the final product. Council members particularly objected to the inspector's inclusion of individuals with less than one-sixteenth Cherokee ancestry because the tribe's amended charter excluded them. In addition, the council argued that families who were legal residents of Georgia when the court awarded them the lands now held by their corporation were not eligible for citizenship or funds because they were not residents of North Carolina in 1874, as stipulated in the decision. Using these ancestral and residential criteria to protest the enrollment of individuals they saw as outsiders, the council insisted that fewer than 1,910 of the names on Churchill's list were legitimate.[35] Over the next decade, the tribe and federal officials hotly contested citizenship criteria. Two separate commissions headed by Special Agents Charles L. Davis and O. M. McPherson traveled to North Carolina to investigate citizenship claims. Applicants, lawyers, bureaucrats, and Eastern Band citizens fought over the tribe's requirements for inclusion.

During the enrollment controversies of the 1910s, the Eastern Band did its best to solidify its citizenship criteria and to defend them against outsiders. The Cherokees needed clear ways to distinguish between genuine citizens and individuals only interested in Cherokee identity for economic reasons. They also needed criteria that they could explain and defend to federal officials. The enrollment decisions the tribal council made reflected its efforts to merge traditional ideas of belonging with new legalistic citizenship criteria. Emerging racial ideas about "blood" shaped traditional Cherokee ways of defining community members through kin ties. New residency requirements incorporated older ideas of cultural affiliation as a marker of Cherokee identity. By using language that white officials understood, the Cherokees hoped to uphold their own roll. In some cases the new criteria appeared to contradict the old and to exclude individuals whom the tribe earlier might have included. Ultimately, however, the council made the decisions it deemed best for the long-term survival of the tribe and the preservation of its political rights and economic resources.

In the eighteenth and early nineteenth centuries, Cherokees had defined their communities by kinship.[36] As a matrilineal society, the Cherokees had long traced tribal belonging through female kin. According to this system, anyone born of a Cherokee mother was automatically a full member of the community, no matter the father's racial identity. Over the years, however, kinship patterns changed as the Cherokees interacted with non-Indians and became acquainted with patriarchal customs. Even before the removal of the 1830s, Cherokee men had secured the rights of citizenship in the Cherokee Nation for their children born of non-Cherokee mothers. Cherokees who remained in the east following removal continued to intermarry with non-Indians, and many of them considered their children to be Cherokee, regardless of the sex of their Cherokee parent. This expanded definition of what it meant to be Cherokee ultimately undermined the desire of the Eastern Band to limit tribal citizenship in order to protect resources for core community members. Traditional matrilineal practices, new assertions of paternal rights, and developing ideas of racial "otherness" interacted to produce new ideas about who belonged.

Overrun by the claims of white Indians and fearful that intermarriage would weaken the tribe by diluting shares of tribal resources, the tribal council made efforts to police the sexual relationships of tribal citizens. In 1886, the tribal council passed a resolution that required all tribal citizens "to be subject to the laws of the State in which they reside concerning marriage, that no man and woman shall live or cohabit together except they be married according to the laws of the State in which they reside."[37] Since state laws prohibited marriage between whites and Indians, this resolution presumably restricted marriages solely to the tribal community. In addition to limiting white intermarriage, the council proposed a resolution in 1909 that barred from citizenship "the children of any member of the Eastern Band of Cherokee Indians who marries an outside negro or person of negro blood."[38] Despite these efforts, libido trumped law. The proportion of western North Carolinians claiming Cherokee blood increased during these years, through legal marriages, common-law relationships, and temporary trysts.

In earlier times, "illegitimacy" had been meaningless in Cherokee society. Children belonged to their mother's clan and their parents' marital status had no bearing on their identity. As intermarriages and cross-racial sexual encounters grew increasingly common in the late nineteenth and early twentieth centuries, however, these ideas changed. Doubts about the paternity of children born out of wedlock led the council to acknowledge the children of non-Cherokee mothers only if the Cherokee father claimed the child as his own. Ute Crowe, for example, denied that he had fathered Mandy Crowe, the daughter of a white woman. The tribal council honored his declaration and contested Mandy's enrollment in the Eastern Band. As council members later testified, "We believed him on the ground we stood on behalf of the tribe, and we took it for granted that what he said was the truth, so we filed the contest."[39] By insisting that only the acknowledged children of Cherokee fathers could claim Eastern Band citizenship, the tribal council tried to make certain that children with recognized kin ties to the tribe—not merely alleged blood connections—received the benefits of citizenship. Fortunately for them, some American ideas of inheritance and illegitimacy overlapped with their traditional notions about matrilineal descent. As one of the Band's lawyers argued in 1910, "under the laws of the State of North Carolina, in the descent of real property, the rule is, that an illegitimate child can inherit only from its mother."[40]

By denying citizenship rights to unacknowledged children, the tribal council sought to protect the Eastern Band from dubious claims filed by non-Cherokee women and their alleged "mixed-blood" offspring. In 1915, the tribal council ruled that no illegitimate child could be enrolled "before the mother of said child shall have first appeared before [the Cherokee Boarding School] Superintendent and under oath declared the name of the father of the child."[41] Even after women made these assertions, neither the tribe nor the superintendent necessarily believed them. With so much money at stake in the tribal bank account, the council wanted to avoid doubtful claims that jeopardized the shares of recognized citizens. When Rebecca Davis filed for citizenship, claiming she was the illegitimate child of tribal citizen Charley Hornbuckle, for example, council member James Blythe protested that "She was a woman about thirty years old when she first began to claim she was of Indian blood." In his view, "she had no further use for the Tribe" than the payments she hoped to receive.[42] From the perspective of the tribal council, these individuals were not legitimate Cherokees. Even if their mothers had engaged in brief relationships with Cherokee men, a presumption of blood alone was not enough to make someone an Eastern Band citizen.

Ideas about race, which grew ever more prevalent in the context of the Jim Crow South, complicated the tribal council's efforts to limit Eastern Band citizenship. In a region that divided people into categories of "colored" and "white," Cherokees were not always free to define their citizenship in ways that adhered to their traditional concepts of kinship or their emerging ideas of political belonging. From the perspective of white agents and government officials, children who showed phenotypically Indian characteristics had to be Cherokee because they certainly were not white. Racially defined, such individuals belonged on tribal rolls, they thought, because they did not fit into Jim Crow's racial binary: they were not white but neither were they black. On the other hand, officials tended to lump children of mixed black and Cherokee ancestry into the category of "colored," for they did have African ancestry. Government agents more readily accepted the judgments of the tribal council on the status of individuals of African and Cherokee descent because their exclusion from the Eastern Band of Cherokee Indians did not threaten the South's racial categories as would have occurred for those whose ancestors were Indian and white. Beyond the boundaries of the reservation, children of Cherokees and African Americans simply became "colored," whereas children of Indians and whites challenged the color line.

As the enrollment process got under way, federal officials encouraged Cherokees to think about applicants racially. When applicants came before the enrolling committees of the 1910s, agents, lawyers, and tribal citizens scrutinized their racial identities to determine their Cherokee blood. Often they depended on phenotype to decide questions of eligibility. In the case of Harriet A. Mashburn, a white lawyer appointed by the Interior Department to serve as advisory counsel during enrollment asked committee members to "look at this lady, as we will make a statement about her appearance." The lawyer described Mashburn as "of a very dark brunette complexion" and used this to prove her assertion of Indian identity. The Cherokee committee members questioned Mashburn's background and noted that her father was no more than "three eights" Cherokee blood by "the general reputation." When the lawyer pressed them, however, they conceded that "she is darker, and her hair is black, she would be taken for a half breed anywhere." Giving in to the lawyer's argument that the woman's physical appearance demanded her enrollment, the committee decided that she was "a little more than one quarter."[43]

Over time, racial ideologies modified traditional understanding of kinship and led to prejudice against a number of claimants on account of their race. Tribal citizens' feeling "toward the colored race" proved particularly detrimental to black-Cherokee applicants.[44] Although kin ties could overcome racial prejudice in some cases—for example, in the 1890s the superintendent reported that Cherokees took in and raised the orphaned son of a Cherokee man and his black-Cherokee wife—in other instances, racial feeling was too strong to surmount.[45] In 1909 the tribal council objected to the enrollment of the family of Acey James on the grounds that they were "said to be part negro, and claim to be of Portuguese descent."[46] Cherokees did not always use race so overtly to limit an individual's rights to citizenship; instead, prejudice against blacks more subtly barred applicants from the tribal rolls.

A useful case study of Cherokee attitudes toward and relationships with racial "others" is the Driver family. Russell B. Driver and James Goliath Driver, two full-blood Cherokee brothers, left Qualla to attend the Carlisle Indian Industrial School in Pennsylvania sometime in the last years of the nineteenth century. While they were away from North Carolina, both brothers met and married non-Cherokee women. James Goliath married a white woman, fathered a child, and moved his small family to Indiana where he worked as a baker. Russell, on the other hand, married a "Negro woman," stayed in Pennsylvania, and had several children. By the time the McPherson Committee reviewed their enrollment cases in the mid-1910s, neither brother had brought his family back to North Carolina, although both returned for visits without their wives or children. In the committee's view, both full-blood brothers were eligible for inclusion on the roll, but their children were not due to non-residence and non-affiliation with the tribe.[47]

On the surface, the cases of the Driver brothers appeared "almost identical," but a closer look at their circumstances reveals profound differences.[48] Tribal citizen James Blythe asked Russell, on one of his visits back to Qualla, "if he would not bring his family here." Russell replied that "he guessed he would not as she was a little too dark to bring here."[49] Even though later testimony revealed that his wife, Sophia Price, was of mixed African and Mohawk ancestry, Russell evidently believed her black heritage would prevent her acceptance by the Cherokees.[50] Although Russell applied for funds for his children through Cherokee claim payments, he chose to live out his life away from his kinsmen in order to protect Sophia and their growing family from racial prejudice.

In contrast to his brother, James Goliath Driver ended up returning to Qualla in later years, where he worked for a time at the Cherokee Boarding School and then in Bryson City as a baker.[51] Although his white wife was not well-liked by the Cherokee community (one letter described her as "a menace to the peace and good feeling wherever she goes"), James did not share his brother's qualms about bringing his family back to North Carolina, perhaps because their racial identity was more acceptable to the Cherokees.[52] His half-white daughter, Helen, graduated from the Cherokee Boarding School on the Qualla Boundary and later enrolled in the Haskell Institute as a Cherokee Indian.[53] When questions of tribal enrollment resurfaced in the 1920s, officials used the fact that Helen "did return and affiliate and associate with her tribe" to recommend her for enrollment.[54] Although Helen ended up marrying a white man and moving to Pennsylvania to work in a silk mill, the time she spent on the Qualla Boundary assured her of Cherokee tribal enrollment. Helen's white-Cherokee racial identity afforded her opportunities denied to her African-Mohawk-Cherokee cousins. Although officials applied the same tests—residency and affiliation—to both cases, attitudes toward race shaped the outcomes for these two blood-connected but racially divided families.

The story of the Coleman family reveals other ways that race influenced enrollment decisions and highlights the complicated intersections of illegitimacy, slavery, and "blood." Harrison Coleman, born around 1853 or 1854 near the Qualla Boundary in Swain County, was the son of Rebecca Coleman, "a negro slave, who belonged to a white man named Mark Coleman."[55] Harrison Coleman claimed that his father was Kah-soo-yo-keh Littlejohn, a full-blood Cherokee, but his parents never legally married and Kah-soo-yo-keh was in fact married to a Cherokee woman at the time of Coleman's conception.[56] The Eastern Cherokees did not know quite what to make of Coleman, partly due to his early servile status (he, like his mother, was the slave of Mark Coleman until emancipation) and partly due to his alleged father's refusal either to confirm or to deny his parentage. Hester included Coleman on his 1884 roll, as did Churchill in 1908, but a number of Cherokees consistently challenged his right to citizenship.[57] Until tribal citizenship debates erupted following the sale of the Love Tract, Harrison Coleman had an ambiguous status, sometimes included, sometimes rejected. He received a tract of land on the Qualla Boundary from the tribal council, which he farmed with the help of his mixed-ancestry wife, Mourning Coleman, who later claimed that she was of "white, Portuguese, African, and Indian" descent, although she never applied for enrollment in her own right. The couple's children attended the Cherokee school at Birdtown until the tribal council contested their admission in the wake of the Churchill Roll.[58]

For those Cherokees who denied Harrison Coleman's Indian ancestry, family issues were certainly at play. Recognizing Coleman as kin meant acknowledging Kah-soo-yo-keh's failings as a husband and father. Coleman's alleged half-brother, Saunooke Littlejohn, for example, insisted that "when we are talking together we do not call each other brother. . . . I do not regard him as my brother."[59] Yet even more insidious was the issue of race. Although Coleman, according to one government official, showed "some characteristics of all three races, white, colored, and Indian" and even showed "Indian the most," his African ancestry along with his illegitimacy made him a pariah in the Cherokee community.[60] As one Cherokee noted, "the young people of the Indian community would have little to do with the Coleman young people, and by reason of such the Coleman young people have affiliated with the colored young people."[61] Excluded from full community participation due to their black ancestry, the Colemans were forced to socialize elsewhere. Ultimately they associated with and married into the surrounding black community, which further distanced them from the Cherokees.[62]

Despite years of rejection, Harrison Coleman and his family clung firmly to their Cherokee identity. Coleman maintained that he was the son of Kah-soo-yo-keh by blood, his children attended the Cherokee day school at Birdtown, and the family claimed to "visit some with the Indians, eat with them and go to their churches."[63] Government officials who reviewed the Colemans' case in the 1910s were hard-pressed to find a legitimate reason to deny the family citizenship rights. Seeing that the Colemans "undoubtedly have Indian blood," and recognizing that "there was a strong prejudice against them" among the Cherokees "because of their negro blood," Superintendent Frank Kyselka and Special Agent Davis challenged the tribal authorities to "support their charges by formal evidence." They warned them that "the burden of proof rests with the tribe and not on the contestees." When the tribal council did not respond, Kyselka assumed their silence was a "tacit withdrawal of the protest against enrollment" and thus included the Colemans on the Love Tract payroll of April, 1910.[64] For a time, at least, it seemed the Colemans would be enrolled.

The tribal council, however, was not easily dissuaded from its effort to protect Cherokee citizenship rights for only undisputedly "legitimate" Cherokees. Over the next few years, councilmen searched for legal tools that played on white society's own prejudices in order to exclude contested black-Indian families like the Colemans. What they found was an argument that resonated in the Jim Crow South: Harrison Coleman, the illegitimate son of a slave woman, "could have no other status than that of a slave, and by no possible construction could it have an inheritable interest in the lands and property of the Eastern Band of Cherokee Indians." Arguing that the "illegitimate child of a bond woman" followed the status of his mother—which also corresponded to Cherokee ideas of matrilineal descent—tribal citizens denied Coleman's right to enrollment, even if his father were Cherokee.[65] In 1913, James Blythe made this argument before the McPherson Committee and insisted that former slaves were "one class of claimants [the tribe] would never recognize."[66]

Although this position challenged the spirit of the US Constitution's Fourteenth and Fifteenth Amendments, which had provided African Americans with US citizenship and stipulated that their right to vote could not be denied based on "race, color, or previous condition of servitude," the Interior Department was happy to agree that "the immemorial custom of the Cherokee people [was] to include only free persons in the [tribal] citizenship."[67] Willing to accept the Cherokees' own requirements when they excluded people that white America also found objectionable, the Interior Department revealed its fickle tendency to defer to tribal authority over citizenship matters only when convenient. Indeed, the Cherokees' rejection of former slaves by claiming the sovereign right to define tribal citizenship outside the bounds of US citizenship criteria may have gratified southern whites who at the time were also searching for loopholes to get around the dictates of the Fourteenth and Fifteenth Amendments.

Although the racial prejudices of Eastern Cherokees pushed them to use any available tools to deny citizenship to individuals of black ancestry, they were equally invested in protecting citizenship rights from claimants who had white "blood." Cherokees borrowed ideas about "blood" from US policymakers and reformers who used the term to measure the competency of Indian people during the allotment era. In the view of white officials, the more "white blood" an Indian had, the more capable he or she presumably would be in managing affairs in the "civilized" world. Cherokees rejected this notion but manipulated ideas of blood to serve their own purposes. "Blood," for the Cherokees—as for the Mississippi Choctaws—carried cultural as well as racial connotations. They applied the term "full blood" to someone who adhered to traditional Cherokee practices and behaved in culturally appropriate ways regardless of whether that person actually had only Cherokee ancestors. "Mixed bloods," on the other hand, acted "white."[68] Although a person's recorded blood quantum did not necessarily correspond to his or her behavior, "blood" served as a litmus test that the tribal council used to defend the Eastern Band against the claims of so-called white Indians.

White Indian families based their claims on previous rolls that often had included white families—either because individuals had married into the tribe, or because they managed to get their names listed fraudulently. Charles L. Davis complained to the Indian Office in 1911: "All the old rolls carry many whites—the Hester rolls hundreds of them. Out of all this it is not to be wondered there are hundreds of people in this region who believe they have Indian blood. Are not the names of their ancestors on the old rolls? And have not their parents told them they have Indian blood? Then of course they do not hesitate to take solemn oath to such things." Some may have had Cherokee ancestry, but they were several generations removed from their Cherokee progenitors, had intermarried exclusively with whites for years, and had few connections to the core Cherokee community. Despite this, they sought a share of tribal lands and funds. "They are perfectly astonished," Davis wrote, "that any other test than blood should be applied. . . . To them a drop of Indian blood gives full right."[69]

Frustrated by the claims of these individuals, tribal citizens from the core Cherokee community rejected the rights of white Indians to Cherokee resources. Indeed, by the 1910s, many tribal citizens referred to these "off-shooting families" as "the 'suckers' to maimed or unhealthy plant life." They believed that "unless the suckers are pruned they will soon so sap the tribal wealth as to leave nothing to sustain the main plant." Cherokees felt particularly frustrated because many of these so-called Indians seemed to value Cherokee identity only for the money they hoped to receive. Davis reported that "except for the little patrimony coming, large numbers would scorn to be known as Indians or of Indian extraction."[70]

In order to curtail the rights of white Indians, Cherokees turned to the blood quantum limitations they had inserted into their amended corporate charter in 1895. They argued that this resolution restricted "tribal rights and membership to persons of not less than one-sixteenth degree Indian blood."[71] Because the resolution was approved by the state of North Carolina and not by the federal government, however, it was unclear whether federal agents making the Cherokee rolls would enforce it. The Indian Office instructed Churchill to ignore the resolution and to enroll "Indians otherwise qualified ... even though they were of one-thirty-second Indian blood or less."[72] The Cherokees protested against this instruction, and in 1910 they issued a new resolution reaffirming that "no person having less than one-sixteenth degree of Indian blood shall be entitled to enrollment as a member to the Band or to participate in any share of any tribal property thereof, except through inheritance of segregated and individual shares."[73] Davis and McPherson appeared to take the limitations set by the tribal council seriously as they investigated enrollment claims. Superintendent Frank Kyselka even proposed an innovative compromise that tribal funds be distributed proportional to the blood quantum of claimants: "Instead of $40 or $45 per head, I would recommend a payment of $60 to full bloods; $30 to half bloods; $15 to quarter bloods, etc."[74] The Indian Office declined to consider his request, and the disputes continued.

Many white Indian applicants hoped that if they pushed their cases hard enough, federal agents eventually would include their names on the rolls and they would receive an equal share of Cherokee resources. The case of one such family, the Raper-Lamberts, illustrates the complexity of the competing claims of federal officials, applicants, and the tribal council. Members of the Raper-Lambert family traced their Cherokee ancestry through the nineteenth-century marriages of three white men (Jesse, Thomas, and James Raper) with the daughters of Alexander McDaniel, a man of reputed Cherokee ancestry. According to the family, each of these daughters had at least one-quarter Cherokee ancestry, though the youngest, Susan, may have had more because she had a different mother than her sisters and "was of darker appearance."[75] In contrast, the tribal council contended that the girls were white: they claimed that Mary (Polly), Catherine (Katy), and Susan all descended from Alexander McDaniel's white wife and her first husband, a white man. The Lambert branch of the family descended from Nancy Lambert, the daughter of Thomas and Catherine Raper, who married a white man named Hugh Lambert. In the late nineteenth century, Hugh Lambert moved his family near to the Qualla Boundary and gained control of some Cherokee land. His children by Nancy almost all married whites and resided both off and on the reservation.[76]

By the early twentieth century, members of the Raper-Lambert family, although they occupied tribal lands, had little association with their supposed Cherokee relatives. All married outside whites, except for two of the great-grandsons of Catherine Raper. According to the McPherson Committee, Jesse B. Lambert married his second cousin, Minnie Stiles, who also claimed Cherokee ancestry, while Hugh N. Lambert married the sister of recognized tribal citizen Sibbald Smith. Other than these exceptions, the committee reported, there had been "no infusion of Cherokee blood, and no claim of infusion of Cherokee blood, in the Lambert Families since the marriage of Thomas Raper with Katy McDaniel (if in fact Katy McDaniel possessed any Cherokee blood, which is not admitted)." In addition, the committee asserted that although the Lambert family lived "on and near the Qualla Boundary," their mere presence in the vicinity of the Cherokee community did not constitute "a proper degree of Cherokee association and affiliation."[77] Due to their limited connection to the Cherokee community as well as their low Indian blood quantum, the tribal council and the McPherson Committee recommended "that the names of all the contested persons be dropped from the rolls of the Eastern Band of Cherokees of North Carolina." They sent their resolution to the Indian Office for approval.[78]

As they reviewed the case, Indian Office officials paid close attention to the blood claims of the Raper-Lamberts. Even though the Cherokee census of 1835 was "blank as to the members of the Raper family," the assistant commissioner of Indian affairs eventually concluded that Mary, Catherine, and Susan Raper must have had between one-quarter and one-half Indian blood. This decision was made "in the absence of all documentary evidence," illustrating the arbitrary nature of blood quantum designations. According to this ruling, some members of the Raper-Lambert family had more than one-sixteenth Cherokee blood; others did not. If the Indian Office applied the Band's blood rule, many individuals would be excluded from the rolls. Ultimately, however, the assistant commissioner declined to do so. He instructed the superintendent of the Cherokee Agency to recognize the Raper-Lamberts and "to accord them all the rights and privileges incident to such enrollment," including "all payments." [79] Much to the chagrin of the Cherokee tribal council, it seemed this white Indian family would gain tribal rights.

Similar to the Raper-Lambert family was the case of the Taylor-Hardin family. Like the Raper-Lamberts, the Taylor-Hardins' claim to Indian identity rested on family tradition. According to their arguments, in the early nineteenth century, an Indian woman married a white man by the name of Bigby. Of their children, one daughter, Polly Bigby, married a white man named Taylor. All the descendants of Taylor and his supposedly mixed-blood wife married whites, yet, McPherson wrote, "this family, of course, think they have Indian blood, for they have been taught it for years, and will swear to such claim to the end of their days."[80] Later, Polly Bigby's son, James Taylor, fathered an illegitimate daughter named Elizabeth Hardin by a white woman. Hardin and thirty-five of her descendants also claimed rights in the Band as descendants of Polly Bigby.[81] Members of the Taylor-Hardin family based their claims to tribal enrollment on their presumed ties to this distant Cherokee ancestor.

The tribal council contested their claims. According to a "well-established rumor and belief all through Cherokee country . . . Polly Bigby was a white girl, raised by the Bigby family, the Bigby mother being part Indian." In earlier times, the adoption of a white child by an Indian mother entitled the child to tribal citizenship, but by the twentieth century, blood superseded adoptive kin bonds in the eyes of the tribal council.[82] Moreover, for generations the family had had no affiliation with the tribe other than through James Taylor, son of Polly Bigby, who became enmeshed in tribal politics after the Civil War. Although presumably recognized as Cherokee by the tribe in the late nineteenth century, Taylor had a bad reputation among tribal citizens due to his divisive politics, his removal schemes, his appropriation of over $10,000 of tribal funds for services he supposedly rendered the Band, and his eventual removal west. Few were willing to grant that his brand of affiliation with the tribe entitled any of his relatives to citizenship.

When the enrollment case came before federal agents in the 1910s, both sides vehemently defended their positions. Members of the Taylor-Hardin family swore that they had Indian blood and pointed out the names of their ancestors on earlier tribal rolls. Those who occupied tribal land refused to leave and, according to McPherson, would "doubtless have to be litigated off."[83] The tribal council, on the other hand, insisted that they were whites who had fraudulently obtained rights in the Band. One witness described Polly Bigby as "fair skinned and freckle-faced. . . . [She] looked like a big Irish woman." According to the Cherokees, Polly Bigby, although "reared by Indians" was racially white and her descendants "were recognized as white people and enjoyed all the privileges of white people."[84]

The agents who reviewed the case had to agree that phenotypically not much suggested Indian ancestry among the descendants of Polly Bigby. "One and all are blondes," exclaimed Charles L. Davis, "and many with florid complexions and red hair."[85] In addition, the committee noted that "none of the applicants . . . live in an Indian community; that they do not speak or understand the Cherokee language; that they do not attend the tribal councils or meetings; that they have never patronized the Indian schools; that there is not now nor never has been a marriage of any individual of the Taylor family with any recognized member of this band; and that the very large majority of the applicants are wholly unknown and strangers to the present recognized membership."[86] The McPherson Committee recommended the expulsion of members of the Taylor-Hardin family from the Cherokee rolls. As with the case of the Raper-Lambert family, however, the Indian Office had to review the decision. Once again, the issue of the Eastern Band's right to set blood quantum requirements framed the discussion. If the Taylor-Hardins had even a drop of Indian blood, would this not make them Indian and entitled to benefits as Cherokees? In the end, the decision was put aside for future enrollment debates since disagreement among federal officials made disposition of the case impossible at the time.[87] By tabling the issue, the Indian Office revealed its reluctance to accept the judgments of the tribal council and even the government-appointed enrolling committee when it came to issues of white individuals who claimed Indian blood. This wavering on the status of supposed mixed-blood Cherokees contrasted with federal decisions to exclude mixed-blood Mississippi Choctaws from the Choctaw Nation rolls, which reveals how different tribal circumstances and legal contexts could lead to vastly different decisions on who counted as "Indian."

Ancestry was important, but blood alone did not make someone an Eastern Band citizen. The tribal council also restricted citizenship to those Cherokees who had participated in rebuilding the Band's land base in North Carolina. Unlike most reservations, tribal citizens had purchased the Qualla Boundary from non-Indians and won fee simple title to the land in 1874. The tribal council argued that only those Cherokees with "pecuniary interest" in the land should have rights as tribal citizens. To claim citizenship, council members insisted, an applicant "must be a resident, actually or constructively, of the Indian community, reestablished and rehabilitated mainly through the efforts of Colonel Wm. H. Thomas, occupying the Southwestern part of the State of North Carolina."[88] Only in this way could applicants prove that they were communal owners of the tribal land base. In particular, they or their ancestors had to have been present on the land at the time of the 1874 court decision. This stipulation lent legal weight to the Band's residency criterion through the language of the court decision that limited ownership of the Qualla Boundary to Cherokees in North Carolina. The decision to include "pecuniary interest" through residency as one of the criteria for inclusion illustrated that the Eastern Band conceived of itself as more than an ethnic group or racial minority in the South. It was a political organization with economic interests. It was not enough to claim racial heritage as Cherokee; individuals also had to prove their political citizenship in and economic ties to the Band.

Residency requirements added another legal twist to belonging, but they also contained a more traditional cultural element. On the Qualla Boundary and in the Snowbird community, Eastern Band citizens gathered for celebrations, festivals, and games. They spoke the Cherokee language and they taught their children Cherokee stories. In the presence of other Cherokees, children culturally became members of the community. If individuals lived away from the Qualla Boundary and the surrounding Cherokee communities in western North Carolina, they failed to learn the behavior patterns and life ways that defined Cherokee identity. Such people might have been racially "Indian" in the eyes of white America, but in the eyes of other Cherokees, they became "white Indians" who no longer thought nor acted like community members. Residency requirements ensured that only individuals with a cultural connection to the Eastern Band were eligible for tribal citizenship. The tribal council hoped that this stipulation, like the blood quantum requirement, would preserve the Band's resources for those Cherokees who were socially and culturally connected to the Eastern Band community.

Mid-twentieth-century anthropologists identified the "Harmony Ethic" as characteristic of the Eastern Band. According to researchers, this ethic "provided the regulatory norms for the early Cherokee but certain aspects have survived to the present as part of the traditional socialization process."[89] This worldview, or ethos, passed through the generations, emphasized avoidance of confrontations and conflicts. Cherokees socialized through the Harmony Ethic avoided social or economic competition and practiced generosity.[90] "Traditional" Cherokees saw avoidance of conflict as key to maintaining a cohesive society. Because white America's emphasis on individualism and competition so directly contradicted the tenets of the Harmony Ethic, it was nearly impossible for individuals born away from the core community to internalize these Cherokee ideals.

Residency on or near the Qualla Boundary also promoted the acquisition of Cherokee cultural knowledge. Stories, told by parents, grandparents, and community elders to Cherokee children, encouraged a distinct Cherokee worldview that was not always available to people who lived away from the core community. In the late nineteenth century, ethnographer James Mooney recorded a number of these stories. As Mooney noted in his 1900 publication, *Myths of the Cherokees*, Cherokee stories included sacred myths, animal stories, local legends, and historical traditions.[91] These tales taught Cherokee children how to live and connected their identity to the landscape of western North

Carolina. Through stories, Cherokees learned the history of their people and their distinctive place as citizens of the Eastern Band.

Cherokee stories embodied particular worldviews and highlighted ap-propriate forms of behavior. An account of the first man and woman, Kana'ti (the Lucky Hunter) and Selu (Corn), for example, provided the Cherokees with a framework for understanding appropriate roles for men and women.[92] Although by the late nineteenth century Cherokee gender roles had shifted as missionaries and reformers encouraged men to farm and women to con-fine themselves to domestic roles, the story of Kana'ti and Selu and their gen-dered tasks of hunting and farming persisted as a model for Cherokee male and female responsibilities and behavior. In 1882, a news article reported that Cherokee men "work in their fields and do farm work generally," but that they did so "in company with the women."[93] Community members turned to sto-ries to affirm their sense of gender and place in Qualla society.

In addition to teaching children appropriate behavior, many Cherokee sto-ries directly connected the Indians to their landscape.[94] As Mooney explained, "almost every prominent rock and mountain, every deep bend in the river, in the old Cherokee country has its accompanying legend." History was writ-ten into the landscape. A bend in the Tuckasegee River in Swain County, for example, was known as "Gakati'yi," or "Place of setting free." This location recalled the release of captives the Cherokees had taken in war, an act of gen-erosity worth commemorating. "Dunidu'lalunyi," "Where they made arrows," on Straight Creek, a headstream of the Oconaluftee River, was the place where Shawnee warriors had stopped to prepare arrows to use against the Cherokees. It reminded Cherokees to beware of enemies in their midst. Another place on Soco Creek, "Skwan'digu'gun'yi," "Where the Spaniard is in the water," evoked an attack the Cherokees made on a Spanish war party, probably in the sixteenth century. According to oral tradition, the Cherokees threw one of the soldiers into the stream.[95] By walking the trails of their ancestors and listening to the stories of their elders, Cherokee children learned the history of their people and their place in the cycle of life and time. Such knowledge could not be learned from a distance: it was immediate, powerful, and intimately tied to their particular surroundings in western North Carolina.

In addition to stories, nineteenth- and twentieth-century ethnographers and anthropologists recorded a number of uniquely Cherokee folkways, such as interpreting ant hills to predict rain, noting that death followed a large catch of fish, and recognizing that a red northern sky warned of danger.[96] Healing knowledge, such as using spider web to stop a cut from bleeding or rubbing hot coals on the skin to relieve soreness, also came from a deep reservoir of shared Cherokee beliefs, as did collecting, preparing, and applying medicinal plants such as liverwort, ginseng, hoarhound, and nightshade.[97] Technical knowledge came from members of the Cherokee community, but so did faith in the efficacy of traditional medicine. Adhering to traditional ideas about illness that included supernatural elements, Cherokees believed that sickness could not be treated with herbs alone but also had to be healed by spiritual means. Mooney thought that through ceremonies and prayers, medicine men comforted the ailing and "the effect thus produced upon the mind of the sick man undoubtedly reacts favorably upon his physical organization."[98] Cherokees believed that the spiritual power of the medicine healed them, an idea the community reinforced even while outsiders cast aspersions on it.

In many ways the material culture and foodways of Cherokees resembled those of their non-Indian neighbors. They all lived in log or clapboard houses, wore calico dresses or overalls, and ate hominy and pork. But Cherokees also retained lifeways that predated European contact. Most mountain women, for example, made baskets for storage, gathering foodstuffs, or shopping. According to historian Sarah H. Hill, Cherokee basket makers adopted styles and even materials from their white neighbors for their own use and for the market, but one kind of basket remained uniquely Cherokee—those made of river cane, especially the double-weave ones.[99] Cutting and stripping the cane, dying the strips, and weaving the double-walled baskets expressed a Cherokee identity even as the market for baskets shifted to oak for utilitarian containers, and honeysuckle, which could be woven in decorative patterns that tourists preferred.[100] Similarly, Cherokees ate many of the same foods as non-Indian mountain people. Indeed, foodways represented a cultural blending with Indians contributing corn (including grits and hominy), beans, and wild game and Europeans wheat and livestock. But some foods were exclusively Cherokee. Sochan, for example, was a green that formed part of a complex of wild foods that Cherokees gathered seasonally.[101] Children who did not grow up in a Cherokee community would not understand how apparently mundane things such as cane baskets and wild greens set Cherokees apart from non-Cherokees and reinforced their identity.

Participation in community festivals and celebrations was a more obvious marker of belonging. The Cherokees held the Green Corn Dance, for example, every fall to celebrate the harvest.[102] Anthropologist Frank G. Speck explained that the sponsor was an individual Cherokee who wished to make "a ceremonial donation from which he gains prestige and spiritual benefit, as do the participants." The dance itself lasted a day and a night, and Cherokee men and women performed gender-specific tasks. Men danced to the rhythm of a gourd rattle and carried guns that they discharged at specific intervals. Women performed the "Meal Dance" in which they sang and "shuffle[d] with short steps." Men and women danced concurrently and sang stanzas in response to one another, reflecting the Cherokees' cosmology of a gender-balanced world. After

Figure 4.4 Distinctive Cherokee crafts like basket weaving and pottery making helped Eastern Band tribal citizens distinguish their identity from other mountain people in western North Carolina. In this photograph, two Cherokee women demonstrated their pottery-making techniques for ethnographer James Mooney. Photographer: James Mooney. Date: 1888. Courtesy of the National Anthropological Archives, Smithsonian Institution (negative 1033).

performing, everyone feasted together on a meal prepared by the women of the dance's home settlement. The next morning, the Cherokees performed the "corn rite" to ensure a fruitful harvest in the coming year.[103] People gathered from miles around during these festivities to meet friends and neighbors, share food and gossip, and reaffirm their sense of community.

During Booger Dances, Cherokees went even further to assert their separate identity as a people. Young men dressed up in masks representing outsiders, including whites, blacks, and Indians from other tribes. With eyes and moustaches drawn in heavy black paint, woodchuck fur glued to the forehead and chin for hair, exaggerated carved mouths, and red painted cheeks, these masks highlighted the otherness of non-Cherokees.[104] Cherokees believed that the dance was bestowed on them in ancient times by a monster named Stone Coat, who foretold the coming of whites, blacks, and foreign tribes to Cherokee lands. Stone Coat gave the Cherokees the Booger Dance as a means of counteracting the "social and physical contamination" that the arrival of outsiders brought on the Indians.[105] During the dance, the masked figures made obscene gestures toward Cherokee women and chased them with mock phalluses made of gourds or wrapped fabric. They portrayed these others as "awkward, ridiculous, horrid, erotic, lewd and menacing."[106] Through performing this cathartic dance that both recalled earlier invasions of Cherokee lands and mocked the vulgar behavior of the invaders, the Cherokees evoked a shared history that united Eastern Band citizens. The dance also emphasized the survival of the Cherokees despite external threats.

Stickball games served as an additional point of community gathering and as an acceptable outlet for competitive impulses. These games, which were similar to the matches played by the Mississippi Choctaws, involved as many as sixty players and occurred several times a year.[107] Two teams vied to score goals by using rackets to toss a ball through opposing goals erected on a cleared field. The team that first succeeded in throwing the ball through the opponent's goal twelve times won.[108] The games were rough, but they provided young men with an opportunity to show off their physical prowess. The sport included its own rituals, with players holding all night ceremonial dances just before their games to ensure success on the playing field.[109] Stickball united community members of all backgrounds. As the agency superintendent reported to the Indian Office in 1909, "both full blood and mixed blood, educated and uneducated attend the ball games, as well as the dances."[110] By participating in the games, understanding the rituals that preceded them, and meeting up with fellow spectators or players, Cherokees affirmed their sense of belonging to the Eastern Band.

Recognizing the importance of a shared culture, the tribal council denied citizenship to the children of tribal citizens who had moved away from North Carolina and married non-Indians. In 1910, they formalized this decision in a resolution. Although the parents retained their birthrights as Cherokees, the tribal council viewed their children as outsiders, particularly if one of their parents was non-Cherokee. The council argued that "the children born of such marriages are reared in ignorance of the tribe and its language, customs, and traditions, and where such families adopt and accept the customs of the people among whom they live, and take advantage of the nearby schools, churches, and other public institutions that such children are not members of the tribe in fact and are not entitled to enrollment."[111]

The tribal council decided that the child of enrolled tribal citizen Henrietta Crow Batson fit this description. Batson had attended the Carlisle Indian Industrial School and married a white man in Pennsylvania. There she gave birth to a son, Alfred G. Batson. Although her son had one-eighth "Cherokee blood," he was born away from the tribal community and had no "association or affiliation with any member of the Eastern Band of Cherokee Indians, except with his mother, and with his grandmother, Laura J. Smith, on the occasion of

Figure 4.5 Stickball games brought Cherokees together and provided young men with an opportunity to show off their physical prowess. In this photograph, Cherokee men and women gathered for pre-game rituals on the Qualla Boundary. Photographer: James Mooney. Date: 1888. Courtesy of the National Anthropological Archives, Smithsonian Institution (BAE GN 1039 A).

a brief visit to the Qualla Boundary when he was about two years old." Living away from the core Cherokee community and raised by "a White man and citizen of the United States," Alfred "acquired the political status of his father." The tribal council asked to strike his name from the tribal rolls.[112]

The rejection of children with one non-Indian parent born away from the tribe extended equally to the offspring of Cherokee women and Cherokee men. The tribal council barred Henrietta Crow Batson's son, but it also rejected the four children of Noah Ed Smith. Like Batson, Smith was "a regularly enrolled and recognized member of the Eastern Band of Cherokee Indians." After attending the Hampton Institute in Virginia, he married a white woman and "never returned since to establish a residence in the State of North Carolina." Because his children "were born in a distant state and have never resided at any time with the Eastern Band of Cherokee Indians or affiliated with them in any way," the tribal council denied them rights in the Band.[113] In the view of the tribal council, the blood ties of these children did not matter as much as their social and cultural affiliation with the core Cherokee community.

Although residency on or near the Qualla Boundary suggested participation in the core Cherokee community, geographical proximity did not guarantee inclusion in the Eastern Band. In addition to residency requirements, the tribal council insisted that applicants prove their "association and affiliation" with the Band. Unlike residency, association and affiliation were difficult to prove, but the tribal council identified certain markers as good indicators of a person's connection to the Eastern Band. Special Agent Charles L. Davis noted that "one of the principal tests of affiliation we regarded [was] that of marriage." If a family had not married individuals from the core Cherokee community for seventy-five or a hundred years, obviously no affiliation existed.[114] For the Cherokees, marriage established kin ties. Without these familial bonds with other members of the core Cherokee community, individuals lost their Cherokee identity.

Another test was language. Although knowledge of English increased as Cherokee children received Euro-American educations and attended boarding schools, most core Cherokee families used the Cherokee language in their homes.[115] In addition to preserving their spoken language, Cherokees also retained their unique written language that used a syllabary, invented by Sequoyah in 1821. Medicine men recorded their sacred knowledge in formulas written in the syllabary and at the Baptist and Methodist churches that dotted the reservation, community members read Cherokee Bibles and sang from Cherokee hymnals while ministers preached in the Cherokee language.[116] In the late nineteenth century, James Mooney observed that the syllabary was "in daily use among the common people."[117] This knowledge continued into the twentieth century. As one government agent wrote in 1920, "the younger members of the tribe, are, as a rule, able to speak and write the English language." Nevertheless, "the Cherokee tongue is commonly used by them and practically all of them are able to write the Cherokee language, using the Sequoyah alphabet."[118] If an applicant spoke, read, and wrote Cherokee, it suggested that he or she enjoyed a close association with the core community.

"The question of home surroundings" served as a third indicator of affiliation. The enrolling agents and tribal council members asked if families applying for citizenship lived "in an Indian community, [sent] their children to Indian schools, attend[ed] the Indian councils and tribal meetings, [made] frequent trips to the agency," and participated in the political life of the Eastern Band by holding "tribal offices, etc."[119] As Chief John A. Tahquette explained, "The officers of the Band considers the Eastern Band the people who live here together, associate together, elect their officers and take an interest in the affairs of the Eastern Band." The tribal council wanted to grant citizenship rights only to individuals who actively participated in the Band's social and political life. They insisted that citizens should have a stake in the survival of the Eastern Band of Cherokee Indians as a sovereign nation and they objected to individuals who took, in Tahquette's words, "no interest whatever in Band affairs unless you call Band affairs the time when we go to make a roll."[120] This stance was not only about reserving Cherokee resources for core members of the Cherokee community, it also was about protecting Cherokee political rights for individuals who cared about the Band's future. Without its economic base, the Band's political independence would be meaningless. If individuals with no interest in Eastern Band affairs claimed a significant portion of tribal resources, the Band's political structure would collapse.

Despite the tribal council's efforts to limit Band citizenship to core members of the Eastern Cherokee community, numerous individuals from across the South insisted that they too had rights as Eastern Band citizens. A census of Eastern Cherokees completed in 1909 by Guion Miller, a federally appointed lawyer, encouraged many of these applicants. This roll stemmed from a 1905 Court of Claims decision that granted the "Eastern Cherokees" a sum of over $4 million. Arising from an 1893 agreement made by the federal government with the Cherokee Nation in exchange for a land cession in the West, this fund promised to reimburse the Cherokees for everything due to them from treaties dating back to 1817 but wrongly withheld.[121] According to the court, Cherokees east and west of the Mississippi were entitled to per capita payments arising from this fund. On May 28, 1906, the Court of Claims directed the secretary of the interior to determine eligible recipients by developing rolls of all Cherokees by blood.[122] Unlike Eastern Band citizenship that the Council Roll and Churchill Roll had tried to establish, the Guion Miller Roll did not consider Indians as political citizens of a tribe but grounded their identity in their biological descent from Cherokees who had been subject to the removal treaty of 1835. Even if an individual had little or no contact with the twentieth-century Cherokee nations west of the Mississippi and in North Carolina, they had a right to a share in the funds based on trace amounts of Cherokee "blood."

In theory, the Guion Miller Roll of Eastern Cherokees had no legal bearing on the citizenship of the Eastern Band. In the midst of drawing up their Council Roll and protesting extraneous names included on the Churchill Roll, however, the Eastern Band found itself overwhelmed by a surge of new applicants who claimed tribal citizenship "by blood" in the same way that they had on the Guion Miller Roll. When the tribal council denied their rights, applicants hired attorneys. Miller himself got involved in the process and contested the right of the tribal council to set citizenship criteria for the Eastern Band. His true interest lay in the profits he reaped by representing Cherokees claimants and helping them to win a share of the tribe's assets. Like the attorneys of Crews & Cantwell, who were scouring the South for Mississippi Choctaw descendants at around the same time, Miller charged his clients for processing their applications and actively encouraged as many people as possible to apply for Eastern Band citizenship. In later years, some Eastern Band citizens scorned such individuals as "five-dollar Indians."[123]

Lawyers representing applicants unabashedly attacked Eastern Band sovereignty by insisting that the tribal council had no authority to determine citizenship criteria, especially when it came to blood quantum requirements. Miller argued that "membership in a tribe is a fundamental right, just as citizenship in a state is," and that only the US Constitution could fix this right of citizenship.[124] Representing 600 or 700 Cherokee claimants, Miller and his colleagues first appealed to Special Agent McPherson's enrollment committee and demanded new hearings for their clients. When the committee recommended that most of these individuals be stricken from the tribal rolls, the lawyers protested that they had "upon one flimsy pretext or another struck from the rolls the names of almost a third of the members of the Band." Unwilling to accept the decisions of the committee or the tribal council, Miller and his associates turned to the commissioner of Indian affairs and succeeded in getting more than 200 of their clients enrolled. Still not satisfied, the lawyers traveled to Washington, DC, to make their case before the assistant secretary of the interior. After examining McPherson's report, the assistant secretary declared it was "too partisan to be used even as a brief in the cases."[125] The Interior Department rendered no decision and enrollment was left at a standstill.

As enrollment debates dragged on into the late 1910s, Cherokee claimants and the Eastern Band grew frustrated with the inaction of the federal government, particularly in regard to the postponed per capita timber payments. Eager to gain permanent control over Cherokee resources, some Cherokees, including members of the tribal council, pushed the US Congress to consider an allotment bill for the Qualla Boundary. On November 6, 1919, the tribal council passed a resolution providing for the final disposition of the Eastern Band's affairs. Councilmen agreed to put corporately owned tribal lands in trust with the federal government in preparation for allotment. According to the council, "the time has been reached . . . when the identity of the membership of the Eastern Band of Cherokees will be lost and destroyed unless final and decisive action is taken to determine the rights of all persons claiming such membership."[126] By finally establishing who belonged to the tribe and clarifying the rights of citizens to tribal lands and resources, the council hoped to protect Eastern Band identity and the individual rights of citizens while essentially dissolving the tribe. Any delay would mean an inflated tribal roll corresponding to a reduced share of resources for each individual tribal citizen.

In response to their request, Congress passed an act in 1924 that promised to bring resolution to the Eastern Band's enrollment debates by sending a new federal official, Fred A. Baker, to western North Carolina to compile a final roll of Cherokees. Baker began his task in November 1926, but it took two years for him to wade through applications, listen to witness testimony, and render decisions on enrollment cases. He began by recording the names of recognized tribal citizens. Upon completing this task, he started processing the claims of unrecognized applicants. This effort put him at odds with the tribal council. The promise of a new roll and the allotment of Eastern Band land had spurred thousands of people to apply for tribal citizenship. Claimants filed 3,833 separate applications, involving 11,979 individuals.[127] The tribal council sent a committee to enrollment hearings to represent the tribe and render opinions on the claims of applicants. Although it approved Baker's findings on 1,924 cases, this committee protested the enrollment of 1,222 applicants who represented roughly twenty family groups.[128] In the eyes of the tribal council, these applicants were not legitimate Eastern Band citizens and they protested their enrollment using the same kinship and cultural criteria—bolstered by legal arguments of "blood" and "residency"—that they had employed during the earlier enrollment controversies.

Despite the tribe's protests, Baker and his agents were not inclined to accommodate Cherokee requirements for enrollment. As Baker noted in his final report, "The right to membership in a tribe of Indians, particularly where there is property involved, is a substantial right. It has a money value to the individuals concerned."[129] Concerned about the rights of individual claimants rather than about the rights of the tribe as a political body about to be dissolved by allotment, Baker insisted that the prerogative to define tribal citizenship ultimately lay with the federal government.

Of particular consternation to the Eastern Band tribal council, the federal government ruled against limiting citizenship to those with one-sixteenth degree or more Indian blood. Although officials recognized that applicants had to have some Cherokee ancestry to be eligible for citizenship, Congress denied the right of the Band to set blood quantum limits approved by the state of North Carolina rather than by the Interior Department. The Act of June 4, 1924, specifically barred the state law that ratified the tribe's criteria from consideration during enrollment, and Baker included numerous individuals of one-thirty-second degree or less Indian blood. From the Cherokee perspective, however, neither North Carolina nor the United States had the right to establish blood quantum criteria. They asserted that only the tribal council had the sovereign authority to set qualifications for citizenship in the Eastern Band.[130] In spite of this, Baker continued to list individuals of questionable ancestry on his roll.

When it came to what Baker referred to as "the vexatious question of association and affiliation and recognition," the Interior Department also overruled the tribal council. The problem, Baker pointed out, was that no one had ever defined the precise amount of association and affiliation necessary to entitle an applicant to enrollment.[131] Trying to make legal sense of the issue, Baker turned to late nineteenth-century congressional acts and court cases—mostly from western tribes—that dealt with the issue of individual Indians' separation from their tribal communities. These statutes, made during the height of the allotment era, encouraged Indians to break their tribal relations by guaranteeing them tribal property rights even if they left their reservations and adopted non-Indian lifestyles.[132] Baker's liberal understanding of affiliation, association, and recognition undermined the tribal council's ability to restrict political and economic rights to individuals associated with the core Cherokee community.

Although federal officials claimed that their objectivity gave them the right to interfere in tribal citizenship debates, they were not unbiased mediators. Indeed, many of the decisions rendered by the Interior Department were highly skewed, especially when it came to questions of race. For individuals of mixed Indian-white ancestry, the department concluded that "appearances are deceptive and inconclusive." They asserted that it was "common knowledge" that some members of an Indian family resembled their white ancestors, while others inherited the physical characteristics of their Indian forebears.[133] Even if these individuals looked white and lived in white communities, evidence of or claims to Indian ancestry precluded them from a pure white racial identity. Therefore, the government was more willing to grant them citizenship in the Eastern Band where they could escape the legal strictures imposed by the South's largely biracial system of segregation.

Individuals of black-Indian ancestry, on the other hand, fell more neatly into the era's black-white binary and government officials comfortably ignored their Indian ancestry in favor of a black racial identity. In his decision on the family of Harrison Coleman, Baker wrote, "It is evident from the appearance of the members of this family that they are largely of negro blood. They have intermarried exclusively among the members of the negro race, and while some them show faint traces of Indian blood by their physical appearance, they are predominantly of negro ancestry."[134] Baker could have made the same statement for a number of enrolled families—exchanging the word "negro" for "white"—yet he accepted white Indians on the roll while rejecting black Indians.

Baker also more readily enrolled the illegitimate "mixed-blood" Cherokee children of white mothers than the children of black mothers. Baker proclaimed the relationship of Rebecca Coleman and Kah-soo-yo-keh as "merely intermittent and casual." Therefore, Harrison Coleman, an illegitimate child, followed the status of his mother. In contrast, Baker deemed the relationship between James Taylor and Betsy Parker that produced Elizabeth Hardin "tantamount to a legal marriage."[135] Baker's decision to validate Elizabeth Hardin's patrilineal Cherokee ancestry strengthened her claims to citizenship, despite her technical illegitimacy. He rejected Harrison Coleman, who probably had one-half Cherokee blood quantum, but accepted Elizabeth Hardin, who may have had no Cherokee ancestry at all. These contradictions highlighted the overarching fallacy of the Interior Department's assumption that federal officials would make more objective enrollment decisions than interested tribal citizens. Although they did not have a stake in tribal assets as did the Cherokees, these officials had a stake in racial politics—with lasting effects for the tribe.

As members of the tribal council agonized about their inability to defend their citizenship against the Interior Department's claims to authority, they searched for other ways to protect Cherokee property. They had agreed to the allotment of their lands in 1919, but after seeing the results of the roll, the council appealed to Washington against proceeding further.[136] The tribal council believed that if allotment went ahead as planned, the land would be so divided as to become practically useless. Councilmen begged the secretary of the interior to suspend final action on the disputed Baker Roll, which, they complained, "appears to permit almost anybody of Cherokee blood, no matter how small the degree, to become enrolled." To prevent these individuals from gaining access to tribal resources, they boldly asserted that they did *not want to be so allotted.*"[137]

In response to their letter, the commissioner of Indian affairs wrote to the Band and requested "more definite information relative to the prevalent attitudes of the Eastern Band of Cherokee Indians regarding the congressional enrollment and allotment act of June 4, 1924." The tribal council replied by entreating the federal government to continue to hold their lands in trust. They also insisted that the Baker Roll be completed as approved by the tribal council with just 1,924 tribal citizens. Appealing once more for justice, the Cherokees maintained that it had been the consistent policy of the tribal council to deny citizenship to any individual with less than one-sixteenth degree of Eastern Cherokee blood. They protested that they would never have agreed to placing their corporately held lands in trust had it not been for the blood quantum requirement. They blamed the omission of this provision from the 1924 act on the attorneys for the applicants.[138] The Cherokees demanded just resolution of the issue and insisted that "the objection of the Council should have been sufficient to cause the rejection of a claimant."[139]

Although the Interior Department was unwilling to reverse its decisions on enrollments, officials made some concessions to the Band. By this time, Indian policy was changing in Washington. The 1928 publication of the Meriam Report had revealed the disastrous effects of allotment on western tribes. In addition, a new generation of reformers, led by soon-to-be-appointed Commissioner of Indian Affairs John Collier, argued for a full-scale congressional investigation of Indian policy and suggested that tribes should have more control over their affairs.[140] In a nod to these shifts in federal Indian policy, the Interior Department agreed to amend the Act of 1924.[141] In 1931, Congress followed the Department's recommendation and passed an act that suspended the allotment of the Qualla Boundary and provided that, from then on, no person with less than one-sixteenth Eastern Cherokee blood could enroll in the Band.[142] This compromise validated federal authority over the Band in the government's previous decisions but recognized the right of the tribal council to have a voice in citizenship debates. Although the individuals listed on the Baker Roll remained regardless of their blood quantum, in the future the government observed the tribe's own requirements. Moreover, Eastern Band lands remained intact for the tribe. The Cherokees may not have won the battle, but ultimately they won the war by preserving their land and their sovereignty.

By protesting against fraudulent claims, contesting enrollments, hiring lawyers, and writing fervent appeals to the Interior Department, the Eastern Band of Cherokee Indians was able to forestall allotment and wait out the era's assimilationist agenda until federal Indian policy shifted in its favor. The federal government's 1931 revision of the 1924 act recognized the Band's right to set its own citizenship criteria. Later in the twentieth century, the Eastern Band took advantage of this sovereign power. In the mid-1950s, a group of culturally conservative Cherokees known as the Qualla Association sent representatives to Washington and called for a purging of the tribal roll of citizens with less than one-sixteenth Cherokee ancestry. In response, Congress authorized a revision of the Baker Roll. The new roll, begun in 1959, specified a minimum of one-thirty-second degree Cherokee blood. After some fractious internal debates, however, the tribal council returned the minimum to one-sixteenth degree in 1963.[143] From then on, individuals had to prove sufficient blood quantum to qualify for Eastern Band citizenship.

In recent years, the Eastern Band's venture into the world of gaming has revived tribal enrollment controversies. Harrah's Cherokee Casino opened in 1997, following on the heels of a profitable tribal bingo parlor established in the early 1980s.[144] By 2005, the casino attracted up to 4 million tourists a year to the Qualla Boundary and provided the Band with much-needed revenue, including funds for health care, education, and housing. In addition, the Eastern Band began paying enrolled citizens small biannual per capita payments.[145] In the same way that money from timber and land sales put an economic premium on tribal citizenship in the early twentieth century, casino profits gave those enrolled in the Eastern Band "monetary perks." As in the past, this development raised concerns about who could legitimately claim a share of tribal assets. Some Cherokees worried that over the years "outsiders" had "finagled enrollment status." These fears magnified when official Eastern

Band enrollment spiked by nearly 700 new citizens in 1995, the year after the secretary of the interior approved the Band's gaming compact with the state of North Carolina.[146]

In a 2002 referendum, 57 percent of Eastern Band voters gave the tribal council permission to begin an audit of the Band's citizenship rolls.[147] The purpose of the audit, as one tribal citizen explained, was "to ascertain the validity of people whose names appear on our tribal rolls" and to weed out imposters.[148] Begun in 2005, the final enrollment audit was completed in October 2009, when the Falmouth Institute—the external agency hired to go over the records—submitted its report to the tribal council.[149] According to the agency's findings, 303 people listed on the rolls had no clear link to the Baker Roll; a few of these individuals were adopted and had no biological tie to enrolled Cherokees, some had ancestors that the auditors could not locate on the Baker Roll, and others lacked sufficient documentation, such as parents' birth certificates, to verify their lineage. The auditors identified another 629 people with the "incorrect blood quantum." Of these, around fifty had a revised blood degree lower than one-sixteenth, which disqualified them from tribal citizenship.[150]

The findings of the Falmouth Institute revived old debates about the meaning of Cherokee identity and Eastern Band citizenship. At community club meetings held across the Qualla Boundary, tribal citizens engaged in "spirited discussion[s]" about how the tribal council should act on the report.[151] Some used the public debates as an opportunity to air long-held grievances about federal interference in the construction of tribal rolls. Tribal council member Terri Henry, for example, pointed out that at the time of the Baker Roll's construction, "the tribe felt its membership should be a smaller group than the one the federal government recognized."[152] Others, however, protested that the Baker Roll "was actually intended to disenfranchise community members from our community and our property." By accepting the Baker Roll as the legal standard for tribal belonging, tribal citizen B. Lynne Harlan contended, the Eastern Band had betrayed "the basic principle of family and community."[153] Families that stood to lose tribal citizenship as a result of the audit were particularly dismayed. Some even took out large advertisements in the tribal newspaper "to set the record straight," prove their family's lineage, and to warn other Cherokees to "keep [their] guard up" since their "family may be next on their list."[154]

The tribal council, meanwhile, responded to the audit by passing an amendment that prevented any new citizens, except infants under three years old and youths aged eighteen to nineteen, from enrolling in the Band until the audit process ended.[155] The Band also required new applicants to submit a certified DNA test to prove their parentage.[156] In addition to tightening enrollment procedures, the tribal council also discussed what to do about people deemed illegitimately enrolled. What would happen to the property and per capita payments of these individuals? Although the Eastern Band's lawyers confirmed that the council had the ability "to take away the right of per capita payments from disenrolled persons," it was less clear whether the tribe could expel them from the Qualla Boundary or repossess their land without providing compensation.[157] Tribal lawyers warned that there was little legal precedent for such actions.[158] Some representatives, like Tommye Saunooke from the Painttown community, cautioned the tribal council not to be "hasty with the disenrollment hearings." In his view, the tribe needed to thoroughly review all available documents before reaching a decision on contested citizens. Others worried about their responsibilities to their constituents, who were "definitely wanting to move forward with it."[159] The fallout from the enrollment audit is ongoing. As of yet, it has not led the Eastern Band to change its citizenship criteria from those laid out in 1963, only to ponder how best to enforce those requirements moving forward.

Today the Eastern Band of Cherokee Indians sets two major criteria for citizenship: the ability to trace a direct lineal ancestor to the Baker Roll of 1924 and proof of at least one-sixteenth degree Cherokee blood for individuals born after 1963.[160] Blood quantum is calculated on the basis of the degree of Cherokee Indian blood recorded by the Baker enrolling committee, not on modern DNA or blood tests, which cannot provide such information. DNA testing is used, however, to confirm descent from enrolled parents, which eliminates problems presented by illegitimacy and helps guard against enrollment fraud. Citizens may adopt children from outside the tribe, but these children are not considered Band citizens unless they biologically descend from enrolled tribal citizens. Although a tribal resolution in 1977 extended citizenship to individuals adopted from other federally recognized tribes, in 1996 the Band rescinded this exception, perhaps in response to fears about inflated tribal numbers following the casino compact.[161] Only proven descent from citizens listed on the Baker Roll along with a sufficient Eastern Cherokee blood quantum permits tribal enrollment. Currently, there are more than 14,600 enrolled tribal citizens, of whom approximately 8,100 reside on the Qualla Boundary.[162]

The struggle of the Eastern Band of Cherokee Indians to define citizenship in the late nineteenth and early twentieth centuries reflected its unique economic situation and political position as a state-chartered corporation and a federally recognized tribe. The sale of tribal timber and the threat of allotment put an economic value on citizenship, leading outsiders to demand rights as tribal citizens based on alleged claims to Cherokee blood. Faced with a flood of applicants and determined to protect its economic interests and political independence from non-Cherokees, the Eastern Band tribal council developed enrollment criteria that limited citizenship to the core Cherokee community. Modifying traditional concepts of kinship and cultural affiliation, the Cherokees developed blood quantum and residency requirements for those they considered true Cherokees. An ongoing federal presence, however, made this task more difficult. Not only did the Cherokees have to decide who deserved citizenship, but they also had to justify those decisions to outsiders.

The citizenship decisions the Cherokees made in the 1910s and the federal rulings they protested in the 1920s factored into the development of the Band's modern citizenship criteria. Tribal citizenship debates were central to Eastern Band efforts to protect Cherokee land, resources, and political identity in North Carolina. By developing legalistic citizenship criteria, defending its decisions, and protesting the interference of federal officials, the Eastern Band of Cherokee Indians was able to survive in the South. The Eastern Band experience reveals that despite the power of the federal government over recognized tribes, Indians have not submitted passively. Instead of allowing outsiders to control its tribal rolls, the Eastern Band of Cherokee Indians demanded the right to determine its citizenry, defended its tribal sovereignty, and ultimately won.

5

Nation Building and
Self-Determination

The Seminole Tribe of Florida and the Miccosukee
Tribe of Indians of Florida

On July 16, 1953, W. O. Roberts, the area director of the Muskogee Office of the Bureau of Indian Affairs, wrote to Kenneth A. Marmon, the superintendent of the Seminole Agency in Florida, to discuss plans for the termination of federal responsibilities to the Seminole Indians. He needed to know whether the tribe had an official political structure in order to implement termination, but he ran into a problem. "With your Indians living on three reservations, two of which support the cattle program and with some Indians living along the Trail," Roberts explained to Marmon, "the composition of the Tribe is rather complex, thus raising a question of the relative rights of the members in the overall tribal interests."[1] Indeed, the Florida Seminoles had an intricate society complicated by linguistic differences, internal political divisions, and divergent responses to relations with the federal government. Although kin ties and clan identities instilled a sense of community belonging in the Indians, the Florida Seminoles disagreed about the political future of their tribe. Their challenge was not only to define *who* belonged to the tribe but also to determine to *what* tribe they belonged.

A remnant population like the Eastern Cherokees and Mississippi Choctaws, the Florida Seminoles had isolated themselves in the Everglades and Big Cypress Swamp after the Second and Third Seminole Wars, which had sent the majority of the tribe west in the mid-nineteenth century. In the years that followed, the Indians who remained in Florida devised strategies to deal with the threats posed by outsiders. They lived in scattered households that formed loosely linked bands, and they limited contact with white and black people, in part by developing a unique racial philosophy. Changes in Florida

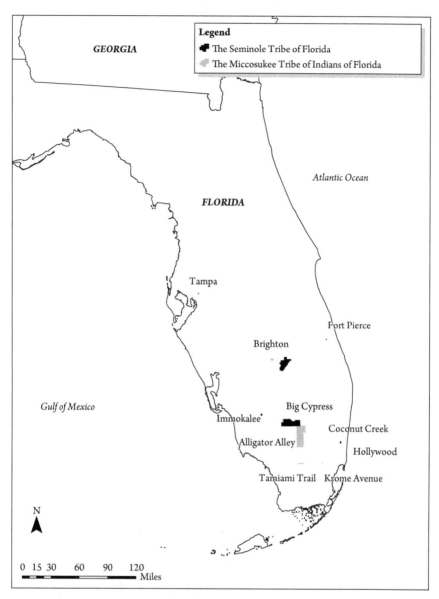

Figure 5.1 Beginning in the late nineteenth century, white allies of the Seminoles pressured both the state and federal governments to set aside reservations for the Florida Indians. By 1930, these reserved lands comprised the Brighton, Big Cypress, and Dania (later renamed Hollywood) reservations and contained more than 123,000 acres, although this acreage was later reduced when the federal government created the Everglades National Park. Since the late 1970s, the Seminole Tribe of Florida has added three additional reservations at Immokalee, Tampa, and Fort Pierce, as well as trust land at Coconut Creek. Today the Seminole Tribe of Florida lands consist of more than 89,000 acres. Although the Miccosukees initially resisted moving to reservations, they eventually gained reservation land as well along the Tamiami Trail, Alligator Alley, and Krome Avenue. In addition, the tribe holds off-reservation trust land near the Brighton Reservation and in the northwest corner of the Big Cypress Reservation. Today the Miccosukee Tribe of Indians of Florida lands consist of nearly 75,000 acres. Map prepared by Christian Adams.

over the course of the late nineteenth and early twentieth centuries, however, brought the Seminoles into increased contact with white America. Exposure to outsiders forced the Seminoles to re-conceptualize notions of belonging. By the 1950s, they had acquired state and federal reservation lands as well as a superintendent from the Bureau of Indian Affairs.[2] Federal officials encouraged the Seminoles to think about the formal political organization of their community. Some Seminoles believed an official tribal government and federal recognition would protect their interests in Florida, while others preferred to keep their loosely organized structure of bands led by medicine men. The political decisions Seminoles made in the mid-twentieth century reflected their history in Florida and the diverse nature of their society. Ultimately, divergent political visions led to a split in the tribe in the late 1950s, with the Seminole Tribe of Florida and the Miccosukee Tribe of Indians of Florida emerging as separate political entities and other Seminoles refusing to join either tribe. Each recognized tribe established its own citizenship criteria and tribal rolls that reflected the beliefs and goals of its citizens. Although they shared a distant past, recent history shaped decisions about who belonged to which tribe.

Unlike the Pamunkeys, Catawbas, Mississippi Choctaws, and Eastern Band Cherokees, the Florida Seminoles did not have a deeply rooted sense of tribal identity in the nineteenth century. The descendants of Creek Indian entrepreneurs and political dissenters who migrated south from Georgia and Alabama for a variety of reasons, the Seminoles underwent a process of ethnogenesis in Florida that was incomplete by the removal era. Creeks began entering Florida in 1717 following the end of the Yamasee War. Attracted by cattle herds and farm lands abandoned by enslaved Apalachee Indians, these migrants built new towns and established their own internal organizations modeled on Creek political systems.[3] Between 1740 and 1812, they founded at least six villages in northern Florida, while smaller parties traveled farther south in search of game and made contact with Cuban fishermen.[4] Later, Red Stick refugees from the Creek War of 1813–14 joined these migrants and increased the Florida Indian population from 4,000 to about 6,000 individuals. The settlers shared similar cultural backgrounds, but they had little interest in forging a common political identity. Indeed, many moved to Florida to escape the political centralization of the Creek Nation. In an effort to collectivize these disparate groups, outsiders called them "Seminoles," which derived from a Creek word used to describe wild varieties of plants and animals. The Seminoles did not use this term themselves.[5]

The migrating bands that entered Florida brought with them different languages. Although Muskogee (Creek) was the dominant language used by the Creeks, many lower Creek towns internally spoke Hitchiti, a related but mutually unintelligible tongue. Hitchiti-speakers named one of their earliest towns

[margin note: Ideas of race & belonging]

in Florida Mikasuki. Over the years, the language these Seminoles spoke became known by the name of the town.[6] By the time of the Second Seminole War, the Seminoles spoke two distinct languages: Muskogee and Mikasuki.[7] They used Muskogee as a trade language and many Seminoles were bilingual.[8] Typically Mikasukis learned to speak Muskogee rather than the other way around, but limited intermarriage encouraged bilingualism in both groups.[9] Each linguistic community contributed to the survival of the Seminoles in Florida. According to oral tradition, "the Muskogees gave us the songs, and the Miccosukees gave us the leaders."[10]

Although Creeks migrated to Florida in part to escape problems posed by Euro-American expansion in the South, trouble followed them to their new homes. In addition to Indians, escaped African slaves had poured into Florida since the early eighteenth century where Spanish officials welcomed them as a buffer against British and later American hostilities. These "Maroons," as they came to be known, forged friendly relationships with the Indians who entered the region, often serving as interpreters for their Seminole allies. White Americans, however, found this situation intolerable. Pressured by plantation owners who wanted to reclaim their "property" and frontier settlers who blamed Seminole "banditti" for border violence, US troops led by General Andrew Jackson invaded northern Florida in 1816 and again in 1818, instigating what became known as the First Seminole War.[11] Both blacks and Indians suffered heavy casualties in the conflict. Survivors fled farther south and joined existing Seminole communities or founded new towns. Following the end of the war, the already weak affiliation of Seminole settlements with the Creek Confederacy ended.[12] The 1823 Treaty of Moultrie Creek negotiated between the United States and the Seminoles marked this official political separation.[13] Seminoles and their black allies forged new identities.

The realities of eighteenth- and nineteenth-century slaveholding complicated the relationship between Africans and Seminoles. Like many southern Indians before the Civil War, some Seminoles owned black slaves. This practice began in the eighteenth century as Seminoles noted the value that Europeans attached to owning slaves. During Britain's rule of Florida from 1763 to 1783, Seminoles purchased their first Africans from European settlers. Unlike the Cherokees or even their Creek ancestors, however, the Seminoles had no intention of devoting their time to managing slaves.[14] Instead, the Seminoles' black slaves lived under a form of vassalage, paying annual tributes of corn to their Seminole masters but often living in separate communities. Like the Maroons, Seminole slaves adopted many of the Indians' customs and habits. They lived in palmetto cabins and dressed like their masters, but these Africans were never full members of Seminole society. Only a few, through adoption or intermarriage, received Seminole clan membership or lived in

Seminole towns.[15] Due to matrilineal rules of descent, the Indians considered children born to Seminole women and African men as Seminoles. Conversely, those children born to African mothers, no matter their paternity, were always outsiders despite their close ties to the Indians.[16]

Interactions with whites and blacks encouraged Florida Indians to think about race. To make sense of racial others, the Seminoles turned to stories. In 1825, a Seminole leader named Neamathla gave one of the earliest recorded versions of the Seminole race creation story. Neamathla spoke of the "Great Spirit's" creation of men from dust. His first attempt was a failure: a white man appeared who looked "pale and weak." His second attempt ended in another disappointment: the man was "black and ugly." Finally, in his third attempt, the Great Spirit got it right—a "red man!"[17] The Seminoles repeated this story well into the twentieth century, although the details varied. In some versions, the Great Spirit (often called Breathmaker) told the men to select from three boxes: the white man chose a box filled with "pens, and ink, and paper, and compasses," the red man chose a box of "tomahawks, knives, war-clubs, traps, and such things as are useful in war and hunting," and the black man was left with a box of "axes and hoes, with buckets to carry water in, and long whips for driving oxen."[18] In another version recalled by a Seminole elder in the 1970s, Breathmaker also gave the Seminoles "medicinal herbs."[19] The story of Breathmaker reassured Seminoles of the validity of their customs and provided them with a framework for understanding their relationships with outsiders, one that they turned to again in the years following the Second and Third Seminole Wars.[20]

ideas of RACE

Like the Choctaws and Cherokees, the Seminoles faced expulsion from their southeastern homelands following the 1830 Indian Removal Act. In contrast to the Cherokees' legal battles to remain in the East, however, the Seminoles took a direct-action approach. No strangers to warfare against the United States, the Seminoles engaged American forces in a brutal seven-year war to resist removal policy. On May 9, 1832, fifteen Seminole leaders signed a removal agreement at Payne's Landing on the Ocklawaha River. The Indians believed the treaty binding only if the tribe as a whole approved the Seminoles' new lands in Indian Territory following a visit west by an appointed delegation of chiefs. In contrast, whites declared the agreement final as soon as the western delegation signaled its approval.[21] Seminoles ridiculed the treaty-signers and refused to abide by the terms.[22] When the US Army stepped in, warfare broke out. By the end of the Second Seminole War in 1842, the United States had spent between $30 million and $40 million and lost the lives of over 1,600 troops and civilians. The Seminoles also experienced heavy losses, including the forced westward removal of nearly 4,000 Indians and their black allies.[23] Only 400 or 500 Seminoles remained in Florida.

response to removal

The Seminoles left in Florida insisted on their right to stay in their homeland. A portion of their argument rested on an agreement signed by sixty-six Seminoles and Major General Alexander Macomb in 1839. At this point in the war, US troops had captured nearly 2,000 Seminoles and killed another 400. Congress authorized Macomb to persuade the remaining Indians to move to a temporary reservation in southwestern Florida until they agreed to remove permanently. Only one of the four Seminole bands left in southern Florida signed the agreement to suspend hostilities, and warfare continued until the United States realized the impossibility of total Seminole removal. Gradually Congress withdrew troops from Florida and fighting ceased. The federal government authorized Colonel William Worth to negotiate a new treaty, but because officials still hoped to persuade the Seminoles to migrate west, they did not outline firm boundaries for the proposed reservation. In 1842, Worth signed an agreement with the remaining Indians that allowed them to occupy the lands stipulated by Macomb, which included over 5 million acres in south Florida.[24] The US Senate failed to ratify either the Macomb or the Worth agreements as treaties. In the view of the Seminoles, however, these agreements combined with the fraudulent nature of earlier treaties gave them rights to practically the entire state.[25]

The Florida Seminoles had little contact with the federal government after the war. As whites moved near their reserved lands, officials tried to restrict the Indians' movement and to secure their removal to Indian Territory as soon as possible.[26] The Seminoles, however, refused to negotiate with whites. They distrusted US officials and resented white intruders. Brief skirmishes between white settlers and the Indians broke out occasionally. The largest of these conflicts resulted in the Third Seminole War from 1855 to 1858. At its conclusion, the United States sent another 200 Seminoles west.[27] The remaining Seminoles retreated to the Everglades and the Big Cypress Swamp, where they began to regard themselves as distinct from those Seminoles whom the United States had forced west.[28] Layers of identity—linguistic, band, busk group, and clan—helped these Indians to understand who belonged to their communities and shaped their views of outsiders.

Although the Seminoles joined together to fight the United States, in the years that followed the Third Seminole War, they returned to their dispersed settlement patterns and decentralized political system. Muskogee-speakers, who represented about 35 percent of the tribe, settled north of Lake Okeechobee, while Mikasuki-speakers retreated to the swamps and the Everglades.[29] Members of the two linguistic groups welcomed each other as visitors to their separate Green Corn ceremonies, but they maintained distinct political and socioeconomic arrangements.[30] Linguistic differences, according to tribal citizen Buffalo Tiger, were "the kind of situation that keeps us separate." Muskogees were proud to speak Muskogee, and Mikasukis considered their group superior. In the Mikasuki language, Muskogees were known as the "weak people" because supposedly they were more susceptible to white influence.[31] In the 1970s, a white artist who had spent time among the Seminoles described the mild rivalry between the Muskogees and Mikasukis as a "Southern-Yankee type thing."[32]

Within their linguistic regions, the Seminoles divided into separate bands. When Richard Henry Pratt visited the tribe in 1879, he observed four groups. Chipco, an old Seminole chief, governed a band of Muskogee-speakers near Fort Clinch. Tuscanugga, also Muskogee-speaking, had a village on the western border of Lake Okeechobee. Chief Tiger Tail led a community of Mikasuki-speakers on the margins of the Big Cypress Swamp. His son, Young Tiger Tail, oversaw a fourth band on the Atlantic coast, near Miami.[33] A few years later, ethnographer Clay MacCauley named these communities the Cat Fish Lake settlement, the Fish Eating Creek settlement, the Big Cypress Swamp settlement, and the Miami River settlement. MacCauley also identified a fifth band: a small Muskogee settlement he called Cow Creek. Each group lived forty to seventy miles apart from any other settlement in an otherwise uninhabited region.[34]

Band members belonged to ceremonial organizations called busk groups under the political and religious leadership of medicine men. By 1900, there were usually five busks, one for the Muskogee-speakers north of Lake Okeechobee, and the others for Mikasuki-speakers farther south.[35] Trained for seven years, medicine men acted as priests and doctors as well as political leaders, and Seminoles respected them for their spiritual knowledge and temporal governance.[36] One of their most important responsibilities was to care for the tribe's medicine bundles, which were collections of sacred objects with curative properties. According to anthropologist Louis Capron, the Seminoles believed that these bundles held great power that directly contributed to the survival of the tribe. Without proper care, the medicine bundles could lose their power or become harmful instead of helpful.[37] Medicine men also had a political function as tribal leaders, a role that grew more important in the late nineteenth century as the authority of war chiefs faded. They passed judgments on crimes, prescribed spiritual remedies to restore balance, and became spokesmen for their group when dealing with outsiders. Each Seminole fell under the jurisdiction of one of these busk groups and owed allegiance to a particular medicine man.[38] Busk group membership was central to Seminole conceptions of their identity.

Medicine men performed their most important function during the tribe's annual Green Corn Ceremony, also known as the busk. Held each June during the week of the full moon when the corn was ready to roast, the Green Corn

Ceremony provided Seminoles with an opportunity to restore friendships and renew community bonds.[39] As one Seminole explained in the 1970s, "the responsibilities we had to one another, we had to renew during the annual Green Corn Dance."[40] Medicine men from the disparate bands selected locations for the ceremony and sent runners to announce the time to scattered family camps.[41] To coordinate the arrival of the groups, each village hung up a number of small sticks, removing one each day until the time of the festival, at which point they traveled to the chosen spot.[42] Although each busk group held its own Green Corn Ceremony, they welcomed members of other busk groups as visitors. At the ceremony, medicine men held council and ruled on criminal cases in the tribe. Seminoles forgave old animosities after lawbreakers purified themselves by taking a medicine known as the black drink.[43] Older men initiated young boys into the mysteries of Seminole manhood.[44] Through ball playing, dancing, fasting, feasting, purifying rituals, and tests of endurance, the Seminoles ritually reaffirmed their relationship with each other and the spiritual world.[45] Participation in the ceremony clearly identified individuals as members of the community.

Although loosely organized into bands and busk groups, Seminole families lived in separate camps, generally a half mile to two or more miles apart.[46] These camps consisted of matrilineal households: one or two wives (often sisters), their husband, their daughters and sons-in-law, and their unmarried sons.[47] Married sons moved to the camps of their wives. This arrangement reflected another element central to Seminole understandings of belonging: clan identity. The Seminoles organized their society around a matrilineal clan system similar to those of other southeastern tribes. By the 1880s there remained at least nine clans among the Florida Seminoles: the Wind, Tiger, Otter, Bird, Deer, Snake, Bear, Wolf, and Alligator Clans.[48] Certain clans had special responsibilities within the tribe. The Bird Clan, for example, served in a judicial capacity, in consultation with the Tiger Clan, while the Wind Clan enforced these decisions.[49] Within the clan system, the Seminoles recognized descent through the female line. Children belonged to their mother's clan and had special obligations toward their maternal relatives.[50] The Seminoles prohibited and strictly punished incest within clans, although their marriages appeared close according to Euro-American standards.[51] Cousins could marry so long as they belonged to different clans.[52] Clan membership gave Seminoles a defined place within the community and helped establish roles and responsibilities for tribal citizens.

Clan membership established kinship. Even if a Seminole had never before met someone belonging to his or her clan, they automatically considered each other relatives and had to treat each other as such.[53] In particular, maternal uncles played an important role in the upbringing of Seminole children by teaching them how to behave to their relatives.[54] In each camp, the oldest man usually had the greatest authority, and strict social rules governed individual behavior.[55] Personal surveillance helped enforce appropriate conduct, and although punishments were rare, clan members knew they faced censure if they stepped out of line.[56] According to a 1913 government report, the Seminoles' home life was "always happy and no friction [was] ever seen among the different members of the family; each member, even the small children, having clearly defined duties, which they never shirk."[57] Clan members also protected one another by vowing to avenge harm done to fellow clan members. If they could not find the individual who committed the crime, they punished another member of that person's clan.[58] By teaching appropriate behavior and exacting vengeance from the clan of a wrongdoer, clan members pressured Seminoles both within and outside their clan to keep the peace. Clan belonging provided Seminoles with a strong sense of identity that also helped distinguish them from surrounding populations.

Linguistic affiliation, band, busk group, and clan membership defined Seminole identity in the late nineteenth century. Although these sociopolitical structures linked them, Seminoles did not necessarily see themselves as belonging to a unified tribe. Nevertheless, the Seminoles developed certain cultural practices in the late nineteenth century that separated them—as Indians—from other people in Florida. As historian Harry A. Kersey Jr. has explained, in the years after the Third Seminole War, the Seminoles completed the last stage of their "ethnoecologic adaptation" to the environment of southern Florida.[59] They learned to live in the swamps and grasslands by building homes, planting gardens, sewing garments, and constructing canoes that were suited to the terrain—and unique to them. They used these cultural practices as ethnic markers that helped identify them as indigenous to Florida. Although their ancestors had been migrants, the Seminoles now considered themselves the rightful owners of the land, and they consciously presented themselves as different from the whites and blacks who later made homes there.

Seminoles may not have shared a common tribal identity, but they knew who they were not. Like their own identities, Seminole ideas about outsiders developed from specific historical experiences. Decades of warfare between the Seminoles and Americans influenced the attitudes of Florida Indians toward whites. Elderly Seminoles passed down stories of the wars so that they were "as fresh with many today as they were when they happened."[60] In the 1970s, for example, Billy Osceola insisted that during the Second Seminole War, "The white men would lie and trick the Indians."[61] Other Seminoles remembered that when the Indians were rounded up for shipment to Indian Territory, "if an old man or child was too old to walk anymore, or to go any further, they say that the soldiers took their bayonets and killed them right on the spot."[62] The

Seminoles held particularly bitter memories about Andrew Jackson. As a general, Jackson had personally launched the invasion of Florida that provoked the First Seminole War. Later on, after he became president, Jackson signed the Indian Removal Act, which instigated the Second Seminole War. In the 1970s, a Seminole woman recalled that Jackson "sent off his soldiers down here in Florida and told them to kill the Indians like dogs—kill every one of them, even children and women, even old men and all of them." In her estimation, Jackson "was no better than Hitler."[63] The anger and fear provoked by these wartime stories contributed to an ongoing dread of removal that lasted well into the twentieth century.

Determined to stay in their homeland in the years that followed removal, the Seminoles developed a foreign policy of conflict-avoidance.[64] Small in number, the Seminoles recognized the futility of further military action. According to W. Stanley Hanson, who worked extensively with the Seminoles in the early twentieth century, "The desire uppermost in the teachings of the medicine men has been to avoid friction with the whites."[65] This attitude carried into the twentieth century. By choosing to retreat rather than fight, the Seminoles created a powerful strategy designed to keep them in Florida. By following this foreign policy and developing a common political habit of mind, Seminoles from disparate settlements created an informal tribal identity expressed by their ongoing opposition to whites.[66]

Seminole leaders actively discouraged younger kinsmen from interacting with whites or adopting their habits. Doing so called into question the tribal belonging of such individuals. Billy Osceola remembered that his father urged him to avoid white people.[67] A reporter observed that the "old chiefs . . . are immovable in their determination not to have the tribes contaminated by adopting the customs of the white men."[68] Seminoles who chose to live with whites met with disapproval from their relatives. In the late nineteenth century a young man named Ko-nip-hat-cho traveled to Fort Myers to pursue a Euro-American education. Upon hearing of his departure, his kinsmen fell into an uproar.[69] Regarding him as a traitor, some Seminoles demanded his execution, and, according to Billy Cypress, only the pleadings of his father saved him.[70] Although Ko-nip-hat-cho returned to his people unharmed, other Seminoles were not as fortunate. According to a 1913 government report, the Seminoles punished those who learned to read and write English by cropping their ears.[71] Part of the Seminoles' negative reaction to Euro-American education may have stemmed from historic events when certain Seminoles had signed treaties that did not represent the goals of the group at large.[72] Fearful that whites would use literacy against them, the Seminoles rejected it altogether.

The Seminoles also expressed their separation from white Americans by living in ways that clearly marked their difference. They resided in open-sided houses with palmetto-thatched roofs known as chickees. Easily built and torn down, chickees allowed the Seminoles visibility of their surroundings, while vegetation obscured them from outsiders.[73] Even when government agents built board houses for the Seminoles, the Indians overwhelmingly preferred to remain in their traditional abodes. The nineteenth-century design persists into the twenty-first century with one exception—the introduction of nails in the late nineteenth century—and even modern homes usually have a chickee or two adjacent to them.[74] Chickees have become so closely identified with Seminoles that many Floridians assume only Seminoles can legally build them.[75]

Gendered subsistence practices also helped distinguish Seminoles from outsiders. Seminole men hunted deer, turkeys, bears, alligators, and other wild game, and traded with outsiders, while women managed the camps, which included tending gardens, raising livestock, preparing food, and caring for children.[76] The Seminoles placed a particular emphasis on hunting and herding, perhaps because large-scale agricultural production had proved impractical during times of conflict with the United States.[77] Every four years the Indians celebrated hunting with a special dance, which included feasting and ball games. As part of the ceremony, "Each morning of the festival, every member of the camp, down to the wee child, must hunt. . . . The men hunt large game; the boys go for rabbits, birds and squirrels; while women hunt the hogs and dig potatoes, and the very small children 'hunt' water, and bring in sticks of wood."[78] Symbolically, hunting affirmed Seminole mastery of the south Florida landscape and contributed to their survival strategy of mobility and conflict-avoidance. As a white trader commented in the early twentieth century, the "normal condition" of the Seminoles was "hunting and independency."[79]

Despite the symbolic emphasis placed on hunting, farming remained essential to Seminole subsistence strategies as well. The Indians planted fields on "swampy hammocks" near their camps with "corn over six feet high," as well as pumpkins, beans, potatoes, squash, melons, sugarcane, and a variety of fruit trees.[80] Like their Creek ancestors, Seminole women farmed, but men increasingly participated in agricultural production as well. In particular, men helped to clear away underbrush, pines, and sawgrass from new fields.[81] They often accompanied their wives and children to more distant gardens to protect them from intruders.[82] In addition to farming, women gathered wild plants like coontie roots and swamp cabbage. Women also took charge of cooking. Although the Seminoles produced most of their own food, they also depended on trade goods they purchased by selling deer, alligator, and otter skins, plumes from Florida's exotic birds, and coontie starch.[83] Subsistence activities meant different things for men and women, but members of both genders derived a sense of personal identity from economic contributions that distinguished them from non-Seminoles.

Seminoles also expressed their separation from outsiders with clothing. The Seminoles' unique style helped mark individuals' status within the group as well as express their clan identity. According to one report, "Seminole clans adhere strictly to the clan colors in their dress, so one familiar with clan history knows at sight to which clan an Indian belongs."[84] Seminole men wore deerskin leggings and moccasins, embroidered shirts, and brightly colored turbans.[85] These turbans served as status markers: "the more important the occasion, the more enormous the turban."[86] In the late nineteenth century, women acquired sewing machines, which they used to construct colorful patchwork garments that men as well as women wore.[87] Women also adorned themselves with hundreds of strings of beads. These necklaces, which sometimes weighed as much as thirty pounds, were "her chief glory and . . . worn constantly."[88] By dressing in their unique styles, the Seminoles laid claim to their identity as Indian. Their clothing helped separate them from outsiders, especially at a time when "colored" people suffered under Florida's strict Jim Crow laws.[89]

Seminole attitudes toward whites in the late nineteenth and early twentieth centuries found their most virulent expression in their reactions to sexual relations with whites. White men who eyed Seminole women met hostility and "it would be well for that man never to appear in the presence of the tribe again."[90] According to an Oklahoma Creek-Seminole woman who lived at the Brighton Reservation in the 1950s, if the Florida Seminoles caught a white man who raped a Seminole woman, they killed him.[91] The Seminoles also repelled the advances of friendly whites. When a white trader named Joe Bowers fell in love with a Seminole woman in the early twentieth century, for example, the tribal council refused his request to marry her.[92] Although discouraged, Bowers vowed to prove his worth by living among the Seminoles and showing them that he could be "just as good an Indian." He built a chickee and adopted a Seminole lifestyle for six months, but nobody paid any attention to him. Unimpressed by Bowers's attempts to become culturally Seminole, the Indians insisted that his racial identity barred him from marriage rights in the tribe. Eventually Bowers gave up.[93]

Seminoles did not tolerate sexual relationships with whites because they threatened notions of who belonged to the community. Although the Seminoles strictly punished both men and women for sexual infidelity, women who willingly associated with white men faced the worst censure.[94] As members of a matrilineal society, Seminole women could bring outsiders into Seminole communities in a way that Seminole men could not. If a Seminole man became involved with a white woman, neither she nor her children could

Figure 5.2 In the late nineteenth century, the Seminoles acquired sewing machines and bright calicos from white traders through the exchange of pelts, plumes, and hides. By producing and wearing unique patchwork clothing, the Seminoles laid claim to a distinctive identity in Florida, one that marked them as indigenous and distinguished them from African Americans. In this photograph, three Seminole girls posed in a Seminole camp in the Everglades. Photographer: Julian A. Dimock. Date: 1907. Courtesy of the American Museum of Natural History Library (image no. 48238).

become part of the tribe. If a Seminole woman united with a white man, however, their children would be clan members with the right to live in Seminole camps and participate in tribal affairs. Determined to protect their resources and independence from people they perceived as morally weak and treacherous, the Seminoles did their utmost to prevent such unions.

According to a government agent who surveyed the tribe in the 1880s, Seminole women who had children by white fathers faced execution.[95] The women's female relatives reportedly enforced this sentence. If such punishments were indeed carried out, they were rare. In the late nineteenth century, observers reported that the Seminoles had accused only two women of sexual relations with whites. One woman died at the hands of "the women of her tribe, who hung her," while the other's high status as the wife of a chief saved her from a similar fate.[96] In the twentieth century, there was one other report of this nature. According to a white nurse, the tribal council ordered the poisoning of Thelma Jim because she had two half-white children.[97]

Babies born to Seminole women and white men also faced death at the hands of their female relatives.[98] According to Betty Mae Tiger Jumper, "the Seminoles believed that half-breeds were evil 'Ho-la wa-gus!' (bad spirits) who could endanger the tribe and bring on bad spells."[99] James Billie, who was born in the 1940s, asserted that previous generations of Seminoles "didn't want no mixed-bloods with them" because "the ill-feeling toward the white was still stronger."[100] According to matrilineal rules of descent these children belonged to the tribe as clan members, but the Seminoles recognized that white men customarily exercised control over their children, which threatened the tribe's independence. Older female relatives took responsibility for dealing with this dangerous situation and drowned the children of white men. Infanticide continued into the early years of the twentieth century. Jumper reported that her baby cousin met this fate in Fort Lauderdale in 1920.[101]

As with whites, the Seminoles' historical experiences with African Americans shaped their attitudes toward black people. Following the Third Seminole War, Seminoles remained aloof from outside blacks, just as they avoided sustained contact with whites. Oral tradition suggests that Seminole men may have occasionally had sexual encounters with outside black women, but any children these unions produced were kept by their black mothers and the Seminoles did not consider them kin.[102] Black women who had remained with the Seminoles as slaves following the wars, however, were another story. The Seminoles had acquired these African American women as girls and by the 1880s they were middle-aged with children of their own.[103] Molly Pitcher and her half-Seminole son, Charlie Dixie, for example, lived among the Mikasuki-speakers.[104] Pitcher may also have had a black-Seminole daughter, Tonagi, although few records of this girl survive.[105] More black Seminoles lived with the Muskogee-speakers north of Lake Okeechobee. These included Poq-ti, also known as Nagey Nancy, her two black-Seminole children, and another black woman named Si-Si, along with her children, Han-ne and Me-le.[106] Census takers reported that another half-black woman, Fikee Jumper, born in 1879, also lived among the Muskogee-speakers.[107] She may have been related to Funke, a black woman who lived with the family of Frank Willie.[108] The Seminoles adopted various and sometimes conflicting strategies to incorporate these anomalous women and their children into the community.

The black women who lived among the Seminoles held an ambiguous position in the tribe. Southern whites spread rumors that the Indians continued to hold blacks in slavery even after the Civil War ended.[109] Other observers, however, claimed that these women lived as community members. Clay MacCauley noted in the 1880s that the "negresses in the tribe live apparently on terms of perfect equality with the other women."[110] A white journalist asserted that "their thriftless owners treat them more as companions than slaves, and about the severest work the men are required to perform is hunting, which is a pleasant pastime rather than a labor, while the slight agricultural pursuits are shared about equally between the Indian and the negro women."[111]

Despite the uncertain status of blacks who remained with the tribe, Seminoles married and had children with them. These children had Seminole fathers, but without matrilineal clan ties they were not fully Seminole. The Seminoles resolved the problem of clanless community members by adopting the remaining black women living among them.[112] In this way, the women received clan membership, usually that of their "mistresses," which they in turn passed on to their children.[113] Si-si, Han-ne, and Me-le, who lived with a Seminole man named Tallahassee, probably became members of his wife's clan, the Deer Clan. Early twentieth-century censuses listed Molly Pitcher's half-black son, Charlie Dixie, as a member of the Bird Clan. Billy Bowlegs III and his half-siblings Lewis Tucker and Lucy Pearce, the grandchildren of Nagey Nancy, belonged to the Snake Clan.[114] Seminole understandings of race, however, complicated the clan identities of black-Seminole children. According to Betty Mae Tiger Jumper, the Seminoles understood the children and grandchildren of Nagey Nancy as belonging not to the Snake Clan proper, but to the "Little Black Snake Clan."[115] Modification of the Snake Clan name revealed that these black-Seminole children did not belong to Seminole clans in the same way as did racially Indian Seminoles.[116]

Although the Seminoles tolerated relationships between Seminole men and adopted black women, they were less accepting of unions between Seminole women and men with African ancestry. For the Seminoles, such marriages represented unacceptable racial mixing because they threatened to bring black-Seminole children fully into the tribe's matrilineal clan system. Efforts to block the marriage prospects of black-Seminole men carried consequences. On February 15, 1889, Nagey Nancy's son, Jim Jumper, sought revenge after a Seminole named Big Tommie rejected him as a suitor for Big Tommie's daughter. Jumper took a shotgun to the camp of the Snake Clan and murdered at least five Seminoles, including his black-Seminole sister, Old Nancy, who tried to stop him.[117] The massacre came to an end when Jumper was fatally shot by another Seminole man.[118] In the months following the tragedy, the Seminole tribal council tried to resolve any additional problems from interracial marriages by officially prohibiting black-Seminole men from taking Seminole wives.[119]

The effects of the massacre reverberated across the tribe. The camp affected by the killings included both Muskogee- and Mikasuki-speaking Seminoles, and Mikasuki-speakers farther south took the tragedy to heart. Compared to the Muskogee-speaking Seminoles, very few people of African descent lived with the Mikasuki-speakers.[120] Molly Pitcher, who was captured by the

Seminoles as a child, was the only black individual among them who had no Seminole ancestry. Initially kept as a slave by John Osceola, she later married a Seminole man named Miami Billie.[121] The relationship did not last, but it produced a son.[122] According to oral tradition, when Seminoles in the Big Cypress Swamp learned of Jim Jumper's actions, "They held court . . . to see about killing this 'un [Charlie Dixie] on this side." Fiercely protective of her teenage son, Molly Pitcher vowed to kill anyone who touched him. As a compromise, John Osceola took Dixie into his camp and had the young man wait on him. This arrangement apparently continued until Osceola married, and he then let Dixie go free.[123]

Although the Mikasuki-speakers spared his life, they forbade Charlie Dixie from taking a Seminole wife. Circumstances conspired, however, to overturn this ruling. According to oral tradition, Dixie's father, Miami Billie, had left his mother years before and married a Seminole woman named Aklohpi. The couple had at least two children, Dixie's half-siblings. According to Seminole ideas of kinship, however, these children—a son named Charlie Billie and a daughter named Jim Sling—belonged to their mother's Panther Clan, and were thus not closely related to Dixie, who belonged to the Bird Clan. When they grew up, the Seminoles uncovered a shocking secret: Charlie Billie had impregnated Jim Sling. Whereas Dixie may not have counted as kin, the Seminoles considered the behavior of Charlie Billie and Jim Sling incestuous since it occurred between full siblings in the same clan. Strictly taboo among the Seminoles, incest was a severe crime, punishable by death.[124]

The Seminoles knew what they had to do. First, Jim Sling's mother disposed of the infant.[125] Next, the tribe dealt with the couple. After deliberations at the annual Green Corn Ceremony in 1893, tribal council members decided to spare Jim Sling, but to execute Charlie Billie.[126] The councilmen appointed Charlie Dixie to carry out the killing, enticing him with a reward: if he executed Charlie Billie, he could marry Jim Sling.[127] Dixie reluctantly performed the task—according to one report the men cried together before Dixie shot Billie through the chest and throat—and, soon after, he and Jim Sling married.[128] Although half-black, Charlie Dixie had a Seminole wife.[129]

Although "He lived as an Indian; he lived with the Indians, and his wife was a pure blood Indian," the Seminoles only gradually regarded Charlie Dixie as one of them.[130] Memories of Jim Sling's past combined with Dixie's racial background made the couple a pariah among Mikasuki-speakers for many years. Ethel Cutler Freeman, who visited the tribe in the 1940s, reported that the Seminoles barred Dixie and his family from participating in tribal festivities and social games.[131] According to W. Stanley Hanson Jr., whose father worked with the Indians, other Seminoles never seemed to interact much with the Dixie family.[132] Over time, these attitudes softened as Charlie Dixie's and Jim

Sling's children grew up and interacted with other Seminoles. In later years, "things gradually changed and he was treated more kindly."[133]

The experiences of Billy Bowlegs III, another black Seminole, both contrasted with and reflected those of Charlie Dixie. Unlike Dixie, Bowlegs spoke Muskogee. Muskogee-speakers north of Lake Okeechobee tended to accept outsiders more readily than did the Mikasuki-speakers in the Everglades and Big Cypress Swamp. Billy Bowlegs was also more phenotypically Indian than Charlie Dixie. One white commentator exclaimed that Bowlegs "doesn't look any more Negro than I do."[134] Indeed, in 1929 Superintendent Lucien

Figure 5.3 Charlie Dixie (pictured) was the son of Molly Pitcher, a black woman captured by the Seminoles as a child, and a Seminole man named Miami Billie. Due to his black ancestry, Dixie held an anomolous position among the Mikasuki-speakers. Although he married a Seminole woman and fathered children who belonged to their mother's matrilineal clan, he remained a social outsider for much of his life. Photographer: Irvin M. Peithmann. Date: c. 1950. Courtesy of the State Archives of Florida (image no. PE0381).

A. Spencer listed both Bowlegs and his half-sister as "full blood" on an agency census.[135] In contrast, whites remarked that Dixie was "absolutely coal black."[136] Bowlegs's circumstances and appearance meant that the Seminoles treated him with a greater degree of equality than they did Charlie Dixie. Like Dixie, however, Bowlegs continually had to prove his worth as a Seminole and the tribe denied him some of the privileges of tribal citizenship on account of his ancestry.

Billy Bowlegs III was born in 1862, the son of Old Nancy, the black-Seminole daughter of Osän-a-ha-tco, a Seminole man of the Otter Clan, and Nagey Nancy.[137] Old Nancy died at the hands of her brother in the 1889 massacre; Bowlegs was away from home that day.[138] Billy Bowlegs's father, Billie Fewell (also known as Key West Billy), was a Mikasuki-speaking trader and traveler familiar with whites.[139] Unlike most Seminoles of his generation, Bowlegs learned to read and write.[140] Other Indians faced punishment if they adopted white ways, but the tribe did not censure Bowlegs for these skills, perhaps on account of his black ancestry. Indeed, Seminoles appreciated his knowledge: "He took the Sears, Roebuck and Montgomery Ward catalog and placed orders" for illiterate Seminoles. A white couple familiar with the Seminoles described him as "the ambassador to the Indians."[141] His black ancestry made Bowlegs an anomaly in the tribe, and he took advantage of this position to carve out a space for himself.

Billy Bowlegs married a Seminole woman, Pillhooll of the Deer Clan, some time before the massacre of 1889 and the tribal ban on intermarriage. That year the couple had a son named Eli Morgan. No evidence suggests that the marriage of Bowlegs and Pillhooll was unusual. She was sixteen years his senior, but it was common for Seminole men to marry older women due to a shortage of suitable spouses in the small community.[142] Bowlegs and Pillhooll lived together as husband and wife until her death in 1928. His half-sister, Lucy, also married a Seminole named John Pearce, and the couple had at least four children.[143] These children developed a close relationship with their uncle, as was typical in the matrilineal society of the Seminoles, and after the death of Bowlegs's wife they lived together in the same camp. His niece, Ada Pearce, took care of Bowlegs in his old age.[144]

People who knew Billy Bowlegs asserted that he was universally liked.[145] Seminoles respected him as an ambassador and as a hunter, and whites visited him when they had questions for the tribe.[146] Despite the skills he offered the Seminoles, however, Bowlegs, like Charlie Dixie, faced discrimination on account of his ancestry.[147] One observer described him as "a loner."[148] When asked by a white visitor why Bowlegs lacked a leadership role in the tribe despite his talents, a group of Seminoles replied, "Billy Bowlegs [is an] African waterboy."[149] Although Bowlegs made a successful life for himself among the

Seminoles, he could not escape his ancestry or the racial climate of the Jim Crow South. Like Charlie Dixie, he made the best of his situation, but remained one step removed from full tribal acceptance.

Although Charlie Dixie and Billy Bowlegs struggled for full inclusion, their children had better luck. Seminoles occasionally denigrated them on account of their black ancestry, but they belonged to the clans of their Indian mothers, which gave them a more secure place in the tribe. Charlie Dixie and Jim Sling's two surviving children, Susie and Walter Huff Dixie, grew up to marry

Figure 5.4 Lucy Pearce and Billy Bowlegs III were the children of Old Nancy, a woman of black and Seminole parentage. Both siblings married Seminole spouses and had children. Bowlegs won respect as a skilled hunter and an ambassador for the tribe. Like Charlie Dixie, however, he faced discrimination due to his black ancestry. Date: 1911. Courtesy of the State Archives of Florida (image no. N032051).

Seminole spouses and raise children of their own.[150] Eli Morgan, the son of Billy Bowlegs and Pillhooll, also married a Seminole woman.[151] As generations passed and Seminoles with black ancestry married "full-blood" Indians, the stigma surrounding their heritage faded. In the 1970s, a Seminole man explained that "Today, you will find some Seminoles with Negro blood. Those who would really know have all died by now."[152]

Changing attitudes toward Seminoles with black ancestry mirrored other social shifts, which ultimately raised new questions about belonging and about what kind of tribe, if any, the Seminoles wanted. Over the years, the Seminoles had used their conflict-avoidance foreign policy to maintain political autonomy from white America. Yet, despite their antagonism toward outsiders, the Seminoles had forged reciprocal economic and social ties with white traders in Florida. Selling pelts, plumes, and hides, the Seminoles earned money to purchase firearms, sewing machines, and foods like flour, sugar, and coffee.[153] They also formed tenuous friendships with white trader families. As more white settlers moved to Florida and Everglade drainage projects commenced in the early twentieth century, the trade economy of the region began to collapse. White traders did not forget their Seminole friends, however, and a number of traders, as well as anthropologists and other concerned Floridians, searched for ways to help the Indians adapt to the new economic conditions.

Beginning in the 1890s, white Floridians interested in helping the Seminoles started to pressure both the state and federal governments to set aside reservation lands for the Indians. In particular, charitable organizations run by white women, such as the Federation of Women's Clubs, made aiding Florida Indians a priority.[154] The federal government responded to the activism of such groups by passing several acts between 1894 and 1910 that enabled the Indian Service to purchase more than 23,000 acres of land south of Lake Okeechobee for the use of the Seminoles. In 1911, President William Howard Taft signed an executive order that set aside another 3,600 acres of public domain land for the Seminoles in Martin, Broward, and Collier Counties. The state of Florida reserved an additional 100,000 acres in Monroe County in 1917. By 1930, federal and state officials had set aside approximately 123,380 acres for the Seminoles, an acreage later reduced when the federal government incorporated some of the land into the Everglades National Park.[155]

Initially, the Seminoles were ambivalent about the reservations. They had practical concerns about the quality of the land. An inspector for the Indian Service reported in 1917 that "95 percent of every foot of land bought by the Federal Government for these Seminoles is covered with water nine months out of twelve."[156] The Seminoles also resented white efforts to confine them to small tracts when they insisted that the entire state was rightfully theirs.[157] As Joe Dan Osceola explained in the 1970s, "The whole State of Florida was ours, but yet wasn't ours."[158] Whites who supported the reservation plans warned the Seminoles that with hundreds of Americans moving into the region, land soon would become scarce.[159] Indeed, drainage projects in the Everglades during these years opened up new swaths of territory to white settlement and development projects. The Seminoles were at a crossroads.

Slowly, some Indians began moving to the reservations. Dania, later re-named the Hollywood Reservation, which consisted of 480 acres in Broward County, was the first to attract Seminole inhabitants. The superintendent of the Seminole Agency, Lucien A. Spencer, persuaded a few families to settle there and provided them with homes and farming equipment.[160] Later, some Seminoles also moved to the Brighton Reservation, north of Lake Okeechobee, which included 36,000 acres of rural land, and to the Big Cypress Reservation, which consisted of 32,000 acres of swampland.[161] For the most part, Muskogee-speakers inhabited the Brighton Reservation, while Mikasuki-speakers moved to Big Cypress. Residents of Dania came from both linguistic groups. A large number of Mikasukis, however, resisted moving to any reservation. The res-ervations set up new divisions within the tribe between reservation and non-reservation Seminoles that only widened as missionaries, white friends, and federal agents established churches, schools, and economic programs for the reservation Indians. Questions of belonging began to swirl around issues other than ancestry and clan membership. At what point did cultural change compromise Seminole identity? Was there room in one tribe for everyone?

Historically, the Florida Seminoles had resisted conversion to Christianity. Episcopal missionaries made a few attempts to woo the Indians in the late nine-teenth and early twentieth centuries, but the Seminoles were not interested.[162] Baptists adopted a different strategy and sent Creek and Seminole missionar-ies from Oklahoma to preach to the Florida Seminoles beginning in 1907 with the arrival of the Reverend Andrew J. Brown, the brother of the principal chief of the Seminole Nation in Oklahoma.[163] Indian missionaries spoke Muskogee and this gave them an entry into Seminole society that white missionaries lacked. They also shared clan ties with the Seminoles in Florida.[164] Despite linguistic and kin connections, however, these missionaries ran into difficul-ties. Willie King, who arrived in Florida in 1923, reported that "on a number of occasions the Indians would run away when they'd see them coming." The Seminoles harassed the missionaries at night by throwing rocks at their camp. They also employed their strategy of avoidance and retreated to the Everglades where the missionaries could not find them.[165] It took years of effort before the Oklahoma Creek and Seminole Baptists won any converts.

Gradually, the persistent efforts of missionaries began to pay off. By 1936, seven Florida Seminoles had converted, including Jimmie Gopher, Mishi (Missy) Tiger, Mary Tiger, and her daughter Ada.[166] Soon after, missionaries established the First Seminole Church on the Dania Reservation.[167] The real coup for the Christians, however, came in 1945 after an internal religious schism divided Mikasuki-speakers. Josie Billie, a prominent Mikasuki medicine man, lost favor with community members after supposedly committing crimes and practicing "black magic." The tribe stripped him of his medicine bundle and bestowed it on his brother instead, although not all Seminoles agreed with this decision. Not long after, Josie Billie "suddenly asked to be baptized" at a Baptist meeting. More than 100 of his Mikasuki supporters followed his example, converted, and moved to reservation land.[168] According to a Baptist missionary, "Some had wanted to before . . . but they did not know what his response might be." After his conversion, "they felt free to come." Josie Billie told the Mikasukis that he could still give them medicine for their bodies, but he was no longer able to help their souls. Over the next decade, missionary work grew and prospered.[169]

Religion divided the Seminoles. Many continued to hold Christianity in contempt and decried the conversion of their relatives. This resentment was especially true of non-reservation Mikasukis who adhered to traditional belief systems. Robert D. Mitchell, a longtime friend of the Seminoles, explained that when some of the Indians on the reservations "accepted this religion, the people south of there were so angry" that converts were afraid to visit their unconverted kinsmen out of fear of retribution.[170] There was also disagreement among Christian Indians. A popular Creek missionary named Stanley Smith stirred up much controversy. Smith worked on the Big Cypress Reservation, and, according to oral tradition, his interests leaned more toward the profane than the sacred. Mitchell claimed that Smith forced Seminole men to find work away from the reservation, telling them it was the will of God. While they were gone, Smith "proceeded to get their wives pregnant."[171] Outraged with his actions, which disrupted Seminole families and threatened community cohesion, Mikasuki leader Ingraham Billie and others vowed to run Smith out of Florida.[172] The breaking point, however, came in 1949, after Smith physically disciplined some Seminole youths. Neither the children's parents nor the Southern Baptist Board approved of his methods, and "there was a big to-do about it."[173] In the wake of the incident, the Southern Baptist Board ousted Smith from his position; he went on to establish his own church nearby, but eventually returned to Oklahoma. These events seemed to confirm the corrupting influence of Christianity on Seminole society for many Indians.

Seminole converts, on the other hand, found new prestige through holding church offices, and social satisfaction through church barbecues and ceremonies.[174] Anthropologist Ethel Cutler Freeman suggested that some of these converts belonged to clans that could not inherit high-status positions within the tribe; Christianity gave them power.[175] By the 1950s, Baptists established new missions on the Big Cypress and Brighton reservations that won a steady stream of converts among both Mikasukis and Muskogees. By the early 1970s, there were approximately 600 professing Christians among the Seminoles.[176] Conversion to Christianity promoted cultural change and influenced some Florida Indians to become more tolerant of contact with outsiders.

Self-avowed white friends of the Indians also encouraged cultural change among the Seminoles. Beginning in 1899, these whites founded private societies to promote the legal rights of the Seminoles, secure permanent reservation lands, and sponsor Euro-American educational programs among the Indians.[177] In particular, they wanted to send Seminole children to school. One of the first Seminole youths to follow their advice was Tony Tommie. Persuaded by Frank and Ivy Stranahan, a white trader and schoolteacher, Tommie entered school in Fort Lauderdale in 1915. After he made quick progress, his teachers sent him to the Carlisle Indian Industrial School in Pennsylvania.[178] The strange environment of Carlisle and cold climate of Pennsylvania disagreed with him. Like many Indian youths who attended boarding schools, he contracted tuberculosis. Suffering and alone, Tommie wrote to Frank Stranahan and discouraged him from sending any more Seminole children to Carlisle.[179] Tommie finally returned to his family in Florida, but he died shortly afterward.[180]

Tony Tommie's death was a setback to Seminole attitudes toward Euro-American education. When whites suggested that other youths move to Fort Lauderdale to attend school, some Seminoles protested: "They said it was alright for Tony Tommie to go to a white school and learn the white people's ways and language, but it wasn't the way for all the Indians and they made the children quit." [181] Older Indians "were satisfied with their life as they lived it" and did not believe a Euro-American education was necessary.[182] White efforts to educate Seminole children, however, continued. In the 1920s, Superintendent Lucien A. Spencer established a new school for Seminole children on the Dania Reservation. The small, one-room reservation school was poorly attended at first, but Spencer persisted in his efforts to encourage school attendance. When the Reverend James L. Glenn became the special commissioner to the Seminoles in 1931, he made the education of Seminole children a priority.[183] Although the Dania Reservation School closed in 1937 due to Depression-era cutbacks, by the early 1950s, 129 of the 198 Seminole children between the ages of six and eighteen were enrolled in other schools. Fifty attended public schools, fifty-four went to day schools, and twenty-five lived at government boarding schools.[184] Like Christian conversion, Euro-American education promoted a gradual shift in Seminole attitudes toward outsiders.

Intermarriage with whites remained rare among the Seminoles into the 1920s. Those who engaged in such relationships faced social marginalization.[185] As religion and education divided the tribe and the power of traditional leaders over Christian converts weakened, however, some Seminoles married and had sexual relationships with outsiders. Betty Mae Tiger Jumper, who later became the chair of the Seminole Tribe of Florida, was born of one of these unions in 1923. Her mother, a Christian convert named Ada Tiger, had a brief relationship with a French trapper. The relationship ended, but Ada received support from her mother and uncle, who had also converted to Christianity. Betty Mae Tiger Jumper recalled, "Before me, all half-breeds were killed as soon as they were born. None were as lucky as I, being born into a family that had received Christ." To avoid punishment by other Seminoles, the family moved to the Dania Reservation in 1928.[186] In the 1930s, a few Seminole men also entered relationships with whites. Willie Willie, for example, married a white woman after spending several years in Miami.[187] The union did not last, but his white wife was included on several tribal censuses.[188] In 1943, another Seminole man, Larry M. Osceola, married a white woman.[189] Around the same time, a Seminole woman named Elizabeth Buster had a child with a black man in the Ochoppe Lumber camp.[190]

Although Seminoles who had relationships with outsiders no longer faced physical punishment, these unions still carried a social stigma. Willie Willie's acceptance of white culture and his marriage to a white woman incurred the wrath of his family. His nephew, Buffalo Tiger, recalled that "When he got sick and die[d], my aunts and my mom didn't go see him. . . . They just hate so much they couldn't forget what he was saying."[191] Ethel Cutler Freeman reported that in the early 1940s the Seminoles shunned a woman named Hot Potato because she had a child by a white man.[192] Although Hot Potato later rejoined the tribe and married Henry Cypress in 1948, the Seminoles' initial reaction to her mixed-ancestry child showed that old attitudes were deep-rooted, especially among culturally conservative Mikasuki-speakers.[193] Lottie Johns Baxley, whose father was white, remembered that other Seminoles called her "a white lady or a white woman or white girl," which they meant as an insult.[194] Freeman speculated that another Seminole woman whom she saw working with African Americans in a tomato field in 1946 was Elizabeth Buster. She suspected that the Seminoles had punished Buster for her union with a black man by making her "stay with negroes."[195]

By the late 1950s, older Seminoles continued to disapprove of intermarriages, but others took them in stride.[196] According to Ross Allen, a white man who worked with the Seminoles, some inflicted "a quiet type of punishment" on Indians who married outsiders, by spreading gossip about them and using other forms of social regulation.[197] In certain cases, however, Seminoles looked for ways to incorporate outside spouses into the community. Buffalo Tiger, for example, married a white woman named Ann. At first his relatives were suspicious, but after they visited the couple's home a number of times, "they

Figure 5.5 Betty Mae Tiger Jumper (pictured) was the daughter of a Seminole woman, Ada Tiger, and a French fur trapper. Relationships with white men were strictly taboo for Seminole women, and prior to Jumper's birth in 1923 the tribe killed most half-white children. Over time, Seminole attitudes toward mixed-ancestry children softened and the tribe accepted the children of Seminole mothers regardless of their father's identity. In 1967, Betty Mae Tiger Jumper was elected as the first female chair of the Seminole Tribe of Florida. Date: 1967. Courtesy of the State Archives of Florida (image no. PR04788).

finally got to like the woman [he] married" and "invited her out to their camp in the Everglades." Ann did her best to make herself agreeable by teaching her husband's family to cut sterile bandages to treat wounds and helping to deliver babies. According to Buffalo Tiger, "those are the kind of things people liked and they kind of accepted her pretty well." Eventually, some of the Mikasuki medicine men told Ann that if she proved herself over the next few years, they could "make [her] brown." Buffalo Tiger explained that "They did not mean skin change to brown, the spirit is brown": Ann would become one of them. Before this transformation occurred, however, Buffalo Tiger and Ann divorced. Later, he married another white woman named Phoebe.[198] Failed marriages brought the common rebuke: "Well, you shouldn't have married outside of your people, because this is added problems."[199]

Despite lingering disapproval of intermarriages, there was always a place for a child in Seminole camps.[200] Seminoles no longer killed or shunned mixed-ancestry children by the mid-twentieth century; instead, they raised them as full community members. Even Indians who previously had scorned children with white fathers adjusted their views once their own family members bore mixed-ancestry children. Lottie Johns Baxley, for example, triumphantly noted that Seminoles who had made fun of her white ancestry "are eating their words today, because of their daughters who ran around and got pregnant. Most of [their children] are part white and most of them are part Mexican."[201] Seminoles came to accept these children regardless of paternity. Traditional matrilineal kinship practices ensured that even those children abandoned by their non-Indian fathers found family support in the tribe. Judie Kannon, a teacher at the Big Cypress Reservation School, for example, remembered the family of one Seminole woman who had children by Indian, Mexican, and white fathers. After the men left her, the woman raised the children with the help of her brother.[202]

Although Seminoles gradually accepted mixed-ancestry children born to Indian mothers, the children of Seminole fathers were a different story. A few Seminole men married non-Indian women, but most children born of unions between Seminoles and outsiders were illegitimate. The tribe accepted the illegitimate children of Seminole mothers, but notions of matrilineal descent ensured that children who resulted from brief affairs between Seminole men and outside women received little consideration. Raised by their non-Indian mothers away from the tribal community, in the view of the tribe, these children did not deserve rights as Seminoles. White officials also denied them tribal citizenship if they lacked proof of paternity, although census takers presumably would have included the recognized children of Seminole men with non-Indian wives.

An example of an individual who asserted Seminole paternity but was denied tribal inclusion was Charles Giddean Stanaland. Stanaland claimed to be the son of a full-blood Seminole "herb doctor" who had practiced medicine across Florida in the late nineteenth century. Whites who knew Stanaland attested to his Indian identity.[203] Stanaland apparently sought enrollment as a Seminole in 1945 so that his eight-year-old daughter could attend a white public school that had denied her admittance on account of her skin color. He believed that enrollment as Seminole would put to rest suspicions that his family had African, rather than Indian, ancestry. Despite his efforts, the Seminoles rejected him since his mother was white. The superintendent of the tribe and the commissioner of Indian affairs agreed.[204] The commissioner asserted that "In the absence of any official records substantiating the contention that Mr. Stanaland is of Indian ancestry," Stanaland was "in the same classification as countless other persons in the United States who possess Indian blood but who cannot be officially recognized as Indians because of lack of proof in the official records."[205] Euro-American concepts of illegitimacy worked in tandem with Seminole ideas of matrilineal kinship to deny Stanaland a place on the tribal censuses.

Questions of tribal belonging grew more important as the Seminoles considered politically organizing their tribe in the mid-twentieth century. Soon after the US Congress passed the Indian Reorganization Act (IRA) in 1934, federal officials, including Commissioner of Indian Affairs John Collier, visited Florida to encourage the Seminoles to write a constitution and establish a formal tribal government. The Seminoles, however, were suspicious of this overture and very few Indians voted on reorganization. Only twenty-one Indians out of 500 or 600 voted, which was far less than the 30 percent of the voting population required for the act to take effect. Despite the Seminoles' lack of enthusiasm, Interior Department officials decided that since all those who voted agreed to accept the act, the Seminoles could organize under its terms. Without broader support from the Indians, officials declined to pursue reorganization activities at that time, but they left the door open for future efforts.[206]

In 1945, officials in Florida renewed attempts to interest the Seminoles in political organization. They discussed plans with the Seminoles that would set up four political districts: the Dania Reservation, the Brighton Reservation, the Big Cypress Reservation, and the area along the Tamiami Trail. Federal agents suggested that each of these districts elect two or three representatives to serve on a constitutional committee. Seminoles living on the reservations took some notice of the plans. Mikasuki-speakers along the Tamiami Trail, however, were not interested. According to Seminole Agency Superintendent Kenneth A. Marmon, "after some effort it was thought best not to continue the idea of setting up a constitution and bylaws for the tribe until a later date."[207]

Although not ready to organize a tribal government, the Seminoles participated in new economic development plans during these years that included a political component. In 1936, the Seminole Agency acquired a foundation cattle herd from a drought-stricken area in the southwestern United States. Although the cattle were in such poor condition that many of them died en route, 500 survived the journey and arrived at the Brighton and Dania reservations.[208] The following year, the agency fenced off trust land in the Brighton area and moved all the cattle to that reservation.[209] Under the terms of the cattle project, the Seminoles elected three men to represent the tribe and to carry on its business in connection with the cattle program. In 1945, the number of elected trustees expanded after the tribe and federal officials split the program into the Brighton Agricultural and Livestock Enterprise and the Big Cypress Agricultural and Livestock Enterprise. Both Seminole men and women voted to elect the trustees.[210] Eventually the cattle committee grew into a three-reservation, twelve-trustee committee, which gave the Seminoles a new political structure that rivaled that of the old medicine men. In 1939, members of the committee met with Jacksonville lawyers to examine tribal claims against the federal government for early land losses. Not all Seminoles agreed with this action: off-reservation Mikasukis objected that money could not replace stolen land.[211] These divisions reflected divergent attitudes among the Seminoles over the best course of action to pursue in response to new pressures. They foreshadowed later political debates in the tribe.

Land claim issues reemerged in 1950. Seminoles argued that the United States had violated nineteenth-century treaties and had taken over more land than stipulated in these documents. In particular, the Indians cited the Macomb agreement of 1839. According to Billy Bowlegs, "the Seminoles understood that the treaty would state that the boundaries of their reservation lands would be along the lines that they (the Seminoles) marked out." Instead, "when the white men had the treaty made up, the map called for a smaller area that did not go so far north." Incensed that the United States had defrauded them, but hopeful that shifts in federal Indian policy like the establishment of the Indian Claims Commission would give them an opportunity for redress, reservation Indians met and discussed their options.[212] These efforts opened tribal divisions. Non-reservation Mikasuki-speakers objected to taking the matter to court because they feared a monetary settlement would strip them of the opportunity to get land.[213] Reservation Indians, on the other hand, saw the actions as necessary for the Seminoles to receive compensation of any kind. The work of reservation Seminoles to organize the claim against the United States also encouraged them to consider the political future of the tribe.

In the early 1950s, Superintendent Kenneth A. Marmon renewed efforts to reorganize the tribe. He wrote to Seminoles involved in the cattle program and proposed that they adopt a constitution and bylaws.[214] Marmon, a Pueblo Indian, wanted to create a ten-year development program for the Seminoles and realized that the tribe could more easily accomplish this task with a formal government in place.[215] W. O. Roberts, the Bureau of Indian Affairs area director in Oklahoma, sent Marmon a draft copy of a proposed constitution and bylaws for the Seminoles, which, on January 20, 1953, Marmon presented to a tribal committee that represented Seminoles from across Florida.[216] According to Marmon, the committee had "a very good meeting" and reviewed more than half of the proposed constitution.[217] When the committee met again in late February 1953, however, they proposed a few changes to the document. In particular, committee members asked that the name of the official governing body of the Seminoles listed in the constitution as "Seminole Business Council" be changed to "Seminole Board of Managers." They reasoned that the word "council" in the constitution might threaten the position of medicine men who governed at Brighton and along the Tamiami Trail, and they did not want the new government to supersede more traditional forms of authority.[218] This revision highlighted ongoing tribal divisions between Seminoles who adhered to more culturally conservative life ways and those who desired political change. The constitutional committee tried to accommodate both perspectives.

The document also delineated citizenship requirements in the proposed "Seminole Nation of Florida." According to the third article of the constitution, "The membership of the Seminole Nation of Florida shall consist of the Tribes of Indians heretofore known as both Miccosuki and Cow Creek Indians" whose names appeared "on the official census roll of the Florida Seminole Agency as of January 1, 1953," and "all children of at least one-half degree of Indian blood born to any member of the Miccosuki and Cow Creek Tribes."[219] The high blood quantum restriction conformed to federal definitions of "Indian" as laid out in the IRA but also reflected Seminole attitudes toward interracial relationships. A fairly recent phenomenon for the Florida Seminoles—at least when it came to white-Indian unions—interracial relationships remained a sensitive issue for many Indians. Although the Seminoles decided to include mixed-ancestry children, they hoped to discourage unions with outsiders by insisting that additions to the tribal roll had close kin ties to recognized, "full-blood" tribal citizens.

Despite the compromises made by members of the constitutional committee, internal tribal divisions stalled the ratification of the proposed constitution. In the meantime, external political forces placed new pressures on the Seminoles. In 1953, Marmon received word that the government wanted to terminate the Seminoles as a tribal group, a move that put their land as well as their federal services in jeopardy. This news created fresh tensions between Seminoles who wanted to organize and those who preferred traditional political systems. In particular, non-reservation Mikasuki-speakers questioned the advisability of an organized political structure that might compete with older forms of authority. They distrusted whites and white forms of governance. Many Seminoles, however, saw political organization as a way to combat termination legislation. Tribal citizens like Betty Mae Tiger Jumper and her husband, Moses Jumper, insisted that political organization was their best chance of survival. At the very least, the Seminoles needed time to work through their political divisions. After the assistant director of the Muskogee office visited the tribe and explained the termination proceedings, Seminoles met and requested that the government take no action on the plans for twenty-five years.[220] With the help of white allies like the Friends of the Seminoles, tribal citizens traveled to Washington, DC, and presented their case before the Bureau of Indian Affairs.[221] After hearing numerous appeals from the tribe, in 1954 the US Congress agreed to suspend Seminole termination.[222]

Although they stalled termination without adopting a tribal constitution and bylaws, many Seminoles continued to press for formal political organization and federal recognition. These Indians, led by "progressive" thinkers like Frank Billie of Big Cypress, believed that a tribal constitution would help them preserve their political autonomy and retain and expand federal services.[223] They reasoned that their old form of tribal government was not as effective as it had been in the past, and they expected a formal tribal government to represent their interests to local, state, and federal officials.[224] Political organization also would enable the tribe to make improvements on the reservations and to have a voice in the direction of the cattle industry.[225] In 1957, after months of negotiations, the Seminole Tribe of Florida achieved federal recognition. Under its constitution and bylaws, the tribe set up two governing bodies: the tribal council, led by a chairman, which dealt with the social and general welfare matters of the tribe, and the board of directors, led by a president, which managed the tribe's business affairs.[226]

When it came to tribal citizenship, the constitution of the Seminole Tribe of Florida stipulated that "any person of Seminole Indian blood whose name appears on the census roll of the Seminole Agency of January 1, 1957, shall be eligible for enrollment, regardless of blood quality or place of residence, upon written application to the tribal council." Historian Harry A. Kersey Jr. has argued that the non-restrictive stance of this citizenship article may have reflected the uncertainty of the constitutional committee over how many "full-blood" Seminoles would vote on the constitution. Hoping to build a consensus by encouraging the broadest participation possible and assuming that "mixed bloods" would approve the document, the committee extended citizenship to Seminoles of all backgrounds. By omitting a residency requirement, the constitutional committee also hoped to attract non-reservation Mikasukis to the tribe.[227] This decision also may have reflected the ambivalent feelings some Seminoles continued to hold toward their reservation lands. In Seminole eyes, kinship mattered more than geography. Very few Seminoles had permanently moved away from Florida in the twentieth century. Most Seminole children who attended boarding schools in other states, for example, returned home after receiving their education.[228] The Seminoles saw no reason to exclude tribal citizens from tribal benefits based on their residency, perhaps in part because such a ruling would have affected so few people.

The 1957 census roll of the Seminole Agency served as the base roll for the new Seminole Tribe of Florida. Since the end of the Third Seminole War, white Floridians had periodically attempted to enumerate the Indians remaining in the state. This was no simple task given the scattered and remote settlement patterns of the Seminoles.[229] Whites complained that "no accurate figures can be obtained, owing to their shyness and dread of anything pertaining to 'red tape.'" According to one story, a Florida cattleman had tried to take a census of the Indians by inviting them to a festival. The Seminoles refused to fall for this trick, however, "and no amount of argument or explanation could convince them that the invitation did not arise for sinister motives."[230] Federal census takers also failed to enumerate the Seminoles. Prior to 1880, census takers ignored them almost entirely, reporting just one Indian in Florida in 1860, and two in 1870.[231] Richard Henry Pratt and Clay MacCauley had better luck in the late 1870s and early 1880s, recording respectively 292 and 208 Seminoles in their surveys of the tribe.[232] It was not until the early twentieth century, however, that officials began to document Seminoles accurately.

The federal census of 1900 was the first in which the United States appointed a special agent specifically to enumerate the Florida Seminoles. Brevard County surveyor J. Otto Fries traveled across Florida with a local guide and recorded 339 Seminoles in a census that Kersey has characterized as "the first accurate one in the modern era of the tribe."[233] Despite this effort, early twentieth-century government censuses contained significant errors due to the way they were compiled and ongoing Seminole suspicions of those making the lists. In particular, Fries characterized Mikasuki-speakers as "not so easy to get information from, but very suspicious about [his] doings."[234] In a 1913 report, anthropologist Alanson Skinner explained that Seminoles preserved a "taboo against telling their names to strangers."[235] Lucien A. Spencer, who took several early twentieth-century censuses of the Seminoles for the Indian Agency in Florida, similarly noted that many of the individuals he enumerated "refused to give name" or "refused to answer."[236] Seminole women were particularly reluctant to talk to census takers: most women merely appeared as "squaws," listed beneath their husbands, or as "unnamed widows" at the end of the documents.[237] In part, the women's reticence may have stemmed from a Seminole custom by which only a woman's mother and older clan relatives had permission to call her by her given name after the birth of her first child. All others had to refer to her in reference to her child's name.[238] The federal government lauded as reliable the 1914 Florida Agency census of the Seminoles, yet even this list was imperfect.[239] On a 1916 census, Spencer reported that he had to strike several duplicate names from the previous year's census because he discovered that the Indians used different names in different localities.[240] This confusion may have resulted from the fact that Seminole men, upon reaching adulthood, often went by various ceremonial or earned titles rather than their childhood names.[241]

Despite the confusion of earlier censuses, determining who belonged to the Seminole Tribe of Florida in 1957 was relatively straightforward. The strict social codes against interracial relationships enforced by the Seminoles in the late nineteenth and early twentieth centuries meant that by the 1950s most Indians either were "full bloods" or could easily trace their ancestry back to a full-blood Seminole. A federal memorandum noted in 1952 that out of a population of approximately 823 individuals, 728 were "full bloods."[242] Little controversy surrounded the development of the official tribal roll of the Seminole Tribe of Florida because there was little question of who legitimately belonged to the community. The main problem was determining to what sort of political entity Florida Seminoles belonged.

Despite the efforts of the Seminole Tribe of Florida to include non-reservation Mikasukis, many Indians remained opposed to formal organization. When federal officials inquired whether Mikasukis along the Tamiami Trail wanted to enroll in the tribe, Indians led by Ingraham Billie told them they wanted nothing to do with the Bureau of Indian Affairs or the reservation Seminoles.[243] Non-reservation Mikasukis considered the new tribal government illegitimate. Buffalo Tiger explained in an oral interview in the 1970s that his people believed that those who signed the constitution "were not really leaders in the first place, and they were not speaking for all the Indians in the first place." In his view, the council of medicine men maintained by non-reservation Mikasukis was the true governing body of the tribe.[244] Unable to convince them otherwise, federal officials abandoned their efforts to include non-reservation Mikasukis in the Seminole Tribe of Florida.

Despite the opposition of some Mikasuki-speakers, especially those living off-reservation along the Tamiami Trail, others chose to join the Seminole Tribe of Florida. Religious conversion helps explain why many Mikasuki-speakers united with Muskogees as citizens of the Seminole Tribe of Florida. Christian Mikasukis worshiped with Muskogee-speakers on the reservations. Indeed, Robert D. Mitchell reported that the reason the Big Cypress Reservation eventually became a Seminole reservation instead of a Miccosukee reservation was that "The Miccosukees who believed the old way pulled out of there, and they went back down the Trail, and they didn't have anything to do with those Indians that were Christians."[245] Christian Seminoles developed a common identity that superseded linguistic differences between Muskogees and Mikasukis.[246]

Economic incentives also encouraged Mikasukis to join the Seminole Tribe of Florida. On the adoption of a tribal constitution by the Seminoles, about $200,000, which had accrued in the tribal funds from the sale of cattle, land, and oil leases, became available for tribal projects. The Bureau of Indians Affairs also offered the tribe a loan from its revolving fund.[247] Seeing the financial benefits of citizenship, some anti-organization Mikasuki-speakers rethought their position. According to Buffalo Tiger, "everytime our Miccosukees got hungry—because money was hard to get and a lot of people were going hungry a long time—well, they went to Hollywood and they got twenty-five dollars. . . . They make the trip, and they got to sign up as a Seminole member so whole family can be member of the Tribe, and they got their money." These Mikasuki-speakers did not necessarily relish the prospect of becoming official tribal citizens, but economic conditions made signing up attractive, especially for those who had children to feed. According to Buffalo Tiger, "That's how we have lost many Miccosukees from here."[248]

Even Mikasuki-speakers who refused to join the Seminole Tribe of Florida began seeing advantages to political organization. Medicine men traditionally led the group, but non-reservation Mikasukis also appointed several other tribesmen to work with county and state authorities for the benefit of the community. Without a formal organization, however, the Mikasukis found this work challenging.[249] Hoping for validation from white officials, Mikasukis led by Buffalo Tiger developed a new constitution separate from that of the Seminole Tribe of Florida. Of the 355 non-reservation Mikasukis, 201 signed the constitution and declared themselves citizens of the Miccosukee Tribe of Indians. The state of Florida recognized their independent political status in 1957; later that year Miccosukee tribal citizens applied for control of a tract of land in a conservation area, as well as state land along US Highway 27. In 1958, the tribal council sent delegates to Washington, DC, to appeal for federal recognition.[250]

Although the federal government accepted the political organization of the Miccosukees, officials were unwilling to grant the tribe federal recognition because, unlike the Seminole Tribe of Florida, the Miccosukee Tribe did not have assets under the trusteeship of the federal government. They had refused to live on reservations or join the Seminole Tribe, so, officials reasoned, they had lost rights to lands the state and federal governments had purchased in the early twentieth century for Seminole use. Miccosukees did not give up their bid for federal acknowledgment or reservation lands easily. They threatened to take their case to the World Court at The Hague, and sent several letters pleading their case to President Dwight D. Eisenhower.[251] To bring publicity to their struggle, a lawyer for the Miccosukees helped arrange a trip to Cuba for tribal leaders in 1959.[252] Fidel Castro lavished the Indians with fancy cars,

sumptuous hotel rooms, and fine wines and granted them recognition from
the Cuban government. Newspapers eagerly followed the story and soon after
the Miccosukee leaders returned to Florida, the state governor agreed to provide them with their own reservation lands. Following more fractious political
debates and lobbying efforts, the federal government finally recognized the
Miccosukee Tribe of Indians of Florida as a separate tribe in 1962.[253]

To join the new tribe, Miccosukees signed their names to a tribal roll. The
Miccosukee constitution permitted only those adults and children of one-half
degree or more Miccosukee blood to enroll automatically; the Miccosukee
general council had to approve those with lesser blood degrees.[254] More restrictive than those for the Seminole Tribe of Florida, these criteria reflected
the culturally conservative perspective of Miccosukee tribal citizens. Some
non-reservation Indians, however, considered the new tribe not conservative
enough. These Mikasuki-speakers remained suspicious of any tribal government and, in particular, of the relationship federal recognition established
between the Miccosukee Tribe and the United States. As Robert D. Mitchell
explained, "they didn't trust the government. . . . They're still Miccosukees, but
they don't belong to the organized tribe." Refusing to join either the Seminole
Tribe or the Miccosukee Tribe, they chose instead to live like their ancestors
had done for generations.[255] This task grew more difficult as white settlement
expanded across Florida, yet these Mikasuki-speakers preferred to remain independent and unenrolled.

As the Miccosukees created their tribal rolls, the Seminole Tribe of Florida
modified its own citizenship requirements. In 1959, after reviewing their governing document, 135 Seminoles signed a petition asking for a revision of the
tribe's constitution. The tribe's new citizenship article, adopted in 1962, provided that "any person of one-fourth or more degree of Seminole Indian blood
born after the adoption of this amendment both of whose parents are members
of the tribe shall be enrolled as a tribal member." It also required applicants for
citizenship to appear on the census roll at the Seminole Agency as of January
1, 1957, and to have their bid for citizenship approved by the tribal council. By
adding blood quantum as a criterion for citizenship and by requiring applicants
to meet the approval of the tribal council, the tribe hoped to prevent individuals of limited Seminole ancestry from applying for citizenship.[256] Interestingly,
while the Seminoles added a blood quantum restriction to tribal citizenship,
the Miccosukees eventually dropped their blood quantum requirement in
favor of returning to a system of belonging based on matrilineal inheritance.[257]

Although the new Seminole constitution did not include a residency requirement for tribal citizenship, it granted those Seminoles who lived on the
reservation certain political rights denied those who lived elsewhere. Like the
Pamunkeys, the Seminoles used residency as a way to distinguish between

tribal citizens with full political rights and those who did not have the same privileges. The original constitution adopted by the tribe in 1957 had provided for at-large seats in the tribal council in recognition of Seminoles who did not live on the three federal reservations; the new constitution limited the right to elect tribal officials to reservation residents.[258] According to Joe Dan Osceola, who served as the president of the Seminole Tribe, Inc. in 1967, "you have to live on the reservation something like four years before you can vote." He described the ruling as "pretty stiff" because "if you live just [a] block, even half a block from the reservation, due to the housing shortage . . . they don't take that into consideration at all." The Seminoles made exceptions, however, for citizens who were away at college or who joined the armed forces.[259] Like the Pamunkeys, the Seminoles ensured that only those Seminoles invested in reservation issues had the power to participate in the politics of the community. This shift also reflected the presence of the new Miccosukee Tribe. Non-reservation Seminoles could join the Miccosukees and achieve political representation there. Residency on the Seminole reservations helped distinguish between the two tribes.

Also like the Pamunkeys, the Seminoles tried to use their new constitution to restrict the access of white men to their land. Although the Seminoles had accepted intermarriage and mixed-ancestry children, tribal leaders worried about the influence of outside spouses on the community. In particular, the Seminoles' long history of conflict-avoidance made them wary of admitting white men into their political and public life. Unable to prevent unions between non-Indians and Seminole women, the tribe did its best to control the consequences of these relationships by prohibiting Seminole women and their non-citizen husbands from living on reservation land.[260] Lottie Johns Baxley, for example, had to move off the reservation to live with her white husband in Okeechobee. The tribe similarly forced two of her cousins who married Mexican men to move away.[261] This residency rule did not extend equally to non-Indian wives: when a Seminole man married an outside woman, she could stay in his parents' camp on the reservation.[262] This practice inverted traditional Seminole residence patterns that called for husbands to join the camps of their wives. The Seminoles, like the Pamunkeys, viewed non-Indian women as less politically threatening than outside men.

The Seminoles hoped that by limiting the access of non-Indian men to tribal land, they could reduce the consequences of intermarriage on the political life of the tribe. Unlike the Pamunkeys, however, Seminole tribal leaders had difficulty enforcing the rule. Compared to the Pamunkeys, the Seminoles held a vast territory difficult to police. Moreover, unlike the Pamunkey tribal council, Seminole leaders did not have a system in place for divvying up land to tribal citizens. Seminole women soon began ignoring the residency restrictions.

Baxley pointed out in 1972 that "nowadays, an Indian girl marries a white man, or an Indian girl marries a Mexican and things like that, they all live out here on the Reservation." The rules had not changed, "it's just the people won't accept the laws of the Tribal Council, that's what it is."[263] By rejecting the rules, these women reinforced traditional Seminole matrilocal practices. They lived in the camps of their mothers rather than moving to the cities or towns of their non-Indian husbands.

By the mid-1960s, the Seminoles had divided into three groups: The Seminole Tribe of Florida, the Miccosukee Tribe of Indians of Florida, and the unorganized Mikasuki-speakers. In an oral interview, Seminole tribal citizen Mary Frances Johns summarized the three political positions of Florida Indians. The Seminole Tribe, she contended, "thought that we should progress ... live like the white people." This did not mean giving up traditional customs or language, but "they thought that we should have walled houses and be educated and be able to work with the white man in what he does." In contrast, the Miccosukee Tribe "wanted to have some of these modern conveniences ... but they wanted to stay where they were." Unwilling to compromise their independence to get federal services, "they figured [if] they needed education, they would educate their children and so forth." Finally, the unorganized Mikasuki-speakers "just decided that they would stay the way they had been for hundreds of years, and so they still do." Rejecting acculturation, "The only thing they depend on are jobs from the outside." These political divisions cut across linguistic boundaries and kin ties. Mikasuki-speakers did not uniformly join the Miccosukee Tribe. Indeed, two-thirds of the citizens of the Seminole Tribe spoke Mikasuki.[264] Occasionally members of the same family joined different tribes. Frank Billie, who became the first president of the Seminole Tribe, was the son of the leader of the anti-reservation Mikasuki movement, Ingraham Billie.[265] Florida Indians simply chose the group that most accurately reflected their political orientation and cultural preferences.

Citizenship between the Seminole and Miccosukee tribes remained fluid into the 1970s. According to Virgil Harrington, who served as the superintendent of the Seminole Indian Agency from 1958 to 1963, those who did not belong to the Seminole Tribe or the Miccosukee Tribe could join either polity, or tribal citizens could petition the councils to be dropped from one tribe to join the other.[266] Although the federal government did not permit Florida Indians to hold dual citizenship in the Seminole and Miccosukee tribes, the ongoing flexibility of the citizenship rolls allowed Mikasuki-speakers in particular to make decisions about which political body most accurately reflected their values. Kersey has argued that these early citizenship shifts helped prevent overt conflict within both tribes between culturally conservative and more acculturated tribal citizens.[267] If an individual was dissatisfied with the tribal government of one polity, he or she joined the other.

The Seminole Tribe of Florida experienced a surge in citizenship applications in the 1970s after the Indian Claims Commission finally settled their case against the federal government. The court awarded the Seminole Indians in Florida and Oklahoma $16 million in recompense for 32 million acres of land due to them by treaty. A researcher who visited the tribe explained the situation: "since word got out that there was some money to be apportioned among the various tribal members in one fashion or another, a number of people who in the past had not seen the need to become formal members of the Seminole Tribe of Florida have now decided that it might be to their advantage to do so."[268] Many people who applied for citizenship at this time were recognizable as Seminole; they simply had chosen not to enroll in previous years. Now enrollment gave them a formal political identity and guaranteed their right to a share of tribal resources. Other independent Mikasuki-speakers refused to enroll, but in 1990, the US Congress agreed that they too could participate in the award as long as they were listed on or were lineal descendants of persons included in the 1957 annotated Seminole Agency census. Enrollment was no longer necessary to participate in the settlement.[269] Legal battles between Seminoles in Florida and Oklahoma delayed the distribution of the awarded funds for several decades. Nevertheless, the promise of financial benefits to tribal citizens alerted people to the economic value of tribal citizenship.

More significant than the Indian Claims Commission settlement to the economic value of tribal citizenship has been the Seminole Tribe of Florida's successful foray into the world of high-stakes gaming. In 1976, the Seminoles opened tribally regulated tobacco sales operations, known as smoke shops. Three years later, they opened Hollywood Seminole Bingo, the first tribally operated high-stakes bingo hall in the United States.[270] Although Florida legislators objected to these new businesses, the Fifth District Court of Appeals recognized the legal right of the Seminoles to operate their gaming enterprise free of state regulation. The *Seminole Tribe of Florida v. Butterworth* (1981) case paved the way for tribal gaming across the United States.[271] In the early 1990s, the tribe installed electronic games, and by 2006, the Seminoles had built new Hard Rock casino-resorts in Florida. Tribal net income from gaming that year surpassed $600 million.[272] As the Seminole Tribe of Florida became rich, tribal citizenship took on a new economic value.

Casino profits have encouraged many Americans to seek citizenship in the Seminole Tribe of Florida. In the early 2000s, the tribal enrollment officer, LaVonne Kippenberger, received thirty to forty phone calls and emails a week inquiring how individuals could join the tribe. According to anthropologist Jessica R. Cattelino, "Some people claim to physically resemble the warrior

Osceola, others say they always knew they were Indian, and still others simply ask about the money." None of these assertions, Kippenberger has maintained, are valid. The tribe also has faced claims by non-Indian women who avow that their children have Seminole fathers. Some Seminoles believe that such women purposely get pregnant by Seminole men in order to profit from their children's casino dividends. Tribal citizens call these children "dividend babies." In response to this threat, the Seminole Tribe of Florida increasingly demands DNA paternity tests before granting children citizenship.[273] Casino profits have benefited the tribe economically, but they have also opened new citizenship controversies.

Today the Seminole Tribe of Florida and the Miccosukee Tribe of Indians of Florida each maintain their own citizenship criteria. Citizens of the Seminole Tribe of Florida must meet three requirements. First, they must be able to trace a direct ancestor to the 1957 tribal census, which the tribe considers its base roll. Second, they must have a minimum of one-quarter Seminole blood. Finally, their petition must be sponsored by a recognized tribal citizen. The Seminoles insist on high blood quantum for citizens because they consider this an indication of close association with the tribe. As the Seminole tribal website explains, one-quarter degree Seminole blood indicates that an applicant for citizenship is "no more than a single generation removed from the cultural heritage."[274] Not all tribal citizens agree with this stipulation. Cattelino reported that in recent years a minority movement in the tribe has advocated a constitutional reform to replace one-fourth blood quantum with clan membership as a necessary qualification for tribal citizenship.[275] The children of Seminole fathers and non-Indian mothers carry no clan, however, so this ruling would disinherit them. Thus far, the tribe has made no serious initiative to change the blood quantum requirement. Sponsorship by a recognized tribal citizen furthers the tribe's goal of maintaining close association between citizens by ensuring that the community recognizes an applicant as a Seminole. It also discourages "dividend babies" from making their way onto the tribal roll.

In contrast to the Seminoles, modern Miccosukees, who also have gaming enterprises, incorporate traditional matrilineal definitions of kinship and identity, which reflect their history of resistance to acculturation.[276] Although the tribe once required citizens to have one-half Miccosukee "blood" in order to qualify as "Indian" under the terms of the IRA, today, according to their website, "Membership in the Miccosukee Tribe of Indians of Florida is open to Indians who have Miccosukee mothers and are not enrolled in any other Tribe."[277] The Miccosukees rely on matrilineal kin ties to ensure that tribal citizens have close relationships with the core Miccosukee communities along the Tamiami Trail, Alligator Alley, and Krome Avenue. This change represents a return to more traditional notions of belonging. As for the unorganized

Mikasuki-speakers, without an officially recognized political status, they do not have formal citizenship criteria. Like the Pamunkeys before the Bureau of Indian Affairs approved their federal recognition bid, they are free to determine belonging as they see fit without outside interference.

Today, the population of the Seminole Tribe of Florida stands at about 3,100. Miccosukees number approximately 600 enrolled tribal citizens.[278] Around 100 individuals known as "Independents" or "Traditionals" continue to reject citizenship in either tribe.[279] Although these groups share a complex history, cultural practices, and kin ties, they are politically distinct. The citizenship criteria developed by the Seminole and Miccosukee tribes reflect the divergent political goals of their citizens and empower them to decide who belongs and what citizenship means. Tribal citizenship has served the Florida Seminoles as a way to create separate political identities for people who share similar ethnic and cultural backgrounds but differing ideas about the future. The histories of the Seminole Tribe of Florida, the Miccosukee Tribe of Indians of Florida, and the unorganized Mikasukis illustrate that tribes do not embody strictly racialized notions of what it means to be "Indian," although race certainly has influenced ideas of belonging over time. Instead, tribal citizenship establishes a legal identity for Indian people—an identity rooted in history but mindful of the present and future political goals of tribal nations and their citizens.

Conclusion

Who Belongs?

In the nearly two centuries since removal left thousands of Indians in the South, many people have shared Sharon Flora's dismay at not gaining acceptance by an Indian tribe. For a host of reasons ranging from romantic notions about Indians to crass opportunism, they have sought tribal citizenship and failed. Knowledge of or belief in Native ancestry makes this failure a particularly bitter pill. Exclusion often strikes applicants as petty, selfish, and mean. Modern tribes, however, base their decisions about admission to tribal citizenship on historically developed criteria. This book has dealt with the process by which six of them—the Pamunkey Indian Tribe, the Catawba Indian Nation, the Mississippi Band of Choctaw Indians, the Eastern Band of Cherokee Indians, the Seminole Tribe of Florida, and the Miccosukee Tribe of Indians of Florida—decided who belonged.

Southeastern Indians struggled for decades after removal to retain their lands and other resources. The Pamunkeys and the Catawbas held state reservations; the Choctaws, although squatters in Mississippi, claimed citizenship in the land-rich Choctaw Nation in the West; the Eastern Cherokees held the Qualla Boundary in common as a tribe, corporation, and federal ward; and the Seminoles, including those who later joined the Miccosukee Tribe, claimed vast acreage in south Florida on which they lived and which they ultimately received, in part, as several smaller reservations. Furthermore, some tribes had income: Catawbas drew an annual state appropriation and Cherokees had proceeds from federal claims and timber sales. These resources, meager though they were, tempted people with few or no ties to the tribes to assert the rights of citizenship, which included access to tribal assets. The fear of losing what little they had left provided tribes with a strong incentive to police the boundaries of their citizenship.

In addition to fearing the loss of tribal resources, Indians worried about losing their political identity in the Jim Crow South. Racial segregation created a black-and-white world that left little room for Indians, who did not fit neatly into either racial category. On the basis of their skin color, whites denied them equal rights, but Indians rejected the label of "colored" and insisted that their historical relationships with state and federal governments warranted them a status separate from African Americans. Indians expected their political identity as tribal citizens to protect them from absorption into a "colored" underclass in the South, but they recognized that their legal rights depended largely on how outsiders perceived them. State-recognized tribes like the Pamunkeys and Catawbas were particularly vulnerable to reclassification as "colored." Without formal ties to the federal government in the late nineteenth and early twentieth centuries, these tribes risked losing their reservations and resources if state officials did not uphold their tribal rights. At the same time, the Seminoles were concerned about whites gaining a foothold within their tribe. All six southeastern tribes established citizenship criteria in this racially charged environment, which their criteria reflected, but they reached different solutions to the problem of race.

As tribes confronted threats to their resources and identities, they searched for new ways to delineate tribal citizenship. Historically, tribes had relied on general markers of belonging such as cultural affinity and ancestry. If someone spoke the tribal language, joined in ceremonies and celebrations, cooked and ate particular foods, perpetuated ancient skills, adhered to certain beliefs and worldviews, and maintained kin ties with other people in the community, Indians recognized that person as a tribal citizen. These factors continued to influence citizenship decisions in the late nineteenth and twentieth centuries, but social changes required Indians to reformulate notions of belonging. Older markers grew difficult to maintain as people left reservation lands to live elsewhere, Indian children went to boarding schools, interactions with non-Indians increased, and tribal citizens began marrying outsiders. In response to these shifts, tribes modified their citizenship rules.

The migration of community members away from tribal lands raised questions about the relative rights of those who left and those who stayed. Over the course of the late nineteenth and twentieth centuries, Indians increasingly left home for a variety of reasons. Some attended federal boarding schools while others joined the military or looked for jobs in cities where their racial identity was not as stigmatized. Still others—like Catawba converts to Mormonism—left for religious reasons. In particular, after the Second World War a steady stream of Indians moved to urban areas. Some took advantage of the federal government's relocation program while others moved on their own. Today, more than two-thirds of Indian people live in and around cities.

Indians worried that if community members moved away, the migrants, and especially their descendants born away from the homeland, eventually would lose their cultural identification with the tribal community and decline to invest in its future. This fear was particularly salient for those Indians who depended on reservation lands and tribal assets for their livelihoods: they worried about empowering non-resident tribal citizens at the expense of reservation-based investment in physical infrastructure, education, law enforcement, and other services.[1] They wanted to ensure that only people invested in the home community had power to make decisions for the tribe.

To deal with the threat of distant people claiming tribal rights, southeastern tribes adopted different strategies. Some, like the Cherokees, refused to include on the base roll the children of tribal citizens who moved away and married outsiders, although the migrants themselves retained their rights. Others, like the Catawbas, insisted that only those who returned to the main tribal body deserved a share of tribal resources. When the Choctaw Nation in Indian Territory made a similar decision, the Mississippi Choctaws were left without a political identity until they insisted that the federal government recognize their separate tribal status in Mississippi. The Pamunkeys established a particularly interesting way to deal with the problem of migration. Those who left still belonged to the tribe, but they could not exercise political rights unless they returned to the reservation. The Seminoles similarly restricted voting in tribal elections to those who lived on tribal land, which also helped to distinguish between Seminole tribal citizens and those who joined the Miccosukee Tribe. Each strategy helped to protect the political cohesion and economic base of the tribes even as circumstances drew some Indians away from home.

Another problem faced by southeastern Indians was that of intermarriage and sexual relationships with outsiders. Tribes in the region had suffered substantial population loss due to years of hardship, disease, and removal. By the late nineteenth century, marriage with outsiders seemed, for some, the only viable way to find non-related partners and to keep up tribal numbers. Yet these unions challenged tribes to redefine their terms of inclusion, especially in the racial context of the Jim Crow South. In the past, most southeastern tribes traced kinship matrilineally, making the children of Indian women tribal citizens no matter the identity of the father, but not the children of Indian men and non-Indian women. Tribes had to decide whether to keep this gendered system, especially as male tribal citizens began demanding rights for their children by non-citizens. Ultimately nearly all southeastern tribes shifted to bilateral inheritance, although culturally conservative Seminoles who joined the Miccosukee Tribe later returned to a matrilineal system. Tribes also looked for ways to limit the influence of non-Indian spouses in reservation communities by passing rules that restricted the access of these outsiders to tribal resources.

Racial segregation in the South encouraged tribes to develop different attitudes toward intermarriage with blacks and whites, which further complicated the question of who belonged. Indians worried that if tribal citizens formed unions with blacks, outsiders would cease to recognize their political status or their racial identity as Indian. State-recognized tribes found this situation especially dangerous due to their already precarious legal status in the South. To prevent amalgamation with blacks and extinction in the eyes of whites, southern tribes seemingly bought into the "hierarchy of color and ancestry" that permeated American discourse, law, and policy.[2] They established segregated institutions, avoided intermarriage, and made difficult choices when it came to family members who crossed the color line. The Pamunkeys, for example, prohibited relationships between blacks and tribal citizens in their late nineteenth-century reservation laws; those who violated the law faced expulsion from the tribe. The Catawbas used social pressure to ensure that tribal citizens did not associate with African Americans. Mississippi Choctaws who married black people simply left the tribal community and merged with the larger African American population; other Choctaws no longer recognized them as tribal citizens. Federally recognized tribes like the Cherokees were less concerned about losing their legal status through amalgamation, but they nonetheless internalized the racial prejudice of the surrounding white population and considered intermarriage with blacks undesirable. The Florida Seminoles proved the one exception to the general trend of southeastern tribes to avoid interactions with blacks. Their historical experiences with escaped African slaves and the ongoing presence of a few black women who remained with the tribe following removal created a unique situation in which the Seminoles tolerated certain relationships with blacks. Even the Seminoles, however, viewed the children of these unions as less-than-equal tribal citizens. American racial ideologies constrained the choices tribes made about their citizenship, which sometimes led to deep divisions and wounds that last to the present day.

Although usually preferred over intermarriage with blacks, relationships with whites posed their own challenges to southeastern tribes. In general, Indians did not worry about losing their identity through white intermarriage because white Americans considered the children of these unions racially Indian, not white. There were, however, exceptions. The Mississippi Choctaws, for example, discovered that diluted Indian "blood" restricted their access to Choctaw Nation citizenship and federal recognition, even though phenotypically Indian "mixed bloods" also were denied the privileges of a white racial identity. As a result of the particular policies they faced in Mississippi and the state's harsh anti-miscegenation laws, Choctaws rarely married whites after the second removal of the early twentieth century. They knew that in order to keep their racial identity and political status as "Indian," they had to convince officials of their presumed racial purity.

Other southeastern Indians, like the Pamunkeys, Catawbas, and Cherokees, did marry whites and sometimes brought white spouses to live with them on tribal lands. They worried, however, about the influence of outsiders on tribal affairs. Tribes developed particular rules to deal with the potential threat of meddling white spouses. Some, like the Pamunkeys, restricted the access of white men to tribal resources by requiring Indian women who married outsiders to leave the reservation. Others, like the Catawbas, initially insisted that traditional rules of matrilineal inheritance dictate the inclusion of the children of tribal citizens who married whites, thereby providing a sense of stability to a potentially volatile situation. Only one tribe, the Seminoles, prohibited intermarriage with whites altogether until well into the twentieth century. This decision, like the one they made about relationships with blacks, reflected their particular historical experiences in Florida.

In addition to their concerns about intermarriage, Indians worried about people who, despite lacking an ongoing political connection to the tribe, claimed distant Indian ancestry in order to demand a share of tribal assets. Remnant tribes like the Mississippi Choctaws and Eastern Band of Cherokees were especially vulnerable to the claims of such individuals because the removal of the Five Tribes to Indian Territory had left people with Indian ancestry scattered across the South. Although most of these individuals did not have a political identity as tribal citizens, many hoped to claim a share of tribal resources by virtue of their assumed ancestry. Tribes dealt with these claimants as best they could. Both the Mississippi Choctaws and the Eastern Band of Cherokees adopted "blood quantum" restrictions to citizenship in the late nineteenth and early twentieth centuries in part as a strategy to distinguish themselves from false claimants and to ensure that only closely related individuals shared in tribal lands and money. The Seminoles followed suit when they organized into two federally recognized tribes in the mid-twentieth century, although the Miccosukees eventually dropped their blood quantum restriction. Smaller tribes like the Pamunkeys and Catawbas, however, rejected blood as a criterion because they recognized that intermarriage with whites was unavoidable for their closely related populations. If these tribes were to survive, they had to include the children of Indians and whites, no matter their blood degree, or risk disappearing in a few generations.

Notions of "blood quantum" entered Indian discourses on tribal citizenship by way of federal officials, who frequently had recorded the degree of "Indian blood" possessed by tribal citizens on nineteenth-century censuses. As the apparatus for managing Indian affairs grew more bureaucratized in the late nineteenth and twentieth centuries, these officials pressed tribes that received services or benefits from state or federal governments to delineate clearly who belonged to the tribe and who was entitled to a share of its resources. Tribes responded to these pressures by turning to legalistic and seemingly objective criteria—like "blood"—to make their citizenship rules. They hoped that if they spelled out their requirements in language white Americans understood, officials would accept tribal decisions on citizenship. By the early twentieth century, many Indians had internalized notions of blood, which they in turn codified in their tribal constitutions.[3]

Indians used ideas of blood, however, for their own purposes. Some, like the Mississippi Choctaws, adopted the language of blood as a strategy to demand federal recognition of their political status as Indian despite losing citizenship in another tribe. Tribes also tied "blood" to "culture": blood became an index for how connected an individual was to the tribal community. The Eastern Band of Cherokee Indians, for example, required that tribal citizens possess a blood quantum of one-sixteenth or more in order to protect its resources from distantly related outsiders who no longer participated in Cherokee social or political life. Indians also used blood as a stand-in for ancestry. Rather than record the general "Indian blood" of tribal citizens, they began to require tribally specific designations of "Choctaw blood," "Cherokee blood," or "Seminole blood." In this way, tribes used blood to assess the kin ties of citizenship applicants to the tribal community.[4]

Somewhat counterintuitively, federal agents occasionally used "blood" to promote more inclusive ideas of tribal citizenship than did the tribes themselves. Wrapped up in the racial ideas of the time, these officials viewed certain people as racially "Indian," even when the tribe questioned their legitimacy as citizens. During the allotment of lands in Indian Territory, for example, the Choctaw Nation did not want to recognize the citizenship claims of Mississippi Choctaws who could not document their descent from beneficiaries of the Choctaw removal treaty. Federal officials insisted, however, that the Choctaw Nation acknowledge "full bloods" in Mississippi as citizens without proof. Similarly, when federal officials compiled the Eastern Cherokee roll in the 1920s, the tribal council wanted to restrict citizenship to those with one-sixteenth or more Indian blood. The Interior Department, however, refused to abide by this rule and instead enrolled hundreds of people without the requisite "blood quantum." For white officials, the racially Indian identity of these individuals equated to tribal citizenship despite the rulings of tribal governments to the contrary.

White officials were not consistent in their application of blood quantum rules, however, or in how liberal they were willing to be when it came to recognizing people as "Indian." In the 1950s in Virginia, for example, state officials imposed blood limitations on whom the state acknowledged as Indian: only those who were more than one-quarter Indian and less than one-sixteenth black made the cut. Similarly, in the 1990s, South Carolina unsuccessfully pressured the Catawba Indian Nation to include a one-eighth blood quantum restriction in its citizenship criteria in the hope that such a rule would eventually reduce the number of Indians the state had to serve. State and federal ideas about "blood" were inconsistent but not illogical. When it came to the distribution of tribal resources, officials did not mind recognizing more people as Indian since the land and money came from the tribe. When it came to questions of who was entitled to state or federal services, however, officials endeavored to reduce the number of recognized tribal citizens. In both cases, blood quantum became an effective tool of "settler-colonial erasure" since tribes and legitimate tribal citizens were the ultimate losers.[5] In the first case, tribes lost land and property to people whom they did not consider citizens and in the second case government officials attempted to deny the legality of certain tribal citizens regardless of the wishes of the tribe.

Although federal and state policies influenced them, tribes did not simply abandon older ways of reckoning belonging in favor of bureaucratized and racialized criteria. Instead, they looked for ways to repackage older concepts into new forms that fit their changing circumstances. Kinship, for example, had always been a key element of belonging to Native communities. People knew who they were based on the relatives they had; kinship defined the social sphere, the rights, and the responsibilities of tribal citizens. Indeed, extended kinship groups or clans formed the basic units of almost all tribal societies.[6] Although definitions of family changed as tribal citizens increasingly married outsiders and adopted Euro-American gender conventions over the course of the nineteenth and twentieth centuries, kinship continued to play a vital role in concepts of tribal identity. To make sure that only recognized relatives were included on the rolls, tribes borrowed concepts of "descent" and "blood" to make these connections clear to white America. Rather than abandon kinship, tribes redefined it in a way that fit Euro-American expectations.

Linguistic and cultural knowledge, political affiliation with the tribe, and participation in tribal life historically also served as markers of belonging. Myths, legends, and stories, for example, provided a foundation for individuals' social identity by tying people to the tribal landscape and explaining their role in the cosmic order.[7] Tribal citizens shared a worldview and a commitment to the well-being of the tribe that they reinforced in tribal ceremonies, dances, and other celebrations. To make these cultural values intelligible to white America in the late nineteenth and twentieth centuries, tribes turned to residency rules as a stand-in for cultural connection.[8] By requiring citizens to live on or near the reservation, tribes ensured that only those in the position to actively participate in tribal life enjoyed the privileges of tribal citizenship. As more tribal citizens moved away from home over the course of the twentieth century and as transportation became cheaper and more widely available, tribes changed their citizenship requirements once again to get rid of residency rules. In this way, tribes adapted "traditions" to changing conditions in order to best guarantee their future survival.

Modern critics sometimes lambaste tribes for abandoning "traditional" ways of defining belonging.[9] As the preceding examples show, this was not the case. Instead, tribes blended tradition and innovation as a strategy to grant older customs new legitimacy in a changed political environment.[10] Moreover, as legal scholar Carole Goldberg has argued, the idea that "tribal law can be authentic and entitled to respect only so long as it adheres to practices that predate European contact" is unrealistic and ahistorical. "Even assuming that membership criteria remained constant before contact, a questionable assumption, it does not follow that Indian nations today should continue to adhere to those criteria."[11] Tribes are living political entities; they are not stuck in the past. They have modified and adapted their "traditions" over time in response to changing conditions and needs.

The transformation of several southeastern peoples into federally recognized tribes during the late nineteenth and twentieth centuries shifted legal definitions of belonging in other ways. The federal government not only required clear criteria for citizenship but also official tribal rolls, which facilitated the distribution of federal benefits and services. Compiled under the supervision of white officials, usually in consultation with the tribes, these rolls captured a mere snapshot of the complex and evolving process of distinguishing tribal citizens, yet they fixed citizenship in place. For tribes that adopted formal rolls, citizenship thereafter relied to a large degree on tracing one's ancestry to an individual listed on the original, or base, roll. The creation of formal tribal rolls effectively negated some of the other criteria developed by tribes to determine belonging, such as reservation residency. Once listed on the roll, individuals migrated away without losing their political status. Rolls freed individual tribal citizens, but they limited the ability of tribes to police their citizenship or reserve tribal resources for those who lived in the community and depended on them for their livelihood. State-recognized tribes like the Pamunkeys exerted more direct control over their citizenship than the five tribes that fell under federal supervision in the nineteenth and twentieth centuries because they could include and exclude people as they saw fit, rather than relying on a base roll to determine belonging. During their recent fight for federal recognition, however, the Pamunkeys conformed to federal requirements and adopted a base roll, which they will use to determine citizenship moving forward.

Although tribal rolls formalized belonging in federally recognized tribes, Indians did not passively accept the citizenship rulings of federal officials. When Indians and agents disagreed on the construction of these rolls, tribal citizens asserted their sovereign right to make their own citizenship decisions. In the case of the Cherokees, this resistance included formal protests and appeals to the Interior Department, which contributed to the federal decision to abandon the plan to allot Cherokee lands. Ultimately the Cherokees reinstated their blood quantum requirement for citizenship, which they viewed as a necessary protection against the claims of "white Indians." The Mississippi Choctaws similarly protested against the way that federal agents handled the Choctaw Nation citizenship rolls. As a result of their political and legal activism, they eventually won recognition as a separate tribe. The Catawbas used their sovereign power to change citizenship requirements in their original tribal constitution and add out-of-state servicemen to their official tribal roll. They chose not to include western Catawbas because they no longer considered these individuals political citizens of the tribe. The Seminoles took the most drastic measures to protect their political identity from federal interference. By refusing to join the Seminole Tribe of Florida, certain Mikasuki-speaking Seminoles asserted their right to determine a different political future. Some became citizens of the Miccosukee Tribe of Indians and added their names to a separate tribal roll. Others refused enrollment altogether, thereby denying the federal government any authority over them. These acts of resistance to federal authority reveal that Indians were active agents in their citizenship decisions even after they fell under federal supervision, and their disparate criteria precluded any common federal standard.

The varying experiences of southeastern tribes belie the notion of an essential "Indian," or of Indians belonging to a homogenous race. The Pamunkeys, the Catawbas, the Mississippi Choctaws, the Eastern Band of Cherokees, the Florida Seminoles, and the Miccosukees developed ideas of belonging in particular historical contexts and made decisions on citizenship for tribally specific reasons. Their experiences reveal that Indians do not live apart from history or construct universal definitions of belonging. Pamunkeys began to police their citizenship carefully only when Jim Crow threatened to reclassify them as "colored." Catawbas altered criteria when some Mormon citizens migrated west, when Catawba fathers of children with white mothers demanded their inclusion, when the federal government required a roll for recognition, and when servicemen were inadvertently left off the rolls. The Mississippi Choctaws learned about the value of tribal citizenship when the federal government allotted Choctaw Nation lands. They used the lessons that federal officials taught them about Indian "blood" to construct a new political identity in the South. Eastern Band Cherokees conceded to expansive rolls when the federal government was paying out claims but moved to restrict the base roll developed originally for the allotment of their reservation. Seminoles and Miccosukees ended up with two tribes and two tribal rolls as well as people who enrolled in neither because of divergent values and goals. Southeastern tribes made different choices about tribal citizenship because each confronted different circumstances.

By making distinctive requirements for tribal citizenship, tribes exerted their sovereign power as independent nations and showed that they were not merely part of a racial or ethnic group. The decisions they made had lasting consequences for tribal belonging, but they were not arbitrary or mean-spirited. Although not always understood by outsiders, tribal choices on citizenship made sense to each tribe given its historical experiences. A fundamental component of tribal sovereignty, tribal citizenship remains a contested and controversial issue today. As the stories of the Pamunkeys, the Catawbas, the Mississippi Choctaws, the Eastern Band of Cherokees, the Florida Seminoles, and the Miccosukees reveal, the only way to understand tribal citizenship decisions is to examine tribes on an individual basis, taking into account their distinctive trajectories and unique goals.[12]

NOTES

Introduction

1. Sharon Flora to Editor, *Cherokee One Feather* (October 19, 1994).
2. In this book, I consciously use the term "tribal citizenship" rather than "tribal member-ship" in order to emphasize the political and legal nature of this aspect of Indian iden-tity. Although the federal government, in Congress and in the courts, has habitually used "member" rather than "citizen" when referring to tribally enrolled Indians, in recent years both tribes and legal scholars have noted that "tribal membership" does not accurately reflect the political status of tribal citizens. As Allison M. Dussias explained, "member" is a sociological term that refers to individuals composing a society or association, while "citizen" is a political term. Citizenship, unlike membership in a club, carries the "right to participate in the actions of a sovereign state and contributes to making the character of a nation." As tribes have fought to defend their sovereign status and nation-to-nation rela-tionship with the United States, many have recognized that the use of the term "member" instead of "citizen" implicitly detracts from tribal sovereignty because it encourages the view of tribal governments "as voluntary societies or sociological units rather than as na-tions or states with territorially-based authority." To avoid this trap and make clear the po-litical and legal status of individuals enrolled in tribal nations, I use "tribal citizenship." See Allison M. Dussias, "Geographically-Based and Membership-Based Views of Indian Tribal Sovereignty: The Supreme Court's Changing Vision," *University of Pittsburgh Law Review*, 55:1 (1993): 92–93; John Rockwell Snowden, Wayne Tyndall, and David Smith, "American Indian Sovereignty and Naturalization: It's a Race Thing," *Nebraska Law Review*, 80 (2001): 237.
3. As legal scholar Matthew Fletcher explains, "Since most Indian nations are treaty tribes, meaning they have been a part of formally ratified treaties with the United States, the legal relationship between Indian nations and the federal government is one between nations: a political relationship. Moreover, because Congress and the executive branch have come to formally recognize some non-treaty tribes, once again as a political matter, even those American Indians who are not members of treaty tribes come within this political rela-tionship." See Matthew L. M. Fletcher, "Race and American Indian Tribal Nationhood," *Wyoming Law Review*, 11: 2 (2011): 321.
4. Tribal sovereignty is based on both the inherent authority of tribes as original sover-eigns and also on federal recognition of that authority in treaties, laws, and court deci-sions. See Rebecca Tsosie, "American Indians and the Politics of Recognition: Soifer on Law, Pluralism, and Group Identity," *Law & Social Inquiry*, 22: 2 (1997): 364; Joseph P. Kalt and Joseph William Singer, "Myths and Realities of Tribal Sovereignty: The Law and Economics of Indian Self-Rule," *Harvard University: Faculty Research Working Paper Series* (March 2004), 9.

5. See N. Bruce Duthu, *American Indians and the Law* (New York: Penguin Group, 2008), xi, xxv–xxvi.

6. In this case, a group of white Bureau of Indian Affairs (BIA) employees challenged the agency's Indian-preference policy in hiring and promotion. They argued that this policy violated prohibitions against racial discrimination in the Equal Employment Opportunity Act. The court found, however, that the BIA did not practice racial discrimination since "Indian" is a political status, not a racial status. See *Morton v. Mancari*, 471 U.S. 535 (1974), discussed in Thomas Biolsi, "Imagined Geographies: Sovereignty, Indigenous Space, and American Indian Struggle," *American Ethnologist*, 32:2 (May 2005): 250. See also Sarah Krakoff, "Inextricably Political: Race, Membership, and Tribal Sovereignty," *Washington Law Review*, 87 (2012): 1054–1056.

7. Alexandra Harmon, "Tribal Enrollment Councils: Lessons on Law and Indian Identity," *Western Historical Quarterly*, 32:2 (Summer 2001): 176.

8. Fletcher, "Race and American Indian Tribal Nationhood," 322. This is not to say that there are no other ways of constructing Indian identity. As Melissa Meyer has pointed out, the question of "Who is an Indian?" has been debated since at least the mid-nineteenth century, and there are many ways of answering that question. Today, there exist people who may or may not be racially and ethnically Indian who are enrolled tribal citizens, but there are also people who have Indian ancestry or who identify as culturally Indian who do not belong to any tribe. Enrollment as a tribal citizen "provides only a partial answer to the question, 'Who is an Indian?'" See Melissa Meyer, "American Indian Blood Quantum Requirements: Blood Is Thicker than Family," in *Over the Edge: Remapping the American West*, edited by Valerie Matsumoto and Blake Allmendinger (Berkeley: University of California Press, 1999), 234. Yet tribal citizenship is a critical factor in determining who is legally recognized as Indian today both by tribes and by the federal government. Most federal services for Indian people, for example, require recipients to have proof of descent and affiliation with an Indian tribe. This legal aspect of tribal citizenship makes it vital to understanding modern constructions of Indian identity. See Bethany Berger, "Race, Descent, and Tribal Citizenship," *California Law Review Circuit*, 4:23 (April 2013): 30–31.

9. Carole Goldberg, "Members Only: Designing Citizenship Requirements for Indian Nations," *American Indian Constitutional Reform and the Rebuilding of Native Nations*, edited by Eric D. Lemont (Austin: University of Texas Press, 2006), 112–113.

10. The Indian Civil Rights Act, enacted by Congress in 1968, made many, but not all, of the guarantees of the United States Bill of Rights applicable within tribes. Martinez argued that the Santa Clara Pueblo's citizenship rules violated her children's "equal protection" under law since it discriminated against them solely on the basis of the sex of their Indian parent. See "Indian Civil Rights Act (1968)," in *Encyclopedia of United States Indian Policy and Law*, edited by Paul Finkelman and Tim Alan Garrison (Washington, DC: CQ Press, 2009), 401–402.

11. *Santa Clara Pueblo v. Martinez*, 436 U.S. 49 (1978). For a brief discussion of the case, see Gary A. Sokolow, *Native Americans and the Law: A Dictionary* (Santa Barbara, CA: ABC-CLIO, 2000), 207, and William T. Hagan, "Full Blood, Mixed Blood, Generic, and Ersatz: The Problem of Indian Identity," *Arizona and the West*, 27:4 (Winter 1985): 314–315.

12. Goldberg, "Members Only," 112–113.

13. To some extent, the federal government continues to do so today by "providing incentives for tribes to design membership criteria in ways that are thought to increase the political cohesion of the group and keep population numbers at a reasonable level." Kirsty Gover, *Tribal Constitutionalism: States, Tribes, and the Governance of Membership* (Oxford: Oxford University Press, 2010), 109. Tribes recognize that although they have the sovereign right to make their own citizenship decisions, Congress technically can override tribal governments by exercising its plenary power over them. So far, Congress has not done so when it comes to tribal citizenship, but it is a risk that keeps tribes careful about the citizenship decisions they make. See Suzanne D. Painter-Thorne, "If You Build It, They *Will* Come: Preserving Trial Sovereignty in the Face of Indian Casinos and the New Premium on Tribal Membership," *Lewis & Clark Law Review*, 14: 1 (2010): 335–336, 339.

14. According to Kirsty Gover, "When they design membership rules, tribes are obliged to make sense, for tribal purposes, of the long and immensely convoluted history of relations between indigenous peoples and settler governments. Likewise, in order to identify tribes and their members, settler governments must grapple (again) with the concept of indigeneity that has been a part of public law since the earliest days of State building. Indigeneity, and indigenous difference, is a constitutive principle of settler States." Gover, *Tribal Constitutionalism*, 9.

15. Despite the fundamental importance of tribal citizenship to tribal sovereignty and although tribal citizenship has increasingly determined who is entitled to federal recognition as "Indian," surprisingly little scholarship has explored how tribes select their citizens and determine their citizenship criteria. Legal scholars have tended to focus on definitions of "tribe" or "indigenous person" in public law and policy, or on particular citizenship controversies within specific tribal nations. Although historians have investigated the racial and cultural dimensions of Indian identity as well as the federal recognition process that provides tribes with an official legal status, few have focused on the political processes that have identified citizens within tribes themselves. Recently, a few scholars have tackled these questions—notably, Kirsty Gover in her comparative study of the governance of tribal citizenship in indigenous nations in the United States, Canada, Australia, and New Zealand; Melissa Meyer in her work on ethnicity and dispossession on the White Earth Reservation; and Alexandra Harmon in her article on tribal enrollment councils on the Colville Reservation. Yet, as Harmon has pointed out, "more historical studies are essential" if scholars, tribes, and the public at large are to understand fully "the influence of U.S. law and racial ideology on the composition of tribes" and how tribes have worked within this colonial framework to change, adapt, and defend their citizenship criteria. This book answers that call and lends an ethnohistorical perspective to the study of tribal citizenship by placing tribes at the center of the narrative. Gover, *Tribal Constitutionalism*; Melissa L. Meyer, *The White Earth Tragedy: Ethnicity and Dispossession at a Minnesota Anishinaabe Reservation, 1889–1920* (Lincoln: University of Nebraska Press, 1999); Harmon, "Tribal Enrollment Councils," 177–178.

16. Kirsty Gover, "Genealogy as Continuity: Explaining the Growing Tribal Preference for Descent Rules in Membership Governance in the United States," *American Indian Law Review*, 33:1 (2009): 244.

17. As Jodi A. Byrd has argued, "These boundaries are absolutely necessary, first and foremost for indigenous peoples because of the genocidal ethnic fraud, and the concomitant speaking as, not to mention the exploitation and mining of indigenous intellectual and cultural subjectivities." Jodi A. Byrd, *The Transit of Empire: Indigenous Critiques of Colonialism* (Minneapolis: University of Minnesota Press, 2011), 144.

18. The federal government has reasoned that it made treaties with Indian tribes, not individual Indians, so it owes most of its responsibilities and duties to tribes and only indirectly to tribal citizens. As a result of this stance, tribal citizenship constitutes the key marker of legal Indian identity in the United States today. See Dussias, "Geographically-Based and Membership-Based Views of Indian Tribal Sovereignty," 84.

19. Francine R. Skenandore, "Revisiting *Santa Clara Pueblo v. Martinez*: Feminist Perspectives on Tribal Sovereignty," *Wisconsin Journal of Law, Gender & Society*, 17:347 (Fall 2002): 357.

20. Joanne Barker, "For Whom Sovereignty Matters," in *Sovereignty Matters: Locations of Contestation and Possibility in Indigenous Struggles for Self-Determination* (Lincoln: University of Nebraska Press, 2005), 26.

21. Charles F. Wilkinson, *American Indians, Time, and the Law: Native Societies in a Modern Constitutional Democracy* (New Haven: Yale University Press, 1987), 55.

22. Circe Sturm, *Becoming Indian: The Struggle over Cherokee Identity in the Twenty-First Century* (Santa Fe: School for Advanced Research Press, 2010), 182.

23. Americans frequently question, for example, if tribal gaming wealth leads to indigenous cultural loss. As Cattelino had pointed out, "It is only a short step from wondering whether Indians are losing their culture to skepticism over whether indigenous people with economic power can and should remain legitimately indigenous and sovereign." The

same forces are at work when it comes to tribal citizenship. If tribes refuse to conform to American expectations of racial "Indianness" they risk losing their claims to separate nationhood based on the idea that they are no longer "really" indigenous. Jessica R. Cattelino, "The Double Bind of American Indian Need-Based Sovereignty," *Cultural Anthropology*, 25:2 (2010): 248.

24. Linda K. Kerber, "The Meanings of Citizenship," *Journal of American History*, 84:3 (December 1997): 834; Snowden, Tyndall, and Smith, "American Indian Sovereignty and Naturalization," 181; Barker, *Sovereignty Matters*, 2–3.

25. Duthu, *American Indians and the Law*, 4.

26. Wilkinson, *American Indians, Time, and the Law*, 54.

27. David E. Wilkins, *American Indian Sovereignty and the U.S. Supreme Court: The Masking of Justice* (Austin: University of Texas Press, 1997), 19–20; David E. Wilkins and K. Tsianina Lomawaima, *Uneven Ground: American Indian Sovereignty and Federal Law* (Norman: University of Oklahoma Press, 2001), 5.

28. *Johnson v. McIntosh*, 21 U.S. 543 (1823); Barker, "For Whom Sovereignty Matters," 7–8.

29. Deborah A. Rosen, *American Indians and State Law: Sovereignty, Race, and Citizenship, 1790–1880* (Lincoln: University of Nebraska Press, 2007), 2.

30. Barker, "For Whom Sovereignty Matters," 4.

31. Barker, "For Whom Sovereignty Matters," 9; see Charles Joseph Kappler, *Indian Affairs: Treaties* (Washington, DC: US Government Printing Office, 1904).

32. Duthu, *American Indians and the Law*, xi.

33. Theda Perdue, *"Mixed Blood" Indians: Racial Construction in the Early South* (Athens: University of Georgia Press, 2003), 40.

34. Perdue, *"Mixed Blood" Indians*, 20.

35. For more on the nationalization of southern tribes in this period, see Duane Champagne, *Social Order and Political Change: Constitutional Governments among the Cherokee, the Choctaw, the Chickasaw, and the Creek* (Stanford, CA: Stanford University Press, 1992).

36. Malinda Maynor Lowery, *Lumbee Indians in the Jim Crow South: Race, Identity, and the Making of a Nation* (Chapel Hill: University of North Carolina Press, 2010), 257.

37. E. Nathaniel Gates, *The Concept of "Race" in Natural and Social Science* (New York: Garland, 1997), vii.

38. Meyer, "American Indian Blood Quantum Requirements," 237–238; for more on the construction of American Anglo-Saxonism as a separate, so-called "superior" race, see Reginald Horsman, *Race and Manifest Destiny: The Origins of American Racial Anglo-Saxonism* (Cambridge, MA: Harvard University Press, 1981).

39. Krakoff, "Inextricably Political," 1118.

40. Circe Sturm, *Blood Politics: Race, Culture, and Identity in the Cherokee Nation of Oklahoma* (Berkeley: University of California Press, 2002), 15.

41. Krakoff, "Inextricably Political," 1041; for more on the racialization of Indians, see Nancy Shoemaker, "How Indians Got to Be Red," *American Historical Review*, 102:3 (June, 1997): 625–644.

42. Byrd, *The Transit of Empire*, 137.

43. In this case, a white man who had married a Cherokee woman and who had himself gained Cherokee citizenship under tribal law argued that federal courts had no criminal jurisdiction over him for crimes committed in Cherokee territory. The Supreme Court disagreed by arguing that his white racial identity made him subject to federal jurisdiction despite his Cherokee citizenship. See *United States v. Rogers*, 45 U.S. 567 (1846), discussed in Fletcher, "Race and American Indian Tribal Nationhood," 300.

44. Paul Spruhan, "A Legal History of Blood Quantum in Federal Indian Law to 1935," *South Dakota Law Review*, 51 (2006): 48.

45. Spruhan, "A Legal History of Blood Quantum in Federal Indian Law to 1935," 48.

46. S. Alan Ray, "A Race or a Nation? Cherokee National Identity and the Status of Freedmen's Descendants," *Michigan Journal of Race & Law*, 12 (Spring 2007): 423–424.

47. Ray, "A Race or a Nation?" 432–436; see also Fay A. Yarbrough, *Race and the Cherokee Nation: Sovereignty in the Nineteenth Century* (Philadelphia: University of Pennsylvania Press, 2008); Sturm, *Blood Politics*; Claudio Saunt, *Black, White, and Indian: Race and*

the Unmaking of an American Family (Oxford: Oxford University Press, 2005); Gary Zellar, *African Creeks: Estelvste and the Creek Nation* (Norman: University of Oklahoma Press, 2007).

48. Ray, "A Race or a Nation?" 430.
49. Charles F. Wilkinson, "Indian Law at the Beginning of the Modern Era," in *Constitutionalism and Native Americans, 1903–1968*, edited by John R. Wunder (New York: Garland, 1996), 24.
50. Duthu, *American Indians and the Law*, xxv–xxvi.
51. Francis Paul Prucha, *The Great Father: The United States Government and the American Indians*, abridged edition (Lincoln: University of Nebraska Press, 1984), 65.
52. Theda Perdue and Michael D. Green, *The Cherokee Nation and the Trail of Tears* (New York: Penguin Group, 2007), 134.
53. C. Joseph Genetin-Pilawa, *Crooked Paths to Allotment: The Fight over Federal Indian Policy after the Civil War* (Chapel Hill: University of North Carolina Press, 2012), 15.
54. "Indian Appropriations Act (1871)," in *Encyclopedia of United States Indian Policy and Law*, 395; Krakoff, "Inextricably Political," 1066, 1069.
55. "Major Crimes Act (1885)," in *Encyclopedia of United States Indian Policy and Law*, 513–514; Spruhan, "A Legal History of Blood Quantum in Federal Indian Law to 1935," 19.
56. "Kagama, United States v. (1886)," in *Encyclopedia of United States Indian Policy and Law*, 472.
57. "General Allotment Act (Dawes Act) of 1887," in *Encyclopedia of United States Indian Policy and Law*, 337–338.
58. Theodore Roosevelt used this phrase to refer specifically to allotment in his First Annual Message to Congress, December 3, 1901; Krakoff, "Inextricably Political," 1067–1068.
59. Kerber, "The Meanings of Citizenship," 833, 841–842.
60. See Clare Sheridan, "Contested Citizenship: National Identity and the Mexican Immigration Debates of the 1920s," *Journal of American Ethnic History*, 21:3 (Spring 2002): 3–35; Brook Thomas, "The Legal and Literary Complexities of U.S. Citizenship around 1900," *Law and Literature*, 22:2 (Summer, 2010): 307–324.
61. See Sam Erman, "Meanings of Citizenship in the U.S. Empire: Puerto Rico, Isabel Gonzalez, and the Supreme Court, 1898 to 1905," *Journal of Ethnic History*, 27:4 (Summer 2008): 5–33.
62. Sheridan, "Contested Citizenship," 3.
63. For more on this topic, see Earl M. Maltz, "The Fourteenth Amendment and Native American Citizenship," *Constitutional Commentary*, 17:3 (Winter 2000): 555–574.
64. "Elk v. Wilkins (1884)," in *Encyclopedia of United States Indian Policy and Law*, 287; Fletcher, "Race and American Indian Tribal Nationhood," 300–301.
65. Kevin Bruyneel, "Ambivalent Americans: Indigenous People and U.S. Citizenship in the Early 20th Century," *American Political Science Association Annual Meeting* (2002): 1–40.
66. John Bloom, "'There Is Madness in the Air': The 1926 Haskell Homecoming and Popular Representations of Sports in Federal Indian Boarding Schools," in *Dressing in Feathers: The Construction of the Indian in American Popular Culture* (Boulder, CO: Westview, 1996), 99. See also Frederick E. Hoxie, *A Final Promise: The Campaign to Assimilate the Indians, 1880–1920* (Lincoln: University of Nebraska Press, 1984).
67. Bruyneel, "Ambivalent Americans," 7.
68. Spruhan, "A Legal History of Blood Quantum in Federal Indian Law to 1935," 49.
69. Indian Citizenship Act, 43 U.S. Stats. At Large, Ch. 233, p. 253 (1924). Boarding school-educated Indian intellectuals welcomed the formal grant of American citizenship in 1924 as a way to secure political rights in the United States, but other Indians remained ambivalent about American citizenship since the act unilaterally incorporated Native people into the American body politic without their consent. See Bruyneel, "Ambivalent Americans," 28–29, and Vine Deloria Jr. and Clifford M. Lytle, *The Nations Within: The Past and Future of American Indian Sovereignty* (Austin: University of Texas Press, 1984), 3–4.
70. See Dussias, "Geographically-Based and Membership-Based Views of Indian Tribal Sovereignty," 1–97; Jean Dennison, "The Logic of Recognition: Debating Osage Nation Citizenship in the Twenty-First Century," *American Indian Quarterly*, 38:1 (Winter

2014): 28; Erin Hogan Fouberg, "Understanding Space, Understanding Citizenship," *Journal of Geography*, 101:2 (2002): 81–85. This shift has had lasting consequences for tribes. As Dennison has argued for the Osage Nation, the separation of citizenship from territory brought into question "the nation's ability to make and enforce laws within its territory." Dennison, "The Logic of Recognition," 29. Tribes today, for example, are largely powerless to prosecute non-Indian offenders on reservations since only tribal citizens fall under tribal jurisdiction. Courts have justified this curtail of tribal sovereignty by arguing that it would be unfair to subject non-Indians to the laws of a tribal government in which they do not participate or have any representation. The Supreme Court upheld this position in *Oliphant v. Suquamish Indian Tribe*, 435 U.S. 191 (1978). In 1990, the Supreme Court extended this decision to hold that tribes also lacked jurisdiction over non-citizen Indians in *Duro v. Reina*, 495 U.S. 676 (1990). Not long after, however, Congress reversed this decision with legislation that held that tribes have inherent criminal jurisdiction over non-citizen Indians as well as citizens of their own tribes but lacked jurisdiction over non-Indians. This legislation was upheld by the Supreme Court in *United States v. Lara*, 541 U.S. 193 (2004). Scholars have criticized these court decisions because they undermine tribal sovereignty, treat tribes differently from other sovereign entities, and promoted race-based definitions of Indian identity. See Dussias, "Geographically-Based and Membership-Based Views of Indian Tribal Sovereignty," 87.

71. Dussias, "Geographically-Based and Membership-Based Views of Indian Tribal Sovereignty," 79.
72. Dennison, "The Logic of Recognition," 3.
73. A number of scholars have made the connection between tribal citizenship and entitlement to property and the ways that these discussions influence tribal citizenship debates. See Charles Park, "Enrollment: Procedures and Consequences," *American Indian Law Review*, 3 (1975): 109; Meyer, "American Indian Blood Quantum Requirements," 231; Harmon, "Tribal Enrollment Councils," 199–200; Kirsty Gover, "Comparative Tribal Constitutionalism: Membership Governance in Australia, Canada, New Zealand, and the United States," *Law & Social Inquiry*, 35:3 (Summer 2010): 690.
74. Political theorists Ayelet Shachar and Ran Hirschl have argued that in a global context, citizenship should be viewed as inherited property since "Securing membership status in a given state or region—with its specific level of wealth, degree of stability, and human rights record—is a crucial factor in the determination of life chances." Like inherited property, citizenship—which worldwide is typically determined either by one's place of birth (*jus soli*) or through one's parents (*jus sanguinis*)—is transferred between generations and affords its holders with benefits and privileges denied to others. The freedoms and opportunities enjoyed by those who inherit citizenship in affluent countries are far greater than the opportunities of those who belong to poor countries, leading to disparities in citizenship that are akin to disparities in inherited property. In other words, some kinds of citizenship are "worth" more than others. These ideas are useful in conceptualizing tribal citizenship and its value for Indian people within the United States since they illustrate why tribal citizenship became something that needed to be defined and defended. As a valuable asset, tribal citizenship was not just a marker of identity but a resource that entitled its "owner" to certain political, legal, economic, and social privileges. See Ayelet Shachar and Ran Hirschl, "Citizenship as Inherited Property," *Political Theory*, 35:3 (June 2007): 253, 255, 258.
75. Laura L. Lovett, "'African and Cherokee by Choice': Race and Resistance under Legalized Segregation," in *Confounding the Color Line: The Indian-Black Experience in North America*, edited by James F. Brooks (Lincoln: University of Nebraska Press, 2002), 193.
76. *Plessy v. Ferguson*, 163 U.S. 537 (1896); Lovett, "'African and Cherokee by Choice,'" 193; for more on postbellum race relations, see C. Vann Woodward, *The Strange Career of Jim Crow* (Oxford: Oxford University Press, 2001, first published in 1955), Joel Williamson, *The Crucible of Race: Black-White Relations in the American South since Emancipation* (New York: Oxford University Press, 1984), and Edward L. Ayers, *The Promise of the New South: Life after Reconstruction* (New York: Oxford University Press, 1992).

77. J. Kēhaulani Kauanui discusses early twentieth-century notions of racial mixing and as-similation in *Hawaiian Blood: Colonialism and the Politics of Sovereignty and Indigeneity* (Durham, NC: Duke University Press, 2008), 133–135.

78. See Angela Gonzales, Judy Kertész, and Gabrielle Tayac, "Eugenics as Indian Removal: Sociohistorical Processes and the De(con)struction of American Indians in the Southeast," *Public Historian*, 29:3 (Summer 2007): 53–67.

79. Ariela J. Gross, *What Blood Won't Tell: A History of Race on Trial in America* (Cambridge, MA: Harvard University Press, 2008), 113; Susan Greenbaum, "What's In a Label? Identity Problems of Southern Indian Tribes," *Journal of Ethnic Studies*, 19:2 (Spring 1991): 112–113.

80. Krakoff, "Inextricably Political," 1070. Some scholars have described this paper erasure of Indians through forced cultural assimilation and blood quantum rules as "ethnocide" or "statistical genocide." See Seena B. Kohl, "Ethnocide and Ethnogenesis: A Case Study of the Mississippi Band of Choctaw, a Genocide Avoided," *Holocaust and Genocide Studies*, 1:1 (1986): 91–100; Michael Yellow Bird, "Decolonizing Tribal Enrollment," in *For Indigenous Eyes Only: A Decolonization Handbook*, edited by Waziyatawin Angela Wilson and Michael Yellow Bird (Santa Fe, NM: School of American Research, 2005), 180.

81. Katherine M. B. Osburn, "The 'Identified Full-Bloods' in Mississippi: Race and Choctaw Identity, 1898–1918," *Ethnohistory*, 56: 3 (Summer 2009): 423.

82. I borrow ideas of racial identity as symbolic property from legal scholar Cheryl Harris. Harris has argued that whiteness and property in America became so closely linked in the nineteenth century that whiteness itself became a form of property. Whiteness accorded those who owned it with rights and privileges denied other racial groups. The value of whiteness as property was reified and legitimized in law. Moreover, whites alone could construct and possess this property, giving them the exclusive right to control group iden-tity. Even after legal segregation ended, "whiteness as property continued to serve as a barrier to effective change as the system of racial classification operated to protect en-trenched power." Cheryl I. Harris, "Whiteness as Property," *Harvard Law Review*, 106: 8 (June 1993): 1707–1791, quote on p. 1709. Although "whiteness" was the most valuable form of racial property in the United States at the time, "Indianness" was a step above "blackness." For those whose phenotype precluded them from inclusion in the category of "white," "Indian" presented a tantalizing alternative to racial marginalization as "black" or "colored." Anthropologist Circe Sturm has called this prospect the "wages of Indianness." Drawing up David R. Roediger's argument that ideas of "whiteness" provided working-class American whites with social and psychological benefits beyond their physical wages and led to the creation of a white working-class identity in opposition to blacks (see David R. Roediger, *The Wages of Whiteness: Race and the Making of the American Working Class* (New York: Verso, 1999)), Sturm has argued that "Indianness" increasingly has symbolic capital that is appealing to individuals who do not formally belong to a tribe but who claim an Indian identity. Although Sturm's work focuses on Indian identity in the late twenti-eth and early twenty-first centuries, her ideas also apply to the late nineteenth and early twentieth centuries when a number of people claimed an Indian identity despite lacking a tribal connection. See Sturm, *Becoming Indian*, 190; J. Kēhaulani Kauanui has also made this connection between indigenous identity and property value in *Hawaiian Blood*, 24.

83. Dennison, "The Logic of Recognition," 19.

84. As William T. Hagan has noted, "The relative affluence of some tribes attracted numerous enterprising non-Indians and the question of Indian identity assumed new significance" Hagan, "Full Blood, Mixed Blood, Generic, and Ersatz," 311. Core members of tribal communities gave these individuals a variety of names. The Eastern Band of Cherokees, for example, called them "white Indians" or "five-dollar Indians," presumably in refer-ence to the amount of money required to bribe census takers to include them on tribal rolls. See Eva Marie Garroutte, "The Racial Formation of American Indians: Negotiating Legitimate Identities within Tribal and Federal Law," *American Indian Quarterly*, 25: 2 (2001): 224.

85. Lovett, "'African and Cherokee by Choice,'" 193.

86. Osburn, "The 'Identified Full-Bloods' in Mississippi," 431.

87. As Eva Marie Garroutte has pointed out, "When tribal affiliation carries with it access to limited material resources, their exploitation by illegitimate recipients occurs at the expense of legitimate ones." Moreover, when individuals self-identify as Indian they threaten tribal sovereignty by denying tribes the right to define their own citizenry. See Eva Marie Garroutte, *Real Indians: Identity and the Survival of Native America* (Berkeley: University of California Press, 2003), 87–97.

88. Osburn, "The 'Identified Full-Bloods' in Mississippi," 431.

89. For more on the professionalization of American institutions, see Burton J. Bledstein, *The Culture of Professionalism: The Middle Class and the Development of Higher Education in America* (New York: W.W. Norton, 1978).

90. For more on the growth and bureaucratization of the Office of Indian Affairs, see Paul Stuart, *The Indian Office: Growth and Development of an American Institution, 1865–1900* (Ph.D. Dissertation, University of Wisconsin, 1979).

91. Spruhan, "A Legal History of Blood Quantum in Federal Indian Law to 1935," 20.

92. See Jesse T. Schreier, "Indian or Freedman? Enrollment, Race, and Identity in the Choctaw Nation, 1896–1907," *Western Historical Quarterly*, 42:4 (Winter 2011): 460.

93. Meyer, "American Indian Blood Quantum Requirements," 232.

94. Schreier, "Indian or Freedman?" 478.

95. Harmon, "Tribal Enrollment Councils," 178.

96. As Rose Stremlau has argued for the Cherokee Nation's base roll, "The Dawes roll is equated with truth. But *whose* truth?" Contested by Cherokees at the time it was cre-ated, the roll did not fully encapsulate what it meant to be Cherokee. Some people were left off the roll, while others made it on the roll illegitimately. Nevertheless, the Dawes Roll has become the modern basis for Cherokee Nation citizenship. See Rose Stremlau, *Sustaining the Cherokee Family: Kinship and the Allotment of an Indigenous Nation* (Chapel Hill: University of North Carolina Press, 2011), 126.

97. According to Kirsty Gover, about 88 percent of tribes in the United States define de-scent by reference to a base roll. See Gover, "Comparative Tribal Constitutionalism," 707. Although technically modern tribes are free to change their enrollment rules or to modify their base roll as a prerogative of their sovereignty, most have not done so in sig-nificant ways. As Carole Goldberg has explained, "Once a roll is established as the basis for citizenship, it becomes politically difficult to expand citizenship beyond its confines" Goldberg, "Members Only," 122.

98. Garroutte, "The Racial Formation of American Indians," 224.

99. Notions of Indian "blood" derived from English common-law conceptions of descent and inheritance. In colonial America, language like "mixed blood" and "half breed" re-ferred to any person of mixed descent. Over time, however, notions of blood became increasingly tied to race as Euro-Americans applied the term to the children of white fur traders and Indian women. By the late eighteenth and early nineteenth centuries, white Americans began to fuse ideas of "blood" and "peoplehood" together and to rank indi-viduals hierarchically into superior and inferior stocks. In this context, "blood" became a marker of racial percentage: the more Indian "blood" a person had, the more "Indian" they appeared to white America. This conception of Indian "blood" was in direct con-trast to notions of hypodescent, which whites applied to individuals with African an-cestry. Whereas any percentage of African "blood" consigned an individual to a black racial identity, whites saw Indian "blood" as diluting whenever it mixed with the "blood" of other populations. As Jean Dennison has pointed out, under this schema, "notions of ancestry are used to create a moment when the percentage of blood is too low to fit within the category of Indian, thus erasing Indian title to land." Blood quantum thus served as a colonial tool of elimination by gradually reducing the number of Indians that the United States recognized as entitled to tribal land, resources, and separate political status as citizens of tribal nations. See Dennison, "The Logic of Recognition," 15–16; Spruhan, "A Legal History of Blood Quantum in Federal Indian Law to 1935," 4–5; Meyer, "American Indian Blood Quantum Requirements," 238–239.

100. Scholars have hotly debated the role the federal government played in imposing notions of "blood" and "blood quantum" on tribal nations. Some have argued that the federal

government enforced blood quantum restrictions on tribal citizenship when it allotted tribal land. Tribes, in turn, adopted these policies and abandoned their old ways of reckoning belonging, becoming "effectively self-colonizing." See Ward Churchill, "The Crucible of American Indian Identity: Native Tradition versus Colonial Imposition in Postconquest North America," *American Indian Culture and Research Journal*, 23:1 (1999): 55. As Kim TallBear has pointed out, the notion that "blood" is a colonial imposition and that tribes are now self-colonizing has become a "standard characterization" that scholars have only recently begun to question. See Kim TallBear, *Native American DNA: Tribal Belonging and the False Promise of Genetic Science* (Minneapolis: University of Minnesota Press, 2013), 55–56. Other scholars, however, have challenged the idea that the federal government imposed the idea of "blood" on tribes by pointing out that the General Allotment Act in fact did not include a blood quantum requirement for tribal citizenship. Instead, Congress made eligibility for allotments dependent on tribes' own citizenship determinations. See John P. LaVell, "The General Allotment Act 'Eligibility' Hoax: Distortions of Law, Policy, and History in Derogation of Indian Tribes," *Wicazo Sa Review* (Spring 1999): 254, 257–258. More recently, scholars like Alexandra Harmon have argued that the adoption of citizenship rules like blood quantum restrictions was more of a give-and-take between tribes and federal officials. Tribes did not blindly accept federal notions of race and blood but engaged in a "conversation" in which they partially conceded to and partially gave their own meaning to these concepts. Harmon, "Tribal Enrollment Councils," 198, 200. According to Kirsty Gover, tribes viewed "blood" as "a pre-existing, well-documented administrative device that conveniently concurs with federal expectations of tribal continuity and political cohesiveness." Gover, *Tribal Constitutionalism*, 156. In this sense, their adoption of blood rules for tribal citizenship was a strategic choice made in order to bolster their political identity and protect their communities from imposters. My work supports this latter position.
101. Gover, "Genealogy as Continuity," 274.
102. Meyer, "American Indian Blood Quantum Requirements," 233.
103. Goldberg, "Members Only," 113.
104. The federal government struggled with how to make blood quantum determinations for the purposes of the IRA. When they could, they turned to documented evidence of descent found in previously compiled censuses and rolls. They also considered additional social and cultural factors not strictly related to biology. The Office of Indian Affair's newly established Anthropological Unit debated the merits of using genealogical versus anthropometric measures to make blood quantum designations. Ultimately, by 1938, the government backed away from these alternative measures and emphasized documentary proof of descent from an ancestor "enrolled on a tribal roll showing degree of Indian blood." See Gover, "Genealogy as Continuity," 282–283; Gonzales et al., "Eugenics as Indian Removal," 61; Paul Spruhan, "Indian as Race/Indian as Political Status: Implementation of the Half-Blood Requirement under the Indian Reorganization Act, 1934–1945," *Rutgers Race & the Law Review*, 8 (2006), 43–45.
105. Gover, "Genealogy as Continuity," 263–264.
106. See Felix S. Cohen, *Handbook of Federal Indian Law*, United States Department of the Interior, Office of the Solicitor (Washington, DC: US Government Printing Office, 1941).
107. Wilkinson, *American Indians, Time, and the Law*, 57.
108. Krakoff, "Inextricably Political," 1076.
109. "House Concurrent Resolution 108 (1953)," in *Encyclopedia of United States Indian Policy and Law*, 384–385.
110. "Public Law 280 (1953)," in *Encyclopedia of United States Indian Policy and Law*, 636–637.
111. Wunder, *Constitutionalism and Native Americans*, xi–xii.
112. Gover, "Genealogy as Continuity," 292.
113. Barker, "For Whom Sovereignty Matters," 1.
114. See Circe Sturm, "Blood Politics, Racial Classification, and Cherokee National Identity," *American Indian Quarterly*, 22: 1/2 (Winter/Spring, 1998): 230–257. In part, they have done so because they continue to fear the federal government's "logic of recognition." Tribes worry about losing their political status if they change their citizenship criteria

and open up the tribe to suspect claimants. As Jean Dennison has argued for the Osage Nation, the "perceived threat of termination" has constrained the choices tribal citizens make about their cultural and political practices. Dennison, "The Logic of Recognition, 11–12. Tribes have also upheld these enrollment criteria to protect themselves from waves of people who claim to be "Indian" despite having tenuous tribal connections. Since the 1970s, thousands of individuals across the United States have sought tribal citizenship for economic, political, social, and psychological purposes. Although many of these individuals are honest in their motivations and wish to reestablish ties with their indigenous heritage, tribes recognize that if they admitted these individuals to citizenship, they would risk losing control of their resources, political structure, and tribal status. For more on the modern phenomenon of these individuals, whom Circe Sturm has called "racial shifters," see Sturm, *Becoming Indian*, and Mark Edwin Miller, *Claiming Tribal Identity: The Five Tribes and the Politics of Federal Acknowledgment* (Norman: University of Oklahoma Press, 2013).

115. Sturm, *Becoming Indian*, 120.
116. Sturm, *Becoming Indian*, 126.
117. Despite popular perceptions, most tribes do not have gaming wealth, and as a whole, Indians remain the poorest population in the United States. Nevertheless, for a few tribes, gaming wealth and the stakes of citizenship are substantial. For these tribes, "gaming distributions can mean the difference between a life of poverty and one of unimaginable wealth." The wealth generated by gaming operations, some have argued, "has increased fights over membership as tribes seek to expel current members or refuse to admit new members." In particular, casino-rich California tribes have engaged in heated debates over the terms of inclusion. In the first decade of the twenty-first century alone, these tribes removed more than 5,000 people from their citizenship rolls. The tribes have argued that these disenrollments correct long-standing mistakes in their citizenship rolls. The individuals excluded, however, contend they were ousted for financial and political reasons. See Painter-Thorne, "If You Build It, They *Will* Come," 311, 319–320; Duthu, *American Indians and the Law*, 157.
118. Sturm, *Becoming Indian*, 126.
119. Gover, "Genealogy as Continuity," 269, 264.
120. Gonzales et al., "Eugenics as Indian Removal," 61; for more on the federal recognition process, see Mark Edwin Miller, *Forgotten Tribes: Unrecognized Indians and the Federal Acknowledgment Process* (Lincoln: University of Nebraska Press, 2004), and Bruce Granville Miller, *Invisible Indigenes: The Politics of Nonrecognition* (Lincoln: University of Nebraska Press, 2003).
121. Gover, "Genealogy as Continuity," 258.
122. Kauanui, *Hawaiian Blood*, 9.
123. On June 29, 2015, the Bureau of Indians Affairs announced a policy change that updated the Federal Acknowledgment Process. According to the new regulations, groups seeking recognition must still show historical identification as an Indian entity, but the evidence is no longer limited "to observations by those external to the petitioner." This allows the BIA to accept and consider all evidence, such as the petitioner's own contemporaneous records, as evidence that the petitioner has been an Indian entity since 1900. This change frees petitioners from some of the burden of proving that outsiders historically regarded them as "Indian," which was often a race-based assessment. A group's historic ability to act as an Indian tribe—even internally—however, often depended on external recognition of their racial identity as "Indian." For more on the BIA's policy change, see Department of the Interior, Bureau of Indian Affairs, *Final Rule for 25 CFR Part 83 Acknowledgment of American Indian Tribes*, June 29, 2015, p. 6, http://www.bia.gov/cs/groups/public/documents/text/idc1-030742.pdf, accessed July 28, 2015. See also "U.S. Makes It Easier for Native American Tribes to Obtain Federal Recognition," *Guardian* (June 29, 2015), http://www.theguardian.com/world/2015/jun/29/indian-tribes-native-americans-federal-recognition, accessed July 28, 2015.
124. As Eastern Band of Cherokee Indian tribal citizen and former employee of the Bureau of Indian Affairs Frell M. Owl explained, "The reason for the difference of definitions

among the several tribes and between tribes and the United States is that each Indian tribe is a distinct political entity, independent of other tribes and possessing extensive powers of self-government." Frell M. Owl, "Who and What Is an American Indian?" *Ethnohistory*, 9:3 (Summer 1962): 275.
125. Gover, *Tribal Constitutionalism*, 109.

Chapter 1

1. R. Lee Fleming, Director of the Office of Federal Acknowledgment, to Robert Gray, April 11, 2011, United States Department of the Interior, Bureau of Indian Affairs, Washington, DC.
2. Helen C. Rountree, *Pocahontas's People: The Powhatan Indians of Virginia through Four Centuries* (Norman: University of Oklahoma Press, 1990), 110, 113, 164.
3. Rountree, *Pocahontas's* People, 187.
4. Rountree, *Pocahontas's* People, 194.
5. A Petition from Citizens of King William County, Virginia, to the General Assembly of Virginia, January 20, 1843, File: Clerk's Correspondence, 1923–1929, Rockbridge County Clerk's Records, Clerk's Correspondence (A. T. Shields) (W. A. Plecker to A. T. Shields), 1872–1936, 1912–1943, Broken Series, Accession 1160754, Box 1, The Library of Virginia, Richmond, Virginia (hereafter The Library of Virginia). This effort came just over a decade after Nat Turner's 1831 insurrection, which prompted increasingly severe restrictions on the state's non-white population, both slave and free.
6. Legislative Petitions, King William County, January 20, 1843. See Rountree, *Pocahontas's People*, 194.
7. Legislative Petitions, King William County, November 26, 1842, and January 12, 1843. See Rountree, *Pocahontas's People*, 194–195.
8. James Mooney, *The Powhatan Confederacy, Past and Present*, Draft of Article, 1907, Manuscript 2199, Smithsonian Institution, National Anthropological Archives, Washington, DC (hereafter NAA Washington).
9. Executive Letter Book 1856–1860, pp. 47–49. See Rountree, *Pocahontas's People*, 198.
10. Kevin K. Washburn, Assistant Secretary, Indian Affairs, "Proposed Finding for Acknowledgment of the Pamunkey Indian Tribe (Petitioner #323), Prepared in Response to the Petition Submitted to the Assistant Secretary—Indian Affairs for Federal Acknowledgment as an Indian Tribe," January 16, 2014, 41, Department of the Interior, Bureau of Indian Affairs, Washington, DC.
11. Mooney, *The Powhatan Confederacy, Past and Present*, Manuscript 2199, NAA Washington.
12. For more information on Pamunkey involvement in the Civil War, see Laurence M. Hauptman, *Between Two Fires: American Indians in the Civil War* (New York: Free Press, 1995).
13. "Letter from Richmond: The Pamunkey and Mattaponi Indians—The Jennings Association," *Baltimore Sun* (March 12, 1877): 4.
14. "An Old Pamunkey Buried," *Atlanta Constitution* (August 6, 1899): 19.
15. Martha Pfaus, *Our Indian Neighbors* (Richmond, VA: Dover Baptist Association, 1947), 7, Helen C. Rountree, Rountree Collection of Virginia Indian Documents, 2005, Accession 42003, Personal Papers Collection, Box 4, The Library of Virginia.
16. Rountree, *Pocahontas's People*, 200.
17. Pfaus, *Our Indian Neighbors*, 7.
18. Robert Reeves Solenberger to Judge J. Hoge Ricks, February 28, 1942, File: IV (20F1g) Speck, Frank G., General and Historical—g. Draft classification of Virginia Indians, 1940–1946, 82 items, Ms. Coll. 126, Frank G. Speck Papers, Sub-Collection 1, Box 13, American Philosophical Society, Philadelphia, Pennsylvania (hereafter APS Philadelphia).
19. Mrs. Thos. P. Bagby, *Tuckahoe: A Collection of Indian Stories and Legends* (New York: Broadway, 1907), 70–71.
20. Helen C. Rountree, "Powhatan's Descendants in the Modern World: Community Studies of the Two Virginia Indian Reservations, with Notes on Five Non-Reservation Enclaves," *The Chesopiean: A Journal of North American Archaeology*, 10 (June 1972): 68.

21. Rountree, *Pocahontas's People*, 201–203; Bagby, *Tuckahoe: A Collection of Indian Stories and Legends*, 70–71.
22. John Garland Pollard, "The Pamunkey Indians of Virginia," *Bureau of American Ethnology, Bulletin 17* (Washington, DC: US Government Printing Office, 1894), 12.
23. Joyce Bradby Krigsvold, quoted by Kenneth Bradby Jr. in *Pamunkey Speaks: Native Perspectives*, edited by Bill O'Donovan (Charleston, SC: BookSurge, 2008), 68.
24. Bagby, *Tuckahoe: A Collection of Indian Stories and Legends*, 70–71.
25. Chief Thomas Cook and Pamunkey Councilmen to Legislators of Virginia, February 13, 1877, Memorial of the Pamunkey Tribe, 1877, File: 15, Box 4, Virginia Secretary of the Commonwealth, Miscellaneous Records, 1872–1906, Accession 25299, State Government Records Collection, The Library of Virginia.
26. "Letter from Richmond," 4.
27. "Powhatan's Men Yet Live," *Washington Evening Star* (April 25, 1894): 6; Albert Samuel Gatschet, *Pamunkey Notebook, post 1893*, Manuscript 2197, NAA Washington.
28. Kermit J. Schmidt, to Senator Ted Dalton, August 19, 1949, File: 5, Bacone College, Oklahoma, Correspondence, 1947–1955, Virginia Department of Education, Indian School Files, 1936–1967, Accession 29632, State Government Records Collection, Box 1, The Library of Virginia; Helen C. Rountree, "The Indians of Virginia: A Third Race in a Biracial State," in *Southeastern Indians since the Removal Era*, edited by Walter L. Williams (Athens: University of Georgia Press, 1979): 44–45, Helen C. Rountree Collection of Virginia Indian Documents, 2005, Accession 42003, Personal Papers Collection, The Library of Virginia.
29. Martha Pfaus, *Our Debt to Virginia Indians* (Richmond, VA: Dover Baptist Association, 1949), 9–10, Helen C. Rountree Collection of Virginia Indian Documents, 2005, Accession 42003, Personal Papers Collection, Box 4, The Library of Virginia.
30. "Tribe of Pamunkey: Conclusion of Their Most Interesting History," *Daily Times*, Richmond, VA (November 2, 1890); Albert Samuel Gatschet, *Pamunkey Notebook, post 1893*, Manuscript 2197, NAA Washington.
31. Bradby, *Pamunkey Speaks*, 28.
32. Interview with Edna Bradby Allmond by Helen C. Rountree, July 19, 1970, File: Helen C. Rountree, Fieldnotes, 1969–1973, Helen C. Rountree Papers, Box 2, NAA Washington.
33. Edgar R. Lafferty Jr., on behalf of Chief T. D. Cook and the Pamunkey Tribal Council, to Helen C. Rountree, October 29, 1971, Helen C. Rountree Papers, Box 1, NAA Washington.
34. "The Pamunkey Indians: Life among Virginia Aborigines on Their Tidewater Reservation," *Baltimore Sun* (September 7, 1889): 6.
35. "Pamunkeys Resent Being Classed as 'Half Niggers,'" *Baltimore Sun* (January 23, 1904): 10.
36. F. Snowden Hopkins, "Modern Survivors of Chief Powhatan: A Virginia Tribe Still Dwells in Its Ancient Stronghold," *Baltimore Sun* (October 16, 1932): M4.
37. Rountree, *Pocahontas's People*, 196.
38. "Pamunkey Indians Angry: Virginia Tribes Object to Riding in 'Jim Crow' Cars," *New York Times* (July 29, 1900): 1.
39. "Validity of Virginia's New Law," *Zion's Herald*, 78 (August 15, 1900): 1028.
40. "Pamunkey Indians Angry," 1.
41. "Jim Crow Car Law Violated: Alleged Abuses on the Southern's Trains—Pamunkey Indians Aggrieved," *Washington Post* (July 29, 1900): 11.
42. Rountree, *Pocahontas's People*, 212.
43. "Pamunkey Indians," *Baltimore Sun* (July 31, 1900): 8; "'Jim Crow' Law to Be Tested: Virginia's Pamunkey Indians Indignant," *New York Times* (August 4, 1900): 1.
44. Rountree, *Pocahontas's People*, 212.
45. "Pamunkey Indians Will Ride with the Whites," *Baltimore Sun* (August 21, 1900): 8.
46. "The Powhatans," *American Antiquarian and Oriental Journal* 31 (June 1, 1909): 147.
47. "Powhatan's Men Yet Live," 6.
48. Pollard, "The Pamunkey Indians of Virginia," 10.
49. "They Want Wives: Indians Are Sending among the Cherokees for Brides," *Atlanta Constitution* (March 24, 1895): 3.

50. James Mooney, "The Powhatan Confederacy, Past and Present," *American Anthropologist*, 9: 1 (January–March, 1907): 145. Copy of article in Helen C. Rountree Collection of Virginia Indian Documents, 2005, Accession 42003, Personal Papers Collection, Box 3, The Library of Virginia.
51. "The Pamunkey Indians: Life among Virginia Aborigines on Their Tidewater Reservation," 6.
52. Pollard, "The Pamunkey Indians of Virginia," 16.
53. Interview with Jesse L. S. Pendleton, February 19, 1971, File: Helen C. Rountree, Fieldnotes, 1969–1973, Helen C. Rountree Papers, Box 2, NAA Washington. For a detailed study on the relationship between African Americans and Native Americans in Virginia, as well as the decisions of Virginia tribes to expel people with black ancestry from their tribal communities, see Arica L. Coleman, *That the Blood Stay Pure: African Americans, Native Americans, and the Predicament of Race and Identity in Virginia* (Bloomington: Indiana University Press, 2013).
54. "Their Origin a Puzzle: Strange Groups of People along the Atlantic Coast," *Washington Post* (November 23, 1902): 17.
55. "The Pamunkey Indians: Life among Virginia Aborigines on Their Tidewater Reservation," 6.
56. "Their Origin a Puzzle," 17.
57. Letter from Edgar R. Lafferty, J., on behalf of Chief T. D. Cook and the Pamunkey Tribal Council, to Helen C. Rountree, October 29, 1971, Helen C. Rountree Papers, Box 1, NAA Washington.
58. "They Want Wives," 3.
59. When two families decided they were distantly related enough to marry, they took advantage of the situation. In 1901, for example, William G. Sweat, a Pamunkey fisherman, took Cruisa A. Bradby as his third consecutive wife. His first wife had been "a sister of his newly-made bride." "Indians Wedded in Church Parsonage," *Washington Post* (January 18, 1901): 9.
60. "They Want Wives," 3.
61. James Mooney, to Albert S. Gatschet, September 20, 1887, File: Albert S. Gatschet, *Letters Received*, Manuscript 4047, NAA Washington.
62. File: IV (21F2h), Theodore Stern, Pamunkey—h. "Pamunkey Pottery," 1941, 1 item, Ms. Coll. 126, Frank G. Speck Papers, Sub-Collection I, Box 14, APS Philadelphia.
63. Photo 74-4898, Jamestown Exposition of 1907, Chief Tecumseh D. Cook, Collection of Pamunkey Photos, Photo-Lot 87-6, NAA Washington.
64. Solenberger to Ricks, February 28, 1942, Ms. Coll. 126, APS Philadelphia.
65. "A Teacher Needed: Difficult to Secure One for the Pamunkey Children," *Baltimore Sun* (October 26, 1900): 8.
66. "They Want Wives," 3.
67. "Looking for New Blood: Mission of the Chief of the Virginia Pamunkeys to Chicago," *Washington Post* (July 7, 1893): 1.
68. Rountree, *Pocahontas's People*, 210.
69. Bradby, *Pamunkey Speaks*, 101.
70. "They Want Wives," 3; "Looking for New Blood," 1.
71. Hopkins, "Modern Survivors of Chief Powhatan," M4.
72. Mooney, *The Powhatan Confederacy, Past and Present*, Manuscript 2199, NAA Washington.
73. "The Last of the Virginia Indians," *Christian Advocate and Journal*, 30 (March 15, 1855): 44.
74. Frank G. Speck, "Chapters on the Ethnography of the Powhatan Tribes of Virginia," *Indian Notes and Monographs*, 1 (New York: Museum of the American Indian, Heye Foundation, 1928): 254, Helen C. Rountree Collection of Virginia Indian Documents, 2005, Accession 42003, Personal Papers Collection, Box 3, The Library of Virginia.
75. "Surviving Indian Tribes," *American Antiquarian and Oriental Journal*, 30 (November/ December 1908): 342.
76. Speck, "Chapters on the Ethnography of the Powhatan Tribes of Virginia," 249.
77. Rountree, *Pocahontas's People*, 211. In a 1972 letter, Rountree wrote that she found the idea of a connection between anthropologist James Mooney's visit to the Pamunkeys

and Mattaponis and the split in the tribes "both intriguing and probable." However, she said, "any definite evidence of influence by Mooney would be hard to ascertain from the Indians, as the Mattaponi have a mild rivalry with the Pamunkey and prefer to establish their own identity by convincing the public that their separate history goes back into aboriginal times." See Helen C. Rountree to William M. Colby, October 19, 1972, Helen C. Rountree Papers, Box 1, NAA Washington.

78. Mooney, *The Powhatan Confederacy, Past and Present*, Manuscript 2199, NAA Washington.

79. Rountree, *Pocahontas's People*, 211.

80. Interview with June Langston, Mattaponi, by Helen C. Rountree, June 19, 1970, File: Helen C. Rountree, Fieldnotes, 1969–1973, Helen C. Rountree Papers, Box 2, NAA Washington.

81. Mooney, "The Powhatan Confederacy, Past and Present," 129–152.

82. Speck, "Chapters on the Ethnography of the Powhatan Tribes of Virginia," 238.

83. "Tribe of Pamunkey: Conclusion of Their Most Interesting History" Manuscript 2197, NAA Washington; Speck, "Chapters on the Ethnography of the Powhatan Tribes of Virginia," 238.

84. Chief Thomas Cook and Councilmen to Governor James L. Kemper, February 9, 1877, File: James L. Kemper, Executive Papers, 1877 February, Virginia, Governor's Office, Executive Papers of Governor James L. Kemper, 1874–1877, Accession 43755, State Government Records Collection, Box 4, The Library of Virginia; "Tribe of Pamunkey: Conclusion of Their Most Interesting History," Manuscript 2197, NAA Washington.

85. "Tribe of Pamunkey: Conclusion of Their Most Interesting History," Manuscript 2197, NAA Washington.

86. "Powhatan's Men Yet Live," *Washington Evening Star* (April 25, 1894): 6, Gatschet, Albert Samuel, *Pamunkey Notebook, Post 1893*, Manuscript 2197, NAA Washington. Pamunkeys continue to vote using corn and bean ballots today. See Minutes of Special Tribal Meeting, July 12, 2012, Appendix 1, "Supplemental Report on Pamunkey Women's 'Voice and Vote' Rights, *Petition for Federal Acknowledgment*, October 19, 2012, 11, United States Department of the Interior, Bureau of Indian Affairs, Washington, DC.

87. Interview with Chief T. D. Cooke, Pamunkey, August 22, 1970, File: Helen C. Rountree, Fieldnotes, 1969–1973, Helen C. Rountree Papers, Box 2, NAA Washington.

88. "Virginia Letter: The Pamunkey Indians and Their Little Reservation," *Washington Chronicle* (December 14, 1890), File: Gatschet, Albert Samuel, *The Pamunkey Indians and Their Little Reservation*, December 14, 1890, Manuscript 55, NAA Washington.

89. "They Want Wives," 3.

90. "Virginia Letter: The Pamunkey Indians and Their Little Reservation," Manuscript 55, NAA Washington.

91. Mooney, "The Powhatan Confederacy, Past and Present," 147.

92. "Virginia Letter: The Pamunkey Indians and Their Little Reservation," Manuscript 55, NAA Washington.

93. Interview with Chief and Mrs. Tecumseh Deerfoot Cook, by Helen C. Rountree, July 15, 1970, File: Helen C. Rountree, Fieldnotes, 1969–1973, Helen C. Rountree Papers, Box 2, NAA Washington; "Tribute from Red Men: Pamunkey Indians Take a Fine Deer to Governor Swanson," *Baltimore Sun* (December 31, 1907): 5.

94. File: IV (21F2d), Speck, Frank G., Pamunkey—d. "Virginia Indians Past and Present," newspaper article, n.d., 1 item, Ms. Coll. 126, Frank G. Speck Papers, Sub-Collection I, Box 14, APS Philadelphia.

95. "They Want Wives," 3.

96. Mooney, "The Powhatan Confederacy, Past and Present," 147.

97. "Tribe of Pamunkey: Conclusion of Their Most Interesting History," Manuscript 2197, NAA Washington.

98. Gatschet, Albert Samuel, *Pamunkey notebook, post 1893*, Manuscript 2197, NAA Washington.

99. "They Want Wives," 3; interview with Chief T. D. Cooke, by Helen C. Rountree, August 22, 1970, File: Helen C. Rountree, Fieldnotes, 1969–1973, Helen C. Rountree Papers, Box 2, NAA Washington.

100. Speck, "Chapters on the Ethnography of the Powhatan Tribes of Virginia," 314.
101. Interview with Chief T. D. Cooke, by Helen C. Rountree, August 22, 1970, File: Helen C. Rountree, Fieldnotes, 1969–1973, Helen C. Rountree Papers, Box 2, NAA Washington.
102. Rountree, "Powhatan's Descendants in the Modern World," 74–75.
103. File: IV (21F2d), Speck, Frank G., Pamunkey—d. "Virginia Indians Past and Present," newspaper article, n.d., 1 item, Ms. Coll. 126, Frank G. Speck Papers, Sub-Collection I, Box 14, APS Philadelphia.
104. Mooney, "The Powhatan Confederacy, Past and Present," 146; File: IV (21F2d), Speck, Frank G., Pamunkey—d. "Virginia Indians Past and Present," newspaper article, n.d., 1 item, Ms. Coll. 126, Frank G. Speck Papers, Sub-Collection I, Box 14, APS Philadelphia.
105. "Pamunkey Indians: Vanishing Remnant of a Once Powerful Tribe," *Los Angeles Times* (June 3, 1894): 9.
106. "Women's Board of Home Missions," *New York Evangelist*, 69 (April 21, 1898): 17; "Pamunkey Indians: Vanishing Remnant of a Once Powerful Tribe," 9.
107. Interview with James Page by Thomas Blumer, 1980s, File: Pamunkey Indians, Oral History, Thomas J. Blumer Collection on the Catawba Nation Native American Studies Collection, Medford Library, the University of South Carolina, Lancaster, South Carolina (hereafter Thomas J. Blumer Collection).
108. File: IV (21F2d), Speck, Frank G., Pamunkey—d. "Virginia Indians Past and Present," newspaper article, n.d., 1 item, Ms. Coll. 126, Frank G. Speck Papers, Sub-Collection I, Box 14, APS Philadelphia.
109. Bagby, *Tuckahoe: A Collection of Indian Stories and Legends*, v.
110. "Pamunkeys' Past Is Obscure: Remnant of the Virginia Aborigines Live, Dress, and Worship like Whites," *Washington Post* (November 26, 1899): 13.
111. Pollard, "The Pamunkey Indians of Virginia," 12.
112. Speck, "Chapters on the Ethnography of the Powhatan Tribes of Virginia," 435.
113. Interview with Chief and Mrs. Tecumseh Deerfoot Cook, by Helen C. Rountree, July 15, 1970, File: Helen C. Rountree, Fieldnotes, 1969–1973, Helen C. Rountree Papers, Box 2, NAA Washington.
114. File: IV (21F2d), Speck, Frank G., Pamunkey—d. "Virginia Indians Past and Present" newspaper article, n.d., 1 item, Ms. Coll. 126, Frank G. Speck Papers, Sub-Collection I, Box 14, APS Philadelphia.
115. Interview with Mrs. T. D. Cooke, assisted by Mrs. Dora Cook Bradby, by Helen C. Rountree, June 17, 1970, File: Helen C. Rountree, Fieldnotes, 1969–1973, Helen C. Rountree Papers, Box 2, NAA Washington.
116. File: IV (21F2h), Stern, Theodore, Pamunkey—h. "Pamunkey Pottery," 1941, 1 item, Ms. Coll. 126, Frank G. Speck Papers, Sub-Collection I, Box 14, APS Philadelphia.
117. Bagby, *Tuckahoe: A Collection of Indian Stories and Legends*, 78.
118. Bagby, *Tuckahoe: A Collection of Indian Stories and Legends*, v.
119. M. R. Harrington, "Catawba Potters and Their Work," *American Anthropologist* (July, August, September, 1908): 406, South Caroliniana Library, University of South Carolina, Columbia, South Carolina (hereafter South Caroliniana Library).
120. "Powhatan's Men Yet Live," 6, Manuscript 2197, NAA Washington. In 1908, anthropologist M. R. Harrington wrote that "the few vessels manufactured now by the Pamunkey for curio hunters are plainly crude attempts to resuscitate the art practiced by the grandmothers of the present generation." See Harrington, "Catawba Potters and Their Work," 406.
121. File: IV (21F2d), Speck, Frank G., Pamunkey—d. "Virginia Indians Past and Present" newspaper article, n.d., 1 item, Ms. Coll. 126, Frank G. Speck Papers, Sub-Collection I, Box 14, APS Philadelphia. The visits of scholars like Frank G. Speck "served as a powerful stimulus in the recollection of elements fast passing into oblivion." See Theodore Stern, "Pamunkey Pottery Making," *Southern Indian Studies*, 3 (October, 1951): 65, Helen C. Rountree Collection of Virginia Indian Documents, 2005, Accession 42003, Personal Papers Collection, Box 4, The Library of Virginia.

122. File: IV (21F2d), Speck, Frank G., Pamunkey—d. "Virginia Indians Past and Present" newspaper article, n.d., 1 item, Ms. Coll. 126, Frank G. Speck Papers, Sub-Collection I, Box 14, APS Philadelphia.

123. File: IV (21F2d), Speck, Frank G., Pamunkey—d. "Virginia Indians Past and Present."

124. File: IV (21F2h), Stern, Theodore, Pamunkey—h. "Pamunkey Pottery," 1941, 1 item, Ms. Coll. 126, Frank G. Speck Papers, Sub-Collection I, Box 14, APS Philadelphia.

125. Interview with Mrs. T. D. Cooke, assisted by Mrs. Dora Cook Bradby, by Helen C. Rountree, June 17, 1970, File: Helen C. Rountree, Fieldnotes, 1969-1973, Helen C. Rountree Papers, Box 2, NAA Washington.

126. File: IV (21F2h), Stern, Theodore, Pamunkey—h. "Pamunkey Pottery," 1941, 1 item, Ms. Coll. 126, Frank G. Speck Papers, Sub-Collection I, Box 14, APS Philadelphia.

127. "Pamunkeys Want a Sea Trip," *Morning Times*, Washington, DC (July 6, 1899), Gatschet, Albert Samuel, *Pamunkey notebook, post 1893*, Manuscript 2197, NAA Washington.

128. "Notice! Powhatan's Pamunkey Indian Braves Will Perform," 1898, Manuscript 4969, NAA Washington.

129. "Pamunkeys Want a Sea Trip," Manuscript 2197, NAA Washington.

130. "Pamunkeys to Go on Warpath in Richmond Colonial Pageant," *Washington Post* (May 29, 1935): 19.

131. The Treaty of 1677 specified that the chiefs of Virginia tribes "in the Moneth of March every year, with some of their Great Men, shall tender their Obedience to the Right Honourable His Majesties Governour at the place of his Residence, wherever it shall be, and there pay the accustomed Tribute of Twenty Beaver Skins to the Governour, and also their Quit-Rent aforesaid, in acknowledgement they hold their Crowns and Lands of the Great King of England." See "May 1677—With Pamunkeys, Weyanocks, Nottoways, Nansemonds, Ratified 1680, with additional signers: Appamattucks, Monacans, Meherrins, Saponis, and a combination of nanzatico/Nanzemunch/Portobaccos," in *Early American Indian Documents: Treaties and Laws, 1609–1789, Vol. 4: Virginia Treaties, 1607–1722*, edited by W. Stitt Robinson (Frederick, MD: University Publications of America, 1983), 82–87, Helen C. Rountree Collection of Virginia Indian Documents, 2005, Accession 42003, Personal Papers Collection, Box 3, The Library of Virginia.

132. "Tribute from Red Men: Pamunkey Indians Take a Fine Deer to Governor Swanson," *Baltimore Sun* (December 31, 1907): 5.

133. "Surviving Indian Tribes," 342.

134. 1901 Pamunkey Census by James Mooney, reprinted in Kevin K. Washburn, Assistant Secretary, Indian Affairs, "Proposed Finding for Acknowledgment of the Pamunkey Indian Tribe (Petitioner #323), Prepared in Response to the Petition Submitted to the Assistant Secretary—Indian Affairs for Federal Acknowledgment as an Indian Tribe," January 16, 2014, Appendix B, Department of the Interior, Bureau of Indian Affairs, Washington, DC.

135. Mooney, *The Powhatan Confederacy, Past and Present*, Manuscript 2199, NAA Washington.

136. Kevin K. Washburn, Assistant Secretary, Indian Affairs, "Proposed Finding for Acknowledgment of the Pamunkey Indian Tribe (Petitioner #323), Prepared in Response to the Petition Submitted to the Assistant Secretary—Indian Affairs for Federal Acknowledgment as an Indian Tribe," January 16, 2014, 88, Department of the Interior, Bureau of Indian Affairs, Washington, DC.

137. Speck, "Chapters on the Ethnography of the Powhatan Tribes of Virginia," 236–237.

138. Rountree, "The Indians of Virginia: A Third Race in a Biracial State," 41.

139. Bureau of Vital Statistics, State Board of Health, *Eugenics in Relation to the New Family and the Law on Racial Integrity* (Richmond: Davis Bottom, Supt. Public Printing, 1924): 6–7, File: Clerk's Correspondence, 1924, Rockbridge County Clerk's Records, Clerk's Correspondence (A. T. Shields) (W. A. Plecker to A. T. Shields), 1872–1936, 1912–1943, Broken Series, Accession 1160754, Box 1, The Library of Virginia, Richmond, Virginia; W. A. Plecker, "The New Virginia Law to Preserve Racial Integrity," *Virginia Health Bulletin*, 56 (March, 1924): 5, File: Clerk's Correspondence, 1924, Rockbridge County Clerk's Records, Clerk's Correspondence (A. T. Shields) (W. A. Plecker to A. T.

Shields), 1872–1936, 1912–1943, Broken Series, Accession 1160754, Box 1, The Library of Virginia.

140. In 1926, Plecker wrote that he and his colleagues at the Bureau of Vital Statistics "expect to bend all of our energies to listing as accurately as possible all who are claiming admittance into the white race, either through the Indian route or directly through extensive white intermixture." See W. A. Plecker, State Registrar, to A. T. Shield, Rockbridge County Clerk's Office, April 2, 1926, File: Clerk's Correspondence, 1923–1929, Rockbridge County Clerk's Records, Clerk's Correspondence (A. T. Shields) (W. A. Plecker to A. T. Shields), 1872–1936, 1912–1943, Broken Series, Accession 1160754, Box 1, The Library of Virginia.

141. Rountree, "The Indians of Virginia: A Third Race in a Biracial State,"41.

142. Bertha Pfister Wailes, *Backward Virginians: A Further Study of the Win Tribe* (Richmond: University of Virginia, 1928); see Helen Rountree's Notes of the Wailes Thesis, Helen C. Rountree Collection of Virginia Indian Documents, 2005, Accession 42003, Personal Papers Collection, Box 3, The Library of Virginia.

143. Plecker, "The New Virginia Law to Preserve Racial Integrity," 4.

144. W. A. Plecker, State Registrar, to John Collier, Commissioner of Indian Affairs, April 6, 1943, File: Pamunkey Indians, 138, 1942–1946, Cherokee Indian Agency, Series 6, General Records, Correspondence, Indian Field Service Filing System, 1926–1952, Box 45, RG 75, National Archives and Records Administration, Atlanta, Georgia (hereafter NARA Atlanta). Plecker's racial ideas were bolstered by the writings of other eugenicists, like Arthur Howard Estabrook and Ivan E McDougle, who disparaged mixed-race communities in their 1926 book, *Mongrel Virginians: The Win Tribe* (Baltimore: Williams & Wilkins, 1926).

145. "Virginia Passes 'One Drop' Bill Unanimously: Designed to Check Mixing in Schools," *Pittsburgh Courier* (February 22, 1930): 20; W. A. Plecker, State Registrar, to Annie Belle Crowder, July 23, 1945, File: 13, General Correspondence, 1945–64, Virginia Department of Education, Indian School Files, 1936–1967, Accession 29632, State Government Records Collection, Box 1, The Library of Virginia.

146. W. A. Plecker, State Registrar, to Annie Belle Crowder, July 23, 1945, File: 13, General Correspondence, 1945–64, Virginia Department of Education, Indian School Files, 1936–1967, Accession 29632, State Government Records Collection, Box 1, The Library of Virginia.

147. "Virginia Passes 'One Drop' Bill Unanimously," 20.

148. William Jones, "Day by Day: Negroid Indians in Virginia," *Baltimore Afro-American* (October 31, 1925): 9.

149. W. A. Plecker, State Registrar, to Annie Belle Crowder, July 23, 1945, File: 13, General Correspondence, 1945–64, Virginia Department of Education, Indian School Files, 1936–1967, Accession 29632, State Government Records Collection, Box 1, The Library of Virginia.

150. James R. Coates to Frank G. Speck, December 2, 1944, File: IV (20F1g) Speck, Frank G., General and Historical—g. Draft classification of Virginia Indians, 1940–1946, 82 items, Ms. Coll. 126, Frank G. Speck Papers, Sub-Collection 1, Box 13, APS Philadelphia.

151. Plecker, "The New Virginia Law to Preserve Racial Integrity," 1

152. W. A. Plecker, State Registrar, to Mary F. Adkins, January 23, 1942, File: Pamunkey Indians, 138, 1942–1946, Cherokee Indian Agency, Series 6, General Records, Correspondence, Indian Field Service Filing System, 1926–1952, Box 45, RG 75, NARA Atlanta.

153. W. A. Plecker, State Registrar, to Martha V. Wood, November 23, 1925, File: Clerk's Correspondence, 1923–1929, Rockbridge County Clerk's Records, Clerk's Correspondence (A. T. Shields) (W. A. Plecker to A. T. Shields), 1872–1936, 1912–1943, Broken Series, Accession 1160754, Box 1, The Library of Virginia.

154. This warning cited the *Encyclopedia Britannica* and the 1843 petition to insist that Pamunkeys were "all mixed-bloods; some negro mixture." Solenberger to Ricks, February 28, 1942, Ms. Coll. 126, APS Philadelphia; Document Issued by Bureau of Vital Statistics, 1947, James R. Coates Papers, 1833–1947, Accession 31577, Personal Papers Collection, The Library of Virginia.

155. Document Issued by Bureau of Vital Statistics, 1947, James R. Coates Papers, 1833–1947, Accession 31577, Personal Papers Collection, The Library of Virginia.

156. W. A. Plecker, State Registrar, to John Collier, Commissioner of Indian Affairs, April 6, 1943, File: Pamunkey Indians, 138, 1942–1946, Cherokee Indian Agency, Series 6, General Records, Correspondence, Indian Field Service Filing System, 1926–1952, Box 45, RG 75, NARA Atlanta.

157. Memorandum No. 336, from State Headquarters from Selective Service, Richmond, VA., to All Local Boards, January 7, 1942, File: IV (20F1g) Speck, Frank G., General and Historical—g. Draft classification of Virginia Indians, 1940–1946, 82 items, Ms. Coll. 126, Frank G. Speck Papers, Sub-Collection 1, Box 13, APS Philadelphia.

158. Lawrence E. Lindley, to John Collier, February 26, 1942, File: IV (20F1g) Speck, Frank G., General and Historical—g. Draft classification of Virginia Indians, 1940–1946, 82 items, Ms. Coll. 126, Frank G. Speck Papers, Sub-Collection 1, Box 13, APS Philadelphia.

159. Council of Pamunkey Tribe of Indians to Colgate W. Darden, Governor of the Commonwealth of Virginia, July 23, 1942, James R. Coates Papers, 1833–1947, Accession 31577, Personal Papers Collection, The Library of Virginia.

160. W. A. Plecker, State Registrar, to John Collier, Commissioner of Indian Affairs, April 6, 1943, File: Pamunkey Indians, 138, 1942–1946, Cherokee Indian Agency, Series 6, General Records, Correspondence, Indian Field Service Filing System, 1926–1952, Box 45, RG 75, NARA Atlanta.

161. Lawrence E. Lindley, to John Collier, February 26, 1942, File: IV (20F1g) Speck, Frank G., General and Historical—g. Draft classification of Virginia Indians, 1940–1946, 82 items, Ms. Coll. 126, Frank G. Speck Papers, Sub-Collection 1, Box 13, APS Philadelphia.

162. W. Carson Ryan, Jr. to William Zimmerman, February 11, 1938, Records of the Offices of Chief Clerk and Assistant Commissioner of Indian Affairs, Correspondence of Assistant Commissioner William Zimmerman, 1935–48, Box 2, RG 75, National Archives and Records Administration, Washington, DC (hereafter NARA Washington).

163. William Zimmerman to Dr. W. Carson Ryan, The Carnegie Foundation for the Advancement of Teaching, New York, March 10, 1938, Records of the Offices of Chief Clerk and Assistant Commissioner of Indian Affairs, Correspondence of Assistant Commissioner William Zimmerman, 1935–48, Box 2, RG 75, NARA Washington.

164. William Zimmerman to B. H. Van Oot, State Supervisor of Trade and Industrial Education, Richmond, VA, March 10, 1938, Records of the Offices of Chief Clerk and Assistant Commissioner of Indian Affairs, Correspondence of Assistant Commissioner William Zimmerman, 1935–48, Box 2, RG 75, NARA Washington.

165. John Collier to W.A. Plecker, May 1, 1943, File: Pamunkey Indians, 138, 1942-1946, Cherokee Indian Agency, Series 6, General Records, Correspondence, Indian Field Service Filing System, 1926-1952, Box 45, RG 75, NARA Atlanta.

166. W. A. Plecker, State Registrar, to John Collier, Commissioner of Indian Affairs, April 6, 1943, File: Pamunkey Indians, 138, 1942–1946, Cherokee Indian Agency, Series 6, General Records, Correspondence, Indian Field Service Filing System, 1926–1952, Box 45, RG 75, NARA Atlanta; W. A. Plecker to John Collier, October 26, 1943, File: Pamunkey Indians, 138, 1942–1946, Cherokee Indian Agency, Series 6, General Records, Correspondence, Indian Field Service Filing System, 1926–1952, Box 45, RG 75, NARA Atlanta.

167. Rountree, "The Indians of Virginia: A Third Race in a Biracial State,"43.

168. J. L. Prince, April 11, 1945, James R. Coates Papers, 1833–1947, Accession 31577, Personal Papers Collection, The Library of Virginia.

169. Petition, March 1, 1945, James R. Coates Papers, 1833–1947, Accession 31577, Personal Papers Collection, The Library of Virginia.

170. James R. Coates to Tribal Chiefs of Virginia Tribes, January 14, 1947, James R. Coates Papers, 1833–1947, Accession 31577, Personal Papers Collection, The Library of Virginia.

171. James R. Coates to Frank G. Speck, November 6, 1945, File: IV (20F1g) Speck, Frank G., General and Historical—g. Draft classification of Virginia Indians, 1940–1946, 82 items, Ms. Coll. 126, Frank G. Speck Papers, Sub-Collection 1, Box 13, APS Philadelphia.

172. Pamunkey Indian Tribe, "Laws of the Pamunkey Indians," circa 1954, reprinted in Pamunkey Indian Tribe Petition for Federal Acknowledgment, Appendix 4: Part A, Pamunkey Tribal Documents, 2010, Department of the Interior, Bureau of Indian Affairs, Washington, DC.

173. Rountree, *Pocahontas's People,* 239.

174. Pamunkey Indian Tribe, "Laws of the Pamunkey Indians," circa 1954, reprinted in Pamunkey Indian Tribe Petition for Federal Acknowledgment, Appendix 4: Part A, Pamunkey Tribal Documents, 2010, Department of the Interior, Bureau of Indian Affairs, Washington, DC.

175. Pamunkey Indian Tribe, "Laws of the Pamunkey Indians," circa 1954, reprinted in Pamunkey Indian Tribe Petition for Federal Acknowledgment, Appendix 4: Part A, Pamunkey Tribal Documents, 2010, Department of the Interior, Bureau of Indian Affairs, Washington, DC.

176. Speck, "Chapters on the Ethnography of the Powhatan Tribes of Virginia," 452–453.

177. Tecumseh Cook to James Coates, December 18, 1944, File: IV (20F1g), Speck, Frank G., General and Historical—g. Draft classification of Virginia Indians, 1940–1946, 82 items, Ms. Coll. 126, Frank G. Speck Papers, Sub-Collection 1, Box 13, APS Philadelphia.

178. Rountree, "The Indians of Virginia: A Third Race in a Biracial State," 45.

179. Helen C. Rountree to W. Grosvenor Pollard, III, August 28, 1972, Helen C. Rountree Papers, Box 1, NAA Washington.

180. In 1901, for example, Mooney recorded at least three Pamunkey men with white wives. Mooney, *The Powhatan Confederacy, Past and Present,* Manuscript 2199, NAA Washington.

181. Rev. E. D. Gooch, April 24, 1945, James R. Coates Papers, 1833–1947, Accession 31577, Personal Papers Collection, The Library of Virginia.

182. Speck, "Chapters on the Ethnography of the Powhatan Tribes of Virginia," 306.

183. Rountree, *Pocahontas's People,* 9–10, 110. For more information on Cockacoeske, see Martha W. McCartney, "Cockacoeske, Queen of Pamunkey: Diplomat and Suzeraine," in *Powhatan's Mantle: Indians in the Colonial Southeast,* edited by Gregory A. Waselkov, Peter H. Wood, and Tom Hatley (Lincoln: University of Nebraska Press, 2006), 243–266.

184. Pamunkey Indian Tribe, "Supplemental Report on Pamunkey Women's 'Voice and Vote' Rights," *Petition for Federal Acknowledgment,* October 19, 2012, 2, United States Department of the Interior, Bureau of Indian Affairs, Washington, DC.

185. Interview with Chief William Miles of the Pamunkey Indian Reservation, by B. Hammje, for Rountree's Virginia Indians Class, October, 1986, Helen C. Rountree Papers, Box 3, NAA Washington.

186. W. A. Plecker, State Registrar, to Annie Belle Crowder, July 23, 1945, File: 13, General Correspondence, 1945–64, Virginia Department of Education, Indian School Files, 1936–1967, Accession 29632, State Government Records Collection, Box 1, The Library of Virginia.

187. Interview with Chief William Miles of the Pamunkey Indian Reservation, by B. Hammje, for Rountree's Virginia Indians Class, October, 1986, Helen C. Rountree Papers, Box 3, NAA Washington.

188. Student fieldnotes by Leslie Willis, October, 1986, File: Helen C. Rountree, Fieldnotes, April 1986–December 1986, Helen C. Rountree Papers, Box 3, NAA Washington.

189. Interview with Chief T. D. Cook, by Helen C. Rountree, August 22, 1970, File: Helen C. Rountree, Fieldnotes, 1969–1973, Helen C. Rountree Papers, Box 2, NAA Washington.

190. Pamunkey Indian Tribe, "Laws of the Pamunkey Indians," circa 1954, reprinted in Pamunkey Indian Tribe Petition for Federal Acknowledgment, Appendix 4: Part A, Pamunkey Tribal Documents, 2010, Department of the Interior, Bureau of Indian Affairs, Washington, DC.

191. Rountree, "Powhatan's Descendants in the Modern World," 72–73.

192. This should perhaps come as no surprise considering that the state of Virginia delayed its own ratification of the Nineteenth Amendment until 1952. Not subject to federal

oversight since it lacked federal recognition, the Pamunkey Indian Tribe maintained the conservative gender policies that it had learned from Anglo-Virginians.

193. One of Helen C. Rountree's anthropology students noted that among the Mattaponi, "wives play a big role in influencing their husbands' vote." Like the Pamunkeys, the Mattaponis limited suffrage to men, but women played political roles behind the scenes. In the early 1980s, the wife of the Mattaponi chief, Gertrude Custalow, exerted "great influence over the chief's decisions." See Notes on Fieldtrip to the Pamunkey and Mattaponi Reservations, November, 1983, File: Helen C. Rountree, Fieldnotes, 1983– 1985, Helen C. Rountree Papers, Box 2, NAA Washington.

194. B. H. Van Oot, State Supervisor of Trade and Industrial Education, to Frank Speck, December 14, 1939, File: IV (21F2s) Speck, Frank G., Pamunkey—s. Correspondence with Informants, 1921–1940, 7 items, Ms. Coll. 126, Frank G. Speck Papers, Sub-Collection I, Box 14, APS Philadelphia.

195. Interview with Mrs. T. D. Cooke, assisted by Mrs. Dora Cook Bradby, June 17, 1970, by Helen C. Rountree, File: Helen C. Rountree, Fieldnotes, 1969–1973, Helen C. Rountree Papers, Box 2, NAA Washington.

196. August 15, 1970, File: Helen C. Rountree, Fieldnotes, 1969–1973, Helen C. Rountree Papers, Box 2, NAA Washington.

197. Interview with Edward Bradby, by Helen C. Rountree, August 15, 1970, File: Helen C. Rountree, Fieldnotes, 1969–1973, Helen C. Rountree Papers, Box 2, NAA Washington.

198. Interview with Chief T. D. Cooke, by Helen C. Rountree, August 22, 1970, File: Helen C. Rountree, Fieldnotes, 1969–1973, Helen C. Rountree Papers, Box 2, NAA Washington.

199. Helen C. Rountree, "Indian Virginians on the Move," in *Indians of the Southeastern United States in the Late 20th Century*, edited by J. Anthony Paredes (Tucaloosa: University of Alabama Press, 1992), 18, Helen C. Rountree Collection of Virginia Indian Documents, 2005, Accession 42003, Personal Papers Collection, Box 5, The Library of Virginia.

200. August 15, 1970, File: Helen C. Rountree, Fieldnotes, 1969-1973, Helen C. Rountree Papers, Box 2, NAA Washington.

201. Interview with Chief T. D. Cooke, by Helen C. Rountree, August 22, 1970, File: Helen C. Rountree, Fieldnotes, 1969–1973, Helen C. Rountree Papers, Box 2, NAA Washington.

202. Pamunkey Indian Tribe, "Supplemental Report on Pamunkey Women's 'Voice and Vote' Rights," 3.

203. Speck, "Chapters on the Ethnography of the Powhatan Tribes of Virginia," 251.

204. Kevin K. Washburn, Assistant Secretary, Indian Affairs, "Proposed Finding for Acknowledgment of the Pamunkey Indian Tribe (Petitioner #323), Prepared in Response to the Petition Submitted to the Assistant Secretary—Indian Affairs for Federal Acknowledgment as an Indian Tribe," January 16, 2014, 25, Department of the Interior, Bureau of Indian Affairs, Washington, D.C.

205. Rountree, *Pocahontas's People*, 205.

206. Interview with Chief T. D. Cooke, Pamunkey, by Helen C. Rountree, August 22, 1970, File: Helen C. Rountree, Fieldnotes, 1969–1973, Helen C. Rountree Papers, Box 2, NAA Washington.

207. Rountree, "Powhatan's Descendants in the Modern World," 74.

208. B. Drummond Ayers, "Last Stand Nears for Tiny Indian Tribe's Identity: 'I Can't Remember When a Pamunkey Last Married a Pamunkey," *New York Times* (January 16, 1989): A8.

209. Joe Volz, "Two Indian Women Fighting Tribal Law that Bars White Husband from Reservation," *Indian Trader* (April, 1989): 16, File: Pamunkey Indians, Clippings, 27 September 1884—August 2001, n.d., Thomas J. Blumer Collection.

210. Hilary Appelman, "Va. Indian Wives Fight to Stay on Reservation: Pamunkey Women Who Marry Outsiders Must Give Up Residency," *Washington Post* (January 14, 1989): B8.

211. Volz, "Two Indian Women Fighting Tribal Law that Bars White Husband from Reservation," 16.

212. Appelman, "Va. Indian Wives Fight to Stay on Reservation," B8.

213. Ayers, "Last Stand Nears for Tiny Indian Tribe's Identity," A8.

214. Volz, "Two Indian Women Fighting Tribal Law that Bars White Husband from Reservation," 16.

215. Appelman, "Va. Indian Wives Fight to Stay on Reservation," B8.

216. Ayers, "Last Stand Nears for Tiny Indian Tribe's Identity," A8.

217. Pamunkey Indian Tribe, "Supplemental Report on Pamunkey Women's 'Voice and Vote' Rights," 3, 5–6.

218. Pamunkey Indian Tribe, "Supplemental Report on Pamunkey Women's 'Voice and Vote' Rights," 6–7.

219. Pamunkey Indian Tribe, "Supplemental Report on Pamunkey Women's 'Voice and Vote' Rights," 8.

220. See Nancy Wright Beasley, "The Pamunkey Legacy: Mildred 'Gentle Rain' Moore Aims to Preserve Her Tribe's Heritage," *Richmond Magazine* (November, 2011), http://www.richmondmagazine.com/articles/the-pamunkey-legacy-01-24-2012.html, accessed April 25, 2014.

221. Pamunkey Indian Tribe, "Supplemental Report on Pamunkey Women's 'Voice and Vote' Rights," 1–2.

222. Pamunkeys felt strongly connected to the reservation. According to Francis Elizabeth Scott Bagby, when confronted with the idea that the tribe should sell their land and "move to a more healthful location" in 1907, the Pamunkey Chief proclaimed that the Pamunkeys could not possibly "sell the graves of our ancestors." Even if they moved away, Pamunkeys recognized the reservation as the home land of their ancestors and gathering point of the tribe. See Bagby, *Tuckahoe: A Collection of Indian Stories and Legends*, vi.

223. Bradby, *Pamunkey Speaks: Native Perspectives*, 106–107.

224. Mooney, *The Powhatan Confederacy, Past and Present*, Manuscript 2199, NAA Washington.

225. Speck, "Chapters on the Ethnography of the Powhatan Tribes of Virginia," 250–251.

226. Bradby, *Pamunkey Speaks: Native Perspectives*, 63.

227. Hopkins, "Modern Survivors of Chief Powhatan," M4. In 1895, a newspaper article reported that twenty Pamunkeys and Mattaponis served "as boatmen on steamers plying the Virginia rivers." See "They Want Wives," 3.

228. Hopkins, "Modern Survivors of Chief Powhatan," M4.

229. "Pamunkey Indian Killed in France," *Atlanta Constitution* (November 26, 1918): 7.

230. G. W. J. Blume, "Present-Day Indians of Tidewater Virginia," *Quarterly Bulletin of the Archaeological Society of Virginia*, 6 (December, 1951): 1–8, Helen C. Rountree Collection of Virginia Indian Documents, 2005, Accession 42003, Personal Papers Collection, Box 4, The Library of Virginia.

231. Lon Tuck, "There's No Wow in Pamunkey Pow: Customs Disappear," *Washington Post, Times Herald* (October 24, 1965): E2.

232. Paul Muse, "Where'd the Indians Go? Mattaponi, Pamunkey Gradually Leaving Reservation," *Virginian-Pilot* (August 29, 1965), File: 19, Historical Data, 1965–66, Virginia Department of Education, Indian School Files, 1936–1967, Accession 29632, State Government Records Collection, Box 1, The Library of Virginia.

233. Interview with Edna Bradby Allmond, by Helen C. Rountree, July 19, 1970, File: Helen C. Rountree, Fieldnotes, 1969–1973, Helen C. Rountree Papers, Box 2, NAA Washington.

234. Blume, "Present-Day Indians of Tidewater Virginia," 1–8.

235. Muse, "Where'd the Indians Go? Mattaponi, Pamunkey Gradually Leaving Reservation."

236. Rountree, "Powhatan's Descendants in the Modern World," 74.

237. Interview with Chief T. D. Cooke, by Helen C. Rountree, August 22, 1970, File: Helen C. Rountree, Fieldnotes, 1969–1973, Helen C. Rountree Papers, Box 2, NAA Washington.

238. Rountree, "Powhatan's Descendants in the Modern World," 71.

239. Gatschet, Albert Samuel, collector, *Yavapai and Havasupai notebook, 1883–1888*, Manuscript 1144, NAA Washington.

240. Rountree, "Powhatan's Descendants in the Modern World," 71.

241. Hopkins, "Modern Survivors of Chief Powhatan," M4.

242. Bradby, *Pamunkey Speaks: Native Perspectives*, 106–107.

243. Thomas Howard, "Attrition Affecting State's Reservation Indians," *Richmond Times—Dispatch* (March 12, 1964): 2B, File: 18, Historical Data, 1951–64, Virginia Department of Education, Indian School Files, 1936–1967, Accession 29632, State Government Records Collection, Box 1, The Library of Virginia.

244. Rountree, "Indian Virginians on the Move," 10.

245. Howard, "Attrition Affecting State's Reservation Indians," 2B.

246. Rountree uses the terms "fringe" and "core" to distinguish between off-reservation and reservation Pamunkeys. See Rountree, *Pocahontas's People*, 276. According to her research, some individuals eligible for citizenship based on their genealogical descent chose not to join the tribe, either because of geographical distance or lack of interest. See Rountree, "Indian Virginians on the Move," 21.

247. Rountree, "Powhatan's Descendants in the Modern World," 74.

248. Fleming to Gray, April 11, 2011.

249. Frances Hubbard, "Pamunkey Indian Tribe Still Awaits Decision on Federal Recognition," *Tidewater Review* (December 24, 2013), www.tidewaterreview.com/news/va-tr-pamunkey-indian-federal-recognition-delayed-20131223,0,3120441.story, accessed January 17, 2014.

250. It seems likely that the "Pamunkey Indian Reservation Census of 1908" mentioned in the 2011 Pamunkey tribal citizenship resolution is drawn from James Mooney's 1901 census, which was published in 1907 and is reprinted as an appendix in the Bureau of Indian Affair's proposed findings for the Pamunkey recognition petition. See 1901 Pamunkey Census by James Mooney, reprinted in Kevin K. Washburn, Assistant Secretary, Indian Affairs, "Proposed Finding for Acknowledgment of the Pamunkey Indian Tribe (Petitioner #323), Prepared in Response to the Petition Submitted to the Assistant Secretary—Indian Affairs for Federal Acknowledgment as an Indian Tribe," January 16, 2014, Appendix B, Department of the Interior, Bureau of Indian Affairs, Washington, DC.

251. Pamunkey Tribal Government, "Resolution to State Membership Criteria of the Pamunkey Indian Tribe," 2011, Department of the Interior, Bureau of Indian Affairs, Washington, DC. On the Pamunkey tribal website, the tribe also warned against individuals who might seek citizenship based on claims of descent from historical Pamunkey figures like Pocahontas. The website stated, "Although Pocahontas was a member of our tribe, the Pamunkey Tribe does not consider her descendants as tribal members nor would these individuals be eligible for membership simply because of this lineage, no matter how well-documented." See Pamunkey Indian Tribe, "Contacting the Pamunkey Indian Tribe," http://www.pamunkey.net/Contact.html, accessed April 25, 2014.

252. Pamunkey Tribal Government, "Resolution to Re-Affirm Laws and Ordinances of the Pamunkey Indian Tribe," 2011, Department of the Interior, Bureau of Indian Affairs, Washington, DC.

253. Pamunkey Indian Tribe, "Ordinances of the Pamunkey Indian Reservation, King William County, Virginia," 2011, 3, Department of the Interior, Bureau of Indian Affairs, Washington, DC.

254. Pamunkey Indian Tribe, "Laws of the Pamunkey Indians," 2011, 1, Department of the Interior, Bureau of Indian Affairs, Washington, DC.

255. Pamunkey Indian Tribe, "Ordinances of the Pamunkey Indian Reservation, King William County, Virginia," 2011, 1, Department of the Interior, Bureau of Indian Affairs, Washington, DC.

256. See "Pamunkeys Deserve Federal Recognition Despite Past Marriage Ban," *Fredericksburg.com, Powered by the Free Lance-Star* (December 10, 2014), http://www.fredericksburg.com/opinion/editorials/pamunkeys-deserve-federal-recognition-despite-past-marriage-ban/article_1bda80b6-7ff9-11e4-ad50-9773c0759d04.html, accessed July 28, 2015.

257. This number represents only those Pamunkeys formally enrolled as tribal citizens. The genealogical database that the Pamunkeys submitted in their recognition petition indicates that "a number of relatives and offspring of current members may not be currently enrolled." These individuals may not have sought formal enrollment, or they may have failed to pass the tribe's "social connection" requirement. Kevin K. Washburn, Assistant Secretary, Indian Affairs, "Proposed Finding for Acknowledgment of the Pamunkey Indian Tribe (Petitioner #323), Prepared in Response to the Petition Submitted to the Assistant Secretary—Indian Affairs for Federal Acknowledgment as an Indian Tribe," January 16, 2014, 10, 90, Department of the Interior, Bureau of Indian Affairs, Washington, DC; National Museum of the American Indian, "Kevin Brown, Chief of the Pamunkey Indian Tribe" (August 22, 2013), http://blog.nmai.si.edu/main/2013/08/kevin-brown-chief-of-the-pamunkey-indian-tribe.html, accessed April 25, 2014.

258. Kevin K. Washburn, Assistant Secretary, Indian Affairs, "Proposed Finding for Acknowledgment of the Pamunkey Indian Tribe (Petitioner #323), Prepared in Response to the Petition Submitted to the Assistant Secretary—Indian Affairs for Federal Acknowledgment as an Indian Tribe," January 16, 2014, 1, Department of the Interior, Bureau of Indian Affairs, Washington, DC.

259. Joe Heim, "Va. Tribe Faces More Hurdles to Recognition," *Washington Post* (April 1, 2015), http://www.washingtonpost.com/local/opposition-to-federal-recognition-of-virginia-tribe-heats-up/2015/03/31/aff6e4f2-d6fb-11e4-b3f2-607bd612aeac_story.html, accessed July 28, 2015.

260. Cheryl Schmit, Director of Stand Up for California, to Kevin K. Washburn, Assistant Secretary for Indian Affairs and R. Lee Fleming, Director of the Office of Federal Acknowledgment, March 25, 2015, http://apps.washingtonpost.com/g/documents/local/pamunkey-research-cover-letter/1498/, accessed July 28, 2015.

261. Elizabeth H. Esty, Louise M. Slaughter, Eddie Bernice Johnson, Rosa L. DeLauro, and Yvette D. Clarke, Members of Congress, to Sally Jewell, Secretary of the Interior, March 17, 2015, http://apps.washingtonpost.com/g/documents/local/letter-in-opposition-of-pamunkey-bid/1495/, accessed April 28, 2015.

262. Joe Heim, "A Renowned Virginia Indian Tribe Finally Wins Federal Recognition," *Washington Post* (July 2, 2015), http://www.washingtonpost.com/local/a-renowned-virginia-indian-tribe-finally-wins-federal-recognition/2015/07/02/40cc0dd4-200a-11e5-aeb9-a411a84c9d55_story.html, accessed July 28, 2015.

263. Joe Heim, "Federal Recognition Put on Hold for Virginia's Pamunkey Indian Tribe," *Washington Post* (October 8, 2015), https://www.washingtonpost.com/local/federal-recognition-put-on-hold-for-virginias-pamunkey-indian-tribe/2015/10/08/479dd9e0-6dcf-11e5-b31c-d80d62b53e28_story.html, accessed January 29, 2016.

264. Joe Heim, "Virginia's Pamunkey Withstand Challenge to Tribe's Federal Recognition," *Washington Post* (February 1, 2016), https://www.washingtonpost.com/local/virginias-pamunkey-withstand-challenge-to-tribes-federal-recognition/2016/02/01/43563890-c924-11e5-a7b2-5a2f824b02c9_story.html, accessed February 2, 2016. Other Virginia tribes, such as the Chickahominy Tribe, Chickahominy Indian Tribe Eastern Division, the Upper Mattaponi, the Rappahannock Tribe, the Monacan Tribe, and the Nansemond Tribe continue to seek recognition, although they hope to bypass the Federal Acknowledgment Process by gaining recognition through an act of Congress. They argue that the effects of the Racial Integrity Act of 1924 make it impossible for them to trace Indian ancestry in a way that sufficiently fulfills the criteria for recognition demanded by the Office of Federal Acknowledgment—although this may now change with the recent updates made to the Federal Acknowledgment Process. See "U.S. Makes It Easier for Native American Tribes to Obtain Federal Recognition," *Guardian* (June 29, 2015), http://www.theguardian.com/world/2015/jun/29/indian-tribes-native-americans-federal-recognition, accessed July 28, 2015. The Mattaponi Tribe, which once shared a political organization with the Pamunkey Indian Tribe, is not currently seeking federal recognition. Mattaponis may not wish to subject themselves to the same level of external scrutiny that the Pamunkeys experienced during their recognition bid. See Jim Nolan, "Virginia's Pamunkey Tribe Seeks Federal Recognition,"

Indian Country News (November, 2010), http://www.indiancountrynews.com/index.php/news/26-mainstream-politics/10369-virginias-pamunkey-tribe-seeks-federal-recognition, accessed April 25, 2014.

Chapter 2

1. Susan J. Stabley, "Lawyer Wants Inclusion on Tribe's Roll," *Herald* (January 31, 2000), in Judy Canty Martin, *My Father's People: A Complete Genealogy of the Catawba Nation* (Cortez, CO: J. Martin, 2002), South Caroliniana Library, University of South Carolina, Columbia, South Carolina (hereafter South Caroliniana Library).
2. James H. Merrell, *The Indians' New World: Catawbas and Their Neighbors from European Contact through the Era of Removal* (Chapel Hill: University of North Carolina Press, 1989), 234, 247.
3. Merrell, *The Indians' New World*, 250.
4. Douglas Summers Brown, *The Catawba Indians: The People of the River* (Columbia: University of South Carolina Press, 1966), 329, 320–321.
5. Louise Pettus, *Leasing Away a Nation: The Legacy of Catawba Indian Land Leases* (Spartanburg, SC: Palmetto Conservation Foundation, 2005), 50.
6. D'Arcy McNickle, Memorandum to the Commissioner, Subject: Catawba Indians, 1937, File: 12492-1930-(011), Central Classified Files, 1907–39, General Service, 81591-1923-011 to 12492-1930-001 Part 2, Box 6, Record Group 75 (hereafter RG 75), National Archives and Records Administration, Washington, DC (hereafter NARA Washington).
7. Charles L. Davis, Special Indian Agent, to Commissioner of Indian Affairs, January 5, 1911, File 8990-1908-052, Central Classified Files, 1907–39, General Service, 41394-1935-051 to 36201-1908-052, Box 193, RG 75, NARA Washington.
8. A Mormon missionary to the Catawbas reported in 1887 that the state funds were "their main dependence" since the Catawbas were only able to cultivate "a small portion of their land." See Joseph Thorup, "The Catawba Nation," *Deseret Evening News* (March 31, 1887), File: Mormons, The Papers of Charles Hudson, Box 17: Completed Research VII: Red, White, & Black, MA Thesis, PhD Dissertation, The Wilson Library, University of North Carolina, Chapel Hill, NC (hereafter Wilson Library, Chapel Hill); see also *Brown, The Catawba Indians*, 322.
9. D'Arcy McNickle, Memorandum to the Commissioner, Subject: Catawba Indians, 1937, File 12492-1930-(011), Central Classified Files, 1907–39, General Service, 81591-1923-011 to 12492-1930-001 Part 2, Box 6, RG 75, NARA Washington.
10. B. S. Massey, *Report to the Governor of South Carolina on the Catawba Indians* (Columbia, SC: R.W. Gibbes, State Printers, 1854), 5, South Caroliniana Library.
11. *Survey of Conditions of the Indians in the United States, Hearings before a Subcommittee of the Committee of Indian Affairs*, United States Senate, 71st Congress, Part 16 (March 28, 1930): 7574-7575, File: Catawba Indians, Administrative, Catawba Indian Nation, Tribal Rolls, 1930, Thomas J. Blumer Collection on the Catawba Nation Native American Studies Collection, Native American Studies Center, the University of South Carolina, Lancaster, South Carolina (hereafter Thomas J. Blumer Collection).
12. Thomas J. Blumer, "A History behind the Catawba Nation Tribal Roll, 1943–1999," in *7th Generation Catawba News*, 1:4 (April 1999), edited by Cynthia A. Walsh, File: Blumer, Thomas J., "A History behind the Catawba Nation Tribal Roll, 1943–1999," mp, Thomas J. Blumer Collection.
13. Davis to Commissioner of Indian Affairs, January 5, 1911, File 8990-1908-052, Central Classified Files, 1907–39, General Service, 41394-1935-051 to 36201-1908-052, Box 193, RG 75, NARA Washington.
14. For a detailed discussion of the development of Catawba racial thought, see James H. Merrell, "The Racial Education of the Catawba Indians," *Journal of Southern History* 50 (1984): 363–384.
15. File IV (18E6), Speck, Frank G., Racial Status, 1938, 3 items, Ms. Coll. 126, Frank G. Speck Papers, Sub-Collection 1, Box 12, IV (18E1)-IV (19E7), American Philosophical Society, Philadelphia, Pennsylvania (hereafter APS Philadelphia).

16. Merrell, "The Racial Education of the Catawba Indians," 380.

17. Davis to Commissioner of Indian Affairs, January 5, 1911, File 8990-1908-052, Central Classified Files, 1907–39, General Service, 41394-1935-051 to 36201-1908-052, Box 193, RG 75, NARA Washington.

18. "Woes of the Catawbas; Charlotte Lawyer to Take Their Appeal for Justice to High Court," *York Inquirer* (August 24, 1929), Manuscript 4639, The National Anthropological Archives, Washington, DC (hereafter NAA Washington).

19. Davis to Commissioner of Indian Affairs, January 5, 1911, File 8990-1908-052, Central Classified Files, 1907–39, General Service, 41394-1935-051 to 36201-1908-052, Box 193, RG 75, NARA Washington.

20. C. A. Callis, "Converted Lamanites," *Liahona, the Elders' Journal*, 6 (June 27, 1908): 48–49, File: Catawba Indians, Mormon Church, Clippings, (1855–1997), Thomas J. Blumer Collection; Life of Chief Samuel T. Blue, July 28, 1955, p. 2, File: Blue, S. T. Autobiography, 1955, Watson, Ian M., Catawba Indian Genealogy Collection, 1750–1986, South Caroliniana Library. According to Mormon missionaries, local white men especially resented the efforts of the Latter-Day Saints because the reservation previously had been "the favorite resort of lecherous whites, who's devilish lusts the young Indian women have been made to satisfy," but following conversion the women resisted these sexual advances. Local white men hoped that by driving the Mormons away, the Catawbas would "return to their former state." See Joseph Thorup, "The Catawba Nation," *Deseret Evening News* (March 31, 1887), File: Mormons, The Papers of Charles Hudson, Box 17: Completed Research VII: Red, White, & Black, MA Thesis, PhD Dissertation, Wilson Library, Chapel Hill.

21. File: Catawba Religious Beliefs, Mortuary Customs, and Dances, 1939, 3 items, Ms. Coll. 126, Frank G. Speck Papers, Sub-Collection 2, Box 21, Series I, Series II: A-E, APS Philadelphia; Brown, *The Catawba Indians*, 341.

22. Callis, "Converted Lamanites," 48–49, Thomas J. Blumer Collection.

23. Stanley Kimball, "Book of Mormon Promises to Indians Coming True, Says Chief," *Desert News* (May 1, 1954): 7, File: Catawba Indians, Mormon Church, Clippings, (1855–1997), Thomas J. Blumer Collection.

24. Life of Chief Samuel T. Blue, July 28, 1955, p. 2, File: Blue, S. T. Autobiography, 1955, Watson, Ian M., Catawba Indian Genealogy Collection, 1750–1986, South Caroliniana Library.

25. Brown, *The Catawba Indians*, 341.

26. Kimball, "Book of Mormon Promises to Indians Coming True, Says Chief," 7, Thomas J. Blumer Collection.

27. William Burton Hopper, "The Pernicious Mormon Doctrines," *Rock Hill Record* (September 23, 1912): 6, File: Catawba Indians, Mormon Church, Clippings, (1855–1997), Thomas J. Blumer Collection.

28. Callis, "Converted Lamanites," 48–49, Thomas J. Blumer Collection.

29. Supplement to Report on Catawba Indian Situation, March, 1935, File 12492-1930-(001), Central Classified Files, 1907–39, General Service, 81591-1923-011 to 12492-1930-001 Part 2, Box 6, RG 75, NARA Washington. Similarly, in 1946, W. R. Bradford noted that "not now, nor at any time in the past, has there been social intermingling between the Catawbas and negroes." He reported that one old Catawba man, upon being asked how the tribe got along with blacks, replied, "Fine. We have nothing to do with them, and they have nothing to do with us. There hasn't been a negro on the Reservation in five years." See W. R. Bradford, "The Catawba Indians of South Carolina," Bulletin of the University of South Carolina, New Series No. XXXIV, February, 1946, File: Catawba Reservation—Withdrawal, 130, 1944–1959, Cherokee Indian Agency, General Records Correspondence, Indian Field Service Filing System, 1926–1952, Box 44, RG 75, National Archives and Records Administration, Atlanta, Georgia (hereafter NARA Atlanta).

30. Davis to Commissioner of Indian Affairs, January 5, 1911, File 8990-1908-052, Central Classified Files, 1907–39, General Service, 41394-1935-051 to 36201-1908-052, Box 193, RG 75, NARA Washington.

31. Hazel Lewis Scaife, *History and Condition of the Catawba Indians of South Carolina* (Philadelphia: Office of Indian Rights Association, 1305 Arch Street, 1896), 14.

32. Joseph Thorup, "The Catawba Nation," *Deseret Evening News* (March 31, 1887), File: Mormons, The Papers of Charles Hudson, Box 17: Completed Research VII: Red, White, & Black, MA Thesis, PhD Dissertation, Wilson Library, Chapel Hill; Catawba Membership Petition, Applications of Viola Elizabeth (Patterson) Garcia Schneider, Brenda Kaye Scheider, Aric Grant Schneider Bartle (minor), Cynthia Ann Schneider Walsh, and Debra Sue Schneider, 1994, Thomas J. Blumer Collection.

33. "The Catawba Indians," *Rock Hill Herald* (March 31, 1887): 3, File: Catawba Indians, Legal, Court Cases, South Carolina (1887), Thomas J. Blumer Collection.

34. Pinkney H. Head, to Secretary of the Interior, January 20, 1909, File 4985-09-211, Central Classified Files, 1907–39, General Service, 73560-1908-211 to 25139-1910, Box 592, RG 75, NARA Washington.

35. Blumer, "A History behind the Catawba Nation Tribal Roll, 1943–1999," Thomas J. Blumer Collection.

36. Agent A. E. Smith to Nancy Harris, January 16, 1892, File: Catawba Indians, Administrative, SC, Agents, Smith, A.E. (1883–1897), Thomas J. Blumer Collection. That year, the financial agent remarked in his report to the Comptroller General of South Carolina that "Heretofore my instructions have been to pay out equally to Catawba Indians, whether residents of this State or not, so long as they maintained their tribal relation. The provisions in the last Act limited appropriation to those living in this State only." See Report of the Comptroller General of the State of South Carolina to the General Assembly for the Fiscal Year Ending October 31, 1892 (Columbia, SC: Charles A. Calvo, Jr., State Printer, 1892), 200, File: Catawba Indians, Administrative, State of SC, Reports, Reports of the Comptroller General, Thomas J. Blumer Collection.

37. "Claims of the Catawba," *Rock Hill Herald* (April 17, 1907):1, File: Catawba Indians, Legal, Court Cases, South Carolina (1905), Thomas J. Blumer Collection.

38. M. P. DeBruhl, Assistant Attorney-General, to J. D. Lesslie, Agent Catawba Indians, April 9, 1909, cited in Report of J. Fraser Lyon, Attorney General to the General Assembly of South Carolina for the Fiscal Year, 1909 (Columbia, SC: Gonzales and Bryan, State Printers, 1910): 64, File Catawba Indians, Legal, Reports, State of South Carolina, Attorney General, Thomas J. Blumer Collection.

39. Davis to Commissioner of Indian Affairs, January 5, 1911, File 8990-1908-052, Central Classified Files, 1907–39, General Service, 41394-1935-051 to 36201-1908-052, Box 193, RG 75, NARA Washington.

40. Nancy Harris, to Governor Tillman, February 10, 1892, File: Catawba Indians, Administrative, SC, Agents, Smith, A. E. (1883–1897), Thomas J. Blumer Collection.

41. Petition and Memorial in the Matter of Claims and Demands of the Catawba Indian Association to the United States (Fort Smith, AR: Thomas A. Higgens, Printers, 15 April, 1895), File: Catawba Indians, Administrative, US-BIA, Correspondence, 18 MS., 10 April 1857—15 April 1895, Thomas J. Blumer Collection.

42. US Senate, Committee on Indian Affairs, *The Catawba Tribe of Indians*, by Richard Franklin Pettigrew (54th Cong., 2nd Sess., February 1, 1897, S.doc.144).

43. Petition and Memorial in the Matter of Claims and Demands of the Catawba Indian Association to the United States (Fort Smith, AR: Thomas A. Higgens, Printers, 15 April, 1895), File: Catawba Indians, Administrative, US-BIA, Correspondence, 18 MS., 10 April 1857—15 April 1895, Thomas J. Blumer Collection. It is unclear whether these Indians ever received homesteads.

44. James Bain, President of the Catawba Indian Association, to Commissioner of Indian Affairs, March 4, 1896, File: Catawba Indians, Administrative, US-BIA, Correspondence, 14 MSS., 18 December 1895—17 April 1905, Thomas J. Blumer Collection.

45. D. M. Browning, Commissioner of Indian Affairs, to R.V. Belt, March 28, 1896, File: Catawba Indians, Administrative, US-BIA, Correspondence, 14 MSS., 18 December 1895—17 April 1905, Thomas J. Blumer Collection.

46. US Senate, Committee on Indian Affairs, *The Catawba Tribe of Indians*, by Richard Franklin Pettigrew (54th Cong., 2nd Sess., February 1, 1897, S.doc.144).

47. J. D. Lesslie, Catawba Agent, to Governor Martin F. Ansel, July 5, 1907, File: Catawba Indians, Administrative, SC, Agents, Lesslie, J.D., (1906–1911), Thomas J. Blumer Collection.

48. Davis to Commissioner of Indian Affairs, January 5, 1911, File 8990-1908-052, Central Classified Files, 1907–39, General Service, 41394-1935-051 to 36201-1908-052, Box 193, RG 75, NARA Washington.

49. Interview with Mae Bodiford Blue, December 30, 1971, Samuel Proctor Oral History Program, Oral History Collections, George A. Smathers Libraries, University of Florida Digital Collections, Gainesville, Florida (hereafter Samuel Proctor Oral History Program).

50. Lesslie to Ansel, July 5, 1907, File: Catawba Indians, Administrative, SC, Agents, Lesslie, J. D. (1906–1911), Thomas J. Blumer Collection.

51. Fred Sanders Biography, in April 1999, 7th Generation Catawba Newsletter, quoted in Judy Canty Martin, *My Father's People: A Complete Genealogy of the Catawba Nation* (Cortez, CO: J. Martin, 2002), 84, South Caroliniana Library.

52. "Claims of the Catawba," 1, Thomas J. Blumer Collection.

53. Scaife, *History and Condition of the Catawba Indians of South Carolina*, 19–20.

54. Interviews taken by Frank Speck with Mrs. Samson Owl, Margaret Wiley Brown, Sally Gordon, and Sam Brown, p. 90, File: Catawba Texts—Page Proofs, 1933, 1 item, Ms. Coll. 126, Frank G. Speck Papers, Sub-Collection 2, Box 21, Series I, Series II, A-E, APS, Philadelphia.

55. South Carolina Economic Association, "Rock Hill, South Carolina: Catawba Indian Reservation" (Rock Hill, SC: S.C.E.A., 1940), South Caroliniana Library.

56. Interview with Nola Campbell, by Frances Wade, October 22, 1973, 1–2, Samuel Proctor Oral History Program.

57. Interview with Mrs. Roy Brown, by Emma Echols, October 14, 1972, 7–8, Samuel Proctor Oral History Program.

58. Robert Harris, "Wild Indians," B. Ward "Children of King Hagler," EH, June 15, 1940, File: Catawba Indians, Folklore, TJB Research Notes, Thomas J. Blumer Collection.

59. Frank G. Speck, *The Catawba Texts* (New York: Columbia University Press, 1934), 27, South Caroliniana Library.

60. Robert Harris, "Wild Indians," B. Ward, "Children of King Hagler," EH, June 15, 1940, File: Catawba Indians, Folklore, TJB Research Notes, Thomas J. Blumer Collection.

61. Speck, *The Catawba Texts*, 27, South Caroliniana Library.

62. Swanton, J. R., *Excerpts from Published Sources*, No. 1 Myths and Customs of the Cherokee, Catawba, and Choctaw, from "Adventures in the Wilds of the United States and British Provinces," by Charles Lanman, 2 vols., Philadelphia, 1856, Manuscript 4146, NAA Washington.

63. John Reed Swanton, *Catawba Linguistic and Miscellaneous Notes*, 1922, Manuscript 4278, NAA Washington.

64. Interview with Nola Campbell, by Frances Wade, October 22, 1973, 1–2, Samuel Proctor Oral History Program.

65. Speck, *The Catawba Texts*, xiv, South Caroliniana Library.

66. File 497.3, Sp3, Speck, Frank G., Catawba Texts, (pt. 1), 1971, 1595 ms, APS, Philadelphia.

67. File 497.3, Sp3, Speck, Frank G., Catawba Texts, (pt. 1), 1971, 1595 ms, APS, Philadelphia.

68. File: Catawba Dances and Musical Instruments, n.d., 2 items, Ms. Coll. 126, Frank G. Speck Papers, Sub-Collection 2, Box 21, Series 1, Series II: A-E, APS, Philadelphia.

69. File: Catawba Dances and Musical Instruments.

70. Charles C. Moore, "An Interview with the Chief of the Catawba Indians: Billy Gilbert Blue," *The Lance: The Literary Magazine of the University of South Carolina, Lancaster, S.C.*, 11 (Fall 1973): 20–30, Thomas J. Blumer Collection.

71. Interview with Jessie Harris and Nola Campbell, by Frances Wade, November 4, 1974, Samuel Proctor Oral History Program; see also Interview at Home of Idle Sanders, September 7, 1962, File: Catawba Notes, First Copy, The Papers of Charles Hudson, Box 17: Completed Research VII: Red, White, & Black, MA Thesis, PhD Dissertation, Wilson Library, Chapel Hill.

72. "Indian Tribe Gradually Fading: Catawbas Drop Old Customs for New," *Chicago Daily Tribune* (August 19, 1962): 38. Catawbas refer to building, not making, pots.

73. D. Ke Wright, "Catawba Pottery Maker: Mrs. Arzada Sanders," *The Lance: The Literary Magazine of the University of South Carolina, Lancaster, S.C.*, 11 (Fall 1973): 31–39, Thomas J. Blumer Collection.

74. Interview with Isabel George, February 6, 1972, Samuel Proctor Oral History Program.

75. Stephen G. Baker, *Catawba Indian Trade Pottery of the Historic Period* (Columbia, SC: Columbia Museum of Art, 1973), South Caroliniana Library.

76. Baker, *Catawba Indian Trade Pottery of the Historic Period*, South Caroliniana Library; Vladimir J. Fewkes, *Catawba Pottery-Making, with Notes on Pamunkey Pottery-Making, Cherokee Pottery-Making, and Coiling* (Philadelphia: University Museum, University of Pennsylvania, 1944), 73, South Caroliniana Library.

77. Interview with Mrs. Roy Brown, by Emma Echols, October 14, 1972, Samuel Proctor Oral History Program.

78. Interview with Frances Canty Wade, August 15, 1963, File: Household History, The Papers of Charles Hudson, Box 17: Completed Research VII: Red, White, & Black, MA Thesis, PhD Dissertation, Wilson Library, Chapel Hill.

79. Scaife, *History and Condition of the Catawba Indians of South Carolina*, 19.

80. Raven I. McDavid, to Eleanor Roosevelt, July 9, 1939, Central Classified Files, 1907–39, General Service, 81591-1923-011 to 12492-1930-001 Part 2, Box 6, RG 75, NARA Washington.

81. File: 497.3, Sp3, Speck, Frank G., Catawba Texts (pt. 1), 1971, 1592ms, APS, Philadelphia.

82. M. R. Harrington, "Catawba Potters and Their Work," *American Anthropologist* (July, August, September, 1908): 402–404, South Caroliniana Library, University of South Carolina, Columbia, South Carolina.

83. Frank G. Speck, "Catawba Medicines and Curative Practices," *Twenty-Fifth Anniversary Studies: Philadelphia Anthropology Society*, edited by D. S. Davidson (Philadelphia: University of Pennsylvania Press, 1937), 180–181, South Caroliniana Library.

84. John Reed Swanton, *Catawba Linguistic and Miscellaneous Notes,* 1922, Manuscript 4278, NAA Washington.

85. Frank G. Speck, *Catawba Texts,* 1921–1928, Manuscript 1777, NAA Washington.

86. Moore, "An Interview with the Chief of the Catawba Indians: Billy Gilbert Blue," 20–30, Thomas J. Blumer Collection.

87. Frank G. Speck, *Catawba Texts,* 1921–1928, Manuscript 1777, NAA Washington.

88. Frank G. Speck, "Catawba Herbals and Curative Practices," *Journal of American Folklore,* 57 (January–March 1944): 37–50, File: Speck, Frank G., Catawba Herbals and Curative Practices, 1937, Frank T. Siebert Papers, Ms. Coll 97, Series II: Catawba, Box 14, APS, Philadelphia.

89. Brown, *The Catawba Indians,* 335; Speck, "Catawba Herbals and Curative Practices," 37–50.

90. Speck, "Catawba Herbals and Curative Practices," 37–50.

91. Carlisle Indian Industrial School—Catawba Chronology (1893–1911), compiled by TJB, File: Catawba Indians, Education, Carlisle Industrial School (1893–1911), Thomas J. Blumer Collection.

92. William M. Goins, editor, *South Carolina Indians Today: An Educational Resource Guide* (Columbia, SC: Phoenix, 1998), 19, South Caroliniana Library.

93. "Strange Conditions of the Indian School," *The State* (Wednesday, January 20, 1904).

94. Thomas J. Blumer, "The Development of the Current Catawba Nation Tribal Roll," March 1997, Thomas J. Blumer Collection. See also Davis to Commissioner of Indian Affairs, January 5, 1911, p. 2, File 8990-1908-052, Central Classified Files, 1907–39, General Service, 41394-1935-051 to 36201-1908-052, Box 193, RG 75, NARA Washington. The superintendent of the Cherokee Boarding School summarized the ongoing problem in 1910: "If the per capita was paid just the same whether the children were on the reservation or elsewhere, no doubt the attitude of the parents regarding sending their children away to be educated would undergo a change." See Frank Kyselka, Superintendent, to Commissioner of Indian Affairs, March 25, 1910, p. 3, File 8990-1908-052, Central Classified Files, 1907–39, General Service, 41394-1935-051 to 36201-1908-052, Box 193, RG 75, NARA Washington.

95. Howard George explained this dilemma in a 1972 oral interview: "Well, in a way if you married your own race of people … down there on the Catawba Indian Reservation, you'd marry your own kin people some way or another 'cause they was all kin one way or another." See interview with Howard George, November 16, 1972, Samuel Proctor Oral History Program.

96. File: Catawba Texts—Page Proofs, 1933, 1 item, Ms Coll. 126, Frank G. Speck Papers, Sub-Collection 2, Box 21, Series I, Series II: A-E, APS, Philadelphia.

97. Interview with Howard George, November 16, 1972, Samuel Proctor Oral History Program.

98. James Mooney to Albert S. Gatschet, September 20, 1887, Manuscript 4047, Gatschet, Albert S., Letters received, 1880–1891, NAA Washington.

99. Notes on James Mooney, File IV (18E15), Cadwalader, John, Catawba Tribal History, n.d., 8 items, Ms. Coll. 126, Frank G. Speck Papers, Sub-Collection 1, Box 12, APS, Philadelphia.

100. Frank G. Speck, *Catawba Texts* (New York: Columbia University Press, 1934), x.

101. Thomas J. Blumer, "Catawba Influences on the Modern Cherokee Pottery Tradition," *Appalachian Journal* (Winter 1987): 156, File: Blumer, Thomas J., Watson, Ian M., Catawba Indian Genealogy Collection, 1750–1986, South Caroliniana Library. Susannah Harris Owl may also have decided to leave the Catawba reservation because, as a Baptist, she disapproved of the influence of the Mormon Church on the tribe. A special thanks to Catawba tribal citizen Brooke Bauer for pointing out this possibility. Personal communication with Brooke Bauer, June 30, 2013.

102. Interview with Sally Brown Beck, by Emma Echols, October 5, 1972, Samuel Proctor Oral History Program.

103. Interview with Cora Ethel Beck Warner, by Frances Wade, October 1, 1975, Samuel Proctor Oral History Program.

104. Interview with Lula Blue Beck, by Emma Echols, March 4, 1994, Samuel Proctor Oral History Program.

105. Interview with Major Beck, September 8, 1963, File: Household History, and Interview at Home of Idle and Arzeda Sanders, June 25, 1963, File: Catawba Notes, First Copy, The Papers of Charles Hudson, Box 17: Completed Research VII: Red, White, & Black, MA Thesis, PhD Dissertation, Wilson Library, Chapel Hill.

106. M. P. DeBruhl, Assistant Attorney-General, to J. D. Lesslie, Agent Catawba Indians, April 9, 1909, cited in *Report of J. Fraser Lyon, Attorney General to the General Assembly of South Carolina for the Fiscal Year, 1909* (Columbia, SC: Gonzales and Bryan, State Printers, 1910): 64, File Catawba Indians, Legal, Reports, State of South Carolina, Attorney General, Thomas J. Blumer Collection.

107. Interview with Sally Brown Beck, by Emma Echols, October 5, 1972, Samuel Proctor Oral History Program.

108. Ian Watson, *Catawba Indian Genealogy* (Geneseo, NY: Geneseo Foundation and the Department of Anthropology, State University of New York at Geneseo, 1995), 86.

109. Charles Davis reported that there was "ample evidence that many members of the tribe marry whites." He noted that "it is about necessary for them to marry outside the tribe by reason of its limited numbers, and all left is the low class of white with which they seem to affiliate somewhat." See Davis to Commissioner of Indian Affairs, January 5, 1911, p. 3, File 8990-1908-052, Central Classified Files, 1907–39, General Service, 41394-1935-051 to 36201-1908-052, Box 193, RG 75, NARA Washington.

110. Interview with Evelyn MacAbee George, by Emma Echols, September 2, 1976, Samuel Proctor Oral History Program.

111. In 1963, a white woman married to a Catawba man recalled that when she told her white son from a previous relationship that she planned on marrying an Indian, "he said that I shouldn't do it." Basing his knowledge of the Catawbas on stereotypes he learned in school, he protested that the Catawbas "live down on the Catawba River in tipis and they hunt and fish for a living. They will scalp you, too." The woman's sister also teased her about the marriage, remarking shortly after the fact, "He ain't scalped you yet." Despite this prejudice against the Catawbas, a number of whites married into

the tribe in the late nineteenth and twentieth centuries. See Interview with Garfield Harris and Olga Fowler Harris, September 11, 1963, The Papers of Charles Hudson, Box 17: Completed Research VII: Red, White, & Black, MA Thesis, PhD Dissertation, Wilson Library, Chapel Hill.

112. Joel Williamson, *After Slavery: The Negro in South Carolina during Reconstruction, 1861– 1877* (New York: W.W. Norton, 1975), 297.

113. Attorney General of South Carolina to Ben P. Harris, April 27, 1918, File 49246, Central Classified Files, 1907–39, General Service, 109179-1916-173.1 to 94533-1920-173.1, Box 542, RG 75, NARA Washington. This reply evidently upset Harris, for not long after, the financial agent for the Catawbas wrote the Interior Department demanding to know if South Carolina's anti-miscegenation laws were constitutional. The assistant commissioner replied that they were. See C. F. Hauke, Acting Assistant Commissioner, to Financial Agent for Catawba Indians, June 20, 1918, File 49246, Central Classified Files, 1907–39, General Service, 109179-1916-173.1 to 94533-1920-173.1, Box 542, RG 75, NARA Washington.

114. Interview at Home of Idle Sanders, August 12, 1963, File: Reconstructed History, The Papers of Charles Hudson, Box 17: Completed Research VII: Red, White, & Black, MA Thesis, PhD Dissertation, Wilson Library, Chapel Hill; Virginia Davis, "It's Illegal, but Red Race Diluted," *Rock Hill Herald* (January 1, 1960), Association on American Indian Affairs Archives, General and Tribal Files, 1851–1983, Part 2: Tribal, Section 5: New York-Wyoming, Subsection Title: South Carolina, File: Catawba 2, 1960–1962, Box 282, File 5, M-1-5665, roll 190, Davis Library, the University of North Carolina at Chapel Hill, NC (hereafter Davis Library, Chapel Hill).

115. Interview with Mrs. Mae Bodiford Blue, December 30, 1971, Samuel Proctor Oral History Program.

116. Interview with Mrs. Mae Bodiford Blue, December 30, 1971.

117. Interview with Nola Campbell, by Emma Echols, September 4, 1992, Samuel Proctor Oral History Program.

118. Whites and the Pottery Tradition (TJB research notes), File: Catawba Indians, Pottery, Non-Indians (Whites) Making, Thomas J. Blumer Collection.

119. Other Catawba women agreed with Doris. According to Wade, Georgia Harris demanded that Mae return one of her borrowed rubbing rocks. See Oral Interview with Frances Wade, May 20, 1977, File: Catawba Indians, Pottery, Non-Indians (Whites) Making, Thomas J. Blumer Collection.

120. Interview with Sallie Wade, February 5, 1981, 9, Samuel Proctor Oral History Program. Mary Jane Watts was a midwife and may have helped the woman give birth. The Watts were childless and welcomed the opportunity to raise the baby. See Interview with Edith Brown, August 16, 1963, File: Household History, and Interview at Home of Idle and Arzeda Sanders, June 25, 1963, File: Catawba Notes, First Copy, The Papers of Charles Hudson, Box 17: Completed Research VII: Red, White, & Black, MA Thesis, PhD Dissertation, Wilson Library, Chapel Hill.

121. Interview with Mamie Blue Adams by Emma Echols, November 9, 1993, 2, and interview with Nelson Blue by Emma Echols, December 31, 1971, 6, Samuel Proctor Oral History Program.

122. Report on Eastern Cherokee Enrollments and Contest for the Commissioner of Indian Affairs by Charles L. Davis, February 21, 1911, p. 443, Copybook of Special Agent Charles L. Davis, 1910–11, Enrollment Records Relating to Enrollment of Eastern Cherokees, Copybook of Special Agent Charles L. Davis, 1910–11, Entry 595, Records of and Concerning the Eastern Cherokee Enrolling Commission, Numerical Index to Enrollment Records, 1929, Entry 596, Box 1, RG 75, NARA Washington.

123. Davis to Commissioner of Indian Affairs, January 5, 1911, p. 3, File 8990-1908-052, Central Classified Files, 1907–39, General Service, 41394-1935-051 to 36201-1908-052, Box 193, RG 75, NARA Washington.

124. *Rock Hill Herald* (May 5, 1894): 3, cited in Judy Canty Martin, *My Father's People: A Complete Genealogy of the Catawba Nation* (Cortez, CO: J. Martin, 2002), 5, South Caroliniana Library.

125. Report of the Comptroller-General of the State of South Carolina to the General Assembly for the Fiscal Year Ending October 31, 1894 (Columbia, SC: Charles A. Calvo Jr., State Printer, 1894), File: Catawba Indians, Administrative, State of SC, Reports, Reports of the Comptroller General, Thomas J. Blumer Collection.
126. "Strange Conditions of the Indian School," *The State* (January 20, 1904). A 1909 report echoed this observation: "In the event of an Indian being the husband of a white woman the husband receives his share but his wife and children are ignored. On the other hand if a white man married an Ind. the rule is reversed." See "A Day with the Catawba Indians," *Rock Hill Herald* (May 1, 1909):1, File: Catawba Indians, General, Clippings, March 25, 1875–July 5, 1951, Thomas J. Blumer Collection.
127. "The True Status of the Catawbas," *Record*, Rock Hill, SC (June 14, 1915), File: Catawba Indians, General, Clippings, March 25, 1875–July 5, 1951, Thomas J. Blumer Collection.
128. "The Catawba Nation," *Columbia Record* (July 19, 1915): 2, File: Catawba Indians, Matrilineal Inheritance, Thomas J. Blumer Collection.
129. File: Thomas J. Blumer, "The Development of the Current Catawba Nation Tribal Roll," March 1997, Thomas J. Blumer Collection.
130. Personal communication with Thomas J. Blumer, Medford Library, Lancaster, South Carolina, May 3, 2011.
131. Interview at the home of Idle Sanders, August 12, 1963, File: Reconstructed History, The Papers of Charles Hudson, Box 17: Completed Research VII: Red, White, & Black, MA Thesis, PhD Dissertation, Wilson Library, Chapel Hill.
132. S. M. Wolfe, Attorney General, to O. K. Williams, Financial Agent for Catawba Indians, May 12, 1921, Annual Report of the Attorney General for the State of South Carolina to the General Assembly for the Fiscal Year ending December 31, 1921, File: Catawba Indians, Administrative, SC, Agents, Williams, O. K. (1915–1923), Thomas J. Blumer Collection.
133. Supplement to Report on Catawba Indian Situation, March, 1935, File: 12492-1930-(001), Central Classified Files, 1907–39, General Service, 81591-1923-011 to 12492-1930-001, Part 2, Box 6, RG 75, NARA Washington.
134. John M. Daniel, Assistant Attorney-General, to Messrs. Dunlap & Dunlap, Attorneys at Law, May 11, 1923, Annual Report of the Attorney General for the State of South Carolina to the General Assembly for the Fiscal Year Ending December 31, 1923, File: Catawba Indians, Legal, Reports, State of South Carolina, Attorney General, Thomas J. Blumer Collection.
135. "The Catawba Indians May Recover Land," *Record* (September 19, 1905):1, File: Catawba Indians, Legal, Court Cases, South Carolina (1905), Thomas J. Blumer Collection.
136. In 1921 the state made an effort to settle with the Catawbas, but this effort fell through. See Thomas J. Blumer, "The Settlement Attempt of 1921," Researched and Written for the Native American Rights Fund, 1981, File: Catawba Indians, Legal, Court Cases, Settlement Attempt (1921–1925), Thomas J. Blumer Collection.
137. Superintendent Frank Kyselka, to Commissioner of Indian Affairs, March 25, 1910, File: 8990-1908-052, Central Classified Files, 1907–39, General Service, 41394-1935-051 to 36201-1908-052, Box 193, RG 75, NARA Washington.
138. W. B. Ardrey, "The Catawba Indians," *American Antiquarian and Oriental Journal*, 16:5 (September 1894): 266.
139. Their financial agent at the time exclaimed that they were in a "pitiful condition," living in "one-room shacks." Some, he said, were "dependent entirely upon charity." See T. O. Flowers, Financial Agent of Catawba Indians, to John Collier, Commissioner of Indian Affairs, August 15, 1933, file: Catawba Indians, Administrative, US-BIA, Correspondence, 45 MSS., June 12, 1933–April 2, 1935, Thomas J. Blumer Collection.
140. Chief Sam Blue to President Franklin D. Roosevelt, February 13, 1934, File: 12492-1930-(011), Central Classified Files, 1907–39, General Service, 81591-1923-011 to 12492-1930-001, Part 2, Box 6, RG 75, NARA Washington.
141. State Auditing Department, Audit of State Institutions, Report on Indebtedness of Catawba Indians, September 7, 1936, File: 55, Catawba Indian Agent, 1936, Governor Johnston, General Subject Files, 1935-1939, Series S540007, RG 540000, Box 1, South

Carolina Department of Archives and History, Columbia, South Carolina (hereafter SCDAH Columbia).

142. T.O. Flowers, Financial Agent of Catawba Indians, to Governor Olin D. Johnston, July 22, 1936, File: 54, Catawba Indian Agent, 1936, Governor Johnston, General Subject Files, 1935-1939, Series S540007, RG 540000, Box 1, SCDAH Columbia.

143. Chief Sam Blue to President Franklin D. Roosevelt, February 13, 1934, File: 12492-1930-(011), Central Classified Files, 1907–39, General Service, 81591-1923-011 to 12492-1930-001, Part 2, Box 6, RG 75, NARA Washington.

144. D'Arcy McNickle, Memorandum to the Commissioner, Subject: Catawba Indians, 1937, File: 12492-1930-(011), Central Classified Files, 1907–39, General Service, 81591-1923-011 to 12492-1930-001, Part 2, Box 6, RG 75, NARA Washington.

145. A Bill to Provide for the Relief of the Catawba Indians in South Carolina, 75th Congress, 1st Session, H.R. 5938, March 25, 1937, File: 12491-1930-(001), Central Classified Files, 1907–39, General Service, 81591-1923-011 to 12492-1930-001, Part 2, Box 6, RG 75, NARA Washington.

146. Memorandum for Secretary Ickes by E. K. Burlew, January 8, 1938, File: 12492-1930-(011), Central Classified Files, 1907–39, General Service, 81591-1923-011 to 12492-1930-001, Part 2, Box 6, RG 75, NARA Washington; William Zimmerman Jr. to J. M. Smith, State Auditor, Columbia, SC, August 28, 1941, File: 12492-1930-(011), Central Classified Files, 1907–39, General Service, 12492-1930-011, Part 2 to 13123-1939-011, Box 7, RG 75, NARA Washington.

147. Memorandum of Understanding between the State of South Carolina, the Catawba Indian Tribe, and the Office of Indian Affairs of the United States Department of the Interior, 1943, File: Catawba Indians—Standard Application for Tribal Lands, 130, 1943–1949, Cherokee Indian Agency, General Records, Correspondence, Indian Field Service Filing System, 1926-1952, Box 44, RG 75, NARA Atlanta.

148. Memorandum for Mr. Armstrong from D'Arcy McNickle, August 14, 1940, File: 12492-1930-(011), Central Classified Files, 1907–39, General Service, 12492-1930-011, Part 2 to 13123-1939-011, Box 7, RG 75, NARA Washington.

149. A 1952 document from Minneapolis Area Office of the Bureau of Indian Affairs stated, "The Federal Government accepted the roll recognized by the State when the Federal Government assumed responsibility." File: Catawba Reservation—Withdrawal, 130, 1944–1959, Cherokee Indian Agency, General Records, Correspondence, Indian Field Service Filing System, 1926-1952, Box 44, RG 75, NARA Atlanta.

150. Blumer, "A History behind the Catawba Nation Tribal Roll, 1943–1999," Thomas J. Blumer Collection.

151. Chief Douglas Harris to Superintendent C. M. Blair, Cherokee, NC, January 18, 1945, File: 063.0 Roll, Tribal—Catawba, Office of the Commissioner, Cherokee Agency, Records Relating to the Catawba Indian Tribe, 1940–62, 061-065, Box 2, RG 75, NARA Washington.

152. Membership and Family Roll of the Catawba Tribe of South Carolina, and Other Related Information Pertaining to Tribal Members as of October 17, 1958, File: 063.0 Rolls, Tribal—Catawba, Office of the Commissioner, Cherokee Agency, Records Relating to the Catawba Indian Tribe, 1940–62, 061-065, Box 2, RG 75, NARA Washington.

153. Copy of the Catawba Membership Petition, Applications of Viola Elizabeth (Patterson) Garcia Schneider, Brenda Kaye Scheider, Aric Grant Schneider Bartle (minor), Cynthia Ann Scheider Walsh, and Debra Sue Scheider, 1994, p. 12, Thomas J. Blumer Collection.

154. Indeed, tribal citizens welcomed the brothers as kin and allowed them to stay in their homes. According to Gladys Thomas, when Edward Guy Garcia arrived in South Carolina "he was taken in immediately." His brother, Ben, "stayed with Douglas Harris. I guess they were 6th or 7th cousins." See Interview at Home of Gladys Thomas, August 30, 1962, File: Catawba Notes, First Copy, The Papers of Charles Hudson, Box 17: Completed Research VII: Red, White, & Black, MA Thesis, PhD Dissertation, Wilson Library, Chapel Hill.

155. Blumer, "A History behind the Catawba Nation Tribal Roll, 1943–1999," Thomas J. Blumer Collection.

156. Wilford M. Canty, Sanford, Colorado, to Office of Indian Affairs, July 11, 1921, File: Catawba Indians, Administrative, US-BIA, Correspondence, 32 MSS., September 21, 1911–June 5, 1933, Thomas J. Blumer Collection.

157. In 1935, Pinkney H. Head wrote the president of the United States requesting that western Catawbas also receive a final settlement that would place them under federal jurisdiction. The commissioner of Indian affairs responded that neither the state's proposal for the tribe nor the congressional bill under consideration made any provision for Catawbas in the West. See F. H. Daiker, Assistant to the Commissioner, to P. H. Head, Farmington, NM, April 3, 1935, File: Catawba Indians, Administrative, United States, BIA Correspondence, 30 MSS., April 3, 1935–August 10, 1937, Thomas J. Blumer Collection.

158. Senator Edwin C. Johnson of Colorado to J. M. Stewart, Director of Land Division, Office of Indian Affairs, November 23, 1937, File: 12492-1930-(001), Central Classified Files, 1907–39, General Service, 81591-1923-011 to 12492-1930-001, Part 2, Box 6, RG 75, NARA Washington.

159. As the commissioner pointed out, they had to consider "whether these benefits are likely to be sufficient to warrant them leaving their present locality and surrendering or losing whatever property, opportunities, etc. which they may have acquired." See William Zimmerman Jr. to Senator Edwin C. Johnson of Colorado, December 7, 1937, File: 12492-1930-(001), Central Classified Files, 1907–39, General Service, 81591-1923-011 to 12492-1930-001, Part 2, Box 6, RG 75, NARA Washington.

160. Elbert Garcia to Senator Edwin C. Johnson of Colorado, December 20, 1937, File: 12492-1930-(001), Central Classified Files, 1907–39, General Service, 81591-1923-011 to 12492-1930-001, Part 2, Box 6, RG 75, NARA Washington.

161. Catawba Membership Petition, Applications of Viola Elizabeth (Patterson) Garcia Schneider, Brenda Kaye Scheider, Aric Grant Schneider Bartle (minor), Cynthia Ann Schneider Walsh, and Debra Sue Schneider, 1994, Thomas J. Blumer Collection.

162. Cynthia Ann Walsh to Thomas J. Blumer, April 15, 1995, File: Catawba Indians, Geneology, Marsh/Mush, Patterson, White, Garcia (Western Band), Thomas J. Blumer Collection.

163. US Department of the Interior, Office of Indian Affairs, *Constitution and By-Laws of the Catawba Indian Tribe of South Carolina, Approved June 30, 1944* (Washington, DC: US Government Printing Office, 1946), File: Catawba Indians, Administrative, Catawba Indians, Constitutions (1944), Thomas J. Blumer Collection.

164. Oscar L. Chapman, Assistant Secretary, Department of the Interior, to Superintendent C. B. Blair, June 30, 1944, quoted in Minutes of Meeting of the Catawba Indian Council, Rock Hill, South Carolina, July 1, 1944, File: Catawba Indians, Administrative, Catawba Indians, Tribal Council Minutes, July 1, 1944, Thomas J. Blumer Collection.

165. "Catawba Indian Tribe Declares War on Axis," *Baltimore Sun* (February 17, 1942): 13.

166. James Andrew Haley, *Providing for the Division of the Tribal Assets of the Catawba Indian Tribe of South Carolina among the Members of the Tribe*, Committee on Interior and Insular Affairs, House, H.rp.910, Congress 86-1 (August 17, 1959), Bill No. 86, H.R. 6128, Public Law No. 86, PL 322, Statutes at Large 73 Stat. 592.

167. Sam T. Blue, "Letter to the Editor," *Rock Hill Evening Herald* (May 9, 1956), File: Catawba Indians, Administrative, Catawba Indians, Tribal Council Minutes, July 1, 1944, Thomas J. Blumer Collection.

168. James Andrew Haley, *Providing for the Division of the Tribal Assets of the Catawba Indian Tribe of South Carolina among the Members of the Tribe*, Committee on Interior and Insular Affairs, House, H.rp.910, Congress 86-1 (August 17, 1959), Bill No. 86, H.R. 6128, Public Law No. 86, PL 322, Statutes at Large 73 Stat. 592.

169. Minutes of Special Meeting of the Catawba Council Held at the Catawba Indian School on Saturday, March 28, 1959, Rock Hill, SC, File: Catawba Indians, Administrative, Catawba Indians, Tribal Council Minutes, July 1, 1944, Thomas J. Blumer Collection.

170. Catawba Tribal Resolution, May 21, 1960, File: Catawba Indians, Administrative, Catawba Indians, Tribal Council Minutes, July 1, 1944, Thomas J. Blumer Collection.

171. Office of the Secretary, Catawba Indian Tribe of South Carolina, Notice of Final Membership Roll, February 7, 1961, File: Catawba Indians, Administrative, Catawba Indians, Tribal Rolls, 1960, Thomas J. Blumer Collection.

172. A Bill (HR 6128), 1959, File: Catawba Reservation—Withdrawal, 130, 1944–1959, Cherokee Indian Agency, General Records, Correspondence, Indian Field Service Filing System, 1926–1952, Box 44, RG 75, NARA Atlanta.

173. Office of the Secretary, Catawba Indian Tribe of South Carolina, Notice of Final Membership Roll, February 7, 1961, File: Catawba Indians, Administrative, Catawba Indians, Tribal Rolls, 1960, Thomas J. Blumer Collection.

174. Catawba Indian Nation, 1961 Tribal Rolls, File: Catawba Indians, Administrative, Catawba Indians, Tribal Rolls, 1961, Thomas J. Blumer Collection.

175. "Indian Tribe Gradually Fading: Catawbas Drop Old Customs for New," *Chicago Daily Tribune* (August 19, 1962): 38.

176. Moore, "An Interview with the Chief of the Catawba Indians: Billy Gilbert Blue," 24, Thomas J. Blumer Collection.

177. The state of South Carolina overturned its 1879 ban on intermarriage between whites and Indians in April 1960 to clarify the state of marriages between Catawbas and whites in anticipation of the termination bill. See Charles Hudson, "A Proposed Study of Catawba Culture Change," 4–5, File: PhD Proposal (Catawba), The Papers of Charles Hudson, Box 17: Completed Research VII: Red, White, & Black, MA Thesis, PhD Dissertation, Wilson Library, Chapel Hill.

178. Moore, "An Interview with the Chief of the Catawba Indians: Billy Gilbert Blue," 24, Thomas J. Blumer Collection.

179. Catawba Regional Planning Council, "Catawba Nation: Overall Economic Development Program" (Rock Hill, SC: 1977), 6, South Caroliniana Library.

180. Prepared Testimony of Gilbert Blue, Chief, Catawba Tribe of Indians of South Carolina, on H.R. 3274, Before the Committee on Interior and Insular Affairs, United States House of Representatives, June 12, 1979, File: Catawba Indians, Richard W. Riley Administration, Catawba Indian Claim, 1977–1983, Series S554019, RG 554000, Box 7, SCDAH Columbia.

181. Constitution and By-Laws of the Catawba Nation of South Carolina, 1975, File: Catawba Indians, Administrative, Catawba Indians, Constitutions (1975), Thomas J. Blumer Collection.

182. Constitution and By-Laws of the Catawba Nation of South Carolina, 1975.

183. "Catawba Indian Nation Votes on New Constitution," *Herald* (July 25, 2015), http://www.heraldonline.com/news/state/south-carolina/article28715047.html, accessed July 30, 2015. The proposed new constitution would not have substantially changed the tribe's citizenship clause from the 1975 constitution. It stated, "The citizenry of the Catawba Indian Nation shall consist of individuals: (1) who are of Catawba blood; and (2) whose name appears on the rolls of July 1, 1943, February 25, 1961, or July 24, 2000. It shall also include such individuals' direct blood descendants." See Constitution of the Catawba Indian Nation, 3, http://catawbaindian.net/wp-content/uploads/Constitution-Final-draft-clean.pdf, accessed July 30, 2015. See also Catawba Indian Nation, "We the First People: Catawba Constitution Initiative," http://catawbaindian.net/constitution-initiative/, accessed August 11, 2014. For the new constitution to go into effect, at least 30 percent of the tribe's more than 2,000 eligible voters had to cast ballots. The turnout, however, was about 100 votes short of that threshold. Thus, although it appeared that the majority of those who voted were in support of the new constitution, the election did not count. See "Not Enough Catawbas Vote to Get New Tribal Constitution," *Herald* (July 26, 2015), http://www.heraldonline.com/news/state/south-carolina/article28760416.html, accessed July 30, 2015.

184. Prepared Testimony of Gilbert Blue, Chief, Catawba Tribe of Indians of South Carolina, on H.R. 3274, before the Committee on Interior and Insular Affairs, United States House of Representatives, June 12, 1979, File: Catawba Indians, Richard W. Riley Administration, Catawba Indian Claim, 1977–1983, Series S554019, RG 554000, Box 7, SCDAH Columbia.

185. William M. Goins, editor, *South Carolina Indians Today: An Educational Resource Guide* (Columbia, SC: Phoenix, 1998), 19, South Caroliniana Library.
186. Prepared Testimony of Gilbert Blue, Chief, Catawba Tribe of Indians of South Carolina, on H.R. 3274, before the Committee on Interior and Insular Affairs, United States House of Representatives, June 12, 1979, File: Catawba Indians, Richard W. Riley Administration, Catawba Indian Claim, 1977–1983, Series S554019, RG 554000, Box 7, SCDAH Columbia.
187. Pettus, *Leasing Away a Nation*, 62. For more on the history behind the 1993 settlement, see Lynn Loftis, "The Catawbas' Final Battle: A Bittersweet Victory," *American Indian Law Review* 19 (1994): 183–215.
188. The federal government contributed $32 million, the state $12.5 million, and York and Lancaster Counties nearly $2.6 million. Local insurance companies and other private donors made up the difference. See Pettus, *Leasing Away a Nation*, 63.
189. Statement of Daniel R. McLeod, Attorney General of South Carolina, before the Committee on Interior and Insular Affairs, Morris K. Udall, Chairman, US House of Representatives, June 12, 1979, File: Catawba Indians, Richard W. Riley Administration, Catawba Indians Claim, 1977–1983, Series S554019, RG 554000, Box 7, SCDAH Columbia.
190. Daniel R. McLeod, Attorney General, to Members of the Catawba Study Commission, August 8, 1980, "Hearings before the South Carolina Legislative Commission to Study Claims of the Catawba Indian Tribe to Certain Lands in South Carolina," Rock Hill, South Carolina, August 13, 1980, South Caroliniana Library.
191. Notice of General Council Meeting, Rock Hill, February 20, 1993, File: Catawba Indians, Administrative, Catawba Indians, Tribal Council Minutes, July 1, 1944, Thomas J. Blumer Collection.
192. Personal communication with Fred Sanders, Catawba Indian Nation, South Carolina, May 4, 2011.
193. "Money Matters: Answers to Your Questions about the Settlement," *News of the Nation: The Official Newsletter of the Catawba Indian Nation*, 1: 2 (February 10, 1994), File: Catawba Indians, Publications, "News of the Nation," Thomas J. Blumer Collection.
194. Catawba Indians, Administrative, Catawba Indians, Tribal Rolls, November 22, 1994, Thomas J. Blumer Collection.
195. Fred Sanders to Roderick Beck, Chair Person of the Committee for the petitioners of the Catawba General Council, April 3, 1997, File: Catawba Indians, Administrative, Catawba Indians, Constitutions (1975), Thomas J. Blumer Collection.
196. Cal Harrison, "Catawba Wants Name on Tribal List," *Rock Hill Herald*, February 14, 1994, File: Catawba Indians, Western Band, Clippings, Thomas J. Blumer Collection.
197. Cal Harrison, "Catawba Wants Name on Tribal List."
198. Personal communication with Fred Sanders, Catawba Indian Nation, SC, May 4, 2011.
199. "Roll Call: The Settlement Means Asking Once Again 'Who Is a Catawba?'" *News of the Nation: The Official Newsletter of the Catawba Indian Nation*, 1: 1 (September 24, 1993), File: Catawba Indians, Publications, "News of the Nation," Thomas J. Blumer Collection.
200. Stabley, "Lawyer Wants Inclusion on Tribe's Roll," in Martin, *My Father's People: A Complete Genealogy of the Catawba Nation*, South Caroliniana Library.
201. Personal communication with Donna Curtis, Catawba Indian Nation, SC, May 4, 2011.
202. Personal communication with Fred Sanders, Catawba Indian Nation, SC, May 4, 2011; Catawba Indian Nation, "Tribal Enrollment," http://catawbaindian.net/services/tribal-enrollment/, accessed August 11, 2014.
203. Personal communication with Chief Donald Rodgers, Catawba Indian Nation, SC, May 4, 2011.
204. Catawba Indian Nation, "Catawba Today," http://catawbaindian.net/about-us/catawba-today/, accessed April 14, 2014.

Chapter 3

1. *Memorial of the Choctaw and Chickasaw Nations relative to the Rights of the Mississippi Choctaws, Submitted for Consideration in Connection with H.R. 19213* (Washington, DC:

US Government Printing Office, 1913), reprinted in P. J. Hurley, *Choctaw Citizenship Litigation: Report of P. J. Hurley, National Attorney for the Choctaw Nation, to Major Victor M. Locke Jr., Principal Chief of the Choctaw Nation* (May 1916), 22.

2. Ronald N. Satz, "The Mississippi Choctaw: From the Removal Treaty to the Federal Agency," in *After Removal: The Choctaw in Mississippi*, edited by Samuel J. Wells and Roseanna Tubby (Jackson: University Press of Mississippi, 1986), 5.

3. The Choctaws had signed the Treaty of Doak's Stand in 1820, in which they ceded about 6 million acres on the western edge of the Choctaw Nation in the southeast for 13 million acres in Arkansas Territory. Although this treaty provided for an exchange of land, it did not require the Choctaws to leave their homes. Most Choctaws remained in Mississippi on the unceded land until the Treaty of Dancing Rabbit Creek in 1830. See Clara Sue Kidwell, *Choctaws and Missionaries in Mississippi, 1818–1918* (Norman: University of Oklahoma Press, 1995), 48–49.

4. Satz, "The Mississippi Choctaw: From the Removal Treaty to the Federal Agency," 5–6; Article 14 of the Treaty of Dancing Rabbit Creek, quoted in US Senate, Committee on Indian Affairs, *Claims of Choctaw Indians of Mississippi* (74th Cong., 1st Sess., 1935, Report No. 781), 1–2.

5. Satz, "The Mississippi Choctaw: From the Removal Treaty to the Federal Agency," 6–8; File: 89 Halbert, H. S. Sketches of Choctaw, Mingoes, Indian Countrymen and their Families, pp. 22–25, *Papers of Henry Sale Halbert, 1837–1916. Montgomery, Alabama: Alabama Department of Archives and History* (hereafter *Papers of Henry Sale Halbert*), M-2167; Mississippi Department of Archives and History, William F. Winter Archives and History Building, Jackson, MS (hereafter MDAH, Jackson); US House of Representatives, Subcommittee of the Committee on Indian Affairs, *Hearings on the Subject of Enrolment in the Five Civilized Tribes, Having under Consideration the Following Bills: 3389, 3390, 6537, 7926, 7974, 8007, 10066, 10140, 12586* (Washington, DC: US Government Printing Office, 1913), 26.

6. US House of Representatives, Committee on Indian Affairs, *Claims of Choctaw Indians of Mississippi* (75th Cong., 3rd Sess., 1938, Report No. 2233), 2.

7. Interview with Charlie Denson, by Sam Proctor, December 3, 1973, 1–2, Samuel Proctor Oral History Program, Oral History Collections, George A. Smathers Libraries, University of Florida Digital Collections, Gainesville, Florida (hereafter Samuel Proctor Oral History Program).

8. David I. Bushnell Jr., "The Choctaw of Bayou Lacomb, St. Tammany Parish, Louisiana," *Bureau of American Ethnology, Bulletin 48* (Washington, DC: US Government Printing Office, 1909), 1; Brian Kiopotek, *Recognition Odysseys: Indigeneity, Race, and Federal Tribal Recognition Policy in Three Louisiana Indian Communities* (Durham, NC: Duke University Press, 2011), 128.

9. US House of Representatives, "Condition of the Mississippi Choctaws," *Hearing before the Committee on Investigation of the Indian Service*, Union, MS, March 16, 1917, Vol. 2 (Washington, DC: US Government Printing Office, 1917), 166.

10. "Tribal Lines Broken: Scattered Groups of Once Powerful Indians," *Washington Post* (February 23, 1902): 14.

11. US House of Representatives, "Condition of the Mississippi Choctaws," *Hearing before the Committee on Investigation of the Indian Service*, Union, MS, March 16, 1917, Vol. 2 (Washington, DC: US Government Printing Office, 1917), 124.

12. Interview with Frank Bell Joe by Lonus D. Hucks, 1970s, 28, Samuel Proctor Oral History Program.

13. File: 179 Halbert, H.S. *Papers of Henry Sale Halbert*. M-3269, MDAH, Jackson.

14. Interview with Baxter York by the Staff of Nanih Waiya, July 8, 1974, 2, Samuel Proctor Oral History Program.

15. "Choctaw Indians in Louisiana: Their Proposed Deportation to the Indian Territory," *Chicago Daily Tribune* (March 24, 1894): 4.

16. Simpson J. Tubby, *Early Struggles* (Walnut Grove, MS: Dawn of Light Print, 1974), 35, reprinted in *Nanih Waiya*, 2:1–2 (Fall–Winter, 1974–75): 35, J. D. Williams Library, University of Mississippi, Oxford, MS (hereafter J. D. Williams Library).

17. Sandra Sam, "Making Bows with Tom Ben," *Nanih Waiya*, 3:4 (Summer, 1976): 149, J. D. Williams Library.
18. Danny Chickaway et al., "Laymon Shumake—Choctaw Craftsman: Rabbit Stick," *Nanih Waiya*, 1:2 (Winter, 1974): 19, J. D. Williams Library.
19. "Playing Ball: Graphic Description of an Indian Amusement," *Atlanta Constitution* (October 28, 1890): 6.
20. Bushnell, "The Choctaw of Bayou Lacomb, St. Tammany Parish, Louisiana," 8–9.
21. File: 26 Halbert, H. S. The Choctaws as Farmers, pp. 22–32, *Papers of Henry Sale Halbert*, M-2137, MDAH, Jackson.
22. Charles Madden Tolbert, *A Sociological Study of the Choctaw Indians in Mississippi* (Ph.D. Dissertation, Louisiana State University, 1958), 155.
23. US House of Representatives, "Condition of the Mississippi Choctaws," *Hearing before the Committee on Investigation of the Indian Service*, Union, MS, March 16, 1917, Vol. 2 (Washington, DC: US Government Printing Office, 1917), 123.
24. Interview with Mary Lou Farmer by Sam Proctor, December 3, 1973, 8–9, Samuel Proctor Oral History Program.
25. Pamela Anne Coe, "Lost in the Hills of Home: Outline of Mississippi Choctaw Social Organization" (M.A. Thesis, Columbia University, February 1960), 72, Association on American Indian Affairs, Box 249, File: 10, Choctaw, 1949–1960, Association on American Indian Affairs Records, Mudd Manuscript Library, Princeton University, Princeton, New Jersey (hereafter Mudd Manuscript Library).
26. File: 26 Halbert, H. S. The Choctaws as Farmers, pp. 17–18, *Papers of Henry Sale Halbert*, M-2137, MDAH, Jackson.
27. Interview with DeLaura Henry by the Staff of Nanih Waiya, January 31, 1974, 4, Samuel Proctor Oral History Program; "Blowgun," *Nanih Waiya*, 1: 2 (Winter 1974): 24, J. D. Williams Library.
28. File: 26 Halbert, H. S. The Choctaws as Farmers, pp. 17–18, *Papers of Henry Sale Halbert*, M-2137, MDAH, Jackson.
29. US House of Representatives, "Condition of the Mississippi Choctaws," *Hearing before the Committee on Investigation of the Indian Service*, Union, MS, March 16, 1917, Vol. 2 (Washington, DC: US Government Printing Office, 1917), 153.
30. Coe, "Lost in the Hills of Home," 46.
31. "A Choctaw Courtship," *Chicago Daily Tribune* (June 24, 1882): 10; File: 34 Halbert, H. S. Choctaw Marriage Customs: Maternity, Punishment of Adultery, *Papers of Henry Sale Halbert*, M-2137, MDAH, Jackson; John R. Swanton, "Source Material for the Social and Ceremonial Life of the Choctaw Indian," *Bureau of American Ethnology, Bulletin 103* (Washington, DC: US Government Printing Office, 1931), 134–135.
32. File: 53 Halbert, H. S. Choctaw Burial and Funeral Custom, Halbert Manuscript, pp. 36–52, *Papers of Henry Sale Halbert*, M-3001, MDAH, Jackson.
33. Frederick Sullens, "The Removal of Indians from Mississippi: The Choctaw Creation Legend," *Atlanta Constitution* (May 12, 1901): A3.
34. "Ball Playing among Indians," *New York Times* (September 9, 1871): 1; Swanton, "Source Material for the Social and Ceremonial Life of the Choctaw Indians," 153.
35. Sullens, "The Removal of Indians from Mississippi," A3.
36. In the early nineteenth century, white missionaries had established several churches and schools among the Choctaws. These moved west with the Choctaw Nation in 1830. For more than fifty years the Choctaws lived without Christian religious instruction, until they once again attracted the attention of missionaries in the late nineteenth century. For more on the relationship between Choctaws and missionaries in Mississippi, see Kidwell, *Choctaws and Missionaries in Mississippi*.
37. John A. Watkins, "The Choctaws in Mississippi," *American Antiquarian and Oriental Journal*, 16: 2 (2 March 1894): 69.
38. Pamela Anne Coe, "More Agency than They Bargained For and Less Land," *Anthropology*, 192 (April 14, 1959): 2, Association on American Indian Affairs, Box 249, File: 10, Choctaw, 1949–1960, Association on American Indian Affairs Records, Mudd Manuscript Library;

File: 53 Halbert, H. S. Choctaw Burial and Funeral Custom, Halbert Manuscript, pp. 55–56, *Papers of Henry Sale Halbert*, M-3001, MDAH, Jackson.

39. Kidwell, *Choctaws and Missionaries in Mississippi*, 181.
40. US House of Representatives, "Condition of the Mississippi Choctaws," *Hearing before the Committee on Investigation of the Indian Service*, Union, MS, March 16, 1917, Vol. 2 (Washington, DC: US Government Printing Office, 1917), 130.
41. Interview with Charlie Denson, by Sam Proctor, December 3, 1973, 30, Samuel Proctor Oral History Program.
42. US House of Representatives, *Additional Land and Indian Schools in Mississippi: Letter from the Secretary of the Interior, Transmitting Report of John T. Reeves, Special Supervisor, Indian Service, on Need of Additional Land School Facilities for the Indians Living in the State of Mississippi* (64th Cong., 2nd Sess., December 7, 1916, Doc. No. 1464), 25, MDAH, Jackson.
43. John H. Peterson Jr., *The Mississippi Band of Choctaw Indians: Their Recent History and Current Social Relations* (Ph.D. Dissertation, University of Georgia, 1970), 78.
44. "The Mississippi Choctaws: How They Are Cared for by a Roman Catholic Mission," *Atlanta Constitution* (September 21, 1892): 4.
45. Coe, "More Agency than They Bargained For and Less Land," 3.
46. In a 1973 oral interview, Louise Willis recalled that her great-grandmother had warned her grandmother "not to look at a white man . . . To never look at a white man because if you do they will come and catch you and take you away." See interview with Louise Willis by John K. Mahon, December 4, 1973, Samuel Proctor Oral History Program.
47. File 42: Halbert, H. S. Choctaw Stories, Papers of Henry Sale Halbert, 1837–1916, Montgomery, Alabama: Alabama Department of Archives and History, M-2137, Media Room, MDAH, Jackson. In the early years of the twentieth century several descendants of slaves claimed to have Choctaw fathers. If such relationships occurred, however, they went unacknowledged by the Indians living in core Mississippi and Louisiana Choctaw communities.
48. Henry S. Halbert to Roland B. Dixon, April 8, 1911, File 163: Halbert, H. S., Letters, 1910–1911, *Papers of Henry Sale Halbert*, M-3464, MDAH, Jackson.
49. Samuel J. Wells, "The Role of Mixed-Bloods in Mississippi Choctaw History," in *After Removal: The Choctaw in Mississippi*, 46, 49.
50. R. Halliburton Jr. "Chief Greenwood Leflore and His Malmaison Plantation," in *After Removal: The Choctaw in Mississippi*, 58–59, 62.
51. Interview of James C. Harris by Commissioner McKennon, Philadelphia, Neshoba County, MS, January 24, 1899, "Records of Proceedings, Commission to the Five Civilized Tribes Identifying Mississippi Choctaws, Sessions at Carthage, Philadelphia, and Decatur, State of Mississippi, January 24th to February 10th, 1899, inclusive," 3–4, 105: Index and Records of Testimony, 1899, P2219: Records Relating to the Identification of Mississippi Choctaws, 1899–1904, M-7RA-16, roll 1, Record Group 75: Records of the Bureau of Indian Affairs (hereafter RG 75), National Archives and Records Administration, Fort Worth, Texas (hereafter NARA Fort Worth).
52. Interview of Tom Tubby by Commissioner McKennon, Philadelphia, Neshoba County, MS, February 2, 1899, "Records of Proceedings, Commission to the Five Civilized Tribes Identifying Mississippi Choctaws, Sessions at Carthage, Philadelphia, and Decatur, State of Mississippi, January 24th to February 10th, 1899, inclusive," 115–116, 105: Index and Records of Testimony, 1899, P2219: Records Relating to the Identification of Mississippi Choctaws, 1899–1904, M-7RA-16, roll 1, RG 75, NARA Fort Worth. Officials spelled the name of the Tubby family in a variety of ways. It appears in the records as "Tubby," "Tubbee," and "Tubbie." I have chosen to spell it as "Tubby" because that is how Simpson Tubby spelled his name in his autobiography (see Tubby, *Early Struggles*). However, I have kept other spellings in quoted material.
53. US House of Representatives, *Additional Land and Indian Schools in Mississippi: Letter from the Secretary of the Interior, Transmitting Report of John T. Reeves, Special Supervisor, Indian Service, on Need of Additional Land School Facilities for the Indians Living in the State of Mississippi* (64th Cong., 2nd Sess., December 7, 1916, Doc. No. 1464), 11, MDAH, Jackson.

54. See Swanton, "Source Material for the Social and Ceremonial Life of the Choctaw Indians."

55. Interview of Wash Bell by Commissioner McKennon, Philadelphia, Neshoba County, MS, February 2, 1899, "Records of Proceedings, Commission to the Five Civilized Tribes Identifying Mississippi Choctaws, Sessions at Carthage, Philadelphia, and Decatur, State of Mississippi, January 24th to February 10th, 1899, inclusive," 118, 105: Index and Records of Testimony, 1899, P2219: Records Relating to the Identification of Mississippi Choctaws, 1899–1904, M-7RA-16, roll 1, RG 75, NARA Fort Worth.

56. An Oral Interview with Barry Davis Jim Sr. by Lana Lohrer, November 12, 1998, Mississippi Band of Choctaw Indians, Volume 727, Interviewer: Lana Lohrer, 1998, Mississippi Oral History Program, Center for Oral History and Cultural Heritage, University of Southern Mississippi, Hattiesburg, MS (hereafter USM Hattiesburg).

57. Interview with Bill Martin by Commissioner McKennon, Philadelphia, Neshoba County, Miss., February 8, 1899, "Applications for Identification as Mississippi Choctaws," *Records of Proceedings, Commission to the Five Civilized Tribes Identifying Mississippi Choctaws, Sessions at Carthage, Philadelphia, and Decatur, State of Mississippi, January 24 to February 10, 1899, inclusive,* 149, 105: Index and Records of Testimony, 1899, P2219: Records Relating to the Identification of Mississippi Choctaws, 1899–1904, M-7RA-116, roll 1, RG 75, NARA Fort Worth.

58. Application of Jim Jack Johnson, Department of the Interior, Commission to the Five Civilized Tribes, Meridian, Mississippi, June 17, 1901, Applications for Enrollment in the Five Civilized Tribes, 1898–1914, M-1301, roll 117, RG 75, NARA Fort Worth.

59. Interview with Billie Willis by Commissioner McKennon, Philadelphia, Neshoba County, Miss., February 1, 1899, "Applications for Identification as Mississippi Choctaws," *Records of Proceedings, Commission to the Five Civilized Tribes Identifying Mississippi Choctaws, Sessions at Carthage, Philadelphia, and Decatur, State of Mississippi, January 24 to February 10, 1899, inclusive,* 109, 105: Index and Records of Testimony, 1899, P2219: Records Relating to the Identification of Mississippi Choctaws, 1899–1904, M-7RA-116, roll 1, RG 75, NARA Fort Worth. Whereas in McKennon's report, Lou was described as half-white and half-Choctaw, the Dawes Commission later recorded her as being "a colored woman." In both cases, however, Willis was recorded as a full-blood Choctaw. See Application of Billy Willis, Department of the Interior, Commission to the Five Civilized Tribes, Philadelphia, Mississippi, May 4, 1901, Applications for Enrollment in the Five Civilized Tribes, 1898–1914, M-1301, roll 110, RG 75, NARA Fort Worth.

60. Interview with Willie Philip by Commissioner McKennon, Philadelphia, Neshoba County, Miss., February 4, 1899, "Applications for Identification as Mississippi Choctaws," *Records of Proceedings, Commission to the Five Civilized Tribes Identifying Mississippi Choctaws, Sessions at Carthage, Philadelphia, and Decatur, State of Mississippi, January 24 to February 10, 1899, inclusive,* 121, 105: Index and Records of Testimony, 1899, P2219: Records Relating to the Identification of Mississippi Choctaws, 1899–1904, M-7RA-116, roll 1, RG 75, NARA Fort Worth.

61. Interview with Willie Philip by Commissioner McKennon, Philadelphia, Neshoba County, Miss., February 4, 1899, "Applications for Identification as Mississippi Choctaws," *Records of Proceedings, Commission to the Five Civilized Tribes Identifying Mississippi Choctaws, Sessions at Carthage, Philadelphia, and Decatur, State of Mississippi, January 24 to February 10, 1899, inclusive,* 121, 105: Index and Records of Testimony, 1899, P2219: Records Relating to the Identification of Mississippi Choctaws, 1899–1904, M-7RA-116, roll 1, RG 75, NARA Fort Worth.

62. Henry S. Halbert to Roland B. Dixon, April 8, 1911. File: 163 Halbert, H. S., Letters, 1910–1911, *Papers of Henry Sale Halbert,* M-3464, MDAH, Jackson.

63. *Memorial of the Choctaw and Chickasaw Nations Relative to the Rights of Mississippi Choctaws, Submitted for Consideration in Connection with H.R. 19213* (Washington, 1913), reprinted in *Choctaw Citizenship Litigation: Report of P. J. Hurley, National Attorney for the Choctaw Nation, to Major Victor M. Locke, Jr., Principal Chief of the Choctaw Nation* (May 1916).

64. "Bill No. 39," *Laws of the Choctaw Nation, Passed at the Regular Session of the General Council, Convened at Tushka Humma, October 3rd, 1892, and Adjourned November 4th, 1892* (Atoka, Indian Territory: Indian Citizen Publishing Co., 1893).

65. Kidwell, *Choctaws and Missionaries in Mississippi,* 184.

66. Some applicants, like Tom Chitto, complained that they didn't "know anything about the treaty. The old folks know but I don't." Others stated that they didn't know the names of their ancestors. For example, Sampson Weshock protested that he didn't "know anything about my grandfather and grandmother." Even if they knew some information, it was often incomplete. For example, William Johnson said, "Don't know much about my grandparents. I know the names. His name was Billie. That is all the name I know." See interviews of Sampson Weshock, William Johnson, and Tom Chitto by Commissioner McKennon, Philadelphia, Neshoba County, MS, January 25, 1899, "Records of Proceedings, Commission to the Five Civilized Tribes Identifying Mississippi Choctaws, Sessions at Carthage, Philadelphia, and Decatur, State of Mississippi, January 24th to February 10th, 1899, inclusive," 20, 23, 105: Index and Records of Testimony, 1899, P2219: Records Relating to the Identification of Mississippi Choctaws, 1899–1904, M-7RA-16, roll 1, RG 75, NARA Fort Worth.

67. US House of Representatives, *Additional Land and Indian Schools in Mississippi: Letter from the Secretary of the Interior, Transmitting Report of John T. Reeves, Special Supervisor, Indian Service, on Need of Additional Land and School Facilities for the Indians Living in the State of Mississippi* (64th Cong., 2nd Sess., December 7, 1916, Doc. No. 1464), MDAH, Jackson.

68. US House of Representatives, Subcommittee of the Committee on Indian Affairs, *Hearings on the Subject of Enrollment in the Five Civilized Tribes, Having under Consideration the Following Bills: 3389, 3390, 6537, 7926, 7974, 8007, 10066, 10140, 12586* (Washington, DC: US Government Printing Office, 1913), 56.

69. US House of Representatives, Subcommittee of the Committee on Indian Affairs, *Hearings on the Subject of Enrollment in the Five Civilized Tribes,* 51.

70. Archibald McKennon, "Mississippi Choctaws, Report of the Problems of Identifying Them," 305, Oklahoma Historical Society, DC (OHS-DC), M-24, roll 11, NARA Fort Worth.

71. US Senate, Committee on Indian Affairs, *Indian Appropriation Bill: Hearings on H.R. 18453, An Act Making Appropriations for the Current and Contingent Expenses of the Bureau of Indian Affairs, for Fulfilling Treaty Stipulations with Various Indian Tribes, and for Other Purposes, for the Fiscal Year Ending June 30, 1918* (64th Cong., 2nd Sess., 1917), 460–461.

72. Interview of Meely Sam by Commissioner McKennon, Philadelphia, Neshoba County, MS, January 25, 1899, "Records of Proceedings, Commission to the Five Civilized Tribes Identifying Mississippi Choctaws, Sessions at Carthage, Philadelphia, and Decatur, State of Mississippi, January 24th to February 10th, 1899, inclusive," 30, 105: Index and Records of Testimony, 1899, P2219: Records Relating to the Identification of Mississippi Choctaws, 1899–1904, M-7RA-16, roll 1, RG 75, NARA Fort Worth.

73. Interview of John Frenchman by Commissioner McKennon, Philadelphia, Neshoba County, MS, February 7, 1899, "Records of Proceedings, Commission to the Five Civilized Tribes Identifying Mississippi Choctaws, Sessions at Carthage, Philadelphia, and Decatur, State of Mississippi, January 24th to February 10th, 1899, inclusive," 131, 105: Index and Records of Testimony, 1899, P2219: Records Relating to the Identification of Mississippi Choctaws, 1899–1904, M-7RA-16, roll 1, RG 75, NARA Fort Worth.

74. Interview of Tom Tubby by Commissioner McKennon, Philadelphia, Neshoba County, MS, February 2, 1899, "Records of Proceedings, Commission to the Five Civilized Tribes Identifying Mississippi Choctaws, Sessions at Carthage, Philadelphia, and Decatur, State of Mississippi, January 24th to February 10th, 1899, inclusive," 115–116, 105: Index and Records of Testimony, 1899, P2219: Records Relating to the Identification of Mississippi Choctaws, 1899–1904, M-7RA-16, roll 1, RG 75, NARA Fort Worth.

75. Interview of Mary Campbell by Commissioner McKennon, Philadelphia, Neshoba County, MS, January 25, 1899, "Records of Proceedings, Commission to the Five Civilized Tribes Identifying Mississippi Choctaws, Sessions at Carthage, Philadelphia,

and Decatur, State of Mississippi, January 24th to February 10th, 1899, inclusive," 23, 105: Index and Records of Testimony, 1899, P2219: Records Relating to the Identification of Mississippi Choctaws, 1899–1904, M-7RA-16, roll 1, RG 75, NARA Fort Worth.

76. Interview with William Billey by Commissioner McKennon, Philadelphia, Neshoba County, MS, January 27, 1899, "Records of Proceedings, Commission to the Five Civilized Tribes Identifying Mississippi Choctaws, Sessions at Carthage, Philadelphia, and Decatur, State of Mississippi, January 24th to February 10th, 1899, inclusive," 59, 105: Index and Records of Testimony, 1899, P2219: Records Relating to the Identification of Mississippi Choctaws, 1899–1904, M-7RA-16, roll 1, RG 75, NARA Fort Worth; interview with Charlie Wiley by Commissioner McKennon, Philadelphia, Neshoba County, MS, January 25, 1899, "Records of Proceedings, Commission to the Five Civilized Tribes Identifying Mississippi Choctaws, Sessions at Carthage, Philadelphia, and Decatur, State of Mississippi, January 24th to February 10th, 1899, inclusive," 37–38, 105: Index and Records of Testimony, 1899, P2219: Records Relating to the Identification of Mississippi Choctaws, 1899–1904, M-7RA-16, roll 1, RG 75, NARA Fort Worth.

77. For an excellent discussion of race and the construction of the McKennon Roll see Katherine M. B. Osburn, "'Any Sane Person': Race, Rights, and Tribal Sovereignty in the Construction of the Dawes Rolls for the Choctaw Nation," *Journal of the Gilded Age and Progressive Era*, 9:4 (October 2010): 451–471.

78. "Application for Identification as Mississippi Choctaws, Philadelphia, Neshoba County, Miss., Wednesday, February 1, 1899," 2, 3–4, 105: Index and Records of Testimony, 1899, RG 75, NARA Fort Worth.

79. "Application for Identification as Mississippi Choctaws, Philadelphia, Neshoba County, Miss., Wednesday, February 1, 1899," 1–2.

80. Conversation between Commissioner A. S. McKennon, Clerk P. G. Reuter, Clerk D. W. Yancey, and Mr. C. F. Winston (Winton) at the Cooper Hotel at Philadelphia, Neshoba County, Mississippi, January 31, 1899, 1–3, 105: Index and Records of Testimony, 1899, RG 75, NARA Fort Worth.

81. Interview with Willie Philip by Commissioner McKennon, Philadelphia, Neshoba County, Miss., February 4, 1899, "Applications for Identification as Mississippi Choctaws," *Records of Proceedings, Commission to the Five Civilized Tribes Identifying Mississippi Choctaws, Sessions at Carthage, Philadelphia, and Decatur, State of Mississippi, January 24 to February 10, 1899, inclusive*, 121, 105: Index and Records of Testimony, 1899, P2219: Records Relating to the Identification of Mississippi Choctaws, 1899–1904, M-7RA-116, roll 1, RG 75, NARA Fort Worth.

82. US House of Representatives, Subcommittee of the Committee on Indian Affairs, *Hearings on the Subject of Enrollment in the Five Civilized Tribes, Having under Consideration the Following Bills: 3389, 3390, 6537, 7926, 7974, 8007, 10066, 10140, 12586* (Washington, DC: US Government Printing Office, 1913), 51.

83. US House of Representatives, Subcommittee of the Committee on Indian Affairs, *Hearings on the Subject of Enrollment in the Five Civilized Tribes*, 78.

84. US Senate, Committee on Indian Affairs, *Choctaw Indians of Mississippi* (76th Cong., 3rd Sess., April 22 and 23, 1940), 15.

85. The Act of May 31, 1900 opened the so-called Mississippi Loophole. Although it cut off applications from individuals not on a tribal roll, it allowed Mississippi Choctaws to continue to enroll until the rolls closed. In this way, the act opened the possibility that anyone who had been denied by the Dawes Commission and the federal courts could now appeal as a Mississippi Choctaw. As a result, thousands of people applied for identification as Mississippi Choctaw. See Clara Sue Kidwell, *The Choctaws in Oklahoma: From Tribe to Nation, 1855–1970* (Norman: University of Oklahoma Press, 2007), 167.

86. US House of Representatives, Subcommittee of the Committee on Indian Affairs, *Hearings on the Subject of Enrollment in the Five Civilized Tribes, Having under Consideration the Following Bills: 3389, 3390, 6537, 7926, 7974, 8007, 10066, 10140, 12586* (Washington, DC: US Government Printing Office, 1913), 78.

87. US Senate, Committee on Indian Affairs, *Rights of the Mississippi Choctaws in the Choctaw Nation* (57th Cong., 1st Sess., 1902, Doc. No. 319), 2.

88. "Fight for a Big Fee: Payment of $750,000 to Indians' Attorneys Contested," *Washington Post* (February 6, 1905): 2.

89. *Memorial of the Choctaw and Chickasaw Nations Relative to the Rights of the Mississippi Choctaws, Submitted for Consideration in Connection with H.R. 19213* (Washington, DC, 1913), reprinted in P. J. Hurley, *Choctaw Citizenship Litigation: Report of P. J. Hurley, National Attorney for the Choctaw Nation, to Major Victor M. Locke Jr., Principal Chief of the Choctaw Nation* (May 1916), 21.

90. US Senate, Committee on Indian Affairs, *Hearings before the Committee on Indian Affairs on the Choctaw and Chickasaw Indians* (59th Cong., 2nd Sess., January 30, 1907, Doc. No. 257), 31–32, MDAH, Jackson; US Senate, Committee on Indian Affairs, *Rights of the Mississippi Choctaws in the Choctaw Nation* (57th Cong., 1st Sess., 1902, Doc. No. 319), 2.

91. "Fight for a Big Fee: Payment of $750,000 to Indians' Attorneys Contested," *Washington Post* (February 6, 1905): 2.

92. *Proposed Legislation for the Full-Blood and Identified Choctaws of Mississippi, Louisiana, and Alabama with Memorial, Evidence, and Brief* (Washington, DC: Judd & Detweiler, Printers, 1913), 34–35, MDAH, Jackson.

93. T. A. Walters, Acting Secretary of the Interior, to Elmer Thomas, Chairman of the Senate Committee on Indian Affairs, April 4, 1935. US Senate, Committee on Indian Affairs, *Claims of Choctaw Indians of Mississippi* (74th Cong., 1st Sess., 1935, Report No. 781), 4.

94. Kidwell, *The Choctaws in Oklahoma,* 164.

95. US Senate, Committee on Indian Affairs, *Indian Appropriation Bill: Hearings on H.R. 18453, An Act Making Appropriations for the Current and Contingent Expenses of the Bureau of Indian Affairs, for Fulfilling Treaty Stipulations with Various Indian Tribes, and for Other Purposes, for the Fiscal Year Ending June 30, 1918* (64th Cong., 2nd Sess., 1917), 460–461.

96. US Supreme Court, *Winton v. Amos,* 255 U.S. 373 (1921).

97. Interview of Charles B. Tinsely, on behalf of Simpson Tubbee, Department of the Interior, Commission to the Five Civilized Tribes, Toles, Mississippi, April 10, 1902, Applications for Enrollment in the Five Civilized Tribes, 1898–1914, M-1301, roll 144, RG 75, NARA Fort Worth.

98. US House of Representatives, Subcommittee of the Committee on Indian Affairs, *Hearings on the Subject of Enrollment in the Five Civilized Tribes, Having under Consideration the Following Bills: 3389, 3390, 6537, 7974, 8007, 10066, 10140, 12586* (Washington, DC: US Government Printing Office, 1913), 53–54.

99. Charles H. Sawyer, Atoka, Indian Territory, to the Commission of the Five Civilized Tribes, Meridian, Mississippi, June 5, 1901, "Letters, Atoka Office, June 5 to September 28, 1901, No. 2," 5, 102: Letters Sent by Enrollment Clerks, Muskogee Area Office, 1901, RG 75, NARA Fort Worth.

100. US Senate, Committee on Indian Affairs, *Indian Appropriation Bill: Hearing on H.R. 18453, An Act Making Appropriation for the Current and Contingent Expenses of the Bureau of Indian Affairs, For Fulfilling Treaty Stipulations with Various Indian Tribes, and for Other Purposes, for the Fiscal Year Ending June 30, 1918* (64th Cong., 2nd Sess., 1917, H.R. 18453), 452.

101. US Supreme Court, *Winton v. Amos,* 255 U.S. 373 (1921).

102. See "Letters, Atoka Office, June 5 to September 28, 1901, No. 2," 102: Letters Sent by Enrollment Clerks, Muskogee Area Office, 1901, RG 75, NARA Fort Worth.

103. Application of Lucy Jim, Department of the Interior, Commission to the Five Civilized Tribes, Meridian, Mississippi, April 3, 1901, Applications for Enrollment in the Five Civilized Tribes, 1898–1914, M-1301, roll 103, RG 75, NARA Fort Worth.

104. Application of Andy Folsom, Department of the Interior, Commission to the Five Civilized Tribes, Muskogee, I.T., March 16, 1903, Applications for Enrollment in the Five Civilized Tribes, 1898–1914, M-1301, roll 162, RG 75, NARA Fort Worth.

105. Application of Charley Farve, Department of the Interior, Commission to the Five Civilized Tribes, Meridian, Mississippi, May 31, 1901, Applications for Enrollment in the Five Civilized Tribes, 1898–1914, M-1301, roll 115, RG 75, NARA Fort Worth.

106. Application of Andy Folsom, Department of the Interior, Commission to the Five Civilized Tribes, Muskogee, I.T., March 16, 1903, Applications for Enrollment in the Five Civilized Tribes, 1898–1914, M-1301, roll 162, RG 75, NARA Fort Worth.

107. Commission to the Five Civilized Tribes, Muskogee, Indian Territory, September 5, 1903, to H. Van V. Smith, Special Agent of the Government, Meridian, Mississippi, September 5, 1903, Applications for Enrollment in the Five Civilized Tribes, 1898–1914, M-1301, roll 140, RG 75, NARA Fort Worth.

108. Application of Charley Farve, Department of the Interior, Commission to the Five Civilized Tribes, Meridian, Mississippi, May 31, 1901, Applications for Enrollment in the Five Civilized Tribes, 1898–1914, M-1301, roll 115, RG 75, NARA Fort Worth.

109. Ultimately the commissioners classed both siblings as "mixed bloods" based on their descent from a half-white mother, but the example illustrates the inherent fallacy of using phenotype as a means to evaluate blood quantum. See Thomas Ryan, Acting Secretary of the Interior, to the Commission to the Five Civilized Tribes, April 11, 1905, 1–3, Applications for Enrollment in the Five Civilized Tribes, 1898–1914, M-1301, roll 144, RG 75, NARA Fort Worth.

110. Application of Susie Cambric, Department of the Interior, Commission to the Five Civilized Tribes, Meridian, Mississippi, April 9, 1901, Applications for Enrollment in the Five Civilized Tribes, 1898–1914, M-1301, roll 105, RG 75, NARA Fort Worth.

111. For numerous examples of these questions, observations on language use, and racial judgments based on an applicant's phenotype, see Applications for Enrollment in the Five Civilized Tribes, 1898–1914, M-1301, RG 75, NARA Fort Worth.

112. Application of Sampson Tubbee, Department of the Interior, Commission to the Five Civilized Tribes, Franks, Mississippi, February 26, 1902, Applications for Enrollment in the Five Civilized Tribes, 1898–1914, M-1301, roll 140, RG 75, NARA Fort Worth.

113. Application of Dick Tubbee, Department of the Interior, Commission to the Five Civilized Tribes, Franks, Mississippi, February 26, 1902, Applications for Enrollment in the Five Civilized Tribes, 1898–1914, M-1301, roll 140, RG 75, NARA Fort Worth.

114. Application of Sampson Tubbee, Department of the Interior, Commission to the Five Civilized Tribes, Franks, Mississippi, February 26, 1902, Applications for Enrollment in the Five Civilized Tribes, 1898–1914, M-1301, roll 140, RG 75, NARA Fort Worth.

115. Application of Tom Stephen, Department of the Interior, Commission to the Five Civilized Tribes, Decatur, Mississippi, May 15, 1901, Applications for Enrollment in the Five Civilized Tribes, 1898–1914, M-1301, roll 112, RG 75, NARA Fort Worth.

116. Department of the Interior, Commissioner to the Five Civilized Tribes, Chickasaw Land Office, Ardmore, Indian Territory, May 20, 1907, In the Matter of the Proof of Continuous Residence within the Choctaw-Chickasaw country for a period of three years of Victoria Lafontain, Applications for Enrollment in the Five Civilized Tribes, 1898–1914, M-1301, roll 111, RG 75, NARA Fort Worth.

117. "Mississippi Choctaw Decisions, Volume 13: June 16, 1904, to November 2, 1904," 110–111, 109: Decisions of the Commission, 1902–1904, RG 75, NARA Fort Worth.

118. US Senate, Committee on Indian Affairs, *Indian Appropriation Bill: Hearing on H.R. 18453, An Act Making Appropriations for the Current and Contingent Expenses of the Bureau of Indian Affairs, for Fulfilling Treaty Stipulations with Various Indian Tribes, and for Other Purposes, for the Fiscal Year Ending June 30, 1918* (64th Cong., 2nd Sess., 1917), 463.

119. P. J. Hurley, *Choctaw Citizenship Litigation: Report of P. J. Hurley, National Attorney for the Choctaw Nation, to Major Victor M. Locke Jr., Principal Chief of the Choctaw Nation* (May 1916), 13–14.

120. Henry S. Halbert was one of the full-blood Choctaws' white allies in Mississippi who encouraged the Indians to send petitions to Congress and to deal with lawyers who were "working for their interests here in Washington." Halbert worked for C. F. Winton, the attorney who had exchanged harsh words with McKennon just a few years before. Although Winton was certainly invested in his own economic interests, he was not simply one of "the parties who have been speculating on their claims without doing anything for them." Instead, he made sure that Choctaw voices were heard in Congress. See

K. S. Murchison to H. S. Halbert, June 17, 1902, File: 159 Halbert, H. S. Letters, 1900–1903, *Papers of Henry Sale Halbert*, M-2343, MDAH, Jackson.

121. US Senate, Committee on Indian Affairs, *Rights of the Mississippi Choctaws in the Choctaw Nation* (57th Cong., 1st Sess., 1902, Doc. No. 319), 3–4.

122. US Senate, Committee on Indian Affairs, *Indian Appropriation Bill: Hearing on H.R. 18453, An Act Making Appropriations for the Current and Contingent Expenses of the Bureau of Indian Affairs, for Fulfilling Treaty Stipulations with Various Indian Tribes, and for Other Purposes, for the Fiscal Year Ending June 30, 1918* (64th Cong., 2nd Sess., 1917), 463; US Supreme Court, *Winton v. Amos*, 255 US 373 (1921).

123. US Senate, Committee on Indian Affairs, *Indian Appropriation Bill: Hearing on H.R. 18453, An Act Making Appropriations for the Current and Contingent Expenses of the Bureau of Indian Affairs, for Fulfilling Treaty Stipulations with Various Indian Tribes, and for Other Purposes, for the Fiscal Year Ending June 30, 1918* (64th Cong., 2nd Sess., 1917), 463.

124. US Congress, "An Act to Ratify and Confirm an Agreement with the Choctaw and Chickasaw Tribes of Indians and for Other Purposes," July 1, 1902 (32 Stats. 641), reprinted in US House of Representatives, Subcommittee of the Committee on Indian Affairs, *Hearings on the Subject of Enrollment in the Five Civilized Tribes, Having under Consideration the Following Bills: 3389, 3390, 6537, 7926, 7974, 8007, 10066, 10140, 12586* (Washington, DC: US Government Printing Office, 1913), 457.

125. US House of Representatives, Subcommittee of the Committee on Indian Affairs, *Hearings on the Subject of Enrollment in the Five Civilized Tribes, Having Under Consideration the Following Bills: 3389, 3390, 6537, 7926, 7974, 8007, 10066, 10140, 12586* (Washington, DC: US Government Printing Office, 1913), 54.

126. "Mississippi Choctaw Decisions, Volume 9: January 2, 1903 to February 19, 1903," 46–48, 109: Decisions of the Commission, 1902–1904, RG 75, NARA Fort Worth.

127. "Mississippi Choctaw Decisions, Volume 1: January 15, 1902, to April 15, 1902," 23–25, 109: Decisions of the Commission, 1902–1904, RG 75, NARA Fort Worth.

128. See "Mississippi Choctaw Decisions, Volume 2, April 15, 1902," 109: Decisions of the Commission, 1902–1904, RG 75, NARA Fort Worth.

129. "Mississippi Choctaw Decisions, Volume 9: January 2, 1903 to February 19, 1903," 130–131, 109: Decisions of the Commission, 1902–1904, RG 75, NARA Fort Worth. For more information on the enrollment of freedmen in the Choctaw Nation, see Jesse T. Schreier, "Indian or Freedman? Enrollment, Race, and Identity in the Choctaw Nation, 1896–1907," *Western Historical Quarterly*, 42: 4 (Winter 2011): 458–479.

130. "Mississippi Choctaw Decisions, Volume 1: January 15, 1902, to April 15, 1902," 916–918, 109: Decisions of the Commission, 1902–1904, RG 75, NARA Fort Worth.

131. "Mississippi Choctaw Decisions, Volume 13: June 16, 1904, to November 2, 1904," 110–111, 113, 109: Decisions of the Commission, 1902–1904, RG 75, NARA Fort Worth.

132. Application of Tom Clemmons, Department of the Interior, Commission to the Five Civilized Tribes, Seale, Mississippi, March 25, 1902, Applications for Enrollment in the Five Civilized Tribes, 1898–1914, M-1301, roll 142, RG 75, NARA Fort Worth.

133. Ralston, Siddons, & Richardson, "In the Matter of Claims of Certain Choctaw Indians Remaining in the States of Mississippi, Louisiana, and Alabama: Brief in Behalf of the Claims of Said Indians to Enrollment as Citizens of the Choctaw Nation and for Their Interest in the Funds and Property in Said Nation" (December 7, 1910), reprinted in *Proposed Legislation for the Full-Blood and Identified Choctaws of Mississippi, Louisiana, and Alabama with Memorial, Evidence, and Brief* (Washington, DC: Judd & Detweiler, Printers, 1913), 28–29, MDAH, Jackson.

134. US Congress, "An Act to Ratify and Confirm an Agreement with the Choctaw and Chickasaw Tribes of Indians and for Other Purposes," July 1, 1902 (32 Stats. 641), reprinted in US House of Representatives, Subcommittee of the Committee on Indian Affairs, *Hearings on the Subject of Enrollment in the Five Civilized Tribes, Having under Consideration the Following Bills: 3389, 3390, 6537, 7926, 7974, 8007, 10066, 10140, 12586* (Washington, DC: US Government Printing Office, 1913), 457.

135. US Senate, Committee on Indian Affairs, *Choctaw Indians of Mississippi* (76th Cong., 3rd Sess., April 22 and 23, 1940), 16.

136. For a thorough discussion of the removal of the identified Mississippi Choctaws in 1903, see Charles Roberts, "The Second Choctaw Removal, 1903," in *After Removal: The Choctaw in Mississippi*, 94–111.

137. US House of Representatives, Subcommittee of the Committee on Indian Affairs, *Hearings on the Subject of Enrollment in the Five Civilized Tribes, Having under Consideration the Following Bills: 3389, 3390, 6537, 7926, 7974, 8007, 10066, 10140, 12586* (Washington, DC: US Government Printing Office, 1913), 61–62.

138. Roberts, "The Second Choctaw Removal, 1903," 99.

139. H. Van V. Smith, Meridian, Mississippi, to John Stockey, Conway, Mississippi, August 4, 1903, "Letters, Special Agent, No. 1," 123, 168: Letters Sent by Special Agent Smith, August–October, 1903, RG 75, NARA Fort Worth.

140. H. Van V. Smith, Meridian, Mississippi, to Commission to the Five Civilized Tribes, Muskogee, Indian Territory, August 12, 1903, "Letters, Special Agent, No. 1," 6, 168: Letters Sent by Special Agent Smith, August–October, 1903, RG 75, NARA Fort Worth.

141. Statement of William E. Richardson, US House of Representatives, Subcommittee of the Committee on Indian Affairs, *Hearings on the Subject of Enrollment in the Five Civilized Tribes, Having under Consideration the Following Bills: 3389, 3390, 6537, 7926, 7974, 8007, 10066, 10140, 12586* (Washington, DC: US Government Printing Office, 1913), 63.

142. H. Van V. Smith, Meridian, Mississippi, to Commission to the Five Civilized Tribes, Muskogee, Indian Territory, August 8, 1903, "Letters, Special Agent, No. 1," 184, 168: Letters Sent by Special Agent Smith, August–October, 1903, RG 75, NARA Fort Worth.

143. H. Van V. Smith, Meridian, Mississippi, to George Thomas, Sanderville, Mississippi, August 7, 1903, "Letters, Special Agent, No. 1," 167, 168: Letters Sent by Special Agent Smith, August–October, 1903, RG 75, NARA Fort Worth.

144. H. Van V. Smith, Meridian, Mississippi, to Emma Pis-ah-ton-tamah, Bayou Lacomb, Louisiana, "Letters, Special Agent, No. 1," 161, 168: Letters Sent by Special Agent Smith, August–October, 1903, RG 75, NARA Fort Worth.

145. H. Van V. Smith, Meridian, Mississippi, to Gill Simpson, Dossville, Mississippi, August 3, 1903, "Letters, Special Agent, No. 1," 80, 168: Letters Sent by Special Agent Smith, August–October, 1903, RG 75, NARA Fort Worth.

146. H. Van V. Smith, Meridian, Mississippi, to John Williams, Baccus, Mississippi, August 6, 1903, "Letters, Special Agent, No. 1," 140, 168: Letters Sent by Special Agent Smith, August–October, 1903, RG 75, NARA Fort Worth.

147. H. Van V. Smith, Meridian, Mississippi, to Jim Wallace, Eady, Mississippi, July 31, 1903, "Letters, Special Agent, No. 1," 66–67, 168: Letters Sent by Special Agent Smith, August–October 903, RG 75, NARA Fort Worth.

148. H. Van V. Smith, Meridian, Mississippi, to Commission to the Five Civilized Tribes, Muskogee, Indian Territory, August 12, 1903, "Letters, Special Agent, No. 1," p. 3–4. 168. Letters Sent by Special Agent Smith, August–October, 1903, ARC ID 2431679, 5-43-1-07-3, RG 75, NARA, Fort Worth.

149. *Proposed Legislation for the Full-Blood and Identified Choctaws of Mississippi, Louisiana, and Alabama with Memorial, Evidence, and Brief* (Washington, DC: Judd & Detweiler, Printers, 1913), 6–7, MDAH, Jackson; William T. Weir, "Brief: Indian Claims Commission of the United States of America: The Mississippi Band of Choctaw Indians, Petititioners, vs. The United States of America, Defendant," (n.d.), 101, MDAH, Jackson.

150. H. Van V. Smith, Meridian, Mississippi, to Commission to the Five Civilized Tribes, Muskogee, Indian Territory, August 12, 1903, "Letters, Special Agent, No. 1," 3–4, 168: Letters Sent by Special Agent Smith, August–October, 1903, RG 75, NARA Fort Worth.

151. US Senate, Committee on Indian Affairs, *Indian Appropriation Bill: Hearings on H.R. 18453, An Act Making Appropriations for the Current and Contingent Expenses of the Bureau of Indian Affairs, for Fulfilling Treaty Stipulations with Various Indian Tribes, and for Other Purposes, for the Fiscal Year Ending June 30, 1918* (64th Cong., 2nd Sess., 1917), 208.

152. H. Van V. Smith, Meridian, Mississippi, to Commission to the Five Civilized Tribes, Muskogee, Indian Territory, August 8, 1903, "Letters, Special Agent, No. 1," 183–184, 168: Letters Sent by Special Agent Smith, August–October, 1903, RG 75, NARA Fort Worth.

153. H. Van V. Smith, Meridian, Mississippi, to Commission to the Five Civilized Tribes, Muskogee, Indian Territory, August 12, 1903, "Letters, Special Agent, No. 1," 3–4, 168: Letters Sent by Special Agent Smith, August–October, 1903, RG 75, NARA Fort Worth.

154. P. J. Hurley, *Choctaw Citizenship Litigation: Report of P. J. Hurley, National Attorney for the Choctaw Nation, to Major Victor M. Locke Jr., Principal Chief of the Choctaw Nation* (May 1916), 21.

155. Winton's estate later sued the Choctaw Nation for compensation for "services rendered" in the removal of these Choctaws. In 1922, the Court of Claims awarded Winton's heirs $175,000 from the tribal funds of the Choctaw Nation as payment. See Kidwell, *The Choctaws in Oklahoma*, 171, 175 and US Senate, *Claim against the Choctaw Nation, Communication from the President of the United States, Transmitting a Copy of a Judgment of the Court of Claims in the Case of Wirt K. Winton, Administrator of Charles T. Winton, Deceased, et al., v. Jack Amos et al. Known as the Mississippi Choctaws Case, in Favor of Robert L. Owen and Associates, Together with a Copy of a Letter from the Assistant Attorney General and a Letter from the Secretary of the Treasury Explaining Status of Tribal Funds of the Choctaw Nation* (67th Cong., 2nd Sess., September 16, 1922, Doc. No. 257), 1.

156. US Senate, Committee on Indian Affairs, *Indian Appropriation Bill: Hearings on H.R. 18453, An Act Making Appropriations for the Current and Contingent Expenses of the Bureau of Indian Affairs, for Fulfilling Treaty Stipulations with Various Indian Tribes, and for Other Purposes, for the Fiscal Year Ending June 30, 1918* (64th Cong., 2nd Sess., 1917), 208.

157. P. J. Hurley, *Choctaw Citizenship Litigation: Report of P. J. Hurley, National Attorney for the Choctaw Nation, to Major Victor M. Locke Jr., Principal Chief of the Choctaw Nation* (May 1916), 21.

158. For a vivid description of what life was like in Indian Territory for the Mississippi Choctaws who removed, see Charles Robert, "A Choctaw Odyssey: The Life of Lesa Phillip Roberts," *American Indian Quarterly*, 14:3 (Summer 1990): 259–276.

159. Velma Sam and Janis Jimmie, "In Memorium: Callie Dixon," *Nanih Waiya*, 1:2 (Winter 1974), 3, J. D. Williams Library.

160. US House of Representatives, "Condition of the Mississippi Choctaws," *Hearing before the Committee on Investigation of the Indian Service*, Union, MS, March 16, 1917, Vol. 2 (Washington, DC: US Government Printing Office, 1917), 138.

161. Enrollment card of Comby Wallace, Card No. 105, Dawes Enrollment Cards for Identified Mississippi Choctaws, M-7RA-173, roll 1, RG 75, NARA Fort Worth.

162. Annuity Rolls for Mississippi Choctaw, 1918–1922, M-38, roll, 2, RG 75, NARA Fort Worth. In 1924, the assistant secretary for the Board of Indian Commissioners noted that around 100 Choctaws in Mississippi had in fact enrolled in the Choctaw Nation and had "property interests in Oklahoma." Many of these individuals had simply abandoned their allotments, but a few had sold them for money. Once the Choctaw Agency was established in Mississippi in 1918, agency superintendents took control of these funds and used them to buy lands and farm equipment for the Indians who remained in Mississippi. In this way, the property was effectively transferred from the Choctaw Nation to the Mississippi Band of Choctaws and the migrants once again became politically associated with the Mississippi Choctaws rather than with the Choctaw Nation. See Earl J. Henderson, Assistant Secretary, Board of Indian Commissioners, to Clement S. Ucker, June 28, 1924, 8, File: 47964, Choctaw, 130, Box 85, Central Classified Files, 1907–1939, RG 75, National Archives and Records Administration, Washington, DC (hereafter NARA Washington).

163. US House of Representatives, Subcommittee of the Committee on Indian Affairs, *Hearings on the Subject of Enrollment in the Five Civilized Tribes, Having under Consideration the Following Bills: 3389, 3390, 6537, 7926, 7974, 8007, 10066, 10140, 12586* (Washington, DC: US Government Printing Office, 1913), 55, 134.

164. T. A. Walters, Acting Secretary of the Interior, to Elmer Thomas, Chairman of the Senate Committee on Indian Affairs, April 4, 1935, US Senate, Committee on Indian Affairs, *Claims of Choctaw Indians of Mississippi* (74th Cong., 1st Sess., 1935, Report No. 781), 4.

165. Mississippi, Alabama, and Louisiana Choctaw Council, *The Mississippi Choctaw Claim* (Washington, DC: Judd & Detweiler, 1914), 2–3.

166. US House of Representatives, Subcommittee of the Committee on Indian Affairs, *Hearings on the Subject of Enrollment in the Five Civilized Tribes, Having under Consideration the Following Bills: 3389, 3390, 6537, 7926, 7974, 8007, 10066, 10140, 12586* (Washington, DC: US Government Printing Office, 1913), 11.

167. P. J. Hurley, *Choctaw Citizenship Litigation: Report of P.J. Hurley, National Attorney for the Choctaw Nation, to Major Victor M. Locke Jr., Principal Chief of the Choctaw Nation*, May, 1916, p. 4.

168. "To Save Indians from Grafters: Sen. Gore Checks Lawyers Who Are after Loot," *Atlanta Constitution* (June 26, 1910): 10.

169. "Rich Heritage for Choctaws: And Chickasaw Tribes of Mississippi," *Atlanta Constitution* (August 28, 1910): 2; see also "Report of Inspector James M'Laughlin in Re Attorneys' Contracts with Mississippi Choctaws, Washington, DC, June 29, 1914," reprinted in US Senate, Committee on Indian Affairs, *Indian Appropriation Bill: Hearings on H.R. 18453, An Act Making Appropriations for the Current and Contingent Expenses of the Bureau of Indian Affairs, for Fulfilling Treaty Stipulations with Various Indian Tribes, and for Other Purposes, for the Fiscal Year Ending June 30, 1918* (64th Cong., 2nd Sess., 1917), 365.

170. "Statement of Harry J. Cantwell, of Crews & Cantwell, Attorneys for the Mississippi Choctaw Claimants, to the Committee on Indian Affairs" (62nd Cong., 2nd Sess., 1912), 12, MDAH, Jackson.

171. US House of Representatives, *Additional Land and Indian Schools in Mississippi: Letter from the Secretary of the Interior, Transmitting Report of John T. Reeves, Special Supervisor, Indian Service, on Need of Additional Land School Facilities for the Indians Living in the State of Mississippi* (64th Cong., 2nd Sess., December 7, 1916, Doc. No. 1464), 26–28, MDAH, Jackson.

172. US House of Representatives, Subcommittee of the Committee on Indian Affairs, *Bill for Enrollment with the Five Civilized Tribes* (63rd Cong., 2nd Sess., July 2, 1914), reprinted in P. J. Hurley, *Choctaw Citizenship Litigation: Report of P. J. Hurley, National Attorney for the Choctaw Nation, to Major Victor M. Locke Jr., Principal Chief of the Choctaw Nation* (May 1916), 428.

173. For a discussion of Pat Harrison's involvement with the Choctaw citizenship rolls, see William Sidney Coker, "Pat Harrison's Efforts to Reopen the Choctaw Citizenship Rolls," *Southern Quarterly*, 3:1 (1965): 36–61.

174. US House of Representatives, Subcommittee of the Committee on Indian Affairs, *Hearings on the Subject of Enrollment in the Five Civilized Tribes, Having under Consideration the Following Bills: 3389, 3390, 6537, 7926, 7974, 8007, 10066, 10140, 12586* (Washington, DC: US Government Printing Office, 1913), 103.

175. US Senate, Committee on Indian Affairs, *Choctaw Indians of Mississippi* (76th Cong., 3rd Sess., April 22 and 23, 1940), 5.

176. US House of Representatives, Subcommittee of the Committee on Indian Affairs, *Hearings on the Subject of Enrollment in the Five Civilized Tribes, Having under Consideration the Following Bills: 3389, 3390, 6537, 7926, 7974, 8007, 10066, 10140, 12586* (Washington, DC: US Government Printing Office, 1913), 140.

177. *Proposed Legislation for the Full-Blood and Identified Choctaws of Mississippi, Louisiana, and Alabama with Memorial, Evidence, and Brief* (Washington, DC: Judd & Detweiler, Printers, 1913), 8–9, 13–14, MDAH, Jackson.

178. US Senate, Committee on Indian Affairs, *Claims of Choctaw Indians of Mississippi* (75th Cong., 1st Sess., 1937, Report No. 997), 2.

179. *Proposed Legislation for the Full-Blood and Identified Choctaws of Mississippi, Louisiana, and Alabama with Memorial, Evidence, and Brief* (Washington, DC: Judd & Detweiler, Printers, 1913), 6, 9–10, MDAH, Jackson.

180. US House of Representatives, Subcommittee of the Committee on Indian Affairs, *Hearings on the Subject of Enrollment in the Five Civilized Tribes, Having under Consideration the Following Bills: 3389, 3390, 6537, 7926, 7974, 8007, 10066, 10140, 12586* (Washington, DC: US Government Printing Office, 1913), 119.

181. J. D. Rogers, Sheriff, Newton County, W. W. Coursey, County Superintendent of Education, J. T. McCune, County Assessor, L. M. Adams, Treasurer, Eugene Carleton, Deputy Chancery Clerk, and T. T. Wells, Decatur, MS, to J. E. Arnold, Washington, DC, March 13, 1914, reprinted in US House of Representatives, Subcommittee of the Committee on Indian Affairs, *Hearings on the Subject of Enrollment in the Five Civilized Tribes, Having under Consideration the Following Bills: 3389, 3390, 6537, 7926, 7974, 8007, 10066, 10140, 12586* (Washington, DC: US Government Printing Office, 1913), 84.

182. Z. C. Hagan, Union, Mississippi, to Congress and Senate of the United States of America, Washington, DC, March 14, 1914, reprinted in US House of Representatives, Subcommittee of the Committee on Indian Affairs, *Hearings on the Subject of Enrollment in the Five Civilized Tribes, Having under Consideration the Following Bills: 3389, 3390, 6537, 7926, 7974, 8007, 10066, 10140, 12586* (Washington, DC: US Government Printing Office, 1913), 84.

183. US House of Representatives, Subcommittee of the Committee on Indian Affairs, *Hearings on the Subject of Enrollment in the Five Civilized Tribes, Having under Consideration the Following Bills: 3389, 3390, 6537, 7926, 7974, 8007, 10066, 10140, 12586* (Washington, DC: US Government Printing Office, 1913), 139–140.

184. US House of Representatives, Subcommittee of the Committee on Indian Affairs, *Hearings on the Subject of Enrollment in the Five Civilized Tribes*, 139–140.

185. Johnson, Wesley, Culbertson Davis, and Emil John (Ahojeobe), *The Mississippi Choctaw Claim* (Washington, DC: Judd & Detweiler, Printers, 1914), 2–3, 11–12, MDAH, Jackson.

186. Johnson, Davis, and John, *The Mississippi Choctaw Claim*, 9.

187. US Senate, Committee on Indian Affairs, *Indian Appropriation Bill: Hearings on H.R. 18453, An Act Making Appropriations for the Current and Contingent Expense of the Bureau of Indian Affairs, for Fulfilling Treaty Stipulations with Various Indian Tribes, and for Other Purposes, for the Fiscal Year Ending June 30, 1918* (64th Cong., 2nd Sess., 1917), 363.

188. US House of Representatives, Subcommittee of the Committee on Indian Affairs, *Hearings on the Subject of Enrollment in the Five Civilized Tribes, Having under Consideration the Following Bills: 3389, 3390, 6537, 7926, 7974, 8007, 10066, 10140, 12586* (Washington, DC: US Government Printing Office, 1913), 380–381.

189. US House of Representatives, Subcommittee of the Committee on Indian Affairs, *Bill for Enrollment with the Five Civilized Tribes*, (63rd Cong., 2nd Sess., July, 2, 1914), reprinted in P. J. Hurley, *Choctaw Citizenship Litigation: Report of P. J. Hurley, National Attorney for the Choctaw Nation, to Major Victor M. Locke Jr., Principal Chief of the Choctaw Nation* (May 1916), 428.

190. *Memorial of the Choctaw and Chickasaw Nations relative to the Rights of the Mississippi Choctaws, Submitted for Consideration in Connection with H.R. 19213* (Washington, DC: US Government Printing Office, 1913), reprinted in P. J. Hurley, *Choctaw Citizenship Litigation: Report of P. J. Hurley, National Attorney for the Choctaw Nation, to Major Victor M. Locke Jr., Principal Chief of the Choctaw Nation* (May 1916), 26–27.

191. P. J. Hurley, *Choctaw Citizenship Litigation: Report of P. J. Hurley, National Attorney for the Choctaw Nation, to Major Victor M. Locke Jr., Principal Chief of the Choctaw Nation* (May 1916), 21.

192. "Report of Inspector James M'Laughlin in Re Attorneys' Contracts with Mississippi Choctaws, Washington, DC, June 29, 1914," reprinted in US Senate, Committee on Indian Affairs, *Indian Appropriation Bill: Hearings on H.R. 18453, An Act Making Appropriations for the Current and Contingent Expenses of the Bureau of Indian Affairs, for Fulfilling Treaty Stipulations with Various Indian Tribes, and for Other Purposes, for the Fiscal Year Ending June 30, 1918* (64th Cong., 2nd Sess., 1917), 365; US House of Representatives, Subcommittee of the Committee on Indian Affairs, *Bills for Enrollment with the Five Civilized Tribes* (63rd Cong., 2nd Sess., July 2, 1914), reprinted in P. J. Hurley,

Choctaw Citizenship Litigation: Report of P. J. Hurley, National Attorney for the Choctaw Nation, to Major Victor M. Locke Jr., Principal Chief of the Choctaw Nation (May 1916), 6.

193. "Report of Inspector James M'Laughlin in Re Attorneys' Contracts with Mississippi Choctaws, Washington, DC, June 29, 1914," reprinted in US Senate, Committee on Indian Affairs, *Indian Appropriation Bill: Hearings on H.R. 18453, An Act Making Appropriations for the Current and Contingent Expenses of the Bureau of Indian Affairs, for Fulfilling Treaty Stipulations with Various Indian Tribes, and for Other Purposes, for the Fiscal Year Ending June 30, 1918* (64th Cong., 2nd Sess., 1917), 366–367.

194. US House of Representatives, Subcommittee of the Committee on Indian Affairs, *Argument of P. J. Hurley against the Enrollment of the So-Called Mississippi Choctaws* (63rd Cong., 2nd Sess., August 11, 1914), reprinted in P. J. Hurley, *Choctaw Citizenship Litigation: Report of P. J. Hurley, National Attorney for the Choctaw Nation, to Major Victor M. Locke Jr., Principal Chief of the Choctaw Nation* (May 1916), 132.

195. "Report of Inspector James M'Laughlin in Re Attorneys' Contracts with Mississippi Choctaws, Washington, DC, June 29, 1914," reprinted in US Senate, Committee on Indian Affairs, *Indian Appropriation Bill: Hearings on H.R. 18453, An Act Making Appropriations for the Current and Contingent Expenses of the Bureau of Indian Affairs, for Fulfilling Treaty Stipulations with Various Indian Tribes, and for Other Purposes, for the Fiscal Year Ending June 30, 1918* (64th Cong., 2nd Sess., 1917), 367.

196. US House of Representatives, Subcommittee of the Committee on Indian Affairs, *Argument of P. J. Hurley against the Enrollment of the So-Called Mississippi Choctaws*, 63rd Congress, 2nd Session (August 11, 1914), reprinted in P. J. Hurley, *Choctaw Citizenship Litigation: Report of P. J. Hurley, National Attorney for the Choctaw Nation, to Major Victor M. Locke Jr., Principal Chief of the Choctaw Nation,* (May 1916), 17.

197. US House of Representatives, Subcommittee of the Committee on Indian Affairs, *Bills for Enrollment with the Five Civilized Tribes,* (63rd Cong., 2nd Sess., July 2, 1914), reprinted in P. J. Hurley, *Choctaw Citizenship Litigation: Report of P. J. Hurley, National Attorney for the Choctaw Nation, to Major Victor M. Locke Jr., Principal Chief of the Choctaw Nation* (May 1916), 6; see also Coker, "Pat Harrison's Efforts to Reopen the Choctaw Citizenship Rolls," 47.

198. "Mississippi Shut Out: Choctaws of That State Are Barred from Tribal Fund," *Washington Post* (July 9, 1914): 13.

199. Coker, "Pat Harrison's Efforts to Reopen the Choctaw Citizenship Rolls," 50.

200. US Congress, House, Subcommittee of the Committee on Indian Affairs, *Report to Reopen the Rolls of the Choctaw-Chickasaw Tribes* (63rd Cong., 3rd Sess., 1915), quoted in Coker, "Pat Harrison's Efforts to Reopen the Choctaw Citizenship Rolls," 54. Evidently, Harrison was disappointed with this decision. According to a newspaper article, when the bill failed to pass, "He shook his fist in the faces of the members of the Oklahoma delegation, and shouted: 'The blackest pages in the history of your State is the way you have treated the Indians.'" See "Mississippi Shut Out," 13.

201. *Memorial of the Choctaw and Chickasaw Nations relative to the Rights of the Mississippi Choctaws, Submitted for Consideration in Connection with H.R. 19213* (Washington, DC: US Government Printing Office, 1913), reprinted in P. J. Hurley, *Choctaw Citizenship Litigation: Report of P. J. Hurley, National Attorney for the Choctaw Nation, to Major Victor M. Locke Jr., Principal Chief of the Choctaw Nation* (May 1916), 26–27.

202. US Senate, Committee on Indian Affairs, *Indian Appropriation Bill: Hearings on H.R. 18453, An Act Making Appropriations for the Current and Contingent Expenses of the Bureau of Indian Affairs, for Fulfilling Treaty Stipulations with Various Indian Tribes, and for Other Purposes, for the Fiscal Year Ending June 30, 1918* (64th Cong., 2nd Sess., 1917), 73; US House of Representatives, *Additional Land and Indian Schools in Mississippi: Letter from the Secretary of the Interior, Transmitting Report of John T. Reeves, Special Supervisor, Indian Service, on Need of Additional Land School Facilities for the Indians Living in the State of Mississippi* (64th Cong., 2nd Sess., December 7, 1916, Doc. No. 1464), MDAH, Jackson.

203. US House of Representatives, "Condition of the Mississippi Choctaws," *Hearing before the Committee on Investigation of the Indian Service,* Union, MS, March 16, 1917, Vol. 2 (Washington, DC: US Government Printing Office, 1917), 172–178.

204. US House of Representatives, "Condition of the Mississippi Choctaws," 163, 156, 124.
205. Katherine M. B. Osburn, "The 'Identified Full-Bloods' in Mississippi: Race and Choctaw Identity, 1898–1918," *Ethnohistory*, 56:3 (Summer 2009): 423.
206. US House of Representatives, "Condition of the Mississippi Choctaws," *Hearing before the Committee on Investigation of the Indian Service*, Union, MS, March 16, 1917, Vol. 2 (Washington, DC: US Government Printing Office, 1917), 118, 125.
207. US Senate, Committee on Indian Affairs, *Indian Appropriation Bill: Hearing on H.R. 18453, An Act Making Appropriation for the Current and Contingent Expenses of the Bureau of Indian Affairs, for Fulfilling Treaty Stipulations with Various Indian Tribes, and for Other Purposes, for the Fiscal Year Ending June 30, 1918* (64th Cong., 2nd Sess., 1917, H.R. 18453), 362–363.
208. US House of Representatives, "Condition of the Mississippi Choctaws," *Hearing before the Committee on Investigation of the Indian Service*, Union, MS, March 16, 1917, Vol. 2 (Washington, DC: US Government Printing Office, 1917), 162, 147.
209. US House of Representatives, *Additional Land and Indian Schools in Mississippi: Letter from the Secretary of the Interior, Transmitting Report of John T. Reeves, Special Supervisor, Indian Service, on Need of Additional Land School Facilities for the Indians Living in the State of Mississippi* (64th Cong., 2nd Sess., December 7, 1916, Doc. No. 1464), 24, MDAH, Jackson. A typical Choctaw day laborer made just 50 cents a day for his work. See US House of Representatives, "Condition of the Mississippi Choctaws," *Hearing before the Committee on Investigation of the Indian Service*, Union, MS, March 16, 1917, Vol. 2 (Washington, DC: US Government Printing Office, 1917), 135–136.
210. US House of Representatives, "Condition of the Mississippi Choctaws," *Hearing before the Committee on Investigation of the Indian Service*, Union, MS, March 16, 1917, Vol. 2 (Washington, DC: US Government Printing Office, 1917), 144, 118, 158–159, 128.
211. US Senate, Committee on Indian Affairs, *Indian Appropriation Bill: Hearing on H.R. 18453, An Act Making Appropriation for the Current and Contingent Expenses of the Bureau of Indian Affairs, for Fulfilling Treaty Stipulations with Various Indian Tribes, and for Other Purposes, for the Fiscal Year Ending June 30, 1918* (64th Cong., 2nd Sess., 1917, H.R. 18453), 452, 429, 470.
212. Cato Sells, Commissioner of Indian Affairs, to Robert H. Marr, January 30, 1918, File: 8953-18, Choctaw, 050, Box 12, Central Classified Files, 1907–1939, Choctaw, RG 75, NARA Washington.
213. US House of Representatives, Committee on Appropriations, *Indian Appropriation Bill: Hearings before a Subcommittee of the Committee on Indian Affairs* (65th Cong., 1918), p. 175.
214. Interview of Simpson Tubby by Commissioner McKennon, Philadelphia, Neshoba County, Miss., January 30, 1899, "Applications for Identification as Mississippi Choctaws," *Records of Proceedings, Commission to the Five Civilized Tribes Identifying Mississippi Choctaws, Sessions at Carthage, Philadelphia, and Decatur, State of Mississippi, January 24 to February 10, 1899, inclusive*, 109, 105: Index and Records of Testimony, 1899, P2219: Records Relating to the Identification of Mississippi Choctaws, 1899–1904, M-7RA-116, roll 1, RG 75, NARA Fort Worth; Indian Census Rolls, 1885–1940, M-595, roll 41, Choctaw (Mississippi), 1926-32, RG 75, NARA Fort Worth.
215. Choctaw (Mississippi), 1927 Narrative Report, Superintendent's Annual Reports, 1920–1935, Choctaw Agency, M-1011, roll 20, RG 75, NARA Washington.
216. Choctaw (Mississippi), 1929 Narrative Report, 15-16, 8, Superintendent's Annual Reports, 1920–1935, Choctaw Agency, M-1011, roll 20, RG 75, NARA Washington. The Choctaw Agency farmer, T. J. Scott, was an active member of the Ku Klux Klan. According to historian Katherine M. B. Osburn, "Scott's long-standing good relationship with the Choctaws may have deflected Klan violence." He encouraged the Choctaws to protect themselves from "accusations of race mixing" by emphasizing their "pure Indian blood." See Katherine M. B. Osburn, *Choctaw Resurgence in Mississippi: Race, Class, and Nation Building in the Jim Crow South, 1830–1977* (Lincoln: University of Nebraska Press, 2014), 90–91.
217. US House of Representatives, *Additional Land and Indian Schools in Mississippi: Letter from the Secretary of the Interior, Transmitting Report of John T. Reeves, Special Supervisor, Indian Service, on Need of Additional Land School Facilities for the Indians Living in the State*

of Mississippi (64th Cong., 2nd Sess., December 7, 1916, Doc. No. 1464), 14, 24, MDAH, Jackson; Indian Census Rolls, 1885–1940, M-595, roll 41, Choctaw (Mississippi), 1926–32, RG 75, NARA Fort Worth.

218. Peterson, *The Mississippi Band of Choctaw Indians*, 155, 162–163; Coe, "More Agency than They Bargained For and Less Land," 3.

219. Joe Jennings, Superintendent of Indian Schools, Eastern Area, Vernon L. Beggs, Supervisor Indian Education, and A. B. Caldwell, Supt. of Ind. Ed, Lake States Area, "A Study of the Social and Economic Condition of the Choctaw Indians in Mississippi in Relation to the Educational Programs, May 1945," 6, File: 38014-37, Choctaw, 806, Box 482, Central Classified Files, 1907–1939, Choctaw, RG 75, NARA Washington.

220. Memorandum to John Collier, Commissioner of Indian Affairs, by Charlotte T. Westwood, Assistant Solicitor, and Joe Jennings, Indian Organization, September 21, 1936, 1, File: 54948-33, Choctaw, 150, Box 87, Central Classified Files, 1907–1939, Choctaw, RG 75, NARA Washington.

221. For more information about the Mississippi Choctaw's effort to reorganize under the terms of the IRA, see Osburn, *Choctaw Resurgence in Mississippi*, 102–130.

222. Indian Census Rolls, 1885–1940, M-595, roll 42, Choctaw (Mississippi), 1933–1939, RG 75, NARA Fort Worth.

223. Constitution and By-Laws of the Mississippi Band of Choctaw Indians, Ratified April 20, 1945 (Washington, DC: US Government Printing Office, 1946), 1, Archives and Special Collections, J. D. Williams Library.

224. US Senate, Committee on Indian Affairs, *Recognition of Mowa Band of Choctaw Indians; Aroostook Band of Mimacs Settlement Act; Ponca Restoration Act; and Jena Band of Choctaw Recognition Act* (101st Cong., 2nd Sess., 1990, S. HRG. 101–762), 45; US Department of the Interior, Bureau of Indian Affairs, "Indian Tribes, Acknowledgment of Existence Determinations for the Jena Band of Choctaw Indians and the Huron Potawatomi, Inc.; Notices," *Federal Register*, 60: 104 (May 31, 1995): 28480-28481. For more information on the Jena Band of Choctaw's effort to gain federal recognition, see Kiopotek, *Recognition Odysseys*.

225. Revised Constitution and Bylaws of the Mississippi Band of Choctaw Indians, 1969, File: 5592-65, Choctaw, 054.3, Box 4, Central Classified Files, 1958–1975, Choctaw, RG 75, NARA Washington; Mississippi Band of Choctaw Indians, "Revised Constitution and Bylaws of the Mississippi Band of Choctaw Indians," reprinted in "Appendix 2" of *Tribal Government: A New Era*, edited by William Brescia (Philadelphia, MS: Choctaw Heritage Press, 1982), x, MDAH, Jackson.

226. Mississippi Band of Choctaw Indians, "Welcome from the Tribal Chief of the Mississippi Band of Choctaw Indians," http://www.choctaw.org/, accessed February 5, 2014.

227. Mississippi Band of Choctaw Indians, "Article II: Membership," *Tribal Constitution*, http://www.choctaw.org/government/court/constitution.html, accessed May 8, 2013.

228. Mississippi Band of Choctaw Indians, "Enrollment," http://www.choctaw.org/government/tribalServices/members/enrollment.html, accessed May 8, 2013.

229. Choctaw Self-Determination: Tribal Profile (Brochure), The Mississippi Band of Choctaw Indians, 2008-37, File 10, Mississippi Band of Choctaw Indians Small Manuscripts Collection, Archives and Special Collections, J. D. Williams Library.

230. *Memorial of the Choctaw and Chickasaw Nations relative to the Rights of the Mississippi Choctaws, Submitted for Consideration in Connection with H.R. 19213* (Washington, DC: US Government Printing Office, 1913), reprinted in P. J. Hurley, *Choctaw Citizenship Litigation: Report of P.J. Hurley, National Attorney for the Choctaw Nation, to Major Victor M. Locke Jr., Principal Chief of the Choctaw Nation* (May 1916), 22.

Chapter 4

1. The 1928 Baker Roll and Records of the Eastern Cherokee Enrolling Commission, 1924-1929, M-2104, roll 2, Record Group 75: Records of the Bureau of Indian Affairs (hereafter RG 75), National Archives and Records Administration, Washington, DC (hereafter NARA Washington).

2. Theda Perdue and Michael D. Green, *The Cherokee Nation and the Trail of Tears* (New York: Penguin Group, 2007), 134.

3. Sharon Flanagan, "The Georgia Cherokees Who Remained: Race, Status, and Property in the Chattahoochee Community," *Georgia Historical Quarterly* 73 (Fall 1989): 586, 605–606.

4. Betty J. Duggan, "Voices from the Periphery: Reconstructing and Interpreting Post Removal Histories of the Duck Town Cherokees," in *Southern Indians and Anthropologists: Culture, Politics, and Identity*, edited by Lisa J. Lefler and Frederic Wright Gleach (Athens: University of Georgia Press, 2002), 45, 55.

5. *Report of Commissioner John D. Lang, Annual Report of the Commissioner of Indian* Affairs (42nd Cong. 2nd sess., December 6, 1871, House doc. 1/ 11), 580–581; John R. Finger, *The Eastern Band of Cherokees, 1819–1900* (Knoxville: University of Tennessee Press, 1984), 114–117.

6. Finger, *The Eastern Band of Cherokees*, 10–11.

7. US House of Representatives, Subcommittee of the Committee on Indian Affairs, *Hearings on the Subject of Enrollment in the Five Civilized Tribes, Having under Consideration the Following Bills: 3389, 3390, 6537, 7926, 7974, 8007, 10066, 10140, 12586* (Washington, DC: US Government Printing Office, 1913), 18–19.

8. See *Eastern Band of Cherokee Indians v. United States and Cherokee Nation*, 117 U.S. 288 (1886), discussed in William T. Hagan, "Full Blood, Mixed Blood, Generic, and Ersatz: The Problem of Indian Identity," *Arizona and the West*, 27:4 (Winter 1985): 312.

9. Finger, *The Eastern Band of Cherokees*, 10–11.

10. Finger, *The Eastern Band of* Cherokees, 13–17. For more information on William Holland Thomas, see Mattie U. Russell and E. Stanley Godbold Jr., *Confederate Colonel and Cherokee Chief: The Life of William Holland Thomas* (Knoxville: University of Tennessee Press, 1990).

11. DeWitt Harris to Commissioner of Indian Affairs, June 24, 1907, Letters of DeWitt Harris, 1-2-07 to 4-13-08, Cherokee Indian Agency, Series 1, General Record Correspondence, Superintendents Letterbooks, Box 5, RG 75, National Archives and Records Administration, Atlanta, Georgia (hereafter NARA Atlanta); Finger, *The Eastern Band of Cherokees*, 120.

12. W. C. McCarthy to Commissioner of Indian Affairs, February 12, 1876, Letters Received by the Office of Indian Affairs, 1824–81, Cherokee Agency, 1836–1880, 1876–1877, M-234, roll 110, RG 75, NARA Washington.

13. B. C. H., "Carolina East Cherokees," *Friends' Review: A Religious, Literary, and Miscellaneous Journal*, 36 (September 2, 1882): 51.

14. Neely, *Snowbird Cherokees: People of Persistence* (Athens: University of Georgia Press, 1991), 26.

15. In a 1962 article, an Eastern Band citizen and veteran employee of the Bureau of Indian Affairs, Frell M. Owl, discussed the origins and meaning of the term "White Indian" among the Cherokees: "The expression 'White Indian' originated among full-bloods. 'White Indian' identifies a tribal member whose physical characteristics are predominantly those of the Whites. Skin is white, eyes are not brown, hair is light colored, speech is English, dress, customs and mannerisms follow the pattern of typical non-Indians. Though White in physical characteristics, the 'White Indian' qualifies as a tribal member. He has identical tribal rights with the full-blood. Full-bloods also apply the expression 'White Indian' to a member of their tribe who has adopted the culture of non-Indians and who has lost typical characteristics of a reservation Indian. A full-blood is not immune to being identified as a 'White Indian.'" From this description, we see that for the Cherokees, the term "white Indian" had both racial and cultural connotations. Although these individuals claimed tribal citizenship—and some ultimately gained it—members of the core Cherokee community doubted their legitimacy as Cherokees. See Frell M. Owl, "Who and What Is an American Indian?" *Ethnohistory*, 9:3 (Summer 1962): 282–283.

16. Testimony of James Blythe, 1913, File Part 20, Exhibit 29, Records of the Bureau of Indian Affairs, Land Division, Correspondence, Reports, and Related Records Concerning Eastern Cherokee Enrollments, 1907–16, Box 5, RG 75, NARA Washington.

17. Finger, *The Eastern Band of Cherokees*, 143.
18. Robert L. Leatherwood, US Indian Agent, to Commissioner of Indian Affairs, February 6, 1889, File 34157-08-053, Records of the Bureau of Indian Affairs, Land Division, Correspondence, Reports, and Related Records Concerning Eastern Cherokee Enrollments, 1907-16, Box 1, RG 75, NARA Washington.
19. Laurence Armand French, *The Qualla Cherokee: Surviving in Two Worlds* (Lewiston, NY: Edwin Mellen Press, 1998), 86.
20. Finger, *The Eastern Band of Cherokees*, 105.
21. Finger, *The Eastern Band of* Cherokees, 125–126, 135.
22. Superintendent to Office of Indian Affairs, September 5, 1944, File 497.3 G41, John Douglas Gillespie, Miscellaneous papers: Cherokee, North Carolina, American Philosophical Society, Philadelphia, Pennsylvania (hereafter APS Philadelphia).
23. Paul Stuart, *The Indian Office: Growth and Development of an American Institution, 1865–1900* (Ph.D. Dissertation, University of Wisconsin, 1978), 40. This act marked the beginning of a process by which the Indian Office abolished the positions of all Indian agents, devolving their duties to reservation school superintendents.
24. Testimony of James E. Henderson, 1913, File Part 20, Exhibit 29, Records of the Bureau of Indian Affairs, Land Division, Correspondence, Reports, and Related Records Concerning Eastern Cherokee Enrollments, 1907–16, Box 5, RG 75, NARA Washington.
25. Neely, *Snowbird Cherokees*, 29.
26. Finger, *The Eastern Band of Cherokees*, 169–170.
27. Henry Spray, Superintendent, Cherokee Agency, NC, to W. R. Maney, Democrat, NC, February 25, 1901, Letters of Supt. Henry Spray, 7-17-99 to 3-5-01, Bureau of Indian Affairs, Cherokee Indian Agency, General Record Correspondence, Superintendents Letterbooks, 1892–1914, Box 3, RG 75, NARA Atlanta.
28. Acting Commissioner to J. L. McLeymore, Murphy, NC, December 20, 1906, File 251, 1906–1941, Bureau of Indian Affairs, Cherokee Indian Agency, Series 6, General Records Correspondence, Indian Field Service Filing System, 1926–1952, Box 64, RG 75, NARA Atlanta.
29. Thomas W. Potter, Superintendent, Cherokee Agency, NC, to the Commissioner of Indian Affairs, June 5, 1895, Letters of Supt. Potter, 10-29-94 to 6-8-95, Bureau of Indian Affairs, Cherokee Indian Agency, Series 1, General Record Correspondence, Superintendents Letterbooks, 1892–1914, Box 2, RG 75, NARA Atlanta.
30. Superintendent Frank Kyselka, Cherokee Agency, NC, to Commissioner of Indian Affairs, October 25, 1909, Letters of Supt. Frank Kyselka, 7-13-09 to 2-18-10, Bureau of Indian Affairs, Cherokee Indian Agency, Series 1, General Record Correspondence, Superintendents Letterbooks, 1892–1914, Box 6, RG 75, NARA Atlanta.
31. John Finger lists the number as 1,479 in *Cherokee Americans: The Eastern Band of Cherokees in the Twentieth Century* (Lincoln: University of Nebraska Press, 1991), 22. The introduction of the Council Roll housed at the National Archives and Records Administration, Washington, DC, however, gives the number as "fifteen hundred twenty eight (1528) inclusive, except No. 1305 on page 38, Samuel Smith, and Mark Wolfe and Mary Emeline entered on page 43 following No. 1465 but not numbered, about which these names this Council is not entirely satisfied that they are proper names from enrollment as members of this Band of Indians." See Census Roll, 1907, Harris, Blythe, & French, Council Roll of Eastern Band of Cherokee Indians, RG 75, NARA Washington.
32. Census Roll, 1907, Harris, Blythe, & French, Council Roll of Eastern Band of Cherokee Indians, RG 75, NARA Washington.
33. DeWitt Harris, Superintendent, Cherokee Agency, NC, to Commissioner of Indian Affairs, September 27, 1907, Letters of DeWitt Harris, 1-2-07 to 4-13-08, Bureau of Indian Affairs, Cherokee Indian Agency, Series 1, General Record Correspondence, Superintendent Letterbooks, 1892–1914, Box 5, RG 75, NARA Atlanta. Churchill began his work on October 24, 1907, at Cherokee, NC, and continued until May 6, 1908.
34. Frank C. Churchill, Report of Census, 1908, Census Roll of Eastern Band of Cherokee Indians, RG 75, NARA Washington.
35. Frank C. Churchill, Report of Census, 1908.

36. Theda Perdue, *"Mixed Blood" Indians: Racial Construction in the Early South* (Athens: University of Georgia Press, 2003).

37. Cherokee Council Grounds, October 9, 1886, Microfilm Z.1.3N: Eastern Band of Cherokees, Council Records, 1902–1907, 1905–1909, 1886–1897, 1899, 1899–1902, North Carolina State Archives, Raleigh, North Carolina (hereafter M-Z.1.3N).

38. Superintendent Frank Kyselka, Cherokee Agency, NC, to Commissioner of Indian Affairs, July 9, 1909, Letters of Supt. Frank Kyselka, 6-3-09 to 10-13-09, Bureau of Indian Affairs, Cherokee Indian Agency, Series 1, General Record Correspondence, Superintendents Letterbooks, 1892–1914, Box 6, RG 75, NARA Atlanta.

39. Testimony of Joseph Saunooke, August 28, 1928, Miscellaneous Testimony in Enrollment Cases, Volume 5, the 1928 Baker Roll and Records of the Eastern Cherokee Enrolling Commission, 1924–1929, M-2104, roll 6, RG 75, NARA Washington.

40. Joseph W. Howell, 1910, File Part 14, Exhibit 23, Records of the Bureau of Indian Affairs, Land Division, Correspondence, Reports and Related Records Concerning Eastern Cherokee Enrollments, 1907–16, Box 4, RG 75, NARA Washington.

41. Cherokee Council Grounds, November 9, 1915, Microfilm Z.1.4: Miscellaneous Records, Eastern Band of Cherokees, 1908–1931, North Carolina State Archives, Raleigh, North Carolina (hereafter M-Z.1.4).

42. Testimony of James Blythe, 1913, File Part 18, Exhibit 27, Records of the Bureau of Indian Affairs, Land Division, Correspondence, Reports, and Related Records Concerning Eastern Cherokee Enrollments, 1907–16, Box 5, RG 75, NARA Washington.

43. Mashburn-Timpson Testimony, 1913, File Part 17, Exhibit 26, Records of the Bureau of Indian Affairs, Land Division, Correspondence, Reports, and Related Records Concerning Eastern Cherokee Enrollments, 1907–16, Box 5, RG 75, NARA Washington.

44. Superintendent, Cherokee Agency, NC, to Commissioner of Indian Affairs, March 24, 1931, File 004 (1), Bureau of Indian Affairs, Cherokee Indian Agency, Series 6, General Records Correspondence, Indian Field Service Filing System, 1926–1952, Box 8, RG 75, NARA Atlanta.

45. Thomas W. Potter, Superintendent, Cherokee Agency, NC, to H. B. Frissel, Hampton, VA, February 5, 1895, Letters of Supt. Potter, 10-29-94 to 6-8-95, Bureau of Indian Affairs, Cherokee Indian Agency, Series 1, General Record Correspondence, Superintendents Letterbooks, 1892–1914, Box 2, RG 75, NARA Atlanta.

46. Superintendent Frank Kyselka, Cherokee Agency, NC, to Guion Miller, Special Commissioner of the Court of Claims, October 6, 1909, Letters of Supt. Frank Kyselka, 7-13-09 to 2-18-10, Bureau of Indian Affairs, Cherokee Indian Agency, Series 1, General Record Correspondence, Superintendents Letterbooks, 1892–1914, Box 6, RG 75, NARA Atlanta.

47. File Part 18, Exhibit 27, 1913, Records of the Bureau of Indian Affairs, Land Division, Correspondence, Reports, and Related Records Concerning Eastern Cherokee Enrollments, 1907–16, Box 5, RG 75, NARA Washington; Commissioner of Indian Affairs to Secretary of the Interior, 1914, File 034 10F2, Records of the Bureau of Indian Affairs, Land Division, Correspondence, Reports, and Related Records Concerning Eastern Cherokee Enrollments, 1907–16, Box 1, RG 75, NARA Washington.

48. Commissioner of Indian Affairs to Secretary of the Interior, 1914, File 034 10F2, Records of the Bureau of Indian Affairs, Land Division, Correspondence, Reports, and Related Records Concerning Eastern Cherokee Enrollments, 1907–16, Box 1, RG 75, NARA Washington.

49. File Part 18, Exhibit 27, 1913, Records of the Bureau of Indian Affairs, Land Division, Correspondence, Reports, and Related Records Concerning Eastern Cherokee Enrollments, 1907–16, Box 5, RG 75, NARA Washington.

50. Decisions in Enrollment Cases, Volume II, the 1928 Baker Roll and Records of the Eastern Cherokee Enrolling Commission, 1924–1929, M-2104, roll 67, RG 75, NARA Washington.

51. Testimony of James Goliath Driver on behalf of his daughter, Helen Esther Driver, February 23, 1928, Miscellaneous Testimony in Enrollment Cases, Volume IV, the 1928

Baker Roll and Records of the Eastern Cherokee Enrolling Commission, 1924–1929, M-2104, roll 66, RG 75, NARA Washington.

52. Superintendent, Cherokee Agency, NC, to Commissioner of Indian Affairs, November 9, 1929, File 004, Bureau of Indian Affairs, Cherokee Indian Agency, Series 6, General Records Correspondence, Indian Field Service Filing System, 1926–1952, Box 7, RG 75, NARA Atlanta.

53. Testimony of James Goliath Driver on behalf of his daughter, Helen Esther Driver, February 23, 1928, Miscellaneous Testimony in Enrollment Cases, Volume IV, the 1928 Baker Roll and Records of the Eastern Cherokee Enrolling Commission, 1924–1929, M-2104, roll 66, RG 75, NARA Washington.

54. Decisions in Enrollment Cases, Volume II, the 1928 Baker Roll and Records of the Eastern Cherokee Enrolling Commission, 1924–1929, M-2104, roll 67, RG 75, NARA Washington.

55. Decisions in Enrollment Cases, Volume II, the 1928 Baker Roll and Records of the Eastern Cherokee Enrolling Commission.

56. Henry Spray, Superintendent, Cherokee Agency, NC, to Commissioner of Indian Affairs, April 3, 1901, Letters of Supt. H.W. Spray, 2-6-01 to 9-17-02, Bureau of Indian Affairs, Cherokee Indian Agency, Series 1, General Record Correspondence, Superintendents Letterbooks, 1892–1914, Box 4, RG 75, NARA Atlanta.

57. Decisions in Enrollment Cases, Volume 1, the 1928 Baker Roll and Records of the Eastern Cherokee Enrolling Commission, 1924–1929, M-2104, roll 67, RG 75, NARA Washington.

58. Testimony of Mourning Coleman, September 20, 1927, Miscellaneous Testimony in Enrollment Cases, Volume III, the 1928 Baker Roll and Records of the Eastern Cherokee Enrolling Commission, 1924–1929, M-2104, roll 66, RG 75, NARA Washington.

59. Sworn Statement of Saunooke Littlejohn, December 26, 1910, File Part 5, Exhibit L, Records of the Bureau of Indian Affairs, Land Division, Correspondence, Reports, and Related Records Concerning Eastern Cherokee Enrollments, 1907–16, Box 2, RG 75, NARA Washington.

60. Statement of Special Agent, Chas. L. Davis, December 27, 1910, File Part 5, Exhibit L, Records of the Bureau of Indian Affairs, Land Division, Correspondence, Reports, and Related Records Concerning Eastern Cherokee Enrollments, 1907–16, Box 2, RG 75, NARA Washington.

61. Sworn Statement of Ropetwister Littlejohn, December 26, 1910, File Part 5, Exhibit L, Records of the Bureau of Indian Affairs, Land Division, Correspondence, Reports, and Related Records Concerning Eastern Cherokee Enrollments, 1907–16, Box 2, RG 75, NARA Washington.

62. Sworn Statement of Joe Stone George, December 26, 1910, File Part 5, Exhibit L, Records of the Bureau of Indian Affairs, Land Division, Correspondence, Reports, and Related Records Concerning Eastern Cherokee Enrollments, 1907–16, Box 2, RG 75, NARA Washington.

63. Sworn Statement of Harrison E. Coleman, December 22, 1910, File Part 5, Exhibit L, Records of the Bureau of Indian Affairs, Land Division, Correspondence, Reports, and Related Records Concerning Eastern Cherokee Enrollments, 1907–16, Box 2, RG 75, NARA Washington.

64. Frank Kyselka, Superintendent, Cherokee Agency, NC, to Commissioner of Indian Affairs, January 19, 1911, Letters of Supt. Frank Kyselka, 2-23-10 to 2-20-11, Bureau of Indian Affairs, Cherokee Indian Agency, Series 1, General Record Correspondence, Superintendents Letterbooks, 1892–1914, Box 7, RG 75, NARA Atlanta.

65. Commissioner of Indian Affairs to Secretary of the Interior, 1914, File 034 10F2, Records of the Bureau of Indian Affairs, Land Division, Correspondence, Reports, and Related Records Concerning Eastern Cherokee Enrollments, 1907–16, Box 1, RG 75, NARA Washington.

66. Testimony of James Blythe, 1913, File Part 20, Exhibit 29, Records of the Bureau of Indian Affairs, Land Division, Correspondence, Reports, and Related Records Concerning Eastern Cherokee Enrollments, 1907–16, Box 5, RG 75, NARA Washington.

67. C. F. Hauke, Acting Assistant Commissioner to the Secretary of the Interior, May 16, 1916, File 034, Records of the Bureau of Indian Affairs, Land Division, Correspondence, Reports, and Related Records Concerning Eastern Cherokee Enrollments, 1907–16, Box 1, RG 75, NARA Washington.

68. For a discussion of some of the social, cultural, and racial meanings western Cherokees have assigned to "blood," see Circe Sturm, *Blood Politics: Race, Culture, and Identity in the Cherokee Nation of Oklahoma* (Berkeley: University of California Press, 2002).

69. Charles L. Davis, Report on Eastern Cherokee Enrollments and Contests for the Commissioner of Indian Affairs, February 21, 1911, Copybook of Special Agent Charles L. Davis, 1910–1911, Records of the Bureau of Indian Affairs, Enrollment Records Relating to Enrollment of Eastern Cherokees, Box 1, RG 75, NARA Washington.

70. Charles L. Davis, Report on Eastern Cherokee Enrollments and Contests for the Commissioner of Indian Affairs, February 21, 1911.

71. Charles L. Davis to Commissioner of Indian Affairs, November 12, 1910, Copybook of Special Agent Charles L. Davis, 1910–1911, Records of the Bureau of Indian Affairs, Enrollment Records Relating to Enrollment of Eastern Cherokees, Box 1, RG 75, NARA Washington.

72. Frank Kyselka, Superintendent, Cherokee Agency, NC, to Commissioner of Indian Affairs, June 3, 1910, Letters of Supt. Frank Kyselka, 2-23-10 to 2-20-11, Bureau of Indian Affairs, Cherokee Indian Agency, Series 1, General Record Correspondence, Superintendents Letterbooks, 1892–1914, Box 7, RG 75, NARA Atlanta.

73. Cherokee Indian Council, October 7, 1910, M-Z.1.4.

74. Superintendent Frank Kyselka, Cherokee Agency, NC, to Commissioner of Indian Affairs, March 1, 1910, Letters of Supt. Frank Kyselka, 1-23-10 to 2-20-11, Bureau of Indian Affairs, Cherokee Indian Agency, Series 1, General Record Correspondence, Superintendents Letterbooks, 1892–1914, Box 7, RG 75, NARA Atlanta.

75. E. B. Merritt to Secretary of the Interior, April 8, 1916, File 034, Records of the Bureau of Indian Affairs, Land Division, Correspondence, Reports, and Related Records Concerning Eastern Cherokee Enrollments, 1907–16, Box 1, RG 75, NARA Washington.

76. File Part 19, Exhibit 28, 1913, Records of the Bureau of Indian Affairs, Land Division, Correspondence, Reports, and Related Records Concerning Eastern Cherokee Enrollments, 1907–16, Box 5, RG 75, NARA Washington.

77. File Part 19, Exhibit 28, 1913, Records of the Bureau of Indian Affairs, Land Division, Correspondence, Reports, and Related Records Concerning Eastern Cherokee Enrollments, 1907–16.

78. E. B. Merritt to Secretary of the Interior, April 8, 1916, File 034, Records of the Bureau of Indian Affairs, Land Division, Correspondence, Reports, and Related Records Concerning Eastern Cherokee Enrollments, 1907–16, Box 1, RG 75, NARA Washington.

79. E. B. Merritt to Secretary of the Interior, April 8, 1916, File 034, Records of the Bureau of Indian Affairs, Land Division.

80. O. M. McPherson, Special Indian Agent, to Guion Miller, September 30, 1913, Letters of Spec. Agents Wadsworth & McPherson, 6-24-13 to 5-1-14, Bureau of Indian Affairs, Cherokee Indian Agency, General Records Correspondence, Special Agents Letterbooks, 1910–1914, Box 1, RG 75, NARA Atlanta.

81. Special Indian Agent to Commissioner of Indian Affairs, July 30, 1910, Letters of Supt. Frank Kyselka, 2-23-10 to 2-20-11, Bureau of Indian Affairs, Cherokee Indian Agency, Series 1, General Record Correspondence, Superintendents Letterbooks, 1892–1914, Box 7, RG 75, NARA Atlanta.

82. Charles L. Davis, December 17, 1910, Copybook of Special Agent Charles L. Davis, 1910–1911, Records of the Bureau of Indian Affairs, Enrollment Records Relating to Enrollment of Eastern Cherokees, Box 1, RG 75, NARA Washington.

83. O. M. McPherson, Special Indian Agent, to Guion Miller, September 30, 1913, Letters of Spec. Agents Wadsworth & McPherson, 6-24-13 to 5-1-14, Bureau of Indian Affairs, Cherokee Indian Agency, General Records Correspondence, Special Agents Letterbooks, 1910–1914, Box 1, RG 75, NARA Atlanta.

84. Testimony of Harvey A. Cooper, August 28, 1928, Miscellaneous Testimony in Enrollment Cases, Volume 5, the 1928 Baker Roll and Records of the Eastern Cherokee Enrolling Commission, 1924–1929, M-2104, roll 66, RG 75, NARA Washington.

85. Charles L. Davis, December 17, 1910, Copybook of Special Agent Charles L. Davis, 1910–1911, Records of the Bureau of Indian Affairs, Enrollment Records Relating to Enrollment of Eastern Cherokees, Box 1, RG 75, NARA Washington.

86. Report of the Committee, 1914, File Part 5, Exhibit G, Records of the Bureau of Indian Affairs, Land Division, Correspondence, Reports, and Related Records Concerning Eastern Cherokee Enrollments, 1907–16, Box 2, RG 75, NARA Washington.

87. Decisions in Enrollment Cases, Volume 1, the 1928 Baker Roll and Records of the Eastern Cherokee Enrolling Commission, 1924–1929, M-2104, roll 67, RG 75, NARA Washington.

88. Proposition in Eastern Cherokee Case, 1915, File No. 034, Records of the Bureau of Indian Affairs, Land Division, Correspondence, Reports, and Related Records Concerning Eastern Cherokee Enrollments, 1907–16, Box 1, RG 75, NARA Washington.

89. Robert K. Thomas, an anthropologist of Cherokee descent, first described the value of "harmony" in Eastern Band culture in his unpublished manuscript, "Cherokee Values and World View" (1958, typescript, North Carolina Collection, Wilson Library, University of North Carolina, Chapel Hill). Drawing on this idea, anthropologist John Gulick coined the term "Harmony Ethic" in *Cherokees at the Crossroads* (Chapel Hill: Institute for Research in Social Science, University of North Carolina, 1960). He argued that "overt and direct expressions of hostility and aggression are definitely minimized" among the Cherokees and contended that the Harmony Ethic was at the core of the "Conservative" Cherokee values system. See Gulick, *Cherokees at the Crossroads*, 134–138. For quoted material, see French, *The Qualla Cherokee*, 35.

90. Neely, *Snowbird Cherokees*, 36.

91. James Mooney, "Myths of the Cherokee," *Nineteenth Annual Report of the Bureau of American* Ethnology (Washington, DC, 1900): 229.

92. Theda Perdue, *Cherokee Women: Gender and Culture Change, 1700–1835* (Lincoln: University of Nebraska Press, 1998), 17–18.

93. B. C. H., "Carolina East Cherokees," 51.

94. For a deeper discussion of the significance land held for Native people, see Nancy Shoemaker, *A Strange Likeness: Becoming Red and White in Eighteenth-Century North America* (Oxford: Oxford University Press, 2004).

95. Mooney, "Myths of the Cherokee," 231, 232, 406, 408.

96. John Douglas Gillespie, Notes from Qualla, May 10, 1952, Item #10 FI.B., File 497.3 G41, No. 3, Miscellaneous Papers: Field Notes of the NC Cherokee, APS Philadelphia.

97. John Douglas Gillespie, June 22, 1952, Item #10 FI.B., File 497.3 G41, No. 3, Miscellaneous Papers: Field Notes of the NC Cherokee, APS Philadelphia; B. C. H., "Carolina East Cherokees," 51.

98. James Mooney, "Sacred Formulas of the Cherokee," *Seventh Annual Report of the Bureau of American Ethnology* (Washington, DC, 1891): 323.

99. Sarah H. Hill, *Weaving New Worlds: Southeastern Cherokee Women and Their Basketry* (Chapel Hill: University of North Carolina Press, 1997), xvii–xviii.

100. Harold W. Foght, Superintendent, to Mrs. S. A. Carnes, Biloxi, Mississippi, May 9, 1936, File, 960–961, Bureau of Indian Affairs, Cherokee Indian Agency, Series 6, General Records, Correspondence, Indian Field Service Filing System, 1926–1952, Box 88, RG 75, NARA Atlanta.

101. John Ellison, "Wild Mountain Greens Are Still Plentiful," *Smoky Mountain News*, March 28, 2001, http://www.smokymountainnews.com/issues/3_01/3_28_01/back_then.shtml, accessed May 1, 2011.

102. John D. Gillespie, Sayings of Carl Standingdeer, October 7, 1948, Item #10 FI. B., File 497.3 G41, No. 3, Miscellaneous papers: Field Notes of the NC Cherokee, APS Philadelphia.

103. Frank G. Speck, Leonard Broom, and Long Will West, *Cherokee Dance and Drama* (Norman: University of Oklahoma Press, 1951), 45–47, 49, 53.

104. Frank G. Speck, Cherokee Music, Dances, and Recordings, 1935–1938, File IV (17D3), Ms. Coll. 126, Frank G. Speck Papers, Sub-Collection 1, Box 11, APS Philadelphia.

105. Speck, Broom, and West, *Cherokee Dance and Drama*, 38.

106. Frank G. Speck, Cherokee Music, Dances, and Recordings, 1935–1938, File IV (17D3), Ms. Coll. 126, Frank G. Speck Papers, Sub-Collection 1, Box 11, APS Philadelphia.

107. For a discussion of Cherokee ball games, see Michael J. Zogry, *Anetso, the Cherokee Ball Game: At the Center of Ceremony and Identity* (Chapel Hill: University of North Carolina Press, 2010).

108. Charles Lanman, "Adventures in the Wilds of the United States and British Provinces," Philadelphia, 1856, Ms. 4146, National Anthropological Archives, Smithsonian Institution, Washington, DC (hereafter NAA Washington).

109. Frank Kyselka, Annual Report of Cherokee Agency, December 6, 1910, Letters of Supt. Frank Kyselka, 2-23-10 to 2-20-11, Bureau of Indian Affairs, Cherokee Indian Agency, Series 1, General Record Correspondence, Superintendents Letterbooks, 1892–1914, Box 7, RG 75, NARA Atlanta.

110. Superintendent Frank Kyselka, Cherokee Agency, NC, to Commissioner of Indian Affairs, October 14, 1909, Letters of Supt. Frank Kyselka, 7-13-09 to 2-18-10, Bureau of Indian Affairs, Cherokee Indian Agency, Series 1, General Record Correspondence, Superintendents Letterbooks, 1892–1914, Box 6, RG 75, NARA Atlanta.

111. Rule for Enrolling Committee, November 1910, M-Z.1.4.

112. File Part 19, Exhibit 28, 1913, Records of the Bureau of Indian Affairs, Land Division, Correspondence, Reports, and Related Records Concerning Eastern Cherokee Enrollments, 1907–16, Box 5, RG 75, NARA Washington.

113. Decisions in Enrollment Cases, Volume VI, the 1928 Baker Roll and Records of the Eastern Cherokee Enrolling Commission, 1924–1929, M-2104, roll 68, RG 75, NARA Washington.

114. Charles L. Davis, Report of Eastern Cherokee Enrollments and Contests for the Commissioner of Indian Affairs, February 21, 1911, Copybook of Special Agent Charles L. Davis, 1910–11, Records of the Bureau of Indian Affairs, Enrollment Records Relating to Enrollment of Eastern Cherokees, Box 1, RG 75, NARA Washington.

115. Charles L. Davis, Report of Eastern Cherokee Enrollments and Contests for the Commissioner of Indian Affairs, February 21, 1911, Copybook of Special Agent Charles L. Davis, 1910–11.

116. James Mooney, "Sacred Formulas of the Cherokee," 308; Thomas W. Potter, Report on Eastern Cherokee Agency and Training School, June 30, 1895, Letters of Supt. Potter & J. Haddon, 6-15-95 to 1-27-96, Bureau of Indian Affairs, Cherokee Indian Agency, Series 1, General Record Correspondence, Superintendents Letterbooks, 1892–1914, Box 2, RG 75, NARA Atlanta.

117. Mooney, "Sacred Formulas of the Cherokee," 309.

118. John Barton Payne, Secretary, to Homer P. Snyder, Chairman, Committee on Indian Affairs, House of Representatives, May 25, 1920, File No. 034 10F2, Records of the Bureau of Indian Affairs, Land Division, Correspondence, Reports, and Related Records Concerning Eastern Cherokee Enrollments, 1907–16, Box 1, RG 75, NARA Washington. For more details on the Cherokee syllabary, see Margaret Bender, *Signs of Cherokee Culture: Sequoyah's Syllabary in Eastern Cherokee Life* (Chapel Hill: University of North Carolina Press, 2002).

119. Charles L. Davis, Report of Eastern Cherokee Enrollments and Contests for the Commissioner of Indian Affairs, February 21, 1911, Copybook of Special Agent Charles L. Davis, 1910–11, Records of the Bureau of Indian Affairs, Enrollment Records Relating to Enrollment of Eastern Cherokees, Box 1, RG 75, NARA Washington.

120. Statement by Chief Tahquette, August 30, 1928, Miscellaneous Testimony in Enrollment Cases, Volume 5, the 1928 Baker Roll and Records of the Eastern Cherokee Enrolling Commission, 1924–1929, M-2104, roll 66, RG 75, NARA Washington.

121. US House of Representatives, *Moneys due the Cherokee Nation* (the Slade-Bender Report) (53rd Cong., 3rd Sess., 1895, H.R. Ex. Doc. 182. Serial 3323). For a discussion of the case

and its effects, see Jill Norgren, *Belva Lockwood: The Woman Who Would Be President* (New York: New York University Press, 2007), 207.

122. "The Cherokee Nation v. The United States, The Eastern Cherokees v. the Same, The Eastern and Emigrant Cherokees v. the Same," in *Cases Decided in the Court of Claims of the United States, at the Term of 1904–5*, Vol. XL (Washington, DC: US Government Printing Office, 1905), 331–332.

123. Finger, *Cherokee Americans*, 48.

124. Memorandum by Miller and Tylor, Attorneys for Lambert and Raper, Murray, and Other Families, July 19, 1916, File 034 20F2, Records of the Bureau of Indian Affairs. Land Division, Correspondence, Reports, and Related Records Concerning Eastern Cherokee Enrollments, 1907–16, Box 1, RG 75, NARA Washington.

125. Ralph M. Moody to Hubert Work, Secretary of the Interior, September 24, 1925, File 311 Part 1 20F2, Records of the Bureau of Indian Affairs, Central Classified Files, 1907–39, Box 61, RG 75, NARA Washington.

126. A Resolution Providing for the Final Disposition of the Affairs of the Eastern Band of Cherokee Indians of North Carolina, November 6, 1919, M-Z.1.4.

127. The 1928 Baker Roll and Records of the Eastern Cherokee Enrolling Commission, 1924–1929, M-2104, roll 1, RG 75, NARA Washington.

128. The 1928 Baker Roll and Records of the Eastern Cherokee Enrolling Commission, 1924–1929, M-2104, roll 2, RG 75, NARA Washington.

129. The 1928 Baker Roll and Records of the Eastern Cherokee Enrolling Commission, 1924–1929, M-2104, roll 2, RG 75, NARA Washington.

130. Joseph W. Howell, Brief on Behalf of the Eastern Band of Cherokees of North Carolina, December 18, 1929, File 93679-1924, Records of the Bureau of Indian Affairs, Central Classified Files, 1907–39, Box 64, RG 75, NARA Washington.

131. The 1928 Baker Roll and Records of the Eastern Cherokee Enrolling Commission, 1924–1929, M-2104, roll 2, RG 75, NARA Washington.

132. See Act of March 3, 1875 (18 Stat. 402), Section 6 of Act of February 8, 1887, Act of August 9, 1888, and Act of June 7, 1897, cited in Decisions in Enrollment Cases, under the Act of June 4, 1924, Volume I, the 1928 Baker Roll and Records of the Eastern Cherokee Enrolling Commission, 1924–1929, M-2104, roll 67, RG 75, NARA Washington.

133. See Act of March 3, 1875 (18 Stat. 402), Section 6 of Act of February 8, 1887, Act of August 9, 1888, and Act of June 7, 1897.

134. See Act of March 3, 1875 (18 Stat. 402), Section 6 of Act of February 8, 1887, Act of August 9, 1888, and Act of June 7, 1897.

135. Decisions in Enrollment Cases, Volume I, the 1928 Baker Roll and Records of the Eastern Cherokee Enrolling Commission, 1924–1929, M-2104, roll 67, RG 75, NARA Washington.

136. Flora Warren Seymour, Eastern Cherokee Allotments, North Carolina, June 11, 1930, File 93679-1924, Records of the Bureau of Indian Affairs, Central Classified Files, 1907–39, Box 64, RG 75, NARA Washington.

137. Emphasis in the original. Officers of the Cherokee Council to Ray Lyman Wilber, February 15, 1930, File 93679-1924, Records of the Bureau of Indian Affairs, Central Classified Files, 1907–39, Box 64, RG 75, NARA Washington.

138. Cherokee Council Grounds, March 19, 1930, M-Z.1.4.

139. Flora Warren Seymour, Eastern Cherokee Allotments, June 11, 1930, File 93679-1924, Records of the Bureau of Indian Affairs, Central Classified Files, 1907–39, Box 64, RG 75, NARA Washington.

140. Francis Paul Prucha, *The Great Father: The United States Government and the American Indians* (Lincoln: University of Nebraska Press, 1984), 279.

141. Memorandum, April 29, 1930, File 93679-1924, Records of the Bureau of Indian Affairs, Central Classified Files, 1907–39, Box 64, RG 75, NARA Washington.

142. This congressional legislation replaced the North Carolina state law that had organized the Eastern Cherokees as a state corporation, thereby reasserting federal control over tribal affairs. See Act of March 4, 1931, c. 494, 46 Stat. 1518, discussed in Paul Spruhan,

"A Legal History of Blood Quantum in Federal Indian Law to 1935," *South Dakota Law Review,* 51 (2006): 45.

143. Finger, *Cherokee Americans,* 145–146.

144. For more on Eastern Band gaming enterprises, see Christopher Arris Oakley, "Indian Gaming and the Eastern Band of Cherokee Indians," *North Carolina Historical Review,* 78:2 (April 2001): 133–155.

145. In 2005, these payments totaled $7,000 per year for each enrolled citizen. Young tribal citizens do not receive their payments, which are held in a trust, until they turn twenty-one, or, if they present a high school diploma, at age eighteen. Eastern Band citizens also receive first priority for jobs at both the casino and adjoining hotels. Sarah Ball, "Welcome to Fabulous Cherokee: Casino Cash Is a Blessing to Cherokee County's Poor," *Chronicle* (December 7, 2005), http://www.dukechronicle.com/article/2005/12/welcome-fabulous-cherokee, accessed September 3, 2015.

146. Ball, "Welcome to Fabulous Cherokee." These new enrollees were legitimately entitled to citizenship based on the Band's criteria; they had simply neglected to submit the necessary paperwork previously, perhaps, in part, because they lacked a financial incentive to do so. The surge in citizenship, however, raised fears about so-called white Indians once again claiming tribal rights only when money was on the table.

147. Ball, "Welcome to Fabulous Cherokee."

148. B. Lynne Harlan, "Audit Raises Old Issues of Who Is Cherokee," *Asheville Citizen-Times* (April 2, 2010), http://www.citizen-times.com/article/20100402/OPINION04/304020062/, accessed September 3, 2015.

149. Legal scholar and Lumbee tribal citizen David E. Wilkins has condemned tribal use of external auditing agencies to police tribal rolls. According to Wilkins, not only does this "outside scrutiny" cost tribes resources and money, but it also exacts "a debilitating toll . . . on the morale and cohesiveness of the community." In his view, deciding who belongs as a bona fide citizen is "one of the most fundamental powers of a tribal nation." To mature as nations, tribes must undertake this task without relying on "third-party corporate entities" that do not share "the same core values, historical understanding, or fundamental commitment that a group of competent, rightly empowered, and fully-trained tribal members possess." See David E. Wilkins, "Auditing Tribal Sovereignty," *Indian Country Today* (August 11, 2014), http://indiancountrytodaymedianetwork.com/2014/08/11/auditing-tribal-sovereignty, accessed September 3, 2015. The use of auditing firms to access and evaluate tribal rolls perhaps marks a new stage in the process of defining tribal citizenship—one that is bound to be as controversial as previous endeavors.

150. "EBCI Enrollment Audit Update," *Cherokee One Feather* (May 12, 2010), http://theonefeather.com/2010/05/ebci-enrollment-audit-update/, accessed September 3, 2015.

151. "EBCI Enrollment Audit Update."

152. Giles Morris, "Enrollment Audit a Slow, Uneasy Process for Cherokee," *Smoky Mountain News* (April 28, 2010), http://www.smokymountainnews.com/news/item/941-enrollment-audit-a-slow-uneasy-process-for-cherokee, accessed September 3, 2015.

153. Harlan, "Audit Raises Old Issues of Who Is Cherokee."

154. Donald Rose, "Enrollment Protest—Setting the Record Straight," *Cherokee One Feather* (August 14, 2014), 15, http://theonefeather.com/files/2013/12/August-14.pdf, accessed September 3, 2015.

155. These exceptions allowed Cherokees to enroll new babies and permitted young adults to enroll themselves on reaching legal maturity if their parents had declined to do so previously. Giles Morris, "Cherokee Enrollment Quandary Leads to Talk of DNA Testing," *Smoky Mountain News* (May 19, 2010), http://www.smokymountainnews.com/news/item/805-cherokee-enrollment-quandary-leads-to-talk-of-dna-testing, accessed September 3, 2015.

156. "Council Passes Several Changes to Enrollment Ordinance," *Cherokee One Feather* (June 23, 2010), http://theonefeather.com/2010/06/council-passes-several-changes-to-enrollment-ordinance/, accessed September 3, 2015.

157. Scott McKie B. P., "Council Discusses Procedures for Enrollment Audit Findings," *Cherokee One Feather* (March 19, 2010), http://theonefeather.com/2010/03/council-discusses-procedures-for-enrollment-audit-findings/, accessed September 3, 2015; Morris, "Enrollment Audit a Slow, Uneasy Process for Cherokee."
158. Morris, "Enrollment Audit a Slow, Uneasy Process for Cherokee."
159. McKie, "Council Discusses Procedures for Enrollment Audit Findings."
160. Section 49–2, Qualifications for Enrollment, the Cherokee Code of the Eastern Band of the Cherokee Nation, Codified through Ordinance No. 322, Enacted June 8, 2010 (Supp. No. 13), http://library1.municode.com/default-now/home.htm?infobase=13359&doc_action=whatsnew, accessed January 18, 2011.
161. Section 49–5, Applications for Enrollment, the Cherokee Code of the Eastern Band of the Cherokee Nation, Codified through Ordinance No. 322, Enacted June 8, 2010 (Supp. No. 13), http://library1.municode.com/default-now/home.htm?infobase=13359&doc_action=whatsnew, accessed January 18, 2011.
162. "EBCI Enrollment Facts," *Cherokee One Feather* (July 11, 2012), http://theonefeather.com/2012/07/ebci-enrollment-facts/, accessed September 3, 2015.

Chapter 5

1. W. O. Roberts, Area Director, to Kenneth A. Marmon, Superintendent, Seminole Agency, Florida, July 16, 1953, File: 064 Councils, Acts of Tribal Constitution, etc., Seminole Agency, Miscellaneous Records, Box 015977, Record Group 75 (hereafter RG 75), National Archives and Records Administration, Atlanta, Georgia (hereafter NARA Atlanta).
2. The Office of Indians Affairs was renamed the Bureau of Indian Affairs in 1947.
3. William C. Sturtevant and Jessica R. Cattelino, "Florida Seminole and Miccosukee," in *Handbook of North American Indians*, Vol. 14: Southeast, volume edited by Raymond D. Fogelson, general editor William C. Sturtevant (Washington, DC: Smithsonian Institution, 2004), 431.
4. James W. Covington, *The Seminoles of Florida* (Gainesville: University Press of Florida, 1993), 5.
5. Sturtevant and Cattelino, "Florida Seminole and Miccosukee," 432, 448.
6. Harry A. Kersey Jr., "Private Societies and the Maintenance of Seminole Tribal Integrity, 1899–1957," *Florida Historical Quarterly*, 56 (January 1978): 298.
7. Although there are a number of ways to spell "Muskogee" and "Mikasuki," I have used these particular spellings to refer to the linguistic groups. I use the term "Miccosukee" to refer to the political citizens of the Miccosukee Tribe of Indians of Florida, which was recognized by the federal government in 1962. Although Miccosukee tribal citizens were Mikasuki-speakers, not all Mikasuki-speakers were Miccosukee tribal citizens.
8. Covington, *The Seminoles of Florida*, 12.
9. Interview with David West, by John Mahon, September 28, 1971, Samuel Proctor Oral History Program, Oral History Collections, George A. Smathers Libraries, University of Florida Digital Collections, Gainesville, Florida (hereafter Samuel Proctor Oral History Program).
10. Jane Wood Reno asserted that she was told this by a Seminole man, either named "Homer" or "Howard." See interview with Jane Wood Reno, by Marcia Kanner, October 21, 1971, Samuel Proctor Oral History Program.
11. For more on the First Seminole War, see Deborah A. Rosen, *Border Law: The First Seminole War and American Nationhood* (Cambridge, MA: Harvard University Press, 2015).
12. Sturtevant and Cattelino, "Florida Seminole and Miccosukee," 432.
13. Rosen, *Border Law*, 112.
14. Kenneth W. Porter, *The Black Seminoles: History of a Freedom-Seeking People* (Gainesville: University Press of Florida, 1996), 4–5. See also Kevin Mulroy, *The Seminole Freedmen: A History* (Norman: University of Oklahoma Press, 2007).
15. Kevin Mulroy, *Freedom on the Border: The Seminole Maroons in Florida, the Indian Territory, Coahuila, and Texas* (Lubbock: Texas Tech University Press, 1993), 19–21.

16. Susan A. Miller, *Coacoochee's Bones: A Seminole Saga* (Lawrence: University Press of Kansas, 2003), 59.

17. Thomas L. McKenney and James Hall, *The Indian Tribes of North America, with Biographical Sketches and Anecdotes of the Principal Chiefs: Volume II* (Edinburgh: John Grant, 1934), 267. See also William G. McLoughlin, "Red Indians, Black Slavery, and White Racism: America's Slaveholding Indians," *American Quarterly* 26 (October 1974): 384.

18. McKenney and Hall, *The Indian Tribes of North America*, 268.

19. Interview with F. S., by Jean Chaudhuri, 1970s, Samuel Proctor Oral History Program.

20. Interview with Mary Frances Johns, by Tom King, May 1, 1973, Samuel Proctor Oral History Program.

21. John K. Mahon, *History of the Second Seminole War, 1835–1842* (Gainesville: University of Florida Press, 1985), 75–79.

22. Covington, *The Seminoles of Florida*, 73.

23. Mahon, *History of the Second Seminole War*, 321.

24. Covington, *The Seminoles of Florida*, 96–97, 106–108, 235.

25. In the late 1940s, the Florida Seminoles began a $50 million claim case against the United States government. They argued that they were owed land and money as a result of the Moultrie Creek Treaty, obtained by fraud and later breached; the Payne's Landing Treaty, made ineffective by dilatory tactics of the United States; the Macomb lands, for which they were never justly compensated; and the fact that the secretary of the interior requested the State of Florida to take land without the consent of the Indians. In total, they claimed the United States owed them 39,132,140 acres, valued at $49,782,995. See Covington, *The Seminoles of Florida*, 234–235.

26. Covington, *The Seminoles of Florida*, 111.

27. Mahon, *History of the Second Seminole War*, 321. See also Dorothy Downs, *Art of the Florida Seminole and Miccosukee Indians* (Gainesville: University Press of Florida, 1995), 63.

28. Minnie Moore-Willson, *The Seminoles of Florida* (New York: Moffat, Yard and Company, 1914), 54.

29. Clay MacCauley, *The Seminole Indians of Florida* (Gainesville: University Press of Florida, 2000), 478. Originally published in the *Fifth Annual Report of the Bureau of American Ethnology*, 1887.

30. Kersey, "Private Societies and the Maintenance of Seminole Tribal Integrity, 1899–1957," 298.

31. Interview with Buffalo Tiger, by Tom King, June 1973, Samuel Proctor Oral History Program.

32. Interview with James Hutchinson, by John Mahon and Tom King, August 1973, Samuel Proctor Oral History Program.

33. Richard Henry Pratt to E. A. Hayt, Commissioner of Indian Affairs, August 20, 1879, reprinted in "R. H. Pratt's Report on the Seminole in 1879," presented and annotated by William C. Sturtevant, *The Florida Anthropologist*, 9 (March, 1956): 5.

34. MacCauley, *The Seminole Indians of Florida*, 478.

35. Sturtevant and Cattelino, "Florida Seminole and Miccosukee," 441.

36. Interview with Louis Capron, by Samuel Proctor, August 31, 1971, Samuel Proctor Oral History Program; File: Taylor, Lyda Averill, III Comparative S.E. Ethnography (incomplete MS and trait lists), 1936–1940, Manuscript 4658, Box 2, Smithsonian Institution, National Anthropological Archives, Washington, DC (hereafter NAA Washington).

37. Louis Capron, "The Medicine Bundles of the Florida Seminole and the Green Corn Dance," *Anthropological Papers, No. 35, Smithsonian Institution, Bureau of American Ethnology, Bulletin 151* (Washington, DC: US Government Printing Office, 1953), 160, 163.

38. Kersey, "Private Societies and the Maintenance of Seminole Tribal Integrity, 1899–1957," 299.

39. "The Green Corn Dance," *Atlanta Constitution* (June 29, 1896): 3; Downs, *Art of the Florida Seminole and Miccosukee Indians*, 72.

40. Interview with Unnamed Seminoles by Jean Chaudhuri, 1970s, Samuel Proctor Oral History Program.

41. Moore-Willson, *The Seminoles of Florida*, 98.

42. Florida Museum of Natural History, *Handbook* (Palm Beach, Fla.: –, 189–), 11, the Newberry Library, Chicago, Illinois (hereafter the Newberry Library).

43. Moore-Willson, *The Seminoles of Florida*, 98.

44. US Department of the Interior, Office of Indian Affairs, *Letter of the Acting Commissioner of Indian Affairs to Senator Duncan U. Fletcher transmitting a copy of a partial report by Lucien A. Spencer, Special Commissioner to the Florida Seminoles, on conditions existing among the Seminole Indians in Florida* (63rd Cong., 1st Sess., 1913. S. Doc. 42), 5.

45. Charles H. Coe, *Red Patriots: The Story of the Seminoles* (Gainesville: University Press of Florida, 1974), 247. First published in Cincinnati: Editor Pub. Co., 1898.

46. MacCauley, *The Seminole Indians of Florida*, 478.

47. Polygamy was not unusual in the late nineteenth century. MacCauley reported that nearly all of the fifty-six women over the age of fifteen he recorded were married to thirty-eight Seminole men. The custom faded, however, by the early twentieth century. See MacCauley, *The Seminole Indians of Florida*, 479.

48. Two other clans, the Buffalo and the Horned Owl, no longer existed in the peninsula because the United States had deported most of their members to Indian Territory. See MacCauley, *The Seminole Indians of Florida*, 507–508.

49. Interview with Billy Osceola, by Jean Chaudhuri, March 1, 1972, Samuel Proctor Oral History Program; interview with Albert DeVane and Jessie Bell DeVane, by Foster L. Barnes and Thelma Boltin, 1960, Samuel Proctor Oral History Program.

50. MacCauley, *The Seminole Indians of Florida*, 507–508.

51. File: Ethel Cutler Freeman, Seminole Indians, Vol. 1, 1940s, Misc. Notes, Florida Seminole, 1942–43, Ethel Cutler Freeman Papers, Box 35, NAA Washington. The tribe punished incestuous women by scratching their arms and legs, or occasionally by cutting off their ears. Incestuous men faced more drastic measures: they might be castrated or even killed. Prohibitions against in-clan incest persisted well into the twentieth century, even after other marriage rules relaxed. In the early 1970s, one observer reported that "a young Seminole girl is far more apt to have sexual relations with a Mexican than with a member of her clan." See interview with Seminole Housewife (E. F.), Bird Clan, interview with David West, by John Mahon, September 28, 1971, and interview with John Belmont, by Tom King, April, 1973, Samuel Proctor Oral History Program.

52. In the nineteenth century, the Seminoles also divided clans into two moieties, one consisting of clans with four-legged totems, and the other with totems of two or no legs. These moieties were also exogamous, but this custom had mostly faded by the twentieth century. See Sturtevant and Cattelino, "Florida Seminole and Miccosukee," 442–443.

53. Buffalo Tiger and Harry A. Kersey Jr., *Buffalo Tiger: A Life in the Everglades* (Lincoln: University of Nebraska Press, 2002), 25.

54. Interview with Unnamed Seminoles by Jean Chaudhuri, 1970s, Samuel Proctor Oral History Program.

55. Alanson Skinner, "Notes on the Florida Seminole," *American Anthropologist*, 15, (January–March 1913): 77.

56. Ethel Cutler Freeman, "Two Types of Cultural Response to External Pressures among the Florida Seminoles," *Anthropological Quarterly*, 38 (April 1965): 56; Economic, geographical, etc., etc. Survey of the Seminole Indians Today, by W. Stanley Hanson, 1940s, File: Ethel Cutler Freeman, Seminole Indians, Survey of the Seminoles Today by Stanley Hanson, Ethel Cutler Freeman Papers, Box 33, NAA Washington; interview with Billy Cypress, by Tom King, October 1, 1972, Samuel Proctor Oral History Program.

57. US Department of the Interior, Office of Indian Affairs, *Letter of the Acting Commissioner of Indian Affairs to Senator Duncan U. Fletcher transmitting a copy of a partial report by Lucien A. Spencer, Special Commissioner to the Florida Seminoles, on conditions existing among the Seminole Indians in Florida* (63rd Cong., 1st Sess., 1913. S. Doc. 42), 4.

58. Interview with Seminole Housewife (E. F.), Bird Clan, Samuel Proctor Oral History Program.

59. Kersey, "Private Societies and the Maintenance of Seminole Tribal Integrity, 1899–1957," 297.

60. US House of Representatives, Committee on Investigation of the Indian Service, *Condition of the Florida Seminoles*, report by Charles D. Carter (65th Cong., 1st Sess., 1917), 57–58.

61. Interview with Billy Osceola, by Jean Chaudhuri, March 1, 1972, Samuel Proctor Oral History Program.

62. Interview with Unnamed Seminoles by Jean Chaudhuri, 1970s, Samuel Proctor Oral History Program.

63. Interview with Seminole Housewife (E. F.) Bird Clan, Samuel Proctor Oral History Program.

64. Minnie Moore-Willson, a white woman interested in Seminole affairs, explained that "they are certainly not foot-sore for the warpath and are fearful of doing anything to arouse the whites." See Moore-Willson, *The Seminoles of Florida*, 75. Anthropologist Ethel Cutler Freeman corroborated this idea in 1939: "The Seminoles of the Big Cypress group give the impression of having a definite cultural goal. Their ideology centers around the concept of avoidance of conflict where consistent with individual integrity and personal dignity." See File: Ethel Cutler Freeman, Seminole Indians, Notes Florida Seminoles, 1939, Volume 1, Ethel Cutler Freeman Papers, Box 35, NAA Washington.

65. Economic, geographical, etc., etc. Survey of the Seminole Indians Today, by W. Stanley Hanson, 1940s, File: Ethel Cutler Freeman, Seminole Indians, Survey of the Seminoles Today by Stanley Hanson, Ethel Cutler Freeman Papers, Box 33, NAA Washington.

66. See Steven C. Hahn's discussion of the creation of Creek national identity through their foreign policy of neutrality in dealing with Europeans in *The Invention of the Creek Nation, 1670–1763* (Lincoln: University of Nebraska Press, 2004), 276.

67. Interview with Billy Osceola, by Jean Chaudhuri, March 1, 1972, Samuel Proctor Oral History Program.

68. "Florida Happenings," *Atlanta Constitution* (July 26, 1891): 7.

69. Moore-Willson, *The Seminoles of Florida*, 169.

70. Interview with Billy Cypress, by Tom King, October 1, 1972, Samuel Proctor Oral History Program.

71. US Department of the Interior, Office of Indian Affairs, *Letter of the Acting Commissioner of Indian Affairs to Senator Duncan U. Fletcher transmitting a copy of a partial report by Lucien A. Spencer, Special Commissioner to the Florida Seminoles, on conditions existing among the Seminole Indians in Florida* (63rd Cong., 1st Sess., 1913. S. Doc. 42), 6. This particular punishment may have served to remind the Seminoles of their duty to listen to the commands of Breathmaker. Whites had chosen the box of paper and ink, the Seminoles had not.

72. Moore-Willson, *The Seminoles of Florida*, 71.

73. US Senate, *A Survey of the Seminole Indians of Florida*, report by Roy Nash (71st Cong., 3rd Sess., 1931. Doc. 314), 5; MacCauley, *The Seminole Indians of Florida*, 499; interview with Reverend Alexander Linn, by Tom King, March 23, 1974, Samuel Proctor Oral History Program.

74. US Senate, *A Survey of the Seminole Indians of Florida*, report by Roy Nash (71st Cong., 3rd Sess., 1931. Doc. 314), 35, 5.

75. I. M. Stackel, "Tradition, Not Laws, Regulate the Business of Chickee Construction," *News from Indian Country* (2002), http://indiancountrynews.info/fullstory.cfm-ID=148. htm, accessed October 31, 2012; "Tradition Calls for Only Indians to Build Chickee Huts," *Florida Times-Union* (December 13, 2004), http://jacksonville.com/apnews/stories/121304/D86UT1FO0.shtml, accessed July 30, 2015.

76. According to Clay MacCauley, women also fished to feed their families. See MacCauley, *The Seminole Indians of Florida*, 503.

77. Indeed, according to some reports, during the Second Seminole War, "the American troops amused themselves by firing at the stems [of Seminole pumpkins] and bringing the pumpkins to the ground." See William A. Read, *Florida Place-Names of Indian Origin and Seminole Personal Names* (Baton Rouge: Louisiana State University Press, 1934), 4.

78. Moore-Willson, *The Seminoles of Florida*, 105.

79. US House of Representatives, Committee on Investigation of the Indian Service, *Condition of the Florida Seminoles*, report by Charles D. Carter (65th Cong., 1st Sess., 1917), 54.

80. Frederick A. Ober, "Ten Days with the Seminoles," *Appletons' Journal of Literature, Science and Art*, 14 (July 31, 1875): 142; "Wild Life in Florida," *Forest and Stream: A Journal of Outdoor Life, Travel, Nature Study, Shooting, Fishing, Yachting*, 1 (November 6, 1873): 193; Leonora Beck Ellis, "The Seminoles of Florida," *Gunton's Magazine*, 25 (December 1903): 25.

81. Florida Museum of Natural History, *Handbook*, 9, the Newberry Library.

82. Skinner, "Notes on the Florida Seminole," 76.

83. Harriet Randolph Parkhill, *The Mission to the Seminoles in the Everglades of Florida* (Orlando: Sentinel Print., 1909), 6; Ellis, "The Seminoles of Florida," 25.

84. Mary F. Dickinson, *Seminoles of South Florida* (Federal Writers' Project of the Work Projects Administration for the State of Florida, 1930), 4. Another observer corroborated this report: "A canoe is decorated with the 'family colors' which are used also on dresses and on the yokes of men's blouses." See File 4690, Densmore, Frances, Seminole Music, Manuscript 4690, Densmore, Frances, Seminole, Box 2, NAA Washington. The Seminoles perhaps also used clothing to punish transgressing individuals. According to Lawrence E. Will, an amateur historian familiar with the Seminoles, "there were some cases which I'd heard of where an Indian was sentenced to wear a white shirt. The Indian, if he'd murdered somebody or anything as bad as that, was not allowed to wear that colored uniform" that Seminoles usually sported. Although Will claimed to have seen "one or two other white shirts," including one worn by a Seminole outcast known as Crop Eared Charlie, these cases were "very, very rare." If they occurred, it suggests that the Indians used clothing to exclude as well as include tribal citizens. White shirts may have served to shame Seminoles into appropriate forms of behavior. See interview with Lawrence E. Will, by Tom King, November 29, 1972, Samuel Proctor Oral History Program.

85. Florida Museum of Natural History, *Handbook*, 6, the Newberry Library.

86. Moore-Willson, *The Seminoles of Florida*, 88–89.

87. Florida Museum of Natural History, *Handbook*, 9–10, the Newberry Library.

88. Moore-Willson, *The Seminoles of Florida*, 90; Villiers Stuart, *Adventures Amidst the Equatorial Forests and Rivers of South America; also in the West Indies and the Wilds of Florida, to Which Is Added "Jamaica Revisited"* (London: John Murray, Albemarle Street, 1891), 111.

89. As one white reporter noted, the Seminoles made their distinctive clothing "so that they would not be Jim Crowed." Interview with Jane Wood Reno, by Marcia Kanner, October 21, 1971, Samuel Proctor Oral History Program. This strategy apparently worked. According to Roy Nash, who conducted a survey of the Seminoles in 1930, Florida law treated Seminoles as "whites." Nash remarked that "the Seminole . . . can travel on the railroad in coaches reserved for whites. He enters hotels and eats at the same table with whites. He is admitted to white wards in local hospitals." Seminole children rarely attended Euro-American schools before the mid-twentieth century, but a few were admitted to white schools in Fort Lauderdale and Indian Town. See US Senate, *A Survey of the Seminole Indians of Florida*, report by Roy Nash (71st Cong., 3rd Sess., 1931. Doc. 314), 46.

90. Moore-Willson, *The Seminoles of Florida*, 114.

91. Interview with Ms. Rich Sands, by Jean Chaudhuri, 1970s, Samuel Proctor Oral History Program. If they failed to punish a rapist themselves, they pursued legal action against him. In the early twentieth century, Seminoles reportedly took a white man to court for the rape of a Seminole woman. To the frustration of the Indians, a white jury acquitted him. See interview with Ernest Lyons, by R. T. King, August 3, 1973, Samuel Proctor Oral History Program.

92. Interview with Bessie DuBois, by Tom King, December 14, 1973, Samuel Proctor Oral History Program; interview with John DuBois, by Tom King, December 14, 1973, Samuel Proctor Oral History Program.

93. The experience apparently scarred Bowers: he remained single until he was sixty years old, at which point he married a much younger white woman. Sadly for Bowers, this marriage failed shortly afterward. See interview with Bessie DuBois, by Tom King, December 14, 1973, Samuel Proctor Oral History Program.

94. Andrew P. Canova, *Life and Adventures in South Florida* (Palatka, FL: Southern Sun Publishing House, 1885), 93, the Newberry Library. According to Canova, a Seminole man named Billy Bowlegs "was condemned to wander apart from his tribe, for a long time, as punishment" for adultery. Such strict rules about "social virtue" may have arisen from the small number of Seminoles remaining in Florida. With few marriage partners to choose from, the Seminoles may have thought it important to enforce marital fidelity in order to promote social harmony and ensure the tribe's survival. If this were the case, it was a historically specific circumstance, as among southeastern groups there was traditionally room for more flexibility in choice of sexual and marital partners.

95. MacCauley, *The Seminole Indians of Florida*, 479. Other white observers corroborated this report. Minnie Moore-Willson insisted that "the Seminole girl who would unwisely bestow her affections would be killed outright by the squaws." See Moore-Willson, *The Seminoles of Florida*, 114. As Robert D. Mitchell, a longtime friend of the Seminoles put it, "if an Indian girl became pregnant . . . why that was the end of it. That'd settle that monkey business." See interview with Bob Mitchell, by Harry Kersey, July 15, 1971, Samuel Proctor Oral History Program.

96. I M'Queen, "The Seminole Indians," *Atlanta Constitution* (February 27, 1885): 5; Moore-Willson, *The Seminoles of Florida*, 114.

97. Death Decrees, Informant—Miss Conrad, Ind. Off, Nurse, March 1940, File: Ethel Cutler Freeman, Seminole Indians, Seminole Killing, Ethel Cutler Freeman Papers, Box 31, NAA Washington.

98. The Seminoles traditionally did not consider infanticide murder. The Seminoles' forebears, the Creeks, put newborn infants to death if they were deformed or if the family could not care for the child. The Seminoles, like the Creeks, resorted to infanticide for medical reasons and in times of desperation. During the Second Seminole War, mothers occasionally killed their infants rather than risk the baby crying and giving away the family's location to the US Army. See Charles Hudson, *The Southeastern Indians* (Knoxville: University of Tennessee Press, 1976), 231, 467; interview with Joe Dan Osceola, by Mark Bass, 1977, Samuel Proctor Oral History Program.

99. Betty Mae Jumper and Patsy West, *A Seminole Legend: The Life of Betty Mae Tiger Jumper* (Gainesville: University Press of Florida, 2001), 39.

100. Interview with James Billie, by Tom King, February 1972, Samuel Proctor Oral History Program.

101. Jumper and West, *A Seminole Legend*, 39. See also interview with Seminole Housewife (E. F.), Bird Clan, 1970s, Samuel Proctor Oral History Program.

102. Interview with John Belmont, by Tom King, April 1973, Samuel Proctor Oral History Program.

103. Jumper and West, *A Seminole Legend*, 12.

104. Reconstructed Florida Seminole Census of 1914, Records of the Statistics Division, Census Rolls and Supplements, 1885–1940, Box 846, PI-163, Entry 964, RG 75, National Archives and Records Administration, Washington, DC (hereafter NARA Washington).

105. Seminole Clan and Kinship Data, 1942, File: Ethel Cutler Freeman, Seminole Indians, Notes: Florida Seminoles, 1942, Volume II, Kinship, Ethel Cutler Freeman Papers, Box 38, NAA Washington.

106. MacCauley, *The Seminole Indians of Florida*, xlvii–xlviii.

107. Reconstructed Florida Seminole Census of 1914, Records of the Statistics Division, Census Rolls and Supplements, 1885–1940, Box 846, PI-163, Entry 964, RG 75, NARA Washington.

108. Census of Seminoles, Indians of Miami Agency, Florida, taken by Lucien A. Spencer, Special Commissioner, July 1915, National Archives Microfilm Publications, Microcopy No. 595, Indian Census Rolls, 1885–1940, roll 486, Seminole (Florida), 1913–29, NARA Washington.

109. An 1889 article, for example, reported that two white men had "the pleasure of meeting the only genuine slaveholder in the land of the free, namely the Hon. Cypress Tiger, of the Everglade Seminoles." See "A Holdover Slaveholder," *Atlanta Constitution* (June 27, 1889): 4. According to another article, Florida cowboys recommended that visitors to

the Seminoles bring an African American with them because one could "sell the negro to the Indians for enough to pay all of [one's] expenses." See "The Florida Everglades," *New York Times* (10 March 1889): 10. Whites familiar with the Indians also remarked on the servile status of the blacks they saw with the Indians. Minnie Moore-Willson, for example, asserted that Si-Si and Han-ne, who lived with a man named Tallahassee, performed all "the drudgery for the family" after Tallahassee's wife died. See Moore-Willson, *The Seminoles of Florida*, 107. Oral tradition supports the idea that the Seminoles viewed blacks among them as less than equals, although not necessarily as slaves. In the 1970s, Mikasuki-speaker Mary Frances Johns recalled that in her grandmother's day, blacks who lived with the Indians "weren't even allowed to sit at the same table and eat with 'em." See interview with Mary Frances Johns, by Tom King, January 5, 1973, Samuel Proctor Oral History Program.

110. MacCauley, *The Seminole Indians of Florida*, 526.
111. M'Queen, "The Seminole Indians," 5.
112. MacCauley, *The Seminole Indians of Florida*, 479, xlvii, li.
113. Jumper and West, *A Seminole Legend*, 13.
114. Reconstructed Florida Seminole Census of 1914, Records of the Statistics Division, Census Rolls and Supplements, 1885–1940, Box 846, PI-163, Entry 964, RG 75, NARA Washington.
115. Jumper and West, *A Seminole Legend*, 13.
116. In a 1973 oral interview, John Belmont asserted that "the clans can be broken down in sort of sub-clans where the relationship between the people is considered to be of a different order." The Little Black Snake Clan may have been one of these sub-clans. See interview with John Belmont, by Tom King, April 1973, Samuel Proctor Oral History Program.
117. Jumper and West, *A Seminole Legend*, 13–15; interview with Lawrence E. Will, by Tom King, November 29, 1972, Samuel Proctor Oral History Program.
118. "Victims of an Insane Indian," *New York Times* (March 3, 1889): 5.
119. US Senate, *A Survey of the Seminole Indians of Florida*, report by Roy Nash (71st Cong., 3rd Sess., 1931. Doc. 314), 26.
120. Interview with Milton D. Thompson, by John Mahon, June 25, 1975, Samuel Proctor Oral History Program.
121. February 24, 1942, File: Ethel Cutler Freeman, Seminole Indians, Notes Florida Seminoles, 1939, Volume 2, Ethel Cutler Freeman Papers, Box 35, NAA Washington.
122. Reconstructed Florida Seminole Census of 1914, Records of the Statistics Division, Census Rolls and Supplements, 1885–1940, Box 846, PI-163, Entry 964, RG 75, NARA Washington.
123. Interview with Rose Kennon, by Harry Kersey, September 24, 1971, Samuel Proctor Oral History Program.
124. Interview with Bob Mitchell, by Harry Kersey, July 15, 1971, Samuel Proctor Oral History Program.
125. Supposedly Aklohpi strangled the baby. See February 24, 1942, File: Ethel Cutler Freeman, Seminole Indians, Notes Florida Seminoles, 1939, Volume 2, Ethel Cutler Freeman Papers, Box 35, NAA Washington. According to another version of the story, Charlie Dixie's mother, Molly Pitcher, executed the child by leaving it near an alligator hole. See interview with Rose Kennon, by Harry Kersey, September 24, 1971, Samuel Proctor Oral History Program.
126. Deaconess Bedell, 1939, File: Ethel Cutler Freeman, Seminole Indians, Negro Relations with Seminoles, Ethel Cutler Freeman Papers, Box 32, NAA Washington. According to information collected by Ethel Cutler Freeman in the 1940s, there may have been a scarcity of Indian women of marriageable age in the tribe at the time, which helps explain the incestuous relationship and also why the council spared Jim Sling. See File: Ethel Cutler Freeman, Seminole Indians, Negro Relations with Seminoles, Ethel Cutler Freeman Papers, Box 32, NAA Washington. According to Will Curry, a city gardener in Fort Myers who knew Charlie Billie, medicine man John Osceola issued the execution decree. See "Death Decrees, Informant—Miss Conrad, Ind. Off, Nurse, March 1940,"

File: Ethel Cutler Freeman, Seminole Indians, Seminole Killing, Ethel Cutler Freeman Papers, Box 31, NAA Washington.

127. "Death Decrees, Informant—Miss Conrad, Ind. Off, Nurse, March 1940," File: Ethel Cutler Freeman, Seminole Indians, Seminole Killing, Ethel Cutler Freeman Papers, Box 31, NAA Washington; E. C. Freeman, 1940, File: Ethel Cutler Freeman, Seminole Indians, Vol. 1, 1940s, Misc. Notes, Florida Seminole (1942–43), Ethel Cutler Freeman Papers, Box 35, NAA Washington; Hanson "R" Liddle, August 8, 1936, File: Ethel Cutler Freeman, Seminole Indians, Notes Florida Seminoles, 1940, Volume 1, Ethel Cutler Freeman Papers, Box 36, NAA Washington.

128. "Death Decrees, Informant—Miss Conrad, Ind. Off, Nurse, March 1940," File: Ethel Cutler Freeman, Seminole Indians, Seminole Killing, Ethel Cutler Freeman Papers, Box 31, NAA Washington; interview with Bob Mitchell, by Harry Kersey, July 15, 1971, Samuel Proctor Oral History Program.

129. According to another version of the tale, Jim Sling was the unfaithful wife of a Seminole man. Her husband punished her for her infidelity by cropping her nose and her ears, but she continued the extramarital relationship. The Seminole man finally decided that she was no longer worth anything to him, so he made a bargain with Charlie Dixie, who, according to the story, was held as a slave by the tribe. He promised Dixie he could take Jim Sling as his wife if Dixie killed her lover. Dixie performed the execution, married Jim Sling, and thereafter became a citizen of the tribe. This version of the story was recounted by tribal citizen Howard Osceola to white journalist Jane Wood Reno in 1955 or 1960. See interview with Jane Wood Reno, by Marcia Kanner, October 21, 1971, Samuel Proctor Oral History Program.

130. Interview with Kirby Storter, by Don Pullease, September 18, 1971, Samuel Proctor Oral History Program.

131. E. C. Freeman, 1940, File: Ethel Cutler Freeman, Seminole Indians, Vol. 1, 1940s, Misc. Notes, Florida Seminole (1942–43), Ethel Cutler Freeman Papers, Box 35, NAA Washington.

132. Interview with W. Stanley Hanson Jr. by John Mahon, June 25, 1975, Samuel Proctor Oral History Program.

133. Interview with Bob Mitchell, by Harry Kersey, July 15, 1971, Samuel Proctor Oral History Program.

134. Interview with Robert D. Mitchell, by John K. Mahon, March 26, 1975, Samuel Proctor Oral History Program.

135. Census of the Seminole Indians of Florida Agency, taken by Lucien A. Spencer, Special Commissioner, on June 30th, 1929, National Archives Microfilm Publications, Microcopy No. 595, Indian Census Rolls, 1885–1940, roll 486, Seminole (Florida), 1913–29, NARA Washington.

136. Interview with Jane Wood Reno, by Marcia Kanner, October 21, 1971, Samuel Proctor Oral History Program.

137. MacCauley, *The Seminole Indians of Florida*, xlvii–xlviii.

138. Jumper and West, *A Seminole Legend*, 14–15.

139. Reconstructed Florida Seminole Census of 1914, Records of the Statistics Division, Census Rolls and Supplements, 1885–1940, Box 846, PI-163, Entry 964, RG 75, NARA Washington.

140. Billy Bowlegs may have learned this skill from his paternal uncle, Ko-nip-hat-cho, who had received a Euro-American education at Fort Myers. He may also have learned from Minnie Moore-Willson and her husband following a visit to their home in Kissimmee in the mid-1890s. During this visit, Bowlegs "expressed an eagerness to learn to read and write, and followed a copy with remarkable exactness." As Moore-Willson noted, "With the desire to read and write, however, ended all ambition to be like the white man." See Moore-Willson, *The Seminoles of Florida*, 86, 169.

141. Interview with Albert DeVane and Jessie Bell DeVane, by Foster L. Barnes and Thelma Boltin, 1960, Samuel Proctor Oral History Program.

142. There is also no indication why the tribe tolerated this marriage but objected to the proposed marriage of Bowlegs's maternal uncle, Jim Jumper. Perhaps tribal citizens saw

Bowlegs as more "Seminole" than Jumper due to his appearance and due to his status as a third-generation community member.

143. Reconstructed Florida Seminole Census of 1914, Records of the Statistics Division, Census Rolls and Supplements, 1885–1940, Box 846, PI-163, Entry 964, RG 75, NARA Washington.

144. Interview with Albert DeVane and Jessie Bell DeVane, by Foster L. Barnes and Thelma Boltin, 1960, Samuel Proctor Oral History Program.

145. Interview with James Hutchinson, by John Mahon and Tom King, August 1973, Samuel Proctor Oral History Program.

146. During one such visit, a white man asked Bowlegs how the weather was going to be that day, expecting a sage response. Bowlegs jokingly replied that he couldn't tell them because "the picture tube had blown out on his TV." Evidently, he enjoyed playing with white assumptions of what it meant to be "Indian." See interview with Bessie DuBois, by Tom King, December 14, 1973, Samuel Proctor Oral History Program.

147. Interview with James Hutchinson, by John Mahon and Tom King, August 1973, Samuel Proctor Oral History Program.

148. Interview with Sister St. Anthony, by R. T. King, August 28, 1976, Samuel Proctor Oral History Program.

149. Interview with John Durham, by John K. Mahon, November 3, 1975, Samuel Proctor Oral History Program.

150. Reconstructed Florida Seminole Census of 1914, Records of the Statistics Division, Census Rolls and Supplements, 1885–1940, Box 846, PI-163, Entry 964, RG 75, NARA Washington.

151. Seminoles in Florida Census, taken by F. J. Scott, January 1, 1937, National Archives Microfilm Publications, Microcopy No. 595, Indian Census Rolls, 1885–1940, roll 487, Seminole (Florida), 1930–40, NARA Washington.

152. Interview with Mr. Osceola, by Jean Chaudhuri, 1970s, Samuel Proctor Oral History Program.

153. For more information about trade between Seminoles and whites in the late nineteenth and early twentieth centuries, see Harry A. Kersey Jr., *Pelts, Plumes, and Hides: White Traders among the Seminole Indians, 1870–1930* (Gainesville: University Press of Florida, 1975).

154. Interview with Ivy Julia Cromartie Stranahan, by Samuel Proctor, October 25, 1970, Samuel Proctor Oral History Collection. In 1891, for example, the Women's National Indian Association established a mission station for the Seminoles. This project was later taken over by the Missionary Board of the Protestant Episcopal Church of South Florida. See H. G. Cutler, *History of Florida, Past and Present, Vol. 1* (Chicago: Lewis Publishing Company, 1923), 52–53, the Newberry Library. For more information on white women's activism on behalf of Indians during the Progressive Era, see Valerie Sherer Mathes, editor, *The Women's National Indian Association: A History* (Albuquerque: University of New Mexico Press, 2015).

155. Report on the Seminole Indians of Florida, by Clement S. Ucker, May 26, 1929, File: 4525, Hugh L. Scott, Seminole, Hugh Lenox Scott Papers, Box 6, Manuscript 4525, NAA Washington; Economic, Geographical, etc., etc. Survey of the Seminole Indians Today, by W. Stanley Hanson, File: Ethel Cutler Freeman, Seminole Indians, Survey of the Seminoles Today by Stanley Hanson, Ethel Cutler Freeman Papers, Box 33, NAA Washington.

156. Statement of W. S. Coleman, Inspector, Indian Service, *Hearings before the Committee on Investigation of the Indian Service, House of Representatives: Condition of the Florida Seminoles, Vol. 1* (Washington, DC: US Government Printing Office, 1917), 10, the Newberry Library.

157. The Claim, 1950: Meeting in Relation to the Seminole Indians of Florida's Claim against the US Government for Broken Treaties and Land Taken from Them without Sufficient Compensation, File: Ethel Cutler Freeman, Seminole Indians, Seminole "Claim" against US Govt., ECF Own Information and Corr., Ethel Cutler Freeman Papers, Box 33, NAA Washington.

158. Interview with Joe Dan Osceola, by Tom King, August 31, 1972, Samuel Proctor Oral History Program.
159. Interview with Josie Billie and Abraham Lincoln Clay, by Billy Cypress, December 24, 1970, Samuel Proctor Oral History Program.
160. Interview with Ivy Julia Cromartie Stranahan, by Samuel Proctor, October 25, 1970, Samuel Proctor Oral History Program.
161. Interview with Robert C. Davis, by Harry Kersey, August 5, 1970, Samuel Proctor Oral History Program.
162. James W. Covington, "Florida Seminoles: 1900–1920," *Florida Historical Quarterly*, 53 (October 1974): 184–191.
163. Covington, "Florida Seminoles: 1900–1920," 191.
164. Jumper and West, *A Seminole Legend*, 27.
165. Interview with Genus Crenshaw, Baptist Missionary appointed by Home Mission Board of the Southern Baptist Convention, by Tom King, August 3, 1973, Samuel Proctor Oral History Program.
166. Jumper and West, *A Seminole Legend*, 38.
167. Interview with Genus Crenshaw, Baptist Missionary appointed by Home Mission Board of the Southern Baptist Convention, by Tom King, August 3, 1973, Samuel Proctor Oral History Program.
168. Freeman, "Two Types of Cultural Response to External Pressures among the Florida Seminoles," 59.
169. Interview with Genus Crenshaw, Baptist Missionary appointed by Home Mission Board of the Southern Baptist Convention, by Tom King, August 3, 1973, Samuel Proctor Oral History Program. Muskogee-speakers on the Brighton Reservation resisted conversion longer due to their loyalty to their own medicine man, Frank Shore. After the Southern Baptists and the Independent Baptists erected churches on the reservation in 1951, however, conversions swiftly followed. Converts included members of the medicine man's family. See Harry A. Kersey Jr. *An Assumption of Sovereignty: Social and Political Transformation among the Florida Seminoles, 1953–1979* (Lincoln: University of Nebraska Press, 1996), 212.
170. Interview with Robert D. Mitchell, by John K. Mahon, March 26, 1975, Samuel Proctor Oral History Program.
171. Interview with Bob Mitchell, by Harry Kersey, July 15, 1971, Samuel Proctor Oral History Program.
172. Interview with Robert D. Mitchell, by John K. Mahon, March 26, 1975, Samuel Proctor Oral History Program.
173. Interview with David West, by John Mahon, September 28, 1971, Samuel Proctor Oral History Program.
174. Freeman, "Two Types of Cultural Response to External Pressures among the Florida Seminoles," 59.
175. Ethel Cutler Freeman, "Cultural Stability and Change among the Seminoles of Florida," in *Men and Cultures: Selected Papers*, edited by Anthony F. C. Wallace (Philadelphia: University of Pennsylvania Press, 1960), 251.
176. Interview with Genus Crenshaw, Baptist Missionary appointed by Home Mission Board of the Southern Baptist Convention, by Tom King, August 3, 1973, Samuel Proctor Oral History Program.
177. According to Harry A. Kersey Jr., three major associations formed to aid the Seminoles. In 1899, Bishop William Cane Gray, F. A. Hendry, P. A. Vans Agnew, Indian Agent Jacob E. Brecht, Senator C. A. Carson, and George W. Wilson founded the "Friends of the Florida Seminoles." Among the organization's most prominent members was Minnie Moore-Willson, author of *The Seminoles of Florida*. Ivy Cromartie Stranahan and other Christian women in south Florida established a similar association, called the "Friends of the Seminoles" in 1934. In 1913, a lesser-known organization, the "Seminole Indian Association," was chartered at Fort Myers by Francis A. Hendry, C. W. Carlton, W. Stanley Hanson, and R. A. Henderson. Although this organization faded not long after its founding, it reorganized in 1933. See Kersey, "Private Societies and the Maintenance of Seminole Tribal Integrity, 1899–1957," 297–316.

178. Interview with Sara Crim, by Don Pullease, May 1, 1969, Samuel Proctor Oral History Program.
179. Interview with Lawrence E. Will, by Tom King, November 29, 1972, Samuel Proctor Oral History Program.
180. Interview with Sara Crim, by Don Pullease, May 1, 1969, Samuel Proctor Oral History Program.
181. Interview with Lawrence E. Will, by Tom King, November 29, 1972, Samuel Proctor Oral History Program.
182. Interview with Louis Capron, by Samuel Proctor, August 31, 1971, Samuel Proctor Oral History Program.
183. Jumper and West, *A Seminole Legend*, 64, 66.
184. Memorandum to Band Chiefs, Muskogee Area Office, February 18, 1952, File: 072, Feasts, Fiestas, Festivals, Celebrations, etc., 1937–1949, Seminole Indian Agency, General Records, Correspondence, 1936–1952, Box 1, RG 75, NARA Atlanta.
185. Interview with John Belmont, by Tom King, April 1973, Samuel Proctor Oral History Program.
186. Jumper and West, *A Seminole Legend*, 39, 43.
187. File: Ethel Cutler Freeman, Seminole Indians, Notes Florida Seminoles, 1939, Volume 2, Ethel Cutler Freeman Papers, Box 35, NAA Washington.
188. Census of the Seminole Indians of Florida Agency, taken by Lucien A. Spencer, Special Commissioner, on June 30th, 1926, 1927, 1928, 1929, National Archives Microfilm Publications, Microcopy No. 595, Indian Census Rolls, 1885–1940, roll 486, Seminole (Florida), 1913–29, NARA Washington.
189. *Miami Herald* (November 16, 1943), File: Ethel Cutler Freeman, Seminole Indians, Negro Relations with Seminoles, Ethel Cutler Freeman Papers, Box 32, NAA Washington.
190. May 1946, File: Ethel Cutler Freeman, Seminole Indians, Negro Relations with Seminoles, Ethel Cutler Freeman Papers, Box 32, NAA Washington.
191. Interview with Buffalo Tiger by Harry Kersey, July 2, 1998, Samuel Proctor Oral History Program.
192. File: Ethel Cutler Freeman, Seminole Indians, Sex, Ethel Cutler Freeman Papers, Box 32, NAA Washington.
193. Interview with John Belmont, by Tom King, April 1973, Samuel Proctor Oral History Program.
194. Interview with Lottie Johns Baxley, by Tom King, September 27, 1972, Samuel Proctor Oral History Program.
195. May 1946, File: Ethel Cutler Freeman, Seminole Indians, Negro Relations with Seminoles, Ethel Cutler Freeman Papers, Box 32, NAA Washington.
196. Interview with Ms. Rich Sands, by Jean Chaudhuri, 1970s, Samuel Proctor Oral History Program.
197. Interview with Ross Allen, by John Mahon, November 11, 1970, Samuel Proctor Oral History Program.
198. Interview with Buffalo Tiger, by Harry Kersey, November 19, 1998, Samuel Proctor Oral History Program.
199. Interview with Ms. Rich Sands, by Jean Chaudhuri, 1970s, Samuel Proctor Oral History Program.
200. Interview with Lester Blain and Laura Blain, by Dr. John Mahon, December 13, 1975, Samuel Proctor Oral History Program.
201. Interview with Lottie Johns Baxley, by Tom King, September 27, 1972, Samuel Proctor Oral History Program.
202. Interview with Judie Kannon, by Dr. John Mahon, February 15, 1975, Samuel Proctor Oral History Program.
203. Kenneth A. Marmon, Superintendent, to Commissioner of Indian Affairs, November 1, 1945, File: 063, Tribal Relations—Enrollment, Citizenship, Degree of Indian Blood, 1945–1952, Seminole Indian Agency, General Records, Correspondence, 1936–1952, Box 1, RG 75, NARA Atlanta; Sworn Statement by White Citizens on Behalf of Charles Giddean Stanaland, November 5, 1945, File: 063, Tribal Relations—Enrollment,

Citizenship, Degree of Indian Blood, 1945–1952, Seminole Indian Agency, General Records, Correspondence, 1936–1952, Box 1, RG 75, NARA Atlanta.

204. Kenneth A. Marmon, Superintendent, to Commissioner of Indian Affairs, November 1, 1945, File: 063, Tribal Relations—Enrollment, Citizenship, Degree of Indian Blood, 1945–1952, Seminole Indian Agency, General Records, Correspondence, 1936–1952, Box 1, RG 75, NARA Atlanta.

205. Commissioner of Indian Affairs to Kenneth A. Marmon, Superintendent of Seminole Agency, November 21, 1945, File: 063, Tribal Relations—Enrollment, Citizenship, Degree of Indian Blood, 1945–1952, Seminole Indian Agency, General Records, Correspondence, 1936–1952, Box 1, RG 75, NARA Atlanta.

206. Interview with Paul G. Rogers, by Harry Kersey, March 23, 1988, Samuel Proctor Oral History Program. For more information on the Seminoles during the New Deal era, see Harry A. Kersey Jr., *The Florida Seminoles and the New Deal, 1933–1942* (Boca Raton: Florida Atlantic University Press, 1989).

207. Kenneth A. Marmon, Superintendent, to Commissioner of Indian Affairs, March 22, 1951, File: 064 Tribal Council Matters, 1940–1952, Seminole Indian Agency, General Records, Correspondence, 1936–1952, Box 1, RG 75, NARA Atlanta.

208. Interview with Fred Monsteoca, by Tom King, December 4, 1972, Samuel Proctor Oral History Program.

209. Memorandum to Band Chiefs, Muskogee Area Office, February 18, 1952, File: 072, Feasts, Fiestas, Festivals, Celebrations, etc., 1937–1949, Seminole Indian Agency, General Records, Correspondence, 1936–1952, Box 1, RG 75, NARA Atlanta.

210. Kenneth A. Marmon, Superintendent, to Commissioner of Indian Affairs, March 22, 1951, File: 064, Tribal Council Matters, 1940–1952, Seminole Indian Agency, General Records, Correspondence, 1936–1952, Box 1, RG 75, NARA Atlanta. See also Interview with Fred Monsteoca, by Tom King, December 4, 1972, Samuel Proctor Oral History Program.

211. Freeman, "Two Types of Cultural Response to External Pressures among the Florida Seminoles," 57.

212. The Claim, 1950: Meeting in Relation to the Seminole Indians of Florida's Claim against the US Government for Broken Treaties and Land Taken from Them without Sufficient Compensation, File: Ethel Cutler Freeman, Seminole Indians, Seminole "Claim" against US Gov, ECF Own Information and corr, Ethel Cutler Freeman Papers, Box 33, NAA Washington.

213. Interview with Roy Struble, by Tom King, August 18, 1972, Samuel Proctor Oral History Program.

214. Memorandum to Trustees and Business Committee of Brighton Indian Reservation, by Kenneth A. Marmon, Superintendent, September 15, 1950, File: 060 Tribal Relations—Business Transactions, 1939–1951, Seminole Indian Agency, General Records, Correspondence, 1936–1952, Box 1, RG 75, NARA Atlanta.

215. Jumper and West, *A Seminole Legend*, 137.

216. The committee included Mike Larry Osceola, Buffalo Tiger, and Henry Cypress from the Tamiami Trail and Miami, Josie Jumper from Dania, Frank Shore, John Josh, and Will Henry Jones from Brighton and Fort Pierce, and Jimmy Osceola and Little Tigertail from Big Cypress. See K. A. Marmon, Superintendent, Seminole Agency, to W. O. Roberts, Area Director, Muskogee, Oklahoma, January 23, 1953, File: 064 Councils, Acts of Tribal Constitution, etc., Seminole Agency, Miscellaneous Records, Box 015977, RG 75, NARA Atlanta.

217. K. A. Marmon, Superintendent, Seminole Agency, to W. O. Roberts, Area Director, Muskogee, Oklahoma, January 23, 1953, File: 064 Councils, Acts of Tribal Constitution, etc., Seminole Agency, Miscellaneous Records, Box 015977, RG 75, NARA Atlanta.

218. K. A. Marmon, Superintendent, Seminole Agency, to W. O. Roberts, Area Director, Muskogee, Oklahoma, February 26, 1953, File: 064 Councils, Acts of Tribal Constitution, etc., Seminole Agency, Miscellaneous Records, Box 015977, RG 75, NARA Atlanta.

219. "Proposed Constitution and By-Laws for the Seminole Nation of Florida," March, 1953, File: 064 Councils, Acts of Tribal Constitution, etc., Seminole Agency, Miscellaneous Records, Box 015977, RG 75, NARA Atlanta.
220. Jumper and West, *A Seminole Legend*, 138–140.
221. Interview with Ivy Julia Cromartie Stranahan, by Samuel Proctor, October 25, 1970, Samuel Proctor Oral History Program.
222. Jumper and West, *A Seminole Legend*, 141.
223. Jumper and West, *A Seminole Legend*, 142.
224. K. A. Marmon, Superintendent, Seminole Agency, to R. A. Gray, Secretary of State, June 23, 1954, File: 064 Councils, Acts of Tribal Constitution, etc., Seminole Agency, Miscellaneous Records, Box 015977, RG 75, NARA Atlanta.
225. Merwyn S. Garbarino, *Big Cypress: A Changing Seminole Community* (New York: Holt, Rinehart and Winston, 1972), 4.
226. Jumper and West, *A Seminole Legend*, 156.
227. Kersey, *An Assumption of Sovereignty*, 65.
228. One of the few exceptions was a Seminole woman named Agnes Parker. After attending boarding school in Cherokee, North Carolina, Parker married a Ute Indian and moved west. Despite the distance, she maintained her kinship ties to her relatives in Florida and was "still an enrolled member of the Seminole Tribe" in the 1970s, and got "her dividends, her benefits." Interview with William D. Boehmer, by John Mahon, February 23, 1971, Samuel Proctor Oral History Program.
229. Florida Museum of Natural History, *Handbook*, 6, the Newberry Library.
230. Canova, *Life and Adventures in South Florida*, 89–90, the Newberry Library.
231. Harry A. Kersey Jr., "Florida Seminoles and the Census of 1900," *Florida Historical Quarterly*, 60 (October 1981): 146.
232. Richard Henry Pratt to E. A. Hayt, Commissioner of Indian Affairs, August 20, 1879, 13; MacCauley, *The Seminole Indians of Florida*, 478.
233. Kersey, "Florida Seminoles and the Census of 1900," 151, 158.
234. J. O. Fries to Hon. J. M. Cheney, Supervisor of Census 2nd District, August 20, 1900, reproduced in Kersey, "Florida Seminoles and the Census of 1900," 157.
235. Skinner also asserted that the Indians "strongly objected to the taking of written notes" by white visitors to their camps, which made the task of census takers more difficult. See Skinner, "Notes on the Florida Seminole," 64, 77.
236. Census of the Seminole Indians of Florida Agency, taken by Lucien A. Spencer, Special Commissioner, June 30, 1920, National Archives Microfilm Publications, Microcopy No. 595, Indian Census Rolls, 1885–1940, roll 486, Seminole (Florida), 1913–29, NARA Washington.
237. Census of the Florida Seminoles, Indians of Florida Agency, taken by Lucien A. Spencer, Special Commissioner, July 1913, National Archives Microfilm Publications, Microcopy No. 595, Indian Census Rolls, 1885–1940, roll 486, Seminole (Florida), 1913–29, NARA Washington.
238. The Seminole Tribe of Florida, http://www.semtribe.com/FAQ/, accessed September 6, 2015.
239. Kersey, *An Assumption of Sovereignty*, 144.
240. Census of Florida Seminoles, Indians of Miami Agency, Florida, taken by Lucien A. Spencer, Special Commissioner, June 30, 1916, National Archives Microfilm Publications, Microcopy No. 595, Indian Census Rolls, 1885–1940, roll 486, Seminole (Florida), 1913–29, NARA Washington.
241. The Seminole Tribe of Florida, http://www.semtribe.com/FAQ/, accessed September 6, 2015.
242. Memorandum to Band Chiefs, Muskogee Area Office, February 18, 1952, File: 072, Feasts, Fiestas, Festivals, Celebrations, etc., 1937–1949, Seminole Indian Agency, General Records, Correspondence, 1936–1952, Box 1, RG 75, NARA Atlanta.
243. Interview with Reginald W. Quinn, by R. T. King, September 27, 1978, Samuel Proctor Oral History Program.

244. Interview with Buffalo Tiger, by Tom King, June 1973, Samuel Proctor Oral History Program.
245. Interview with Robert D. Mitchell, by John K. Mahon, March 26, 1975, Samuel Proctor Oral History Program.
246. Interview with Bob Mitchell, by Harry Kersey, July 15, 1971, Samuel Proctor Oral History Program.
247. Freeman, "Two Types of Cultural Response to External Pressures among the Florida Seminoles," 58.
248. Interview with Buffalo Tiger, by Tom King, June 1973, Samuel Proctor Oral History Program.
249. Interview with Buffalo Tiger, by Tom King, June 1973, Samuel Proctor Oral History Program.
250. Kersey, *An Assumption of Sovereignty*, 177–178.
251. Kersey, *An Assumption of Sovereignty*, 178–179.
252. Interview with Paul G. Rogers, by Harry Kersey, March 23, 1988, Samuel Proctor Oral History Program. See also Harry A. Kersey Jr., "The Havana Connection: Buffalo Tiger, Fidel Castro, and the Origin of Miccosukee Tribal Sovereignty, 1959–1962," *American Indian Quarterly*, 25 (Autumn 2001): 491–507.
253. Interview with Buffalo Tiger, by Tom King, June 1973, Samuel Proctor Oral History Program.
254. Kersey, *An Assumption of Sovereignty*, 187.
255. Interview with Robert D. Mitchell, by John K. Mahon, March 26, 1975, Samuel Proctor Oral History Program.
256. Kersey, *An Assumption of Sovereignty*, 88–89.
257. Sturtevant and. Cattelino, "Florida Seminole and Miccosukee," 444.
258. Kersey, *An Assumption of Sovereignty*, 213.
259. Interview with Joe Dan Osceola, by Tom King, August 31, 1972, Samuel Proctor Oral History Program.
260. As a white couple familiar with the Seminoles explained, "they still distrust the white people. When a girl marries a white man she had to leave the reservation." See Interview with Jack and Charlotte Baxter, by Tom King, January 4, 1973, Samuel Proctor Oral History Program.
261. Interview with Lottie Johns Baxley, by Tom King, September 27, 1972, Samuel Proctor Oral History Program.
262. Interview with Jack and Charlotte Baxter, by Tom King, January 4, 1973, Samuel Proctor Oral History Program.
263. Interview with Lottie Johns Baxley, by Tom King, September 27, 1972, Samuel Proctor Oral History Program.
264. Interview with Mary Frances Johns, by Tom King, August 16, 1972, Samuel Proctor Oral History Program.
265. Jumper and West, *A Seminole Legend*, 142.
266. Interview with Virgil Harrington, by William Boehmer, October 12, 1971, Samuel Proctor Oral History Program.
267. Kersey, *An Assumption of Sovereignty*, 218.
268. Monologue by Robert Thomas King, field notes, March 26, 1976, Samuel Proctor Oral History Program.
269. Kersey, *An Assumption of Sovereignty*, 151.
270. Jessica R. Cattelino, *High Stakes: Florida Seminole Gaming and Sovereignty* (Durham, NC: Duke University Press, 2008), 54. See also Sturtevant and Cattelino, "Florida Seminole and Miccosukee," 446.
271. Julian M. Pleasants and Harry A. Kersey Jr., *Seminole Voices: Reflections on Their Changing Society, 1970–2000* (Lincoln: University of Nebraska Press, 2010), 2.
272. Cattelino, *High Stakes*, 8–9.
273. Cattelino, *High Stakes*, 91–93.
274. Seminole Tribe of Florida, http://www.semtribe.com/FAQ/, accessed November 3, 2011.

275. Cattelino, *High Stakes*, 93.
276. The Miccosukee Tribe does not make public gaming revenues. Recently they have been involved in a controversy with the US Internal Revenue Service over non-payment of federal income tax. See Jay Weaver, "Federal Judge: Miccosukees Must Turn over Financial Records to IRS," *Miami Herald* (August 2, 2011), http://www.miamiherald.com/2011/08/02/2342387/federal-judge-miccosukees-must.html#storylink=misearch, accessed, January 21, 2012.
277. Miccosukee Tribe of Indians of Florida, http://www.miccosukeeresort.com/tribe.htm, accessed November 3, 2011.
278. Miccosukee Tribe of Indians of Florida, "Tribe: History," http://www.miccosukee.com/tribe/, accessed September 6, 2015.
279. Seminole Tribe of Florida, http://www.semtribe.com/FAQ/, accessed November 3, 2011.

Conclusion

1. For more on the issue of balancing tribal resources between resident and non-resident tribal citizens, see Carole Goldberg, "Members Only: Designing Citizenship Requirements for Indian Nations," *American Indian Constitutional Reform and the Rebuilding of Native Nations*, edited by Eric D. Lemont (Austin: University of Texas Press, 2006), 129.
2. Malinda Maynor Lowery, *Lumbee Indians in the Jim Crow South: Race, Identity, and the Making of a Nation* (Chapel Hill: University of North Carolina Press, 2010), 21.
3. Tribal use of blood quantum rules has increased over the course of the twentieth century. Whereas just 44 percent of tribes used blood quantum as a criterion of citizenship before 1941, nearly 70 percent of tribes depend on blood to define who belongs today. At first glance, this increase appears counterintuitive. As tribes gained greater recognition of their sovereignty in the 1960s and 1970s, they had more freedom to decide who belonged as tribal citizens and could have decided to reject colonially imposed criteria. Instead they chose to add blood quantum restrictions. Kirsty Gover has proposed that they did so as a response to increasing rates of outmigration and intermarriage in this period. As Indians moved to cities and integrated into non-tribal communities, tribes had to find ways to determine the citizenship rights of children born away from the home base. Blood quantum rules provided tribes with a tool to limit the pool of eligible children without necessitating the reintroduction of residency requirements. See Kirsty Gover, *Tribal Constitutionalism: States, Tribes, and the Governance of Membership* (Oxford: Oxford University Press, 2010), 85, 113, 153.
4. As Kirsty Gover has explained, tribal blood quantum is different from Indian blood quantum because it "does not rest on an Indian/non-Indian dichotomy, but rather serves as a device for counting the number of a person's *tribal* ancestors." Although tribal blood quantum is more restrictive than Indian blood quantum in cases where individuals have multiple tribal backgrounds, it points to one way that tribes have pushed back against "the colonial concept of an undifferentiated Indian population" defined by race. Kirsty Gover, "Genealogy as Continuity: Explaining the Growing Tribal Preference for Descent Rules in Membership Governance in the United States," *American Indian Law Review*, 33:1 (2009): 252. Tribes have reframed the meaning of "blood" to make it an index of ancestry, kinship, and political belonging to a specific tribe. As Jean Dennison has argued for the Osage Nation, "'Osage blood' can be understood as a metaphor of connection, a way of linking a population spread out 'racially,' 'culturally,' and 'geographically.'" Jean Dennison, "The Logic of Recognition: Debating Osage Nation Citizenship in the Twenty-First Century," *American Indian Quarterly*, 38: 1 (Winter 2014): 21. According to Gover, this use of tribal blood quantum indicates that a form of "retribalization" is under way as tribal communities act "to extricate themselves from the racial category used by the federal government ... and to reassert themselves as descent-based, self-governing polities." Gover, *Tribal Constitutionalism*, 156. Similarly, Bethany Berger has argued that tribes' "reliance on descent in general comes from efforts to maintain

political continuity and cohesion in the face of persistent and racist efforts to destroy tribes." Bethany Berger, "Race, Descent, and Tribal Citizenship," *California Law Review Circuit*, 4: 23 (April 2013): 26.

5. Dennison, "The Logic of Recognition," 18.

6. Goldberg, "Members Only," 123.

7. John J. Chiodo, "Citizenship: The Cherokee Indian Perspective," *National Social Science Journal*, 36: 2 (July 2011): 28.

8. Goldberg, "Members Only," 126.

9. Cedric Sunray, a MOWA Choctaw citizen, for example, has written, "Many tribes in North American have simply lost their way today. They have abandoned every traditional aspect of inclusion that has ever existed." Cedric Sunray, "Tribes Abandon Traditional Aspects of Inclusion," *Indianz.com* (October 20, 2014), http://www.indianz.com/News/2014/015388.asp, accessed October 22, 2014.

10. Erik M. Zissu has made a similar argument for the tribal constitutional governments adopted by the Five Tribes in the nineteenth century. Creating citizenship criteria, like creating constitutional governments, was part of a process of nationalization that tribes underwent over the course of the nineteenth and twentieth centuries that allowed them to better exercise their political sovereignty. Erik M. Zissu, *Blood Matters: The Five Tribes and the Search for Unity in the Twentieth Century* (New York: Routledge, 2001), 14.

11. Goldberg, "Members Only," 107, 122–123.

12. Over the years, scholars have proposed a variety of ways to "fix" tribal citizenship and combat the legacies that colonialism has left on Indian identity and tribal belonging. Scholars have widely critiqued blood quantum, for example, as a colonial imposition that divides tribes, reifies nineteenth-century categories of race, and promotes the eventual elimination of Indians through paper erasure. See Russell Thornton, "Tribal Membership Requirements and the Demography of 'Old' and 'New' Native Americans," *Population Research and Policy Review*, 16 (1997): 40; J. Kēhaulani Kauanui, *Hawaiian Blood: Colonialism and the Politics of Sovereignty and Indigeneity* (Durham, NC: Duke University Press, 2008), 9; Dennison, "The Logic of Recognition," 19. Scholars have also criticized lineal descent from tribal rolls as a criterion for citizenship since these rolls are "inaccurate indicators of Native American ancestry for those listed," and, more important, "recapitulate a system of race hierarchies based on bogus science." See S. Alan Ray, "A Race or a Nation? Cherokee National Identity and the Status of Freedmen's Descendants," *Michigan Journal of Race & Law*, 12 (Spring 2007): 442; Rose Stremlau, *Sustaining the Cherokee Family: Kinship and the Allotment of an Indigenous Nation* (Chapel Hill: University of North Carolina Press, 2011), 136. These scholars urge tribes to resist the racialization of tribal identities that occurred in the late nineteenth and early twentieth centuries and to look instead for other solutions to the question of who belongs. Yet tribes have not found easy replacements for blood quantum or descent rules. Cultural tests, as Bethany Berger has pointed out, are untenable since many tribes experienced culture and language loss as a result of years of contact and assimilationist policies. If such tests became a standard for tribal citizenship, German hobbyists might beat out indigenous teenagers for tribal inclusion. Berger, "Race, Descent, and Tribal Citizenship," 36. Some scholars, notably sociologist Eva Marie Garroutte, have proposed that tribes return to kinship principles as a basis for recognizing and incorporating tribal citizens, whether or not they are racially "Indian." Garroutte's model for Indian identity includes two kinship principles: (1) relationship to ancestry based either on blood ties through descent or ceremonial adoption, and (2) the responsibility of kin to forge and maintain reciprocal relationships with one another. By creating kin ties and maintaining those bonds through good behavior, individuals could effectively become tribal citizens. Eva Marie Garroutte, *Real Indians: Identity and the Survival of Native America* (Berkeley: University of California Press, 2003), 118–133. Although this solution is appealing, it may prove difficult to put into practice without opening the floodgates to anyone who wants to be "Indian." In the end, modern tribes face the same conundrum they did a century ago: how do they define citizenship in such a way as to ensure that the right people are included while preventing outsiders from usurping their identity, sovereignty, and resources? As long as tribes lack territorial control or real

independence, descent rules and blood quantum "whether in combination with residence or cultural requirements or alone, may be one of the only feasible paths" for tribal citizenship. See Berger, "Race, Descent, and Tribal Citizenship," 36; Pauline Turner Strong and Barrik Van Winkle, "'Indian Blood': Reflections on the Reckoning and Refiguring of Native North American Identity," *Cultural Anthropology*, 11:4 (November 1996): 565. For some scholars, the ultimate solution to the problem of tribal citizenship is for tribes to exert more sovereignty. They urge tribes to "act like nations" and once again think of themselves as territorially based rather than membership-based political entities. According to legal scholar Matthew Fletcher, tribes need to move beyond racial conceptions of tribal identity and instead become "domestic nations" like Monaco or the Vatican. Under such a construction, tribes would have to find ways to incorporate non-Indians within their territorial bounds, whether by naturalizing them as tribal citizens or by having them consent to tribal jurisdiction as resident aliens. See Matthew L. M. Fletcher, "Race and American Indian Tribal Nationhood," *Wyoming Law Review*, 11:2 (2011): 324–327. Such an exercise of tribal sovereignty, however, is largely dependent on the willingness of the United States to tolerate it. Once again, the logic of recognition is at play. If tribes incorporate outsiders and insist on territorial jurisdiction, will the United States continue to recognize them? Without federal recognition and support for tribal sovereignty can tribes continue to function? Practically speaking, tribes remain constrained in their options.

BIBLIOGRAPHY

Manuscript Collections

Atlanta, Georgia
  National Archives and Records Administration
    Record Group 75
      Cherokee Indian Agency
        General Records, Correspondence, Indian Field Service Filing
          System, 1926–1952
        General Records Correspondence, Special Agents Letterbooks,
          1910–1914
        General Record Correspondence, Superintendents Letterbooks,
          1892–1914
      Seminole Indian Agency
        General Records, Correspondence, 1936–1952
        Miscellaneous Records
Chapel Hill, North Carolina
  Davis Library
    The Association on American Indian Affairs Archives
      General and Tribal Files, 1851–1983
  Wilson Library, University of North Carolina
    North Carolina Collection
      Robert K. Thomas, "Cherokee Values and World View"
        (1958, typescript)
    The Papers of Charles Hudson
      Completed Research VII: Red, White, & Black, MA Thesis, PhD
        Dissertation
Chicago, Illinois
  The Newberry Library
    Edward E. Ayer Collection
Columbia, South Carolina
  South Carolina Department of Archives and History
    Governor Johnston, General Subject Files, 1935–1939
    Richard W. Riley Administration, Catawba Indians Claim, 1977–1983
  South Caroliniana Library, The University of South Carolina
    Watson, Ian M., Catawba Indian Genealogy Collection, 1750–1986
    Judy Canty Martin, "My Father's People: A Complete Genealogy
      of the Catawba Nation" (2002, typescript)

Fort Worth, Texas
National Archives and Records Administration
Oklahoma Historical Society, DC (OHS-DC), Microfilm 24
Record Group 75
Annuity Rolls for Mississippi Choctaw, 1918–1922, Microfilm 38
Applications for Enrollment in the Five Civilized Tribes, 1898–1914, Microfilm 1301
Dawes Enrollment Cards for Identified Mississippi Choctaws, Microfilm M-7RA-173
Decisions of the Commission, 1902–1904
Letters Sent by Enrollment Clerks, Muskogee Area Office, 1901
Letters Sent by Special Agent Smith, August–October, 1903
Index and Records of Testimony
Records Relating to the Identification of the Mississippi Choctaws, 1899–1904, Microfilm M-7RA-116
Indian Census Rolls, 1885–1940, Microfilm M-595
Gainesville, Florida
George A. Smathers Libraries, University of Florida Digital Collections
Samuel Proctor Oral History Program (http://www.history.ufl.edu/oral/)
Hattiesburg, Mississippi
The Center for Oral History and Cultural Heritage, The University of Southern Mississippi
Mississippi Oral History Program
Jackson, Mississippi
Mississippi Department of Archives and History, William F. Winter Archives and History Building
Papers of Henry Sale Halbert, 1837–1916
Lancaster, South Carolina
Medford Library, The University of South Carolina
Thomas J. Blumer Collection on the Catawba Nation Native American Studies Collection
Catawba Indians, Administrative
Constitutions, 1944, 1975
SC, Agents, Lesslie, J.D., 1906–1911
SC, Agents, Smith, A.E., 1883–1897
SC, Agents, Williams, O.K., 1915–1923
State of SC, Reports, Reports of the Comptroller General
Tribal Council Minutes
Tribal Rolls, 1930, 1961
US-BIA, Correspondence
Catawba Indians, Education
Carlisle Industrial School, 1893–1911
Catawba Indians, Folklore, TJB Research Notes
Catawba Indians, Genealogy, Marsh/Mush, Patterson, White, Garcia (Western Band)
Catawba Indians, Legal, Court Cases
Settlement Attempt, 1921–1925
South Carolina, 1887, 1905
Catawba Indians, Legal, Reports
State of South Carolina, Attorney General
Catawba Indians, Matrilineal Inheritance
Catawba Indians, Mormon Church, Clippings, 1855–1997
Catawba Indians, Pottery, Non-Indians (Whites) Making
Pamunkey Indians, Clippings, 27 September 1884–August 2001
Pamunkey Indians, Oral History

Oxford, Mississippi
　J. D. Williams Library, The University of Mississippi
　　Archives and Special Collections
　　　Mississippi Band of Choctaw Indians Small Manuscripts Collection
　　　Constitution and By-Laws of the Mississippi Band of Choctaw
　　　　Indians, Ratified April 20, 1945
Philadelphia, Pennsylvania
　American Philosophical Society
　　Frank G. Speck Papers
　　　Sub-Collection 1
　　　Sub-Collection 2
　　Frank T. Siebert Papers
　　John Douglas Gillespie Papers
Princeton, New Jersey
　Mudd Manuscript Library, Princeton University
　　Association on American Indian Affairs Records
Raleigh, North Carolina
　North Carolina State Archives
　　Eastern Band of Cherokees, Council Records, 1902–1907, 1905–1909, 1886–
　　　1897, 1899, 1899–1902, Microfilm Z.1.3N
　　Miscellaneous Records, Eastern Band of Cherokees, 1908–1931, Microfilm
　　　Z.1.4
Richmond, Virginia
　The Library of Virginia
　　Helen C. Rountree Collection of Virginia Indian Documents, 2005, Personal
　　　Papers Collection Accession 42003
　　James R. Coates Papers, 1833–1947, Personal Papers Collection, Accession
　　　31577
　　Rockbridge County Clerk's Records, Clerk's Correspondence (A. T. Shields)
　　　(W. A. Plecker to A. T. Shields), 1872–1936, 1912–1943, Broken Series,
　　　Accession 1160754
　　State Government Records Collection
　　　Virginia Department of Education, Indian School Files, 1936–1967,
　　　　Accession 29632
　　　Virginia, Governor's Office, Executive Papers of Governor James L.
　　　　Kemper, 1874–1877, Accession 43755
　　　Virginia Secretary of the Commonwealth, Miscellaneous Records,
　　　　1872–1906, Accession 25299
Washington, DC
　National Archives and Records Administration
　　Record Group 75
　　　Census Roll, 1907, Harris, Blythe, & French, Council Roll of Eastern
　　　　Band of Cherokee Indians
　　　Central Classified Files, 1907–39
　　　　General Service
　　　　Choctaw
　　　Central Classified Files, 1958–75
　　　　Choctaw
　　　Cherokee Agency
　　　　Records Relating to the Catawba Indian Tribe, 1940–62
　　　Frank C. Churchill, Report of Census, 1908, Census Roll of Eastern
　　　　Band of Cherokee Indians
　　　Indian Census Rolls, 1885–1940, Microfilm 595
　　　Letters Received by the Office of Indian Affairs, 1824–81, Cherokee
　　　　Agency, 1836–1880, 1876–1877, Microfilm 234

Narrative Report, Superintendent's Annual Reports, 1920–1935, Choctaw Agency, Microfilm 1011

Records of and Concerning the Eastern Cherokee Enrolling Commission

Copybook of Special Agent Charles L. Davis, 1910–11

Records of the Bureau of Indian Affairs, Land Division
  Correspondence, Reports, and Related Records Concerning Eastern Cherokee Enrollments, 1907–16

Records of the Offices of Chief Clerk and Assistant Commissioner of Indian Affairs, Correspondence of Assistant Commissioner William Zimmerman, 1935–48

Records of the Statistics Division, Census Rolls and Supplements, 1885–1940
  Reconstructed Florida Seminole Census of 1914

The 1928 Baker Roll and Records of the Eastern Cherokee Enrolling Commission, 1924–1929, Microfilm 2104

Smithsonian Institution, National Anthropological Archives
  Albert S. Gatschet, Letters received, 1880–1891
  Albert Samuel Gatschet, *Pamunkey notebook, post 1893*
  Albert Samuel Gatschet, *Yavapai and Havasupai notebook, 1883–1888*
  Collection of Pamunkey Photos
  Ethel Cutler Freeman Papers
  Frances Densmore Papers
  Helen C. Rountree Papers
  Hugh Lenox Scott Papers

United States Department of the Interior, Bureau of Indian Affairs
  Esty, Elizabeth H., Louise M. Slaughter, Eddie Bernice Johnson, Rosa L. DeLauro, and Yvette D. Clarke, Members of Congress, to Sally Jewell, Secretary of the Interior, March 17, 2015

  Final Rule for 25 CFR Part 83 Acknowledgment of American Indian Tribes, June 29, 2015

  Fleming, R. Lee, Director, Office of Federal Acknowledgment, to Robert Gray, April 11, 2011

  Pamunkey Indian Tribe, *Petition for Federal Acknowledgment,* October 19, 2012

  Schmit, Cheryl, Director, Stand Up for California, to Kevin K. Washburn, Assistant Secretary for Indian Affairs and R. Lee Fleming, Director of the Office of Federal Acknowledgment, March 25, 2015

  Washburn, Kevin K., Assistant Secretary, Indian Affairs, "Proposed Finding for Acknowledgment of the Pamunkey Indian Tribe (Petitioner #323), Prepared in Response to the Petition Submitted to the Assistant Secretary—Indian Affairs for Federal Acknowledgment as an Indian Tribe," January 16, 2014

U.S. Supreme Court Cases

Cherokee Nation v. Georgia, 30 U.S. 1 (1831).

Duro v. Reina, 495 U.S. 676 (1990).

Eastern Band of Cherokee Indians v. United States and Cherokee Nation, 117 U.S. 288 (1886).

Elk v. Wilkins, 112 U.S. 94 (1884).

Johnson v. McIntosh, 21 U.S. 543 (1823).

Morton v. Mancari, 471 U.S. 535 (1974).

Oliphant v. Suquamish Indian Tribe, 435 U.S. 191 (1978).

Plessy v. Ferguson, 163 U.S. 537 (1896).

Santa Clara Pueblo v. Martinez, 436 U.S. 49 (1978).

United States v. Lara, 541 U.S. 193 (2004).
United States v. Rogers, 45 U.S. 567 (1846).
Winton v. Amos, 255 U.S. 373 (1921).
Worcester v. Georgia, 31 U.S. 515 (1832).

Government Documents and Petitions

Bureau of Vital Statistics, State Board of Health. *Eugenics in Relation to the New Family and the Law on Racial Integrity.* Richmond: Davis Bottom, Supt. Public Printing, 1924.

Choctaw Nation. "Bill No. 39." *Laws of the Choctaw Nation, Passed at the Regular Session of the General Council, Convened at Tushka Humma, October 3rd, 1892, and Adjourned November 4th, 1892.* Atoka, Indian Territory: Indian Citizen Publishing Co., 1893.

Cohen, Felix S. *Handbook of Federal Indian Law.* United States Department of the Interior, Office of the Solicitor. Washington, DC: US Government Printing Office, 1941.

Hurley, P. J. *Choctaw Citizenship Litigation: Report of P.J. Hurley, National Attorney for the Choctaw Nation, to Major Victor M. Locke Jr., Principal Chief of the Choctaw Nation* (May, 1916).

Indian Citizenship Act, 43 U.S. Stats. At Large, Ch.233, p.253 (1924).

Massey, B. S. *Report to the Governor of South Carolina on the Catawba Indians.* Columbia, SC: R.W. Gibbes & Co., State Printers, 1854.

Memorial of the Choctaw and Chickasaw Nations relative to the Rights of the Mississippi Choctaws, Submitted for Consideration in Connection with H.R. 19213. Washington, DC: US Government Printing Office, 1913.

Mississippi, Alabama, and Louisiana Choctaw Council. *The Mississippi Choctaw Claim.* Washington, DC: Judd & Detweiler, 1914.

Petition and Memorial in the Matter of Claims and Demands of the Catawba Indian Association to the United States. Fort Smith, Ark.: Thomas A. Higgens, Printers, 15 April, 1895.

Proposed Legislation for the Full-Blood and Identified Choctaws of Mississippi, Louisiana, and Alabama with Memorial, Evidence, and Brief. Washington, DC: Judd & Detweiler, Inc., Printers, 1913.

Report of Commissioner John D. Lang, Dec. 6, 1871, Annual Report of the Commissioner of Indian Affairs. House doc. 1/ 11. 42nd Congress. 2nd Session (1871).

Report of J. Fraser Lyon, Attorney General to the General Assembly of South Carolina for the Fiscal Year, 1909. Columbia, SC: Gonzales and Bryan, State Printers, 1910.

Report of the Comptroller-General of the State of South Carolina to the General Assembly for the Fiscal Year Ending October 31, 1892. Columbia, SC: Charles A. Calvo Jr., State Printer, 1892.

Report of the Comptroller-General of the State of South Carolina to the General Assembly for the Fiscal Year Ending October 31, 1894. Columbia, SC: Charles A. Calvo Jr., State Printer, 1894.

"The Cherokee Nation v. The United States, The Eastern Cherokees v. the Same, The Eastern and Emigrant Cherokees v. the Same," in *Cases Decided in the Court of Claims of the United States, at the Term of 1904–5, XL.* Washington, DC: US Government Printing Office, 001905.

US Department of the Interior. Bureau of Indian Affairs. "Indian Tribes, Acknowledgment of Existence Determinations for the Jena Band of Choctaw Indians and the Huron Potawatomi, Inc.; Notices." *Federal Register,* 60: 104 (May 31, 1995).

US Department of the Interior. Office of Indian Affairs. *Constitution and By-Laws of the Catawba Indian Tribe of South Carolina, Approved June 30, 1944.* Washington, DC: US Government Printing Office, 1946.

US Department of the Interior. Office of Indian Affairs. *Letter of the Acting Commissioner of Indian Affairs to Senator Duncan U. Fletcher transmitting a copy of a partial report by Lucien*

A. Spencer, Special Commissioner to the Florida Seminoles, on conditions existing among the Seminole Indians in Florida. 63rd Congress. 1st Session (1913). S. Doc. 42.

US House of Representatives. *Additional Land and Indian Schools in Mississippi: Letter from the Secretary of the Interior, Transmitting Report of John T. Reeves, Special Supervisor, Indian Service, on Need of Additional Land School Facilities for the Indians Living in the State of Mississippi.* 64th Congress. 2nd Session (December 7, 1916). Doc. No. 1464.

US House of Representatives. Committee on Investigation of the Indian Service. *Condition of the Florida Seminoles.* Report by Charles D. Carter. 65th Congress.1st Session (1917).

US House of Representatives. Committee on Indian Affairs. *Claims of Choctaw Indians of Mississippi.* 75th Congress. 3rd Session (1938). Report No. 2233.

US House of Representatives. "Condition of the Mississippi Choctaws." *Hearing before the Committee on Investigation of the Indian Service.* Union, MS, March 16, 1917, Vol. 2. Washington, DC: US Government Printing Office, 1917.

US House of Representatives. *Moneys due the Cherokee Nation* (the Slade-Bender Report). 53rd Congress. 3rd Session (1895). H.R. Ex. Doc. 182. Serial 3323.

US House of Representatives. Committee on Interior and Insular Affairs. *Providing for the Division of the Tribal Assets of the Catawba Indian Tribe of South Carolina among the Members of the Tribe.* Report by James Andrew Haley. 86th Congress 86. 1st Session (August 17, 1959). Bill No. 86, H.R. 6128, Public Law No. 86, PL 322, Statutes at Large 73 Stat. 592.

US House of Representatives. Subcommittee of the Committee on Indian Affairs. *Argument of P.J. Hurley Against the Enrollment of the So-Called Mississippi Choctaws.* 63rd Congress. 2nd Session (August 11, 1914).

US House of Representatives. Subcommittee of the Committee on Indian Affairs. *Bill for Enrollment with the Five Civilized Tribes.* 63rd Congress. 2nd Session (July 2, 1914).

US House of Representatives. Subcommittee of the Committee on Indian Affairs. *Hearings on the Subject of Enrolment in the Five Civilized Tribes, Having under Consideration the Following Bills: 3389, 3390, 6537, 7926, 7974, 8007, 10066, 10140, 12586.* Washington, DC: US Government Printing Office, 1913.

US House of Representatives. Subcommittee of the Committee on Indian Affairs. *Report to Reopen the Rolls of the Choctaw-Chickasaw Tribes.* 63rd Congress. 3rd Session (1915).

US Senate. *A Survey of the Seminole Indians of Florida.* Report by Roy Nash. 71st Congress. 3rd Session (1931). Doc. 314.

US Senate. *Claim against the Choctaw Nation, Communication from the President of the United States, Transmitting a Copy of a Judgment of the Court of Claims in the Case of Wirt K. Winton, Administrator of Charles T. Winton, Deceased, et al., v. Jack Amos et al. Known as the Mississippi Choctaws Case, in Favor of Robert L. Owen and Associates, Together with a Copy of a Letter from the Assistant Attorney General and a Letter from the Secretary of the Treasury Explaining Status of Tribal Funds of the Choctaw Nation.* 67th Congress. 2nd Session (September 16, 1922). Doc. No. 257.

US Senate. Committee on Indian Affairs. *Choctaw Indians of Mississippi.* 76th Congress, 3rd Session (April 22 and 23, 1940).

US Senate. Committee on Indian Affairs. *Claims of Choctaw Indians of Mississippi.* 74th Congress. 1st Session (1935). Report No. 781.

US Senate. Committee on Indian Affairs. *Claims of Choctaw Indians of Mississippi.* 75th Congress. 1st Session (1937). Report No. 997.

US Senate. Committee on Indian Affairs. *Indian Appropriation Bill: Hearings on H.R. 18453, An Act Making Appropriations for the Current and Contingent Expenses of the Bureau of Indian Affairs, for Fulfilling Treaty Stipulations with Various Indian Tribes, and for Other Purposes, for the Fiscal Year Ending June 30, 1918.* 64th Congress, 2nd Session (1917).

US Senate. Committee on Indian Affairs. *Recognition of Mowa Band of Choctaw Indians; Aroostook Band of Mimacs Settlement Act; Ponca Restoration Act; and Jena Band of Choctaw Recognition Act.* 101st Congress. 2nd Session (1990). S. HRG. 101-762.

US Senate. Committee on Indian Affairs. *Rights of the Mississippi Choctaws in the Choctaw Nation.* 57th Congress. 1st Session (1902). Doc. No. 319.

US Senate. Committee on Indian Affairs. *The Catawba Tribe of Indians.* By Richard Franklin Pettigrew. 54th Congress. 2nd Session (February 1, 1897). S.doc.144

US Senate. Subcommittee of the Committee of Indian Affairs. *Survey of Conditions of the Indians in the United States.* 71st Congress. Part 16 (March 28, 1930).

Newspapers and Periodicals

American Antiquarian and Oriental Journal, 1880–1914
Asheville Citizen-Times, April 2, 2010
Atlanta Constitution, 1868–1925
Baltimore Afro-American, 1893–1988
Baltimore Sun, 1837–1986
Cherokee One Feather, 1990–2012
Chicago Daily Tribune, 1872–1922
Christian Advocate and Journal, 1833–1865
Chronicle, December 7, 2005
Columbia Record, July 19, 1915
Daily Times, November 2, 1890
Deseret Evening News, March 31, 1887
Desert News, May 1, 1954
Florida Times-Union, December 13, 2004
Forest and Stream: A Journal of Outdoor Life, Travel, Nature Study, Shooting, Fishing, Yachting, November 6, 1873
Free Lance-Star, December 10, 2014
Friends' Review: A Religious, Literary, and Miscellaneous Journal, 1847–1894
Guardian, June 29, 2015
Gunton's Magazine, December 1903
Herald, January 31, 2000
Huffington Post, September 3, 2010
Indian Country News, November, 2010
Indian Country Today, March 9, 2007, August 11, 2014
Indian Trader, April, 1989
Indianz.com, October 20, 2014
Liahona, the Elders' Journal, June 27, 1908
Lance: The Literary Magazine of the University of South Carolina, Lancaster, SC, 1973
Los Angeles Times, 1881–1988
Miami Herald, August 2, 2011
Morning Times, July 6, 1899
Nanih Waiya, 1974–1976
News from Indian Country, 2002
News of the Nation: The Official Newsletter of the Catawba Indian Nation, September 24, 1993, February 10, 1994
NewsOK, September 22, 2011
New York Evangelist, 1830–1902
New York Times, 1951–1999
Pittsburgh Courier, 1911–1950
Richmond Magazine, November, 2011
Richmond Times, March 12, 1964
Rock Hill Evening Herald, May 9, 1956
Rock Hill Herald, 1887–2015
Rock Hill Record, September 19, 1905, September 23, 1912, June 14, 1915
Smoky Mountain News, March 28, 2001, April 28, 2010
State, January 20, 1904
Tidewater Review, December 24, 2013

Tulsa World News, November 25, 2011
Virginian-Pilot, August 29, 1965
Washington Chronicle, December 14, 1890
Washington Evening Star, April 25, 1894
Washington Post, 1877–2016
York Inquirer, August 24, 1929
Zion's Herald, 1868–1910

Published Sources

Ayers, Edward L. *The Promise of the New South: Life after Reconstruction.* New York: Oxford University Press, 1992.

Bagby, Frances Elizabeth Scott. *Tuckahoe: A Collection of Indian Stories and Legends.* New York: Broadway, 1907.

Baker, Stephen G. *Catawba Indian Trade Pottery of the Historic Period.* Columbia, SC: Columbia Museum of Art, 1973.

Barker, Joanne. "For Whom Sovereignty Matters." In *Sovereignty Matters: Locations of Contestation and Possibility in Indigenous Struggles for Self-Determination,* edited by Joanne Barker. Lincoln: University of Nebraska Press, 2005.

Beard-Moose, Christina Taylor. *Public Indians, Private Cherokees: Tourism and Tradition on Tribal Ground.* Tuscaloosa: University of Alabama Press, 2009.

Bender, Margaret. *Signs of Cherokee Culture: Sequoyah's Syllabary in Eastern Cherokee Life.* Chapel Hill: University of North Carolina Press, 2002.

Bethany Berger. "Race, Descent, and Tribal Citizenship." *California Law Review Circuit,* 4:23 (April 2013): 23–37.

Biolsi, Thomas. "Imagined Geographies: Sovereignty, Indigenous Space, and American Indian Struggle." *American Ethnologist,* 32: 2 (May 2005): 239–259.

Bledstein, Burton J. *The Culture of Professionalism: The Middle Class and the Development of Higher Education in America.* New York: W.W. Norton, 1978.

Bloom, John. "'There Is Madness in the Air': The 1926 Haskell Homecoming and Popular Representations of Sports in Federal Indian Boarding Schools." In *Dressing in Feathers: The Construction of the Indian in American Popular Culture.* Boulder, CO: Westview, 1996.

Blume, G. W. J. "Present-Day Indians of Tidewater Virginia." *Quarterly Bulletin of the Archaeological Society of Virginia,* 6 (December 1951): 1–8.

Blumer, Thomas J. "A History behind the Catawba Nation Tribal Roll, 1943–1999." 7th *Generation Catawba News,* 1 (April 1999).

Blumer, Thomas J. "Catawba Influences on the Modern Cherokee Pottery Tradition." *Appalachian Journal* 14 (Winter 1987): 153–173.

Bradby, Kenneth Jr. *Pamunkey Speaks: Native Perspectives.* Edited by Bill O'Donovan. Charleston, SC: BookSurge, 2008.

Bradford, W. R. "The Catawba Indians of South Carolina." *Bulletin of the University of South Carolina, New Series,* 34 (February, 1946).

Brescia, William, editor. *Tribal Government: A New Era.* Philadelphia, MS: Choctaw Heritage Press, 1982.

Brown, Douglas Summers. *The Catawba Indians: The People of the River.* Columbia: University of South Carolina Press, 1966.

Bruyneel, Kevin. "Ambivalent Americans: Indigenous People and U.S. Citizenship in the Early 20th Century." *American Political Science Association Annual Meeting* (2002): 1–40.

Bushnell, David I. Jr. "The Choctaw of Bayou Lacomb, St. Tammany Parish, Louisiana." *Bureau of American Ethnology, Bulletin 48.* Washington, DC: US Government Printing Office, 1909.

Byrd, Jodi A. *The Transit of Empire: Indigenous Critiques of Colonialism.* Minneapolis: University of Minnesota Press, 2011.

Canova, Andrew P. *Life and Adventures in South Florida*. Palatka, FL: Southern Sun Publishing House, 1885.

Capron, Louis. "The Medicine Bundles of the Florida Seminole and the Green Corn Dance." *Anthropological Papers, No. 35, Smithsonian Institution, Bureau of American Ethnology, Bulletin 151*. Washington, DC: US Government Printing Office, 1953.

Carney, Virginia Moore. *Eastern Band Cherokee Women: Cultural Persistence in Their Letters and Speeches*. Knoxville: University of Tennessee Press, 2005.

Catawba Regional Planning Council. *Catawba Nation: Overall Economic Development Program*. Rock Hill, SC: Catawba Regional Planning Council, 1977.

Cattelino, Jessica R. *High Stakes: Florida Seminole Gaming and Sovereignty*. Durham, NC: Duke University Press, 2008.

Cattelino, Jessica R. "The Double Bind of American Indian Need-Based Sovereignty." *Cultural Anthropology*, 25:2 (2010): 235–262.

Champagne, Duane. *Social Order and Political Change: Constitutional Governments among the Cherokee, the Choctaw, the Chickasaw, and the Creek*. Stanford, CA: Stanford University Press, 1992.

Chiodo, John J. "Citizenship: The Cherokee Indian Perspective." *National Social Science Journal*, 36: 2 (July 2011): 24–34.

Churchill, Ward. "The Crucible of American Indian Identity: Native Tradition versus Colonial Imposition in Postconquest North America." *American Indian Culture and Research Journal*, 23:1 (1999): 39–67.

Coe, Charles H. *Red Patriots: The Story of the Seminoles*. Gainesville: University Press of Florida, 1974. First published in Cincinnati: Editor Pub. Co., 1898.

Coe, Pamela Anne. "Lost in the Hills of Home: Outline of Mississippi Choctaw Social Organization." M.A. Thesis, Columbia University, 1960.

Coker, William Sidney. "Pat Harrison's Efforts to Reopen the Choctaw Citizenship Rolls." *Southern Quarterly*, 3:1 (1965): 36–61.

Coleman, Arica L. *That the Blood Stay Pure: African Americans, Native Americans, and the Predicament of Race and Identity in Virginia*. Bloomington: Indiana University Press, 2013.

Covington, James W. "Florida Seminoles: 1900–1920." *Florida Historical Quarterly*, 53 (October 1974): 181–197.

Covington, James W. *The Seminoles of Florida*. Gainesville: University Press of Florida, 1993.

Cutler, H. G. *History of Florida, Past and Present*, Vol. 1. Chicago: Lewis Publishing, 1923.

Deloria, Vine Jr., and Clifford M. Lytle. *The Nations Within: The Past and Future of American Indian Sovereignty*. Austin: University of Texas Press, 1984.

Dennison, Jean. "The Logic of Recognition: Debating Osage Nation Citizenship in the Twenty-First Century." *American Indian Quarterly*, 38:1 (Winter 2014): 1–35.

Dickinson, Mary F. *Seminoles of South Florida*. Federal Writers' Project of the Work Projects Administration for the State of Florida, 1930.

Downs, Dorothy. *Art of the Florida Seminole and Miccosukee Indians*. Gainesville: University Press of Florida, 1995.

Duggan, Betty J. "Voices from the Periphery: Reconstructing and Interpreting Post Removal Histories of the Duck Town Cherokees." In *Southern Indians and Anthropologists: Culture, Politics, and Identity*. Edited by Lisa J. Lefler and Frederic Wright Gleach. Athens: University of Georgia Press, 2002.

Dussias, Allison M. "Geographically-Based and Membership-Based Views of Indian Tribal Sovereignty: The Supreme Court's Changing Vision." *University of Pittsburgh Law Review*, 55:1 (1993): 1–97.

Duthu, N. Bruce. *American Indians and the Law*. New York: Penguin Group, 2008.

Erman, Sam. "Meanings of Citizenship in the U.S. Empire: Puerto Rico, Isabel Gonzalez, and the Supreme Court, 1898 to 1905." *Journal of Ethnic History*, 27:4 (Summer 2008): 5–33.

Estabrook, Arthur Howard, and Ivan E McDougle. *Mongrel Virginians: The Win Tribe*. Baltimore: Williams & Wilkins, 1926.

Fewkes, Vladimir J. *Catawba Pottery-Making, with Notes on Pamunkey Pottery-Making, Cherokee Pottery-Making, and Coiling.* Philadelphia: University Museum, University of Pennsylvania, 1944.

Finger, John R. *Cherokee Americans: The Eastern Band of Cherokees in the Twentieth Century.* Lincoln: University of Nebraska Press, 1991.

Finger, John R. *The Eastern Band of Cherokees, 1819–1900.* Knoxville: University of Tennessee Press, 1984.

Finkelman, Paul, and Tim Alan Garrison, editors. *Encyclopedia of United States Indian Policy and Law.* Washington, DC: CQ Press, 2009.

Flanagan, Sharon. "The Georgia Cherokees Who Remained: Race, Status, and Property in the Chattahoochee Community." *Georgia Historical Quarterly* 73 (Fall 1989): 584–609.

Fletcher, Matthew L. M. "Race and American Indian Tribal Nationhood." *Wyoming Law Review,* 11:2 (2011): 295–327.

Florida Museum of Natural History. *Handbook.* Palm Beach, Fla.: –, 189–.

Fouberg, Erin Hogan. "Understanding Space, Understanding Citizenship." *Journal of Geography,* 101:2 (2002): 81–85.

Freeman, Ethel Cutler. "Cultural Stability and Change among the Seminoles of Florida." In *Men and Cultures: Selected Papers.* Edited by Anthony F. C. Wallace. Philadelphia: University of Pennsylvania Press, 1960.

Freeman, Ethel Cutler. "Two Types of Cultural Response to External Pressures among the Florida Seminoles." *Anthropological Quarterly,* 38 (April 1965): 55–61.

French, Laurence. *The Qualla Cherokee Surviving in Two Worlds.* Lewiston, NY: E. Mellen Press, 1998.

Garbarino, Merwyn S. *Big Cypress: A Changing Seminole Community.* New York: Holt, Rinehart and Winston, 1972.

Garroutte, Eva Marie. "The Racial Formation of American Indians: Negotiating Legitimate Identities within Tribal and Federal Law." *American Indian Quarterly,* 25:2 (2001): 224–239.

Garroutte, Eva Marie. *Real Indians: Identity and the Survival of Native America.* Berkeley: University of California Press, 2003.

Gates, E. Nathaniel. *The Concept of "Race" in Natural and Social Science.* New York: Garland, 1997.

Genetin-Pilawa, C. Joseph. *Crooked Paths to Allotment: The Fight over Federal Indian Policy after the Civil War.* Chapel Hill: University of North Carolina Press, 2012.

Goins, William M., editor. *South Carolina Indians Today: An Educational Resource Guide.* Columbia, SC: Phoenix, 1998.

Goldberg, Carole. "Members Only: Designing Citizenship Requirements for Indian Nations." In *American Indian Constitutional Reform and the Rebuilding of Native Nations.* Edited by Eric D. Lemont. Austin: University of Texas Press, 2006.

Gonzales, Angela, Judy Kertész, and Gabrielle Tayac. "Eugenics as Indian Removal: Sociohistorical Processes and the De(con)struction of American Indians in the Southeast." *Public Historian,* 29:3 (Summer 2007): 53–67.

Kappler, Charles Joseph. *Indian Affairs: Treaties.* Washington, DC: US Government Printing Office, 1904.

Gover, Kirsty. "Genealogy as Continuity: Explaining the Growing Tribal Preference for Descent Rules in Membership Governance in the United States." *American Indian Law Review,* 33:1 (2009): 243–311.

Gover, Kirsty. "Comparative Tribal Constitutionalism: Membership Governance in Australia, Canada, New Zealand, and the United States." *Law & Social Inquiry,* 35:3 (Summer 2010): 689–762.

Gover, Kirsty. *Tribal Constitutionalism: States, Tribes, and the Governance of Membership.* Oxford: Oxford University Press, 2010.

Greenbaum, Susan. "What's In a Label? Identity Problems of Southern Indian Tribes." *Journal of Ethnic Studies,* 19:2 (Spring 1991): 107–126.

Gross, Ariela J. *What Blood Won't Tell: A History of Race on Trial in America.* Cambridge, MA: Harvard University Press, 2008.

Gulick, John. *Cherokees at the Crossroads.* Chapel Hill: Institute for Research in Social Science, University of North Carolina, 1960.

Hagan, William T. "Full Blood, Mixed Blood, Generic, and Ersatz: The Problem of Indian Identity." *Arizona and the West*, 27:4 (Winter 1985): 309–326.

Hahn, Steven C. *The Invention of the Creek Nation, 1670–1763.* Lincoln: University of Nebraska Press, 2004.

Halliburton, R. Jr. "Chief Greenwood Leflore and His Malmaison Plantation." In *After Removal: The Choctaw in Mississippi.* Edited by Samuel J. Wells and Roseanna Tubby. Jackson, MS: University Press of Mississippi, 1986.

Harmon, Alexandra. "Tribal Enrollment Councils: Lessons on Law and Indian Identity." *Western Historical Quarterly*, 32 (Summer 2001): 175–200.

Harrington, M. R. "Catawba Potters and Their Work." *American Anthropologist* (July, August, September 1908): 399–418.

Harris, Cheryl I. "Whiteness as Property." *Harvard Law Review*, 106: 8 (June 1993): 1707–1791.

Hauptman, Laurence M. *Between Two Fires: American Indians in the Civil War.* New York: Free Press, 1995.

Hill, Sarah H. *Weaving New Worlds: Southeastern Cherokee Women and Their Basketry.* Chapel Hill: University of North Carolina Press, 1997.

Horsman, Reginald. *Race and Manifest Destiny: The Origins of American Racial Anglo-Saxonism.* Cambridge, MA: Harvard University Press, 1981.

Hoxie, Frederick E. *A Final Promise: The Campaign to Assimilate the Indians, 1880–1920.* Lincoln: University of Nebraska Press, 1984.

Hudson, Charles M. *The Catawba Nation.* Athens: University of Georgia Press, 1970.

Hudson, Charles M. *The Southeastern Indians.* Knoxville: University of Tennessee Press, 1976.

Jumper, Betty Mae, and Patsy West. *A Seminole Legend: The Life of Betty Mae Tiger Jumper.* Gainesville: University Press of Florida, 2001.

Kalt Joseph P., and Joseph William Singer. "Myths and Realities of Tribal Sovereignty: The Law and Economics of Indian Self-Rule." *Harvard University: Faculty Research Working Paper Series*, March, 2004.

Kauanui, J. Kēhaulani. *Hawaiian Blood: Colonialism and the Politics of Sovereignty and Indigeneity.* Durham, NC: Duke University Press, 2008.

Kerber, Linda K. "The Meanings of Citizenship." *Journal of American History*, 84:3 (December 1997): 833–854.

Kersey, Harry A. Jr. "Private Societies and the Maintenance of Seminole Tribal Integrity, 1899–1957." *Florida Historical Quarterly*, 56 (January 1978): 297–316.

Kersey, Harry A. Jr. *The Florida Seminoles and the New Deal, 1933–1942.* Boca Raton: Florida Atlantic University Press, 1989.

Kersey, Harry A. Jr. "Florida Seminoles and the Census of 1900." *Florida Historical Quarterly*, 60 (October 1981): 145–160.

Kersey, Harry A. Jr. "The Havana Connection: Buffalo Tiger, Fidel Castro, and the Origin of Miccosukee Tribal Sovereignty, 1959–1962." *American Indian Quarterly*, 25 (Autumn 2001): 491–507.

Kersey, Harry A. Jr. *An Assumption of Sovereignty: Social and Political Transformation among the Florida Seminoles, 1953–1979.* Lincoln: University of Nebraska Press, 1996.

Kersey, Harry A. Jr. *Pelts, Plumes, and Hides: White Traders among the Seminole Indians, 1870–1930.* Gainesville: University Presses of Florida, 1975.

Kidwell, Clara Sue. *Choctaws and Missionaries in Mississippi, 1818–1918.* Norman: University of Oklahoma Press, 1995.

Kidwell, Clara Sue. *The Choctaws in Oklahoma: From Tribe to Nation, 1855–1970.* Norman: University of Oklahoma Press, 2007.

Kiopotek, Brian. *Recognition Odysseys: Indigeneity, Race, and Federal Tribal Recognition Policy in Three Louisiana Indian Communities.* Durham, NC: Duke University Press, 2011.

Kohl, Seena B. "Ethnocide and Ethnogenesis: A Case Study of the Mississippi Band of Choctaw, a Genocide Avoided." *Holocaust and Genocide Studies,* 1:1 (1986): 91–100.

Krakoff, Sarah. "Inextricably Political: Race, Membership, and Tribal Sovereignty." *Washington Law Review,* 87 (2012): 1041–1132.

LaVell, John P. "The General Allotment Act 'Eligibility' Hoax: Distortions of Law, Policy, and History in Derogation of Indian Tribes." *Wicazo Sa Review* (Spring 1999): 251–302.

Loftis, Lynn "The Catawbas' Final Battle: A Bittersweet Victory." *American Indian Law Review* 19 (1994): 183–215.

Lovett, Laura L. "'African and Cherokee by Choice': Race and Resistance under Legalized Segregation." In *Confounding the Color Line: The Indian-Black Experience in North America.* Edited by James F. Brooks. Lincoln: University of Nebraska Press, 2002.

Lowery, Malinda Maynor. *Lumbee Indians in the Jim Crow South: Race, Identity, and the Making of a Nation.* Chapel Hill: University of North Carolina Press, 2010.

MacCauley, Clay. *The Seminole Indians of Florida.* Gainesville: University Press of Florida, 2000. Originally published in the *Fifth Annual Report of the Bureau of American Ethnology.* Washington, DC: US Government Printing Office, 1887.

Mahon, John K. *History of the Second Seminole War, 1835–1842.* Gainesville: University of Florida Press, 1985.

Maltz, Earl M. "The Fourteenth Amendment and Native American Citizenship." *Constitutional Commentary,* 17:3 (Winter 2000): 555–574.

Mathes, Valerie Sherer, editor. *The Women's National Indian Association: A History.* Albuquerque: University of New Mexico Press, 2015.

McCartney, Martha W. "Cockacoeske, Queen of Pamunkey: Diplomat and Suzeraine." In *Powhatan's Mantle: Indians in the Colonial Southeast.* Edited by Gregory A. Waselkov, Peter H. Wood, and Tom Hatley. Lincoln: University of Nebraska Press, 2006.

McKenney, Thomas Loraine, and James Hall. *History of the Indian Tribes of North America, with Biographical Sketches and Anecdotes of the Principal Chiefs.* Philadelphia: E. C. Biddle, 1836–1844

McLoughlin, William G. "Red Indians, Black Slavery, and White Racism: America's Slaveholding Indians." *American Quarterly* 26 (October 1974): 367–385.

Merrell, James H. "The Racial Education of the Catawba Indians." *Journal of Southern History,* 50 (August 1984): 363–384.

Merrell, James H. *The Indians' New World: Catawbas and Their Neighbors from European Contact through the Era of Removal.* Chapel Hill: University of North Carolina Press, 1989.

Meyer, Melissa. "American Indian Blood Quantum Requirements: Blood Is Thicker than Family." In *Over the Edge: Remapping the American West.* Edited by Valerie Matsumoto and Blake Allmendinger. Berkeley: University of California Press, 1999.

Meyer, Melissa L. *The White Earth Tragedy: Ethnicity and Dispossession at a Minnesota Anishinaabe Reservation, 1889–1920.* Lincoln: University of Nebraska Press, 1999.

Miller, Bruce Granville. *Invisible Indigenes: The Politics of Nonrecognition.* Lincoln: University of Nebraska Press, 2003.

Miller, Mark Edwin. *Forgotten Tribes: Unrecognized Indians and the Federal Acknowledgment Process.* Lincoln: University of Nebraska Press, 2004.

Miller, Mark Edwin. *Claiming Tribal Identity: The Five Tribes and the Politics of Federal Acknowledgment.* Norman: University of Oklahoma Press, 2013.

Miller, Susan A. *Coacoochee's Bones: A Seminole Saga.* Lawrence: University Press of Kansas, 2003.

Mooney, James. "Myths of the Cherokee." *Nineteenth Annual Report of the Bureau of American Ethnology.* Washington, DC: US Government Printing Office, 1900.

Mooney, James. "Sacred Formulas of the Cherokee." *Seventh Annual Report of the Bureau of American Ethnology.* Washington, DC: US Government Printing Office, 1891.

Moore-Willson, Minnie. *The Seminoles of Florida*. New York: Moffat, Yard, 1914.

Mulroy, Kevin. *Freedom on the Border: The Seminole Maroons in Florida, the Indian Territory, Coahuila, and Texas*. Lubbock: Texas Tech University Press, 1993.

Mulroy, Kevin. *The Seminole Freedmen: A History*. Norman: University of Oklahoma Press, 2007.

Neely, Sharlotte. *Snowbird Cherokees: People of Persistence*. Athens: University of Georgia Press, 1991.

Norgren, Jill. *Belva Lockwood: The Woman Who Would Be President*. New York: New York University Press, 2007.

Oakley, Christopher Arris. "Indian Gaming and the Eastern Band of Cherokee Indians." *North Carolina Historical Review*, 78:2 (April 2001): 133–155.

Osburn, Katherine M. B. "The 'Identified Full-Bloods' in Mississippi: Race and Choctaw Identity, 1898–1918." *Ethnohistory* 56 (Summer 2009): 423–447.

Osburn, Katherine M. B. "'Any Sane Person': Race, Rights, and Tribal Sovereignty in the Construction of the Dawes Rolls for the Choctaw Nation." *Journal of the Gilded Age and Progressive Era*, 9:4 (October 2010): 451–471.

Osburn, Katherine M. B. *Choctaw Resurgence in Mississippi: Race, Class, and Nation Building in the Jim Crow South, 1830–1977*. Lincoln: University of Nebraska Press, 2014.

Owl, Frell M. "Who and What Is an American Indian?" *Ethnohistory*, 9:3 (Summer 1962): 265–284.

Painter-Thorne, Suzianne D. "If You Build It, They *Will* Come: Preserving Tribal Sovereignty in the Face of Indian Casinos and the New Premium on Tribal Membership." *Lewis & Clark Law Review*, 14: 1 (2010): 311–353.

Park, Charles. "Enrollment: Procedures and Consequences." *American Indian Law Review*, 3 (1975): 109–115.

Parkhill, Harriet Randolph. *The Mission to the Seminoles in the Everglades of Florida*. Orlando: Sentinel Print., 1909.

Perdue, Theda, and Michael D. Green. *The Cherokee Nation and the Trail of Tears*. New York: Penguin Group, 2007.

Perdue, Theda. *"Mixed Blood" Indians: Racial Construction in the Early South*. Athens: University of Georgia Press, 2003.

Perdue, Theda. *Cherokee Women: Gender and Culture Change, 1700–1835*. Lincoln: University of Nebraska Press, 1998.

Peterson, John H. Jr. *The Mississippi Band of Choctaw Indians: Their Recent History and Current Social Relations*. Ph.D. Dissertation, University of Georgia, 1970.

Pettus, Louise. *Leasing Away a Nation: The Legacy of Catawba Indian Land Leases*. Spartanburg, SC: Palmetto Conservation Foundation, 2005.

Pfaus, Martha. *Our Debt to Virginia Indians*. Richmond, VA: Dover Baptist Association, 1949.

Pfaus, Martha. *Our Indian Neighbors*. Richmond, VA: Dover Baptist Association, 1947.

Pleasants, Julian M., and Harry A. Kersey Jr. *Seminole Voices: Reflections on Their Changing Society, 1970–2000*. Lincoln: University of Nebraska Press, 2010.

Plecker, W. A. "The New Virginia Law to Preserve Racial Integrity." *Virginia Health Bulletin*, 56 (March 1924).

Pollard, John Garland. "The Pamunkey Indians of Virginia." *Bureau of American Ethnology, Bulletin 17*. Washington, DC: Government Printing Office, 1894.

Porter, Kenneth W. *The Black Seminoles: History of a Freedom-Seeking People*. Gainesville: University Press of Florida, 1996.

Pratt, R. H. "R. H. Pratt's Report on the Seminole in 1879," reprinted and annotated by William C. Sturtevant. *Florida Anthropologist*, 9 (March 1956): 1–24.

Prucha, Francis Paul. *The Great Father: The United States Government and the American Indians*. Lincoln: University of Nebraska Press, 1984.

Ray, S. Alan. "A Race or a Nation? Cherokee National Identity and the Status of Freedmen's Descendants." *Michigan Journal of Race & Law*, 12 (Spring 2007): 387–463.

Read, William A. *Florida Place-Names of Indian Origin and Seminole Personal Names.* Baton Rouge: Louisiana State University Press, 1934.

Roberts, Charles. "The Second Choctaw Removal, 1903." In *After Removal: The Choctaw in Mississippi.* Edited by Samuel J. Wells and Roseanna Tubby. Jackson, MS: University Press of Mississippi, 1986.

Roberts, Charles. "A Choctaw Odyssey: The Life of Lesa Phillip Roberts." *American Indian Quarterly,* 14:3 (Summer 1990): 259–276.

Robinson, W. Stitt, editor. *Early American Indian Documents: Treaties and Laws, 1609–1789,* Vol. 4: *Virginia Treaties, 1607–1722.* Frederick, MD: University Publications of America, 1983.

Roediger, David R. *The Wages of Whiteness: Race and the Making of the American Working Class.* New York: Verso, 1999.

Rosen, Deborah A. *American Indians and State Law: Sovereignty, Race, and Citizenship, 1790–1880.* Lincoln: University of Nebraska Press, 2007.

Rosen, Deborah A. *Border Law: The First Seminole War and American Nationhood.* Cambridge, MA: Harvard University Press, 2015.

Rountree, Helen C. "Indian Virginians on the Move." In *Indians of the Southeastern United States in the Late 20th Century.* Edited by J. Anthony Paredes. Tucaloosa: University of Alabama Press, 1992.

Rountree, Helen C. "Powhatan's Descendants in the Modern World: Community Studies of the Two Virginia Indian Reservations, with Notes on Five Non-Reservation Enclaves." *Chesopiean: A Journal of North American Archaeology,* 10 (June 1972): 61–97.

Rountree, Helen C. "The Indians of Virginia: A Third Race in a Biracial State." In *Southeastern Indians since the Removal Era.* Edited by Walter L. Williams. Athens: University of Georgia Press, 1979.

Rountree, Helen C. *Pocahontas's People: The Powhatan Indians of Virginia through Four Centuries.* Norman: University of Oklahoma Press, 1990.

Russell, Mattie U., and E. Stanley Godbold Jr. *Confederate Colonel and Cherokee Chief: The Life of William Holland Thomas.* Knoxville: University of Tennessee Press, 1990.

Satz, Ronald N. "The Mississippi Choctaw: From the Removal Treaty to the Federal Agency." In *After Removal: The Choctaw in Mississippi.* Edited by Samuel J. Wells and Roseanna Tubby. Jackson, MS: University Press of Mississippi, 1986.

Saunt, Claudio. *Black, White, and Indian: Race and the Unmaking of an American Family.* Oxford: Oxford University Press, 2005.

Scaife, Hazel Lewis. *History and Condition of the Catawba Indians of South Carolina.* Philadelphia: Office of Indian Rights Association, 1305 Arch Street, 1896.

Schreier, Jesse T. "Indian or Freedman? Enrollment, Race, and Identity in the Choctaw Nation, 1896–1907." *Western Historical Quarterly,* 42:4 (Winter 2011): 459–479.

Shachar, Ayelet, and Ran Hirschl. "Citizenship as Inherited Property." *Political Theory,* 35:3 (June 2007): 253–287.

Sheridan, Clare. "Contested Citizenship: National Identity and the Mexican Immigration Debates of the 1920s." *Journal of American Ethnic History,* 21:3 (Spring 2002): 3–35.

Shoemaker, Nancy. "How Indians Got to Be Red." *American Historical Review,* 102:3 (June 1997): 625–644.

Shoemaker, Nancy. *A Strange Likeness: Becoming Red and White in Eighteenth-Century North America.* Oxford: Oxford University Press, 2004.

Skenandore, Francine R. "Revisiting *Santa Clara Pueblo v. Martinez*: Feminist Perspectives on Tribal Sovereignty." *Wisconsin Journal of Law, Gender & Society,* 17 (Fall 2002): 347–370.

Skinner, Alanson. "Notes on the Florida Seminole." *American Anthropologist,* 15 (January–March 1913): 63–77.

Sokolow, Gary A. *Native Americans and the Law: A Dictionary.* Santa Barbara, CA: ABC-CLIO, 2000.

Snowden, John Rockwell, Wayne Tyndall, and David Smith. "American Indian Sovereignty and Naturalization: It's a Race Thing." *Nebraska Law Review*, 80 (2001): 171–238.

Speck, Frank G. "Catawba Herbals and Curative Practices." *Journal of American Folklore*, 57 (January–March 1944): 37–50.

Speck, Frank G. "Catawba Medicines and Curative Practices." In *Twenty-Fifth Anniversary Studies: Philadelphia Anthropology Society*. Edited by D. S. Davidson. Philadelphia: University of Pennsylvania Press, 1937.

Speck, Frank G. "Chapters on the Ethnography of the Powhatan Tribes of Virginia." In *Indian Notes and Monographs*, 1. New York: Museum of the American Indian, Heye Foundation, 1928.

Speck, Frank G. *The Catawba Texts*. New York: Columbia University Press, 1934.

Speck, Frank G., Leonard Broom, and Will West Long. *Cherokee Dance and Drama*. Norman: University of Oklahoma Press, 1951.

Spruhan, Paul. "A Legal History of Blood Quantum in Federal Indian Law to 1935." *South Dakota Law Review*, 51 (2006): 1–50.

Spruhan, Paul. "Indian as Race/Indian as Political Status: Implementation of the Half-Blood Requirement under the Indian Reorganization Act, 1934–1945." *Rutgers Race & the Law Review*, 8 (2006): 27–49.

Stern, Theodore. "Pamunkey Pottery Making." *Southern Indian Studies*, 3. Chapel Hill: Archaeological Society of North Carolina, 1951.

Stremlau, Rose. *Sustaining the Cherokee Family: Kinship and the Allotment of an Indigenous Nation*. Chapel Hill: University of North Carolina Press, 2011.

Strong, Pauline Turner, and Barrik Van Winkle. "'Indian Blood': Reflections on the Reckoning and Refiguring of Native North American Identity." *Cultural Anthropology*, 11:4 (November 1996): 547–576.

Stuart, Paul. *The Indian Office: Growth and Development of an American Institution, 1865–1900*. Ph.D. Dissertation, University of Wisconsin, 1978.

Stuart, Villiers. *Adventures Amidst the Equatorial Forests and Rivers of South America; also in the West Indies and the Wilds of Florida, to which Is Added "Jamaica Revisited."* London: John Murray, Albemarle Street, 1891.

Sturm, Circe. "Blood Politics, Racial Classification, and Cherokee National Identity." *American Indian Quarterly*, 22:1/2 (Winter/Spring 1998): 230–257.

Sturm, Circe. *Blood Politics: Race, Culture, and Identity in the Cherokee Nation of Oklahoma*. Berkeley: University of California Press, 2002.

Sturm, Circe. *Becoming Indian: The Struggle over Cherokee Identity in the Twenty-First Century*. Santa Fe: School for Advanced Research Press, 2010.

Sturtevant, William C., and Jessica R. Cattelino. "Florida Seminole and Miccosukee." In *Handbook of North American Indians*, Vol. 14: *Southeast*. Volume edited by Raymond D. Fogelson. General editor William C. Sturtevant. Washington, DC: Smithsonian Institution, 2004.

Swanton, John R. "Source Material for the Social and Ceremonial Life of the Choctaw Indians." *Bureau of American Ethnology, Bulletin 103*. Washington, DC: US Government Printing Office, 1931.

TallBear, Kim. *Native American DNA: Tribal Belonging and the False Promise of Genetic Science*. Minneapolis: University of Minnesota Press, 2013.

Thomas, Brook. "The Legal and Literary Complexities of U.S. Citizenship around 1900." *Law and Literature*, 22:2 (Summer 2010): 307–324.

Thornton, Russell. "Tribal Membership Requirements and the Demography of 'Old' and 'New' Native Americans." *Population Research and Policy Review*, 16 (1997): 33–42.

Tiger, Buffalo, and Harry A. Kersey Jr. *Buffalo Tiger: A Life in the Everglades*. Lincoln: University of Nebraska Press, 2002.

Tolbert, Charles Madden. *A Sociological Study of the Choctaw Indians in Mississippi*. Ph.D. Dissertation, Louisiana State University, 1958.

Tsosie, Rebecca. "American Indians and the Politics of Recognition: Soifer on Law, Pluralism, and Group Identity." *Law & Social Inquiry*, 22:2 (1997): 359–388.

Tubby, Simpson J. *Early Struggles*. Walnut Grove, MS: Dawn of Light Print, 1974.

Wailes, Bertha Pfister. *Backward Virginians: A Further Study of the Win Tribe*. M.A. Thesis, University of Virginia, 1928.

Watson, Ian. *Catawba Indian Genealogy*. Geneseo, NY: Geneseo Foundation and the Department of Anthropology, State University of New York at Geneseo, 1995.

Wells, Samuel J. "The Role of Mixed-Bloods in Mississippi Choctaw History." In *After Removal: The Choctaw in Mississippi*. Edited by Samuel J. Wells and Roseanna Tubby. Jackson, MS: University Press of Mississippi, 1986.

West, Patsy. *The Enduring Seminoles: From Alligator Wrestling to Ecotourism*. Gainesville: University Press of Florida, 1998.

Wilkins, David E. *American Indian Sovereignty and the U.S. Supreme Court: The Masking of Justice*. Austin: University of Texas Press, 1997.

Wilkins, David E., and K. Tsianina Lomawaima. *Uneven Ground: American Indian Sovereignty and Federal Law*. Norman: University of Oklahoma Press, 2001.

Wilkinson, Charles F. "Indian Law at the Beginning of the Modern Era." In *Constitutionalism and Native Americans, 1903–1968*. Edited by John R. Wunder. New York: Garland, 1996.

Wilkinson, Charles F. *American Indians, Time, and the Law: Native Societies in a Modern Constitutional Democracy*. New Haven, CT: Yale University Press, 1987.

Williamson, Joel. *After Slavery: The Negro in South Carolina during Reconstruction, 1861–1877*. New York: W.W. Norton, 1975.

Williamson, Joel. *The Crucible of Race: Black-White Relations in the American South since Emancipation*. New York: Oxford University Press, 1984.

Woodward, C. Vann. *The Strange Career of Jim Crow*. Oxford: Oxford University Press, 2001. First published in 1955.

Yarbrough, Fay A. *Race and the Cherokee Nation: Sovereignty in the Nineteenth Century*. Philadelphia: University of Pennsylvania Press, 2008.

Yellow Bird, Michael. "Decolonizing Tribal Enrollment." In *For Indigenous Eyes Only: A Decolonization Handbook*. Edited by Waziyatawin Angela Wilson and Michael Yellow Bird. Santa Fe: School of American Research, 2005.

Zellar, Gary. *African Creeks: Estelvste and the Creek Nation*. Norman: University of Oklahoma Press, 2007.

Zissu, Erik M. *Blood Matters: The Five Tribes and the Search for Unity in the Twentieth Century*. New York: Routledge, 2001.

Zogry, Michael J. *Anetso, the Cherokee Ball Game: At the Center of Ceremony and Identity*. Chapel Hill: University of North Carolina Press, 2010.

Web Sources

Catawba Indian Nation, "Catawba Today," http://catawbaindian.net/about-us/catawba-today/.

Catawba Indian Nation, "Constitution of the Catawba Indian Nation," http://catawbaindian.net/wp-content/uploads/Constitution-Final-draft-clean.pdf.

Catawba Indian Nation, "Tribal Enrollment," http://catawbaindian.net/services/tribal-enrollment/.

Catawba Indian Nation, "We the First People: Catawba Constitution Initiative," http://catawbaindian.net/constitution-initiative/.

Eastern Band of Cherokee Indians, Section 49-2, Qualifications for Enrollment, the Cherokee Code of the Eastern Band of the Cherokee Nation, Codified through Ordinance No. 322, Enacted June 8, 2010 (Supp. No.13), http://library1.municode.com/defaultnow/home.htm?infobase=13359&doc_action=whats new.

Eastern Band of Cherokee Indians, Section 49-5, Applications for Enrollment, the Cherokee Code of the Eastern Band of the Cherokee Nation, Codified through Ordinance No. 322, Enacted June 8, 2010 (Supp. No.13), http://library1.municode.com/defaultnow/home.htm?infobase=13359&doc_action=whatsnew.

Miccosukee Tribe of Indians of Florida, http://www.miccosukeeresort.com/tribe.htm.

Mississippi Band of Choctaw Indians, "Article II: Membership," *Tribal Constitution*, http://www.choctaw.org/government/court/constitution.html.

Mississippi Band of Choctaw Indians, "Enrollment," http://www.choctaw.org/government/tribalServices/members/enrollment.html.

Mississippi Band of Choctaw Indians, "Welcome from the Tribal Chief of the Mississippi Band of Choctaw Indians," http://www.choctaw.org/.

National Museum of the American Indian, "Kevin Brown, Chief of the Pamunkey Indian Tribe" (August 22, 2013), http://blog.nmai.si.edu/main/2013/08/kevin-brown-chief-of-the-pamunkey-indian-tribe.html.

Pamunkey Indian Tribe, "Contacting the Pamunkey Indian Tribe," http://www.pamunkey.net/Contact.html.

Seminole Tribe of Florida, http://www.semtribe.com/FAQ/.

INDEX

Note: Page numbers in italics indicate photographs or maps.

9 780190 055639